THE PAST AND FUTURE
OF MEDIEVAL STUDIES

NOTRE DAME CONFERENCES IN MEDIEVAL STUDIES
Number IV

Institute of Medieval Studies
University of Notre Dame
John Van Engen, Director

The Past and Future
of Medieval Studies

EDITED BY

John Van Engen

UNIVERSITY OF NOTRE DAME PRESS

Notre Dame   London

Library of Congress Cataloging-in-Publication Data

The past and future of medieval studies / edited by John Van Engen.
    p. cm. — (Notre Dame conferences in medieval studies ; 4)
    Includes bibliographical references.
    ISBN 0-268-03800-7 (alk. paper)
    1. Civilization, Medieval—Study and teaching—Congresses.
2. Middle Ages—Study and teaching—Congresses.   I. Van Engen, John
H. II. Series.
CB351.P324   1994
942.02—dc20   93-13972
                                            CIP

Contents

Foreword

ON 19–21 FEBRUARY 1992 the Medieval Institute at the University of Notre Dame hosted a conference on the "past and future of medieval studies." Twenty-eight scholars reflected for three days on who medievalists are, what they study and teach and write, how they engage their materials (mentally, imaginatively, methodologically), why they do things as they do. Each invited scholar was sent an agenda paper and asked to consider a number of questions about the position of medieval studies in the world of higher education. At Notre Dame such questions arose in the context of an institute established, as its founders put it in 1946, "to acquire exact information about and accurate knowledge of Mediaeval life, thought, and history by utilizing every method and device known to modern scholarship." In various other institutional and disciplinary settings, medieval scholars began raising questions at nearly the same time: Marina S. Brownlee, Kevin Brownlee, and Stephen G. Nichols in *The New Medievalism* (Baltimore, 1991), Allen J. Frantzen in essays on *Speaking Two Languages: Traditional Disciplines and Contemporary Theory in Medieval Studies* (Binghamton, N.Y., 1991), Lee Patterson in an introductory essay on "Critical Historicism and Medieval Studies," *Literary Practice and Social Change in Britain 1380–1530* (Berkeley, 1990), Caroline Walker Bynum in the introduction to her *Fragmentation and Redemption* (New York, 1991)—to mention four distinguished examples. Several of the same people contributed to the discussion of a "new philosophy" in *Speculum* 65 (1990). Questions of this sort can also be asked with a sense of humor: one colleague sent me a short spoof published recently in *Médiévales,* a self-questionnaire to determine by way of thirty items, each with multiple choices, "what kind of medievalist you are." For instance, you consider the least bad medievalist was Michelet, Nerval, Walter Scott, Jeanne Bourin, Péguy, or Hugo; again, you would name your dog Attila, Abelard, Roland, Tristan, Medor, or Rupert of Deutz.

The conference at Notre Dame was designed to include a variety of disciplinary and methodological viewpoints. It was not conceived as a call to arms for beleaguered medievalists, nor did it issue in any such call, though several scholars argued for better representation of our purposes in the schools and to the general public. Neither was it conceived as an invitation to indulge in nostalgia or self-congratulation, though most scholars seemed self-conscious about precedents and puzzled over how best to join past achievements to present questions. What provoked this gathering, drew participants to it, and animated discussion over three days was, quite simply, questions—queries about the place medievalists hold, both intellectually and institutionally, in the present world of higher education, queries too about their preparedness to participate in any re-thinking of humanities education undertaken during the last decade of the twentieth century.

To raise such general questions of purpose and method is to invite a range of responses. Excitement in some: it is past time for medievalists to join the fray, to make their voices heard. Yawns in others: such questions are too tedious, their answers too predictable; better to get on with the work. Dizziness in still others: peering over into the chasm of "what" and "why" and "how" questions can induce vertigo, a sense that one will never again walk along that edge with quite the same sense of confidence. And amusement in still others: the questions are old ones, after all; each generation must have its own try at answering them. Yet, in many or even most medievalists genuine interest—at least so I found among colleagues and graduate students at Notre Dame and among participants in the conference.

That interest springs from a variety of sources, including deeply personal ones, questions within ourselves and our students about what aims we have set as medievalists and what hope we have of realizing them in the academy and among the educated public. Colleagues who stop to reflect in any way on our professional circles express wonder that "medieval studies," virtually unknown to universities in the 1930s or 1940s, should have come so far, with the flyer for this conference mailed to about 4,000 people in North America alone. Just as many colleagues, or more, express an equally strong sense of foreboding, of fear that in the restructuring of higher education over the next generation medievalists will be left behind unless they reposition themselves within the academy. Discussion at this level can quickly become journalistic in character or even confessional, personal expressions of what people see or fear or hope. A few days after the conference, a question put out on the "Chaucer-net" by my colleague Edward Vasta elicited more than forty printed pages of individual responses about the state and mood of medievalists in their home institutions.

My purposes in organizing this conference were twofold, and they are interrelated. First, at a time when many teachers and writers within the academy have become increasingly self-conscious and articulate about their methods and purposes, we medievalists should not hesitate to express our own intentions or self-understandings, various as they may be, and quite particularly should not be content with descriptions imposed on us by others taking the liberty to say what it is that we medievalists supposedly represent or do not represent. The notion of the European Middle Ages has served for generations, or rather for centuries, as a backdrop, a strawman, a figure of the "other"; and sometimes we medievalists get put in the same position—some of us even perversely play upon it. But we should on occasion say for ourselves what it is we study and how and why. In the invitation to this conference, I encouraged our speakers to give voice to those personal questions, what we worry about and hope for in the loneliness of our studies as we read and write, what we worry about publicly in conversation with our colleagues and students.

Second, as a university enterprise we are well into our second generation, and entering our third. I am speaking of medieval studies as an institutionalized activity. Medieval scholars have been at work since the seventeenth century at least. In our individual disciplines or specialties we depend upon, and usually acknowledge, the indispensable work of those early editors, chroniclers, and interpreters. But until Harvard introduced elective courses, Johns Hopkins German-style graduate seminars, and colleges everywhere the system of majors, medieval studies as a professionalized course of study remained inconceivable. It was a good generation later that medievalists in North America began to organize: the Academy was founded in 1925 and Etienne Gilson first proposed an institute at Harvard in 1928–29. The first generation of "medieval-ists," taught by those "founders" and strengthened by outstanding emigré scholars, carried the enterprise forward through the 1950s at least. The transition from that extended first generation to the second took place, as I see it, in the latter 1960s when Toronto's Institute and Centre moved to the fore, the Kalamazoo Congress took wing, the Medieval Academy's Committee on Regional Centers and Associations (CARA) was formed (now some 100 members), and the "old boys" character of the original Medieval Academy first came under serious pressure. Now, however, we are another twenty-five years, another generation, down the road. Many pursue medieval studies with much the same motives and some of the same interests manifest in the first generation. But conditions in higher education and in society at large continue to change. Europe generally looms less large in America's sense of its social and cultural origins, and medieval Europe less so still; medieval literature or history or philosophy, not to say medieval studies generally, may seem an expendable luxury in the face of so many other matters that need studying and teaching.

"Medieval studies," as we have come to call it, shares certain broad characteristics, as I see it, with various other units in American universities that we choose to call "studies." Each of them has arisen at some particular moment in time when the intellectual conventions ruling within departments seemed inadequate to accommodate the whole vision that animated, the whole subject matter that engaged, a given set of teachers and students. Such "studies" people are driven by a vision that combines a relative firmness of purpose, stated or unstated, with a relatively amorphous or all-embracing sense of subject matter (all of the Middle Ages, all of American civilization, all of Europe, all of culture, all women). Through the first generation the original sense of purpose, often articulated or represented by a few gifted writers in the field, carries the program forward, and attracts still others to it. By the second generation, however, assuming universities have by this time given these "studies" some independent status and allowed some institutionalization, those purposes may begin to vary, the amorphous sense of subject matter begins to seem more puzzling or problematic, and the "studies" themselves become transformed virtually into another "discipline" or "department" with its own in-

tellectual conventions and constrictions. If I am right about this ma-
turing process, we in medieval studies, entering upon our third
generation, must face up to the implications of it, and begin talking
about the work of the third generation.

As organizer of the conference, I sent out a short agenda paper several months before these scholars came together. Whatever
its limitations, including that of a tone intended to provoke response, and however many other questions might have been asked,
this agenda paper was implicitly or explicitly presupposed by all
participants and was cited in several of the papers; it therefore
seemed unavoidable to reproduce it here. Readers may judge for
themselves whether the questions posed were useful ones and how
well the speakers took them up. Readers may also observe the variety of responses, some more personal, some more institutional,
some more "disciplinary"—but all, I think, professionally and personally engaged.

The conference, in the nature of such things, dealt with the
papers in organized sessions with prepared responses. The papers
are printed here, without rubrics or thematic divisions, largely in
the order in which they were read. One paper was read *in absentia*
(Marcia Colish); its author thus could not react to the discussions in
any subsequent rewriting, as the others could and to varying extents
did. One paper arose from discussions subsequent to the conference (Wawrykow). Two papers grew out of responses delivered at
the conference, and one paper failed to materialize.

For help organizing this conference and keeping everything
running smoothly, I am deeply indebted to Mark Jordan and Marsha
Kopacz and most especially to Edward English, administrative assistant at Notre Dame's Medieval Institute.

Agenda Paper:
The Future of Medieval Studies

A CENTURY AGO professors in American universities began to treat the history and literatures of medieval Europe as formal subjects for graduate and undergraduate education. These first medieval scholars, few in number and nearly all at Chicago or on the East Coast, contributed significantly, perhaps even disproportionately, to the professionalization of higher education in the humanities. A generation later (1925) medievalists acquired in the Mediaeval Academy of America a professional organization and journal with the declared aim of ensuring the study of medieval Latin language and literature. The organizing scholars moved to separate themselves from the Modern Language Association and to distinguish themselves from classicists, apparently convinced that neither would offer much in the way of support or sympathy for their pursuit of medieval Latin culture. Fifty years ago medieval studies gained an "institute" in Toronto which has subsequently served as both a degree-granting institution and a scholarly resource. Twenty-five years ago Toronto, UCLA, and Cornell, among others, formed "centers" or umbrella organizations for students and scholars drawn from several departments, occasionally providing a home for those whose specialties fit no departmental definition. Since that time interdisciplinary centers and programs of medieval studies have sprung up in nearly one hundred North American colleges and universities. These "centers" have banded together as a distinct interest group (CARA) within the Mediaeval Academy of America, and during the last decade produced an overview of the history and state of *Medieval Studies in North America* (Kalamazoo, 1982). Beyond all this growth in organizational activity, including subsets of specialized interests fostered by separate

1

newsletters and meetings, individual medieval scholars, in absolute numbers, have likewise probably never been so numerous. At the annual meeting of the Academy, between three hundred and five hundred scholars assemble for three days, and at the Kalamazoo international congress held each May some 2,600 medievalists live and work together in student dormitories for four days.

Despite all this organizational activity and the notable number of scholars in the humanities who have chosen to call themselves "medievalists," there exists no scholarly or disciplinary rationale for "medieval studies"; indeed there is no ongoing conversation about such a rationale. Many "departments" in the modern university can claim an ancient disciplinary pedigree. Both in materials and in methodology, departments of language, philosophy, and mathematics can trace their origins back to the ancient liberal arts; the laws, medicine, and theology back to the medieval university; and history back to ancient practice and the Renaissance vision of the liberal arts. Each rests upon a long tradition of scholars asking what the specific object of study in their discipline is and how it is best approached. From the beginning reflection on both the materials that comprise the discipline and the methods to be employed in interpreting those materials has accompanied any formal study of the discipline, and in recent years this self-reflective impulse has become livelier than ever—some would say overpowering the disciplines themselves.

For medieval studies, however, there is nothing comparable, beyond a lecture given in Toronto by Joseph Owens, some remarks in the volume noted above (first written in 1975), and scattered individual observations. In the last few years this situation has become more anomalous than ever. While most disciplines within the humanities have entered upon a period of tumultuous and contentious reassessment, so much so that it regularly attracts the attention of the press (*New York Review of Books, The New Republic,* and many others), medieval studies has remained relatively isolated from this kind of self-analysis, making it all the more attractive to some and still more contemptible to others. In the midst of the so-called "battle over the university," which will inevitably affect the shape of teaching and research in the humanities over the next decade, medieval studies would do well to reflect upon its own place and rationale.

Medieval studies is strongly associated in the public mind—and very often in the scholarly—with the study of received traditions. And it is true that medieval studies appears to have flourished in the immediate aftermath of the two World Wars, when the need to understand and to reclaim traditions—be they political, historical, literary, or religious—seemed crucial. Yet medieval studies also flourished in the midst of the cultural revolutions associated with the 1960s, buoyed then by a search for alternative visions of the world. In reality, ever since the sixteenth century images of the Middle Ages have alternated in the public consciousness between a "dark age" and a lost "golden age," with every conceivable combination in between. The present climate in the humanities seems, once again, less welcoming. In a journalistic account of the most recent meeting of the Modern Language Association, the very organization medievalists left sixty-five years ago, the *New York Times Magazine* listed as "out" or "not hot" at least six items often associated with medieval studies: Beowulf, grammar, textual editing, orthodoxy, the written word, religious allegory. Allowing for journalistic rhetoric—and for all those who would ardently defend these items as "in"—there seems little doubt that one version of medieval studies stirs up deep prejudices in the minds of students and scholars who inhabit the humanities departments of modern universities. Some would respond that these items represent only a caricature of medieval studies; others would argue that medieval studies includes a whole range of interests that are decidedly "in"; and others still would wait cynically for the pendulum of scholarly enthusiasms to swing back in other directions. But in none of these reactions is there a considered account of what medieval studies is, or might be, or should become.

Medievalists should reflect collectively on their enterprise and formulate their purposes and self-understanding in written forms accessible to their colleagues in the humanities. The purpose of this conference is to organize a symposium of leading scholars of differing disciplines and persuasions who will attempt just that. There is no hidden agenda in this gathering, no preferred approach, rationale, or "party line." The strength of the conference will derive rather from the diversity of views represented, and from the debate that will ensue.

Each scholar is asked to project a rationale for medieval studies based in part on the strengths of their own research and teaching. The hope is for presentations rooted in practice, or at least the possibilities for practice, rather than a series of vapid generalizations or platitudes about the character of interdisciplinary studies. Thus, while taking account of the problems and details best known to them from specialized research or teaching, each presenter is to propose a conceptual statement about the role of medieval studies within the modern university.

Each scholar, though drawing upon their own sense of the field and its rationale, should also take into consideration several common questions:

(1) The humanities departments of universities have been overwhelmed by a sense of the pluriformity of human experience. Will this inevitably exclude a special role for the western tradition, and especially for its early stages? If Europe becomes one block alongside several others (Africa, Asia, etc.), does any place remain in the university for the study of early Europe? Would a notion of "Early Europe" save us from prejudices associated in the minds of some with things medieval, or would it only discourage those attracted for whatever reasons to the Middle Ages? Will emphasis upon the pluriformity of medieval experience do more justice to the sources and satisfy those who judge the Middle Ages as uniform and hence uniformly uninteresting?

(2) In the balance between materials and methods, modern scholars of the humanities have swung decidedly toward the interpretive mode and highlighted the subjectivity inevitably present in all interpretation. Medievalists have followed at a distance, if at all. How should medievalists do justice both to the methodological questions of their colleagues and to their medieval materials? Are there methods peculiar to the interpretation of medieval materials which would actually open up new possibilities for colleagues in other fields?

(3) Have medievalists paid anything more than lip service to the notion of interdisciplinary or cross-disciplinary studies? Is there a way to deepen the interdisciplinary approach in a way peculiar or proper to medieval materials?

(4) Careful attention to the artifacts of medieval civilization has often marked the work of medievalists: preparation for medieval studies has therefore meant learning how to proceed knowledgeably in such fields as manuscript studies, paleography, codicology, diplomatics, archeology, and so on. How can this still be maintained—or should it be—in humanities departments which have placed so much emphasis upon the interpretive mode? Will work of this kind (manuscript studies, textual editing, and the like) be judged comparable to that of colleagues in more modern periods? Should medievalists claim a special sanction to undertake work of this kind?

(5) Medieval studies exacts a high price in terms of linguistic preparation. Can that be assumed any more of undergraduates? Must medieval programs build in language components much as institutes for Asian and Slavic studies have done? Or would this only further isolate medievalists from the mainstream of work in the humanities, as is often true of such institutes?

(6) Interdisciplinary efforts have their characteristic emphases, which arise in part from the materials themselves and in part from the past history of the discipline. Thus Renaissance studies have often focused upon literature and the arts. Similarly, Medieval studies has a strong association with philosophy, theology, and intellectual history. Plainly, this was motivated in part by religious interests, as Renaissance studies were often driven in the past by a search for the origins of "modern man." What for good or ill remains of this inspiration and outlook? Has its impact upon the field been salutary or deleterious? Can an approach to religious studies, to include the medieval histories of Judaism and Islam, help bring scholarly focus to these interests?

March 1991

The Future of Medieval Studies
A Retrospective Introduction to the Issues

MICHAEL M. SHEEHAN, C.S.B.

THIS YEAR 1992 marks the five-hundredth anniversary of Christopher Columbus's first voyage to the Americas. That voyage has become symbolic of what may well be the most decisive flanking movement in human history. The anniversary and the realization of the consequences of the process it symbolizes provide a peculiar piquancy, even an urgency, to the discussions that follow.

By the fifteenth century, as we know, the Islamic powers had thrown a crescent around Europe extending from the southernmost part of the Iberian peninsula to the headwaters of the central Russian rivers flowing into the Black and the Caspian Seas. Christian Europe steadily retreated as Islamic armies pressed the center and eastern flanks in an immense movement that—as all history majors once knew!—caused the end of the Middle Ages.

But the western flank of the Islamic world betrayed a weakness, a flaw that the peoples of Iberia had long exploited. Finally Europe, in the person of Iberian sailors, merchants, and missionaries, executed the flanking movement which is commemorated in this year of 1992, with consequences undreamed of by those involved: the Europeanization of this planet was under way.

Today, in the land that is the principal motor of the mighty cultural machine advancing that process of Europeanization, scholars and teachers are examining and debating the consequences of that process and their place in the humanities curricula and programs of our universities. The latter indeed face a major problem: to what degree should the curricula incorporate the study of the indigenous cultures which have been drawn into the unity formed by the flanking movement? And to what extent should the study of the traditions that did so much to bring all of this about yield part of its place to them?

In his preface to this volume, Van Engen sets out the main issues currently faced by medievalists and proposes an agenda to be addressed. A number of specialized problems are to be examined—a wise plan, given the degree of refinement and complexity to which medieval scholarship has come. For these reasons, it seemed best to limit my introductory remarks to some observations and distinctions which might prove useful as the discussion develops; to consider in general terms the scholarly issues as they apply to medievalists by reflecting on the title of the colloquium; and to concentrate on some of the internal and external problems which are currently faced by the medievalists' enterprise.

I

First—and this applies to any scientific enterprise—there is the question of rationale. One commonly accepted meaning of this elusive term involves the notion of fundamental reason for, or rational explanation of, some thing or activity. Within that meaning there is place for an examination of purpose. A second meaning of the term "rationale" is an exposition of the principles or reasons involved in some thing or action. In this latter sense of the word, our host suggests, medievalists have been wanting. That second meaning, of course, is dependent on the first, since it is the exposition of what is or should be already functional. If one approaches the matter from the point of view of the first definition, namely rational explanation, and includes the notion of purpose, several questions present themselves: Why study the Middle Ages? Does the reason for such study change as the culture of which medieval scholars are part evolves? What are the academic and methodological consequences of deciding to undertake or continue such an enterprise? Implicit in the answer to these questions are consequences touching the development of special tools and methods and, at a more theoretical level, of methodology.

Second, there is the matter of the types of activity, some or all of which a scholar can expect to find in institutions and organizations pursuing a scientific enterprise: (1) provision of mutual support, stimulus, criticism, etc., for those already active in the field in question; (2) supplying libraries and other resources required for systematic investigations within the field in question; (3) publication of the results of research; (4) training of advanced students so that they are equipped to participate in research and, eventually, to direct it; and (5) instruction of a wider world, first, on the undergraduate level—here arises the tension between the medieval studies approach to instruction and the departmental organization of that instruction—and, second, on the level of the general population, so that inasmuch as possible society as a whole may be informed.

II

The title of this volume suggests an examination of the past and reflection on the future of medieval studies. At first glance it seems to ignore the fulcrum between the two, namely, the present. But this apparent lacuna will likely attain the purpose of the title more successfully than would have been the case were the word "present" included there. For it is precisely on the present situation that discussion must focus. The world "fulcrum" has been used with an intent that goes beyond the mere seeking of an image; for, in a lever, the fulcrum not only passes the force from one end to the other—in this image, from the past to the future—but also decides the direction that the force will take. The participants in the colloquium, their colleagues, and the graduate students whom they instruct in medieval studies carry within them much of the accomplishment, the power, and purpose of past endeavors in the study of the Middle Ages and transmit it to the future. In addition, through them as through a fulcrum, the angles and approaches of the past are transmitted, angles and approaches that may no longer be suitable.

Now what is to be said of the past? The historiography of medieval Europe and the splendid efforts by scholars over three centuries to make its records available and to understand them, important as they are, will not be treated here.[1] I want rather to reflect on the development of the study of the Middle Ages in terms of three models: the Medieval Academy, institutes such as the one to which I belong, and the development characteristic of the most recent generation, the center for medieval studies.[2] The different categories of support set out a moment ago should be in mind as I proceed.

First, the Medieval Academy: an excellent introduction to its foundation is supplied by the truly exciting account by George R. Coffman in the first number of *Speculum*,[3] an account taken up and enlarged, with the insights that the passage of time permits, by Luke Wenger in the open session of CARA at Nashville in 1979.[4] There are several things to note here. First, the individuals involved were already mature scholars or, occasionally, interested amateurs of things medieval. Second, though drawn from departments of languages and literature for the most part, they had come to the conclusion that there was a specific chronological block of the European past that merited special study. Furthermore they saw that neither in classics departments nor in the Modern Language Association of America was it possible to find the focus on the culture of the Middle Ages that they sought. In the Editor's Preface to the first number of *Speculum,* E. K. Rand expressed the hope that the Academy would become "a rallying point for the cultivation and study of these Middle Ages," and announced that it "would include in its scope the entire civilization and study of the Middle Ages."[5] A rationale is expressed here: first, the recognition of a period during which the culture that lies at the roots of modern European civilization was formed. Second, the founders agreed that knowledge of the Latin language was necessary to approach the Middle Ages. (This agreement was the principal force bringing the founders of the Academy together.) They also realized that, since it was a culture that was to be investigated, various disciplines had to be brought into the process. Four years earlier, at the meeting in Baltimore, it had been proposed that the new institution be called an Academy of Mediaeval Latin Culture.[6] But that was not enough: when the Academy finally came into being it was designed to foster the study of all aspects of medieval Europe and was interdisciplinary in principle. Formal recognition of this was new and represented a major development in scholarship.[7]

The second model is exemplified by the institute of which I have been a member for many years.[8] Here too there was some innovation, but its genesis was different from that of the Medieval Academy. In the early part of this century, St. Michael's College in the University of Toronto was making a serious effort to enhance its offerings in philosophy and the history of philosophy.[9] In the 1920s it was decided to implement the direction given by Pope Leo XIII in 1879 in his encyclical *Aeterni patris* to study medieval thought, especially that of Thomas Aquinas. To assist in this process, several leading European scholars, among them Etienne Gilson, were invited to St. Michael's. Gilson had reflected on and discussed the question of approaches to the Middle Ages with Marc Bloch during the years when they taught at the University of Strasbourg, and they had made some attempts to introduce changes at the Sorbonne along those lines. Gilson believed that the study of the thought of the great scholastics in a cultural vacuum was an error[10] and urged the establishment of an institution that would devote itself to the study of medieval culture in its various aspects—with emphasis, of course, on the history of the ideas of that culture—and that would devote parts of its energies to the formation of students who would in time take up the same task. Since the scholars needed for this enterprise were not available in Toronto, a group of the most promising young men at St. Michael's College were sent off to Harvard, Strasbourg, Paris, Cracow, and Rome to be trained in the subjects required for that interdisciplinary approach. As the instructional dimension of the program was developed, provision was made for a core program which required of all students not only the research skills of Latin and paleography but also the wide-ranging set of introductory studies intended to make the students—whatever their own special disciplines happened to be—conversant with the different facets of medieval culture.

An incident in 1936 throws light on the source of some of the pressure pushing towards the realization of the interdisciplinary approach to the Middle Ages. That year, the Institute sought a charter from the Vatican Congregation of Seminaries and Universities. It was denied because, in the judgment of the Congregation, the Institute was not yet able to provide the wide approach to the Middle Ages that was warranted. Adjustments were made, but the following year there were further objections. First, there must be different professors teaching major subjects. (The temptation with multidisciplinary and the inferior quality of instruction that might result were faced.) Second, there must be more than one professor of vernacular literature: "alter saltem professor assignandus est Litteris medii aevi vernaculis."[11]

One further point should be noted. Almost from the beginning the Institute was so arranged that the offices of the Fellows and the library were under one roof. Later, when the size of the collections and the scale of use forced removal of the library to a distance of about two hundred meters, the housing of medievalists has still remained under one roof.

A key to the rationale of the Institute is provided by the account of its genesis: from the beginning there was an accepted notion that the knowledge of medieval culture, especially its thought, has value for modern people. This purpose can be, and occasionally has been, read as a Catholic or at least a Christian missionary endeavor. In a sense it is, since the culture under examination was profoundly influenced by the Christian religion; but that has never been the purpose of the Institute. (Some bishops have not found this easy to understand.) The experience of scholars and students who have worked there would, I think, agree.

The third type is the center, an invention of the last thirty years. Here the effort to provide for the limitations of the departmental system are most evident. The term "center" is used of many types of organization ranging from those that are essentially switchboards coordinating courses that, in one way or another, can be said to be medieval, to those providing instruction at the graduate level. I wish to reflect on the latter. In some ways, the formation of centers repeated one aspect of the foundation of the Academy: given the diachronic organization of the subject matter of departments and the scale of demands that resulted, many graduate students found little time to acquire the tools necessary to gain direct access to the sources of their study. This deficiency often continued to prevail during the period in which they prepared for comprehensive examinations. Formation of centers for graduate instruction in medieval studies allowed students to provide for both of these needs and to complete a doctorate in reasonable time. This possibility provided the rationale for the specific contribution of the center to medieval studies.

The new program involved some cost: the sacrifice of the broader culture in history, literature, etc., that would likely have been obtained within the departmental system. Furthermore, this abandonment, to a degree at least, of the diachronic approach to subject matter that has been characteristic of most humanities departments carries within it a danger: do medievalists, working under the circumstances described, adopt a synchronic, interdisciplinary approach to medieval culture, or do they simply make themselves responsible for a considerably smaller body of knowledge than would have been the case had they fulfilled the usual departmental requirements? The question of the compatibility of specialization and the interdisciplinary approach to the Middle Ages comes to the fore here. To this we shall return.

III

Organized medieval studies in the form suggested by these three models and variants of them move into the future in the person of you and me and all medievalists in general. It is true that the different institutions in which we work have self-descriptions, statements of purpose, rules of order, even statutes or constitutions that guarantee a certain continuity through time. But we are the vehicle through which they function now, and through us they are given the particular thrust that they will carry into the future. If we look at the medieval field as it can be observed in North America today, there is reason for satisfaction. Gilson remarked in 1930 that there would be many centers of medieval research in the years to come.[12] Still it is hard to believe that he anticipated the extent of the growth that would occur during the last sixty years. The number of persons involved, the publications, the formation of societies of medieval specialists, the quality of instruction at the graduate and undergraduate levels, these and many other things are indications of what has been accomplished. To me, one of the principal signs of the vigor of our enterprise and of its hopes for the future appears regularly in *Medieval Academy News:* the establishment of new journals.

Yet, as John Van Engen has pointed out, we cannot afford to be complacent. There are many questions that need discussion. Some are intrinsic to our enterprise. What are the areas into which study should be extended? This question is the stuff of inaugural lectures.[13] Related to this question is the ever greater specialization of medieval research. This is at once a progress and a problem: how can an interdisciplinary approach be maintained, let alone enhanced, in the face of such specialization? Is insistence on an interdisciplinary approach the solution to the secondary problems that come with specialization? At a deeper level, and more philosophical, is the question of communication across time: to what extent can we share the understanding and the intentions of the medievals we study? Do whole areas of knowledge that have been discussed for generations run the risk of evaporating in the face of critical positions that sometimes seem to make their study irrelevant?

Then there is the question of a theory of medieval studies itself. It is true that the opening of new approaches and new methods has occasioned a methodological discussion of their intent and value; but the more general discussion of medieval studies and its dialogue with contemporary culture has not developed on the scale and at the depth that would seem to be required of such a large and costly enterprise.

Finally, there is the question that confronts each of us, why do it at all? Is it a personal fascination with the period? Is it simply a way of earning a salary? Or do we consider knowledge of the Middle Ages to be valuable, valuable to our self-understanding? valuable to the self-understanding of our society? As we face the problems of the future our stance and our determination will be colored by the answer to these last questions.

It is at this point, when I must draw these remarks to a close, that I return to reflect on that sense of "flanking" with which I began. Here we reflect on threats to our enterprise which are extrinsic to it.[14] It is a commonplace that the university labors under serious financial strain and that humanities components are being asked to carry their share, perhaps more than their share, of the burden. As a result, professors of medieval subjects are not always being replaced at a rate necessary to maintain the levels and types of instruction that have come to be expected. Many services are withdrawn as well. But there is another longer term problem that might lead to a diminished role for medieval studies within the university. We can see now that the European culture whose roots we seek to understand has indeed reached the whole planet. We understand, too, that the process of inculturation[15] is under way on a massive scale. Other cultures claim our attention. They are usually much influenced by the culture of Europe, but still are "other" and give that which is European a statement somewhat different from the one we know.[16] The consequences of this vast cultural shift may well be more important than those internal problems sketched above. Do we face the need to yield space in the humanities curriculum and in the agenda of future research to the study of these cultures? Or is there a greater need than ever for specialists in medieval studies to help others understand the threads that came together to form the dominant culture of our age?[17]

NOTES

[Father Sheehan died unexpectedly on 23 August 1992, before he could complete revisions to the paper read at the conference. For recovering and editing that paper, I am grateful to James Farge, C.S.B., his literary executor. JVE]

1. See David Knowles, *Great Historical Enterprises* (London: Oxford University Press, 1963).

2. Laurence K. Shook, "The Nature and Value of Medieval Studies," in *Studies in Medieval Culture,* Ser. 7, no. 2, ed. John R. Sommerfeldt (Kalamazoo, Mich.: Western Michigan University, 1964), 9–20 and "University Centers and Institutes of Medieval Studies," *Journal of Higher Education* 38 (1967): 484–492, and especially, the essays in *Medieval Studies in North America: Past, Present and Future,* ed. Francis G. Gentry and Christopher Kleinhenz (Kalamazoo, Mich.: Medieval Institute Publications, 1982). For the present discussion Stanley Kahrl's essay in that volume, "On the Desirability of Banding Together" (pp. 41–56) is very useful.

3. "The Mediaeval Academy of America: Historical Background and Prospect," *Speculum* 1 (1926): 5–18.

4. "The Medieval Academy and the Growth of Medieval Studies in North America," in *Medieval Studies in North America,* 23–40.

5. *Speculum* 1 (1926): 3.

6. Coffman, "The Mediaeval Academy of America," *Speculum* 1 (1926): 7.

7. It might be argued that classics departments had already done so.

8. See John F. Quinn, "Pontifical Institute of Medieval Studies," *Anuario de estudios medievales* 6 (1969): 585–598; and Laurence K. Shook, *Catholic Post-secondary Education in English-speaking Canada: A History* (Toronto: University of Toronto Press, 1971), 210–228.

9. See Joseph Owens, *The Philosophical Tradition of St. Michael's College, Toronto* (Toronto: University of St. Michael's College Archives, 1979).

10. See Kenneth L. Schmitz, *What Has Clio to do with Athena? Etienne Gilson: Historian and Philosopher,* Etienne Gilson Series 10 (Toronto: Pontifical Institute of Mediaeval Studies, 1987), 2–5.

11. *Instituti studiorum mediae aetatis statuta* (Toronto: Aedes Instituti Studiorum Mediae Aetatis: Toronto 1963), 36–37.

12. See Shook, *Catholic Post-Secondary Education,* 220.

13. E.g. David Knowles, *The Prospects of Medieval Studies: An Inaugural Lecture, 1947* (Cambridge: Cambridge University Press, 1947) and Walter Ullman, *The Future of Medieval History* (Cambridge: Cambridge University Press, 1973).

14. See the recent discussion by Milton McC. Gatch, "The Medievalist and Cultural Literacy," *Speculum* 66.3 (1991): 591–604.

15. We historians called it "acculturation" in the 1950s when it was all the rage among us.

16. See the discussion of the analogous problem faced by theologians in Claude Geffré, "La théologie européenne à la fin de l'européocentrisme," *Et* 2.1 (1991): 45–64.

17. On the later writings of Christopher Dawson in this regard, see J. Ambrose Raftis, "The Development of Christopher Dawson's Thought," *Chesterton Review* 9.2 (1983): 130–132.

Bede's Blush: Postcards from Bali, Bombay, Palo Alto

KATHLEEN BIDDICK

DREAMING THE MIDDLE AGES

Are MEDIEVALISTS DREAMING the Middle Ages?[1] Umberto Eco has claimed such dreams as "pseudo-medieval pulp midway between Nazi nostalgia and occultism." The dreams have been dreamt fitfully since the Renaissance. In their sleepwalking humanists invented a Middle Ages as a place and a time of non-origin and formed an identity essentially informed by a claim of what it was not.[2] Nation-states of the nineteenth century, in contrast, produced a place and time, a Middle Ages, to stage the cultural origins of the "western animal" (Eco's term). At the end of the twentieth century, such overdetermined constructs of the Middle Ages haunt medieval studies as a double bind of origin and non-origin.

The double bind has divided medieval studies into camps of pastists and presentists who debate over the epoch in which to locate radical "past" alterity instead of questioning desires for such a boundary as an effect of specific historiographical metanarratives. Caught in the divisions of a double bind, medieval studies cycles repetitiously between these poles of loss and plenitude. Humanist fantasies of sublime non-origin return in contemporary debate under the guise of "pastism," a position that argues for radical historical difference between the Middle Ages and the present. Pastism regards the past and the present as bounded temporal objects which cannot come into contact for fear of scholarly contamination. Pastism produces historical difference as moral difference between a medieval exemplarity and an impoverished present. At the other

16

extreme, the pole of plenitude, the Middle Ages becomes a mirror. Presentism looks into the mirror of the Middle Ages and asks it to reflect back histories of modernist or postmodernist identities. Absorbed by these reflections, presentism forgets to examine the privileging of such identities or to question institutional and personal investments in understanding the past as a mirror, however near or distant.[3] Supposedly more neutral versions of this model of historiographical temporality, usually cast as questions of "continuity" and "change," likewise get caught up in problems of pastism and presentism.[4]

As both non-origin and origin, the Middle Ages can be everywhere, both medieval and postmodern, and nowhere, sublime and redemptive. What better material for a dream-frame for popular culture, a truly relative past which can be read as either the present or the future? It is therefore not surprising to find the Middle Ages figured in a near-future space of science-fiction and standing in for contemporary fantasies of the Third World.[5] Recent conference calls, such as our own, express an anxiety about dreaming the Middle Ages in this way. Dreams of disciplinary transformation, however, have mostly repeated problems of pastism and presentism inhering in such a construct. Some scholars sleep with images of Boethius dancing in their heads ("tell them of Boethius, tell them we are all in prison and the world without in ruin. . ."[6]). Others awake moved by desires to colonize popular medievalia for its energy and enthusiasm, unmindful that the cultural construct of the Middle Ages produces this very pseudo-medievalia as an effect. Like Rip Van Winkle we can dream on or, alternatively, use the repetition I am describing as an occasion for dream-work in public culture today.[7]

This essay attempts to negotiate such dream-work. It holds in tension the contradictions of pastism and presentism in order to read along their fault lines for histories which the construct of the Middle Ages as non-origin and origin must defend against through erasure or occultation. I offer you three discrete readings intended to trouble rhetorically, materially, and institutionally the foundational category of the Middle Ages. My vignettes (used here in the dictionary-sense of something that shades off gradually at the edges so as to leave no definite line at the border) engage medieval studies with critical theoretical and pedagogical concerns in public culture today, in the present. In reading along fault lines, I try not demonize our disciplinary problems—such a strategy would render my readings indistinguishable from the processes I seek to trouble. Rather my essay argues for a non-foundational medieval studies which articulates rather than re-presents the Middle Ages as a historical category.[8] This essay seeks to set in motion a non-foundational moment with a blush, the blush of Bede. His blush becomes a performative moment for dream-work in medieval studies, a moment for historical mourning and rememoration. The blush produces a possibility for a history after the end of history as an epistemological concept formed in the nineteenth century and still all too dominant in the North American academy today.[9]

VIGNETTE I:
MISSING BODIES/DISAPPEARING ACTS/
RETURN OF THE COCKFIGHT

The reading of my first vignette begins by stumbling over missing bodies. They begin popping up in the title of our conference, *The Past and Future of Medieval Studies.* Missing is the notion of the critical "present" of medieval studies.[10] The absence of a critical present offers a clue to where to search for the missing bodies disappeared by the title.[11] The clues lead to the classroom where the desires of teachers and students engage and transform the construct of the Middle Ages through pedagogy. Pedagogy, the *embodiment* of "technique" and "method," shapes the future for medieval studies. In missing out on this critical present, we miss possibilities for questioning our institutional practices.[12] We disappear the bodies of our students and their important work in the institutional reproduction of knowledge.

Missing bodies also haunt recent critical essays on the future of medieval studies. One body in particular, that of Clifford Geertz, like a corpse in a detective novel, keeps getting found by the reader of these disciplinary critiques. This body is not just any body of Clifford Geertz. It is his body as emplotted in his famous essay, "Deep Play: Notes on the Balinese Cockfight."[13] How can we read the Geertzian body of deep play as a clue to problems in medieval studies? A warning of his opens the mystery; he pulls no punches when he tells his readers: "every people, the proverb has it, loves its own form of violence" (DP, 449). With this admonition he invites readers to ask about the kinds of violence "Deep Play" might love. The violence produced by the essay can offer insight into the return of medievalists to "Deep Play," twenty years after its publication, as if to the scene of a crime in search of clues.

"Attending cockfights and participating in them is, for the Balinese, a kind of sentimental education" (DP, 449). Reading about Balinese cockfights is, for the reader, a kind of historical education about ethnographic writing in the early 1970s. We learn from Geertz that cockfights are disquieting for their "immediate dramatic shape," their "metaphoric content," and their "social context" (DP, 444). In describing these three registers of disquiet, Geertz offers the reader a way of understanding the forms of violence haunting the anthropological enterprise of the author. Geertz dramatically shapes the essay as a spatial progression. The reader moves from the space of encounter ("The Raid"), to a spectacular space of the cockfight ring ("Of Cocks and Men" and subsequent sections), to a scholarly space of textuality ("Saying Something of Something"). In the space of encounter Geertz uses a fable to produce rapport with his informants. This space of encounter also serves as a kind of map to the rapport desired in the text between the reader and the ethnographer. Presumably, violence is at play here, or at least Geertz has insinuated as much. He tells the fable of encounter as follows.

Geertz opens his essay by telling the story of his arrival together with his wife in a Balinese village in April 1958.[14] He describes himself and his wife initially as "nonpersons, specters, invisible men" (DP, 412); he tells how one "drifts around feeling vaguely disembodied" (DP, 413), doubting "whether you are really real after all" (DP, 413). After ten days of such alienation the Geertzs attend a village cockfight which gets raided by the police. Scattering with the rest of the villagers, Geertz and his wife end up running into a family compound to take cover. The wife of the resident whom the Geertzs had followed quickly sets up a tea-table. The two couples pretend to be deeply engaged in conversation. When the police arrive and see the "White Men" in the yard, meaning Geertz and his wife, they do a "double take." The host, who is unknown to

Geertz, is able to give an accurate and detailed account of the Geertz's scholarly purpose in the village. Convinced that the members of the tea party could not have been cockfight fans, the police leave. Geertz describes the police raid as a turning point for his relations to the villagers.

In a recent critique of historic ways of constituting ethnographic authority, James Clifford cites this story of the police raid as an example of an anthropological fable of rapport. According to Clifford: "The anecdote establishes a presumption of connectedness, which permits the writer to function in his subsequent analyses as an omnipresent, knowledgeable exegete and spokesman."[15] Once connected fabulously to his informants, Geertz disconnects his narrative. Just like magic, a Western anthropologist appears out of the hat of a "non-person." As an anthropological observer he then proceeds to change his rhetorical strategy and plunges his readers into a new section entitled "Of Cocks and Men," where he narrates a spectacular account of the masculine world of the cockfight. The rhetoric conceals the negotiated, interactive historical nature of his ethnographic presence at the cockfights. What little dialogue of his subject-informants he selects for citation, he uses to intensify the spectacular account of the cockfight: " 'I am cock crazy,' my landlord, a quite ordinary *afficionado* by Balinese standards, used to moan as he went to move another cage, give another bath, or conduct another feeding. 'We're all cock crazy.' " (DP, 419).

Does Geertz parody the conventions of what is called the hyper-masculine genre, a genre typically at work in narratives of cockfights, bullfights, etc., or does his essay simply reproduce such conventions? Different readers read the essay differently. My reading, which plays with the kinds of narrative space constructed by Geertz for the representation of the cockfight, shows how his spectacular account genders the production of knowledge in the essay by conforming closely to the space and masculinity typical of this highly conventionalized hyper-masculine genre. Students of the genre (the cockfight, bullfight, classic Western and detective films) have taught us how it internalizes violence as narrative content and opposes it to "emotionalism," which is gendered as feminine. The genre typically relegates women, children, adolescents, and "unfit" men to the edges of its narrative space.

Geertz reproduces this generic social space in the textual space of the essay. He marginalizes discussion of non-participants (women, children, adolescents, unfit men) to his footnotes and to a few brief sentences at the end, or "edge" of his account of the cockfight. The reader only learns from a footnote in the section "Of Cocks and Men" that "women—at least *Balinese* women [Geertz's emphasis]—do not even watch" (DP, n. 4, p. 418). The folktales footnoted by Geertz in the same sections suggest, however, a more complicated gendering that disrupts these conventionalizing margins. In the folktales, women are central to narrative action and set it into motion by resisting or abetting the world of the cockfight. One woman refuses her husband's request to feed her infant girl to the cocks, with consequences (DP, n. 22); in another tale a woman gives her last "rainy day" money to her husband to place a bet and the story unfolds (DP, n. 27).

The rhetorical collusion of the essay with the conventions of the hyper-masculine genre undoubtedly account for much of the familiar pleasure of and repetitious returns to readings of the cockfight. The hyper-masculine genre is an immensely popular one on television, in the movies, and in academia. This collusion helps to perpetuate a specific historical form of anthropological enterprise to be discussed more fully in a moment. Conventions of the hyper-masculine genre work to contain its intense homoerotic charge safely within the orbit of the homosocial. Closeted as such the convention can then mobilize the sexuality of power to "fix" its mobility—cocks in the center, women and children, unfit men to the margins.[16]

The rhetoric of the concluding section of the Geertz essay restores good homosocial order. Geertz writes of *ethnography* as "penetrating a literary text" (DP, 448). It says "something of something." He insists that the saying something of something should be said to *somebody* (DP, 453), but he never broaches the question of who that somebody might be, whether they would give their permission to be penetrated and where. Where would such conversation occur, who would participate, and how would they wish to embody a co-narration?

The fable of rapport enables Geertz to silence the co-narration of fieldwork. His rhetorical construction of the cockfight colludes with the homophobia and misogyny typical of the hyper-masculine genre. The essay is not limited, however, to these forms of violence. Geertz writes in a timeless ethnographic present, which the anthropologist masters as the observer. To suppress temporality, a presentism, Geertz denies a historical, colonial past which informs the present of the Balinese village of Tihingan in 1958. Such suppression also produces Geertz as a "pastist," at the same time. He must invent a "tradition" (people without history have traditions) for the Balinese, a "peasant mentality" (DP, 416), a category which seals them off from the dynamic historical present.[17] These shifting and complementary rhetorical ploys of pastism and presentism enable Geertz to textualize the Balinese villagers. Scholars only repeat these ploys when they take over uncritically the "deep play" of the cockfight disembodied from its historic ethnographic practices.[18] "Every people, the proverb has it, loves its own form of violence" (DP, 449).

The cockfight returned to medieval studies in the 1990s. In recent and important essays advocating disciplinary transformation both Gabrielle Spiegel and Allen Frantzen use the Balinese cockfight to read a disciplinary future.[19] Spiegel, in apparent discomfort with Geertz, attempts to revise "deep play," to rematerialize his approach: "those who bet on the cocks are not only expressing their peculiar understanding of the nature of Balinese social culture (its 'sociomoral hierarchy') but hoping to profit materially from the animal violence that ensues. In its particular mixture of symbolic and material negotiations, the cockfight serves as an apt metaphor for the kind of literary history that we need to begin to elaborate."[20]

Frantzen, discomforted by the disciplinary isolation of medieval studies, uses "deep play" as a methodological way to link medieval studies with cultural studies. The textuality argued for by Geertz (that texts "neither merely relieve nor arouse passions but display power is a proposition that medieval studies, practiced as a form of cultural studies, will be able to explore") forms a bridge for Frantzen to cultural studies.[21] He defines cultural studies as "rooted in ethnography, the study of diverse and remote cultures; keenly aware of the structuring effect of the scholar on his or her subject; and particularly concerned about 'non-literary' genres and discourse."[22]

Spiegel and Frantzen read the cockfight as Geertz writes it, as a representation. Spiegel criticizes precisely this tendency to aestheticize culture, to separate language from reality. She tries to restore the materiality of violence in the Balinese cockfight by bringing the cocks back in. In adding on "materiality," she fails, however, to question the rhetorical frame of the essay that enables the violent disappearance of materiality in the first place. Frantzen, who wishes to link cultural studies to medieval studies, also fails to question the concept of culture which frames the Geertz essay. Is it possible to use that concept of culture as a link, or is the culture of cultural studies also problematic, in need of a critical history? Both the missing bodies in "Deep Play" and the problem of the "return of the cockfight" in medieval studies suggest that we need to read the Geertz essay differently, to articulate it, rather than simply re-represent it.

VIGNETTE II;
SHADOW LINES: BOMBAY/LONDON

To turn "deep play" inside out we need to multiply and bring into a public rhetorical space the many bodies the essay renders missing, the bodies it "disappears." The disappearing acts of deep play deny the "present" of the essay, a particular, historic, present of postcolonial Bali in 1958, during the troubling days of the Sukarno regime which had followed upon the domination of the Dutch and the Japanese. In disappearing as a historical subject himself, Geertz denies his historic relation to the villagers of Tihingan. Rather than mark and hold the ambivalence of the space in between the double relational identities of participant-observer, subject-informant, Geertz erases them. He elides, too, his unnamed wife into a "White Man" in the essay. In the main body of his text, as we have already observed, Geertz mentions women only in the footnotes or toward the conclusion of his account of the cockfight. At the edges of that account he also finally names the village as Tihingan (DP, 435–436). The very textual space of the essay is gendered in the way it relegates both women and the historical space of ethnographic fieldwork to the footnotes and to the edges of spectacular accounts of fighting cocks.

The return of the Balinese cockfight to medieval studies, I argue, rehearses our anxieties about its historically constituted rhetorical violences. Could it be that its violence somehow points to a violence within medieval studies itself—hence our anxiety and fascination with the essay? The concealment of the relation between participant-observer and subject-informant is not unique to this essay by Geertz, although its hyper-masculine spectacle intensified its seductive effects. The rhetorical ploys of the essay are characteristic of the cultural assumptions of an "orientalist" ethnography. Orientalism is historically founded on a notion of cultures as contiguous, synchronous, and representational (world as exhibit).[23] The historical construct of the Middle Ages was invented and re-invented alongside of orientalism, hence, their mutual fascination.[24] The return of the essay to medieval studies in the 1990s can be understood as a symptom of an anxiety arising from the failure to articulate rigorously the intersections between the constructs of orientalism and medievalism.

The reduction of complex, permeable, relational identities to simple, bounded, unitary identities in the Geertz essay repeats the structure of violence that made orientalism historically possible. The terms—orientalism and neo-orientalism—are loaded terms to introduce. They have extensive critical histories and complicated institutional usages.[25] For the purposes of discussion in this paper, I use orientalism to refer to the historically situated Euroamerican project of producing an experience of scholarship, order, truth and management based on the textualization of imaginary others exterior to Europe who inhabit an imaginary space constructed by Europeans through their scholarship, cartography, surveys, photography, exhibitions, administration. Historically this process produced despotically administered texts and territories of the so-called East as well as a fantastic scholarly geography of the origins of Europe. Within European national histories, orientalism produced knowledge of certain epochs, places, and social groups as an orientalism within.[26]

Even in the presumably postcolonial order and supposedly postmodern times, orientalism perdures as a neo-orientalism. The latter acknowledges the decentering of its own imaginary European map without transforming the violent representational strategies that first drew such a map. It abandons the exhausted project of producing anthropological primitives in ethnographic fieldwork; in its stead, it substitutes a search for the "real" native informant to speak the pre-oriental truth. Neo-orientalism now searches for this "real" native in the Third World, and among diasporan scholars and artists resident in Euroamerican metropoles. Just as neo-orientalism looks for a "real" voice from the empires within Euroamerican scholarly and political traditions; it also searches for a "real" *pre-colonial, historical* subject in European archives. This historical informant can speak the truth from within representations of European history.

Medievalists can fall easily into this neo-orientalist trap of searching for a pre-colonial, historical informant, unless we study the cultural construct of the Middle Ages in relation not only to nationalisms (as has already been well done) but to imperialism as well. We need to situate historic nationalism with imperialism in the formation of medieval studies around the cultural construct of the Middle Ages. Such an analysis will regard the nineteenth century as much a neighboring field as medieval studies has traditionally considered Antiquity and the Renaissance.

My second vignette attempts to read such intersections. The founding of the Early English Text Society serves here as a case study which joins gender and imperialism to a traditional founding history of class and nationalism. The reading reconnects London and Bombay.[27]

F. J. Furnivall founded the Early English Text Society in 1864. He lectured on English grammar at the Working Men's College, a college which had grown out of evening classes given by a cadre of professors to working men in London. The society intended to bring the "mass of Old English literature within the reach of the ordinary student...."[28] From the beginning the society eschewed expensive editions such as those published by the Roxburghe Club, so that its volumes could be readily available. The society was particularly interested in "the spread of the study of English in schools" and engaged in the publication of textbooks and the award of annual prizes to encourage the spread of English Studies.[29]

This group of philanthropic professors who taught in the Working Men's movement also concerned themselves with the education of women. In 1848, colleagues from King's College, active in the Working Men's college movement, founded Queen's College for Women. In an inaugural lecture, Charles Kingsley, Professor of

English Studies at Queen's College, described a special affinity between women and the study of English.

> [S]uch a course of history [study of English literature] would quicken women's inborn *personal interest* in the actors of this life-drama, and be quickened by it in return, as indeed it ought: for it is thus that God intended woman to look instinctively at the world. Would to God that she would teach us men to look at it likewise. Would to God that she would in these days claim and fulfil to the uttermost her vocation as the priestess of charity!—that woman's heart would help deliver man from bondage to his own tyrannous and all-too-inclusive brain—from our idolatry of mere dead law and printed books—from our daily sin of looking at men, not as our struggling and suffering brothers, but as mere symbols of certain formulae, incarnations of sets of opinions, wheels in some iron liberty-grinding or Christianity spinning-machine, which we miscall society, or civilisation, or, worst misnomer of all, the Church.[30]

The founding of the Early English Text Society intersected with complex, gendered class interests. The society staunchly identified itself as a middle-class project.[31] The study of Old English constructed complicated gender and class identities around a notion of the "mother-tongue." But class, gender, and national identities were not the only identities under construction. Imperial colonial identities also framed the institutionalization of English studies in the mid-nineteenth century.

The founders of the Early English Text Society wrote about their imperial mission. "We are banded together to trace out the springs, and note the course, of the language that shall one day be the ruling tongue of the world, which is now the speech of most of its free men.[32] It would bring texts into the reach of "every student and boy in the British Empire."[33] Its early membership lists reflect both its metropolitan, class, and imperial mission. From the earliest membership list I was able to examine (1868), I could trace how the volumes edited by the society circulated to mercantile, mechanics, colonial, and dominion libraries.[34] The membership list of 1868 mentions the following subscribers of this type: Baltimore Mercantile Library, the Wakefield Mechanic's Institution, The South African

Library of Cape Town, The India Office Library, The Melbourne Public Library. These types of memberships expanded to include the following additions (listed by year of first appearance in the membership list): Young Men's Association of Troy, New York (1869), The Brooklyn Mercantile Library (1871), The Philadelphia Mercantile Library (1871), Queens College, Benares (1876), The Mercantile Library, St. Louis (1886), Bombay Asiatic Society (1886). The society also recruited private subscribers from its colonies and members of its dominion: Australia, Canada, India, South Africa. Institutional subscribers from the Indian colonial service included the Legislative Council Building, Calcutta (1868), the Madras Civil Service (1869), the Bengal Civil Service (1871), Rajkoomar College, Rajkote, India (1871), Assistant Commissioner of the Punjab (1876).

Of these class and imperial cross-hatchings in the membership list, I would like to focus on the connections between imperialism and medievalism suggested by the EETS volumes which began to fill the shelves of the Bombay Asiatic Society, an affiliate of the Asiatic Society of Bengal, based in Calcutta.[35] Founded in 1784 by Sir William Jones, an Oxford-trained orientalist and lawyer who served as a judge in the Supreme Court of Calcutta, the Asiatic Society gathered together the first generation of British colonial administrators who had learned Sanskrit. Jones is noted for his translation (1789) of the Sanskrit classic *Sakuntala* by Kalidasa, whom the British dubbed the Shakespeare of India. He also participated in a project central to the colonial administration, the establishing of translations of Hindu law texts. He worked on *The Digest of Indian Laws,* which H. T. Colebroke brought to completion in 1798, after Jones's death. The so-called Sanskrit Renaissance is attributed to the members of the Asiatic Society who were also instrumental in the founding of the Royal Asiatic Society in England in 1823. By 1832 Oxford had established a chair of Sanskrit, which H. H. Wilson, a member of the Asiatic Society and the Indian Colonial Service, took up.

In the early days of the Asiatic Society, its members mostly relied on Brahmin pundits to supply them with their Sanskrit manuscripts and language training. Brahmin-English relationships in the late eighteenth and early nineteenth centuries were highly ambivalent. The pundits served as "go-betweens" in the British translation projects and often supplied the British with "padded" texts which served their own purposes. The Asiatic Society of Calcutta did not formally vote to open its membership to Indians until 1829. The Bombay chapter of the society voted against their admission. As Spivak has said of this exchange among British colonials and learned Brahmins in regard to the codification of Hindu law, a central task of their translation work:

> when the law was finally written, the history of the long period of collaboration was effaced, and the language celebrated the noble Hindu who was against the bad Hindu, the latter given to savage atrocities.[36]

The imperial cultural work of the Asiatic Society joined with English studies of the mid-nineteenth century in yet another guise. The new Germanic philology which revolutionized Anglo-Saxon studies at Oxford was introduced by Max Müller (listed as a member of the EETS from its earliest lists), for whom the Chair of Comparative Philology was created in 1868. Müller knew personally the orientalists of the Asiatic Society and had himself translated the *Rig Veda*. The desire of British orientalists to recover India's past—"there, notoriously, the *Vaidic* tradition was, for many centuries, virtually in abeyance"—echoes the desires of the EETS of "wiping away the reproach under which England had long rested, of having felt little interest in the monuments of her early life and language."[37] The ideology and practices of Sanskrit and English text editing have much to do with each other in the mid-nineteenth century and only a positivist linguistics would separate them.

The Bombay Asiatic Society received the publications of the Early English Text Society. The volumes sat on the shelves in colonial libraries in India and also in libraries as diverse and contrasting as the Astor Library and the Brooklyn Mercantile Library in New York. The comments published by English-based contributors in the early EETS volumes enable us to reconstruct the imaginary grid of their libraries which arranged translations of Sanskrit classics undertaken by British colonials resident in the colonial service in India, side by side with medieval English literature.[38]

This juxtaposition of national and colonial members and national and colonial scholarships in the EETS cannot be reduced simply to the eccentricities of mid-nineteenth-century philology. These contiguities show how national, imperial, and gendered identities criss-crossed the formation of EETS. The story of the institutionalization of English studies in nineteenth-century England is typically told as a narrative of aristocratic Oxford founding fathers. A post-orientalist reading, such as this one, questions what fantasies reduce these historically complex borders to a bounded disciplinary object, English studies, and restricts the plot to a story of upper-class English men. As Viswanathan reminds us: "... but less appreciated is the irony that English literature appeared as a subject in the curriculum of the colonies long before it was institutionalized in the home country."[39]

My reading has sought to multiply rather than disappear the bodies in the history of the Early English Text Society. The many bodies conjured pose new challenges. Their multiplicity and heterogeneity challenge the adequacy, indeed, the violence of the foundational categories (nation, class, founding-fathers, mother-tongue) in which we have traditionally told the story of the formation of English studies in the nineteenth century. A paraphrase of an observation made by Salman Rushdie in *Satanic Verses* can aptly conclude this reading of aspects of the formation of the Early English Text Society. Rushdie wrote: "The trouble with the English is that their history happened overseas, so they don't know what it means."[40] The trouble with the formation of medieval English studies in the nineteenth century is that it happened just as much in Bombay and Calcutta, as in London, so it is difficult to know what it means, unless we put these histories in relation.

VIGNETTE III:
BEDE'S BLUSH (731/1992)

So far my readings, a kind of ghostbusting, have brought into relation the non-commensurate times and places. The readings conjure up Balinese women of Tihingan on the pages of *Speculum;* they enable us to watch a Brahmin pundit look over the shoulder of F. J. Furnivall. My conclusion turns to contemporary institutional problems not to bust ghosts but to ensure that we do not go on creating them by disappearing bodies in our contemporary disciplinary practices. My final vignette imagines the transformation of the cultural construct of the Middle Ages in a specific setting. As I mentioned earlier, historians are only just beginning to imagine the kinds of history that "deliberately make visible, within the very structures of its narrative forms, its own repressive strategies and practices."[41] My vignette performs a historical poetics of mourning and rememoration.

I invite us to the reading room of a medieval institute, its walls lined with standard source-collections and reference works for paleography and diplomatics. The economics of the setting are important—what but a medieval institute can make arguments to a dean to hire and retain a paleographer, a diplomatist? The forces of the current job market serve as a strong glue for keeping medieval institutes from coming apart. Can we unglue the construct of the Middle Ages from this economic framework?

Four characters appear in the reading room: the dean of Stanford University, where recently the administration dropped the requirement of Old English; Bede, the author of the eighth-century text, *The History of the English Church and People;* a professor of Old English; and the chair of the Humanities curriculum committee, a self-identified Chicana feminist theorist. These four are talking about the current status of Old English studies in the curriculum.

The dean asks the professor of Old English how her curriculum can respond to the fact that soon less than half of the college students on the West Coast will claim English as their native language. Can Old English rely any longer on the implicit national and imperial argument of "our mother tongue" to justify its claims on the curriculum of the twenty-first century? The professor replies that the study of Old English is useful.

The dean, unpersuaded, tries again. She announces her respect for the technical demands and rigor of Old English scholarship. She does not want to see these tools thrown out of the canonical tool kit. But she warns that unless scholars try to redescribe their discipline outside of its nineteenth-century parameters, it will die out in the curriculum. The dean mentions early medieval thought and scholastic theology as examples of fields which are virtually extinct and serve as a warning to Old English studies.

Meanwhile Bede and the Chicana theorist have been talking to each other. Bede's multilingualism interests the theorist and she wants to learn more about his multilingual world. He pulls the Penguin edition of his history off the shelf and reads to the Chicana theorist: "At the present time there are in Britain, in harmony with the five books of the divine law, five languages and four nations— English, British, Scots, and Picts. Each of these have their own language; but all are united in their study of God's truth by the fifth— Latin—which has become a common medium through the study of the scriptures."[42]

The Chicana theorist asks how is it that all the languages he mentions seem to be dead, with the exception of English. She asks how people communicated in power-charged disagreements during his time. Bede tells her about the importance of exiles and interpreters in this multilingual world and illustrates this with the story of the Synod of Whitby. He describes how there were interpreters there, but English was the dominant language. The Chicana theorist then asks Bede about the politics of writing his history in Latin, how his text works as a go-between, among Mediterranean, Anglo-Saxon, and Celtic churchmen.

Bede asks what she means by "go-between." She describes to him the tensions of being a go-between in her worlds, a go-between among different languages, different racial and sexual identities.[43] She tells Bede the story of Malinche, a go-between who served as an Aztec translator for Cortez, and explains how Chicana feminists have appropriated Malinche to figure their own political, linguistic, sexual, and theoretical exchanges. Traditions of Mexican popular culture have nicknamed Malinche as "The Sell-Out" (La Vendida) or "The Raped One" (La Chingada). She asks Bede if he ever got a similar kind of nickname among his people. Bede blushes.

I wish to pause here in my story and ask about the historicity of Bede's blush. Have I made this blush up for you, my readers, as a presentist? I argue no. The blush marks the return of an affective moment in the history of Old English, which generations of writers and readers, have suppressed. The recent work of Allen Frantzen, Seth Lerer, and Katherine O'Brien O'Keeffe are helping us to understand Bede's blush. Bede created Caedmon, the poet of sacred hymns in Old English, as a textual double in his *History*. Caedmon speaks Old English in his dreams, only at the twice-repeated command of a stranger. Who is this other who appeared to Caedmon? Surely, it is Bede. But Bede never wrote the words of Caedmon's

Hymn in Old English in his *History.* The Old English text exists only as marginalia in the early Latin manuscript versions of Bede's *History.* Old English exists only on the borders of this *History* and the date and the status of the gloss are still open to debate. Indeed, some scholars argue that the glossed Old English text is a translation of Bede's Latin text of Caedmon's *Hymn.* The *History* and the *Hymn,* the story of Old English and Anglo-Saxon Latin lies in the space in between the text and the gloss, between Bede and his double Caedmon. They are the forks of the "mother-tongue," its hybridity. As go-between in his own *History,* Bede could allow Old English only in his dreams. This dream of the *History* and the textual problems of the "first" verse of Anglo-Saxon literature figures uncannily the conditions of the contemporary cultural construct of the Middle Ages, which we have repeated and reinscribed in textual editions until recently.

The Chicana feminist observes Bede's blush. She tries to explain how he might learn something if he began to think of the complex problems of multiple identities involved in the power-charged border-writing and border-speaking that "go-betweens" negotiate.[44] This kind of writing and speaking asks what it means to write and speak without categories, such as the "nation," or the "people." Border-writing also writes with a transformed notion of culture, one which does not simply re-inscribe nineteenth-century notions of culture. Border-writing thinks of culture otherwise and she cites a different way of imagining "culture" from Edward Said:

> Thus to see Others not as ontologically given but as historically constituted would be to erode the exclusivist biases we so often ascribe to cultures, our own not the least. Cultures may then be represented as zones of control or abandonment, of recollection and forgetting, of force or of dependence, of exclusiveness or of sharing, all taking place in the global history that is our element.[45]

The Chicana feminist invites Bede to come to speak to her feminist theory class in order to work through this theoretical issue of his performing as a "go-between." Bede then asks if he should speak in English or Latin. The Chicana theorist laughs. Of course, English, she says. Don't you know that your native language, which was first colonized by Latin literates, paradoxically became the great colonizing language of the nineteenth century?

This paradox inherent in the history of the English language has inspired renewed theoretical interest in the "go-between." Chicana theorists are "re-writing" Malinche differently. Their historical and power-charged experiences of negotiating the border of many languages (formal Spanish, Mexican-Spanish, Tex-Mex, College English, rap English), theories, racial, sexual practices, have given them a historical appreciation of negotiating borders. They have learned that the 'foreigness our language' becomes the "inescapable cultural condition for the enunciation of the mother tongue."[46] She concludes by explaining to Bede that Chicana feminist theorists have a word for this theoretical and political negotiation of borders which power and violence have kept separate and incommensurate. It is called a border consciousness, a *mestiza* consciousness.

Bede says he looks forward to visiting her class and the challenge of rethinking the linguistic negotiations of his text *The History of the English Church and People* as one of negotiating power-charged language borders. Perhaps, he will analyze the famous dream of his *History,* Caedmon's dream, perhaps he has not yet worked through that dream, even after all this time. He admits to his fear and anxiety at the thought of imagining himself as a go-between. He finds the comparison with Malinche particularly unsettling. He will need help to think through these issues. He wonders if the students would be interested in learning Latin and Old English and several other languages to help him? The Chicana feminist says, you will have to ask the students, but I think this engaged historical thinking about the language negotiations of your work will spark their interest.

The Chicana theorist ironically realizes as she speaks to Bede that she too has reenacted the act of go-between. She translates her claims into more formal, theoretical language for Bede. By reconceptualizing Old English and the Latin written by Anglo-Saxon writers, such as Bede, as border writing, we can bring these multidimensional texts into a rich, critical postcolonial field of border writing and theories of border performance. By linking the study of Old English to theories of border-writing we also open up the study of Old English to contemporary historical questions: How did a colonized language come to be the colonizing language of the nineteenth century? How did Old English get taught in the English schools of colonial India, how does Old English get taught in the California university-system today? Do we need to think of a san-skritized Beowulf, as much an anglicized *Sakuntala,* a chicanoized Caedmon's hymn? Deep in conversation, the Chicana feminist and Bede leave the dean and the professor of Old English in the medieval institute library and go out for some coffee. Readers get to make up their own ending to my story.

The time has come to mark my own performance as a go-between between some feminist and postcolonial theory in this paper. I have imagined my own ending to this vignette just conjured for you. How to articulate La Vendida and La Chingada—how to articulate the double bind of the construct of the Middle Ages? To encourage us to think in an utopian mode for the twenty-first century, in the face of contested problems of pedagogy and scholarship in medieval studies, I will end not with a dream, but with the work of dream-work:

> That focal point or fulcrum, that juncture where the *mestiza* stands, is where phenomena tend to collide. It is where the possibility of uniting all that is separate occurs. This assembly is not one where severed or separated pieces merely come together. Nor is it a balancing of opposing powers. In attempting to work out a synthesis, the self has added a third element which is greater than the sum of its severed parts. The third element is a new consciousness—a *mestiza* consciousness—and though it is a source of intense pain, its energy comes from a continual creative motion that keeps breaking down the unitary aspect of each new paradigm.... Et unas pocas centurias, the future will belong to the *mestiza.*[47]

NOTES

I am grateful to the following colleagues who generously read drafts of this paper and offered their criticisms and support: Joe Buttigieg, Ted Cachey, Bill Dohar, Julia Douthwaite, Kent Emery, Ed English, Robert Franklin, Philip Gleason, Barbara Green, Madonna Hettinger, Cyraina Johnson, Mark Jordan, Sandra Joshel, Mark Myerson, Dianne Phillips, Dan Sheerin, John Van Engen, Joseph Wawrykow, Lisa Wolverton. I am also grateful to the participants of the Medieval Studies section of the Cultural Studies Seminar at Rice University for their stimulating exchange and critical support for developing this conference paper for the conference publication. A mini-colloquium with Clare Lees and James W. Earle organized by Sarah Lynn Higley and Tom Hahn (Rochester) offered a much-needed opportunity to deliver a version of this paper to colleagues in medieval literature. The *Exemplaria* session at Kalamazoo (1993) on "Medievalism and Imperialism: The Subject of Appropriation" provided this paper the benefit of two thoughtful comments by Laurie Finke (Kenyon College) and Catherine S. Cox (University of Florida).

1. The material quoted in this paragraph comes from the essay by Umberto Eco, "The Return of the Middle Ages," in his *Travels in Hyperreality,* trans. William Weaver (New York: Harcourt Brace Jovanovich, 1986), 61–85.

2. I am telescoping an important discussion of the historical construction of early-modern identity worked through by Jonathon Dollimore, *Sexual Dissidence: Augustine to Wilde, Freud to Foucault* (Oxford University Press, 1991), 283–289. My thanks to Kari Kalve (Madison) who first urged me to read Dollimore.

3. A large literature exists on the non-originary and originary frames of the Middle Ages. For a selection of recent reflections, see R. Howard Bloch, "Naturalism, Nationalism, Medievalism," *Romantic Review* 76, no. 4 (1985): 341–360; Allen J. Frantzen, *Desire for Origins: New Language, Old English, and Teaching the Tradition* (New Brunswick, N.J.: Rutgers University Press, 1990); *idem,* "Prologue: Documents and Monuments: Difference and Interdisciplinarity in the Study of Medieval Culture," in his *Speaking Two Languages* (Albany: State University of New York Press, 1990), 1–33; Lee Patterson, *Negotiating the Past: The Historical Understanding of Medieval Literature* (Madison: University of Wisconsin Press, 1987); *idem,* "On the Margin: Postmodernism, Ironic History, and Medieval Studies," *Speculum* 65, no. 1 (1990): 87–108; Brian Stock, *Listening for the Text: On the Uses of the Past* (Baltimore: Johns Hopkins University Press, 1990); for a study of medievalism and Catholicism in the United States, important to the cultural history of North American medieval institutes, see Philip Gleason, "American Catholics and the Mythic Middle Ages," *Keeping the Faith: American Catholicism Past and Present* (Notre Dame, Ind.: University of Notre Dame Press, 1987), 11–34. For a strong example of the effects of the pastism-presentism debate, see *Holy Feast and Holy Fast: The Religious Significance of Food to Medieval Women* by Caroline Walker Bynum (Berkeley: University of California Press, 1987); for a critique of pastism in the study of medieval women's history, see Kathleen Biddick, "Genders,

Bodies, Borders: Technologies of the Visible," *Speculum* 68 (2, 1993):389–418. A popular form of "presentism" may be found in the essay by Georges Duby, "The Emergence of the Individual," in *A History of Private Life. II. Revelations of the Medieval World* (Cambridge, Mass: Harvard University Press, 1988), 507–563.

4. The energies devoted to such debate help to contribute to the disciplinary repression of discussion of pressing questions about the significance of other cultural constructions of time in historical practice, notably, transference and time-lag. Dominick LaCapra has made important arguments about the theoretical importance of transference to the practice of history: "I use 'transference' in the modified psychoanalytic sense of repetition-displacement of the past into the present as it necessarily bears on the future. 'Transference' is bound up with a notion of time not as simply continuity or discontinuity but as repetition with variation or change—at time traumatically disruptive change" (from his essay "Is Everyone a *Mentalité* Case?" in his *History and Criticism* (Ithaca: N.Y.: Cornell University Press, 1985), 72; Homi Bhabha has pointed out the importance of the critical concept of *time-lag,* especially for post-colonial, subaltern histories: "There is a continual tension between spatial incommensurability of the articulation of cultural differences, and the temporal non-synchronicity of signification as they attempt to speak, quite literally, in terms of each other" in his essay "Postcolonial Authority and Postmodern Guilt," in *Cultural Studies,* ed. Lawrence Grossberg, Cary Nelson, Paula A. Treichler (New York: Routledge, 1992), 58.

5. For an example of the Middle Ages working as stand-in for neo-colonial representations of the Third World in the present, see my review of the film *The Navigator: A Medieval Odyssey* (Vincent Ward, 1988) *The American Historical Review* 97, no. 4 (1993): 1152–1153.

6. Words of Henry Chadwick quoted by Milton McC. Gatch in a recent essay, "The Medievalist and Cultural Literacy," *Speculum* 66, no. 3 (1991): 604. Lee Patterson drew our attention to such tropes in his comments at the conference.

7. Our disciplinary problems with pastism and presentism could both learn from and contribute to a parallel debate in critical studies—the debates over modernism-postmodernism. The controversy can provide medievalists with productive ways of reading the medieval–early-modern debates. In turn, our own controversies over the medieval–early-modern divide can produce important questions about containment and appropriation for contemporary critical studies of postmodernism. Dollimore, *Sexual Dissidence,* sets out an incisive discussion of debates over containment, resistance, and transgression in cultural politics (81–91).

8. Such a medieval studies would be studies in diffraction: "diffraction is a mapping of interference, not of replication, reflection, or repro-

duction." For important discussion of the difference between articulation and representation as political strategies in disciplines, terms which can be refigured as transgressive knowledge and representation in Dollimore, *Sexual Dissidence,* see Donna Haraway, "The Promises of Monsters: A Regenerative Politics for Inappropriate/d Others," in *Cultural Studies,* 295–337; citation from p. 300. These issues are also raised in Joan W. Scott, "The Evidence of Experience," *Critical Inquiry* 17 (Summer 1991): 773–797.

9. The work of Christina Crosby and Homi Bhabha inspire my thoughts here: Christina Crosby, *The Ends of History: Victorians and "The Woman Question"* (New York: Routledge, 1991); and her "Dealing with Differences," *Feminists Theorize the Political,* ed. Judith Butler and Joan W. Scott (New York: Routledge, 1992), 130–143; Bhabha, "Postcolonial Authority and Postmodern Guilt."

10. It is interesting to note that another conference devoted to disciplinary scrutiny of medieval studies also avoided mention of the present: *The Past and Future of Medieval Studies,* December 1990, Barnard College. My thoughts about missing bodies were set in motion at the Barnard meeting.

11. I have appropriated the unusual uses of the noun, "the disappeared" and the very "to disappear" from the work of the "mother of the disappeared" in Chile. I wish to suggest that meditations on their political work have relevance to issues of pedagogy in medieval studies: "The memory of protest, and the violence enacted against it by the State, best serves the official forces of oppression when the collective nature of memory is broken, when it is fragmented and located not in the public sphere but in the private fastness of the individual self or of the family. There it feeds fear. There it feeds nightmares crippling the capacity for public protest and spirited intelligent opposition. And that is why the actions of the mothers of the disappeared strike me as important. For they create a new public ritual whose aim is to allow the tremendous moral and magical power of the unquiet dead to flow into the public sphere, empower individuals, and challenge the would-be guardians of the Nation-State, guardians of the dead as well as its living, of its meaning and of its destiny." Citation taken from a keynote address for the Smithsonian Columbus Quincentenary Conference by Michael Taussig, reprinted as "Violence and Resistance in the Americas: The Legacy of Conquest," in his *Nervous System* (New York: Routledge, 1992), 48–49.

12. Medieval studies will have to respond to the problems of critical pedagogy as *embodied theory,* as the university approaches the twenty-first century. Allen Frantzen trenchantly comments on the disembodiment of pedagogy when it gets discussed as "approaches" to Old English in his *Desire for Origins,* p. 13 and passim. For critical commentaries on pedagogy that can serve as a starting point for engaged discussion of pedagogy

among medievalists, see the interview between Harold Veeser and Gayatri Chakravorty Spivak which appeared in *The New Historicism,* ed. Harold Veeser (New York: Routledge, 1989); reprinted as "The New Historicism: Political Commitment and the Post-modern Criticism," in Spivak's *The Post-Colonial Critic: Interviews, Strategies, Dialogues,* ed. Sarah Harasym (New York: Routledge, 1990), 152–168; Chandra Talpade Mohanty, "On Race and Voice: Challenges for Liberal Education in the 1990s," *Cultural Critique* (Winter 1990): 179–208; Shoshana Felman, "Psychoanalysis and Education: Teaching Terminable and Interminable," in her *Jacques Lacan and the Adventure of Insight: Psychoanalysis in Contemporary Culture* (Cambridge, Mass.: Harvard University Press, 1987), 69–97; Henry A. Giroux, "Resisting Difference: Cultural Studies and the Discourse of Critical Pedagogy," in *Cultural Studies,* 199–212.

13. I will discuss two examples where Geertz is used in contemporary critiques of medieval studies, see below note 19. I want to note here, too, the uncanny appearance of Geertz in the opening travel story told by Stephen Greenblatt in his introduction to *Marvellous Possessions: The Wonder of the New World* (Chicago: University of Chicago Press, 1991), 3–6. I read Greenblatt's opening travel anecdote of a visit to Bali in 1986 as a story of an emblematic encounter of literary critics (and also historians) with a not-so-new New World of post–World War II anthropology. Like the Columbian encounter, this encounter has yet to be worked through in the academy.

14. Clifford Geertz, "Deep Play: Notes on the Balinese Cockfight," in his *The Interpretation of Culture: Selected Essays* (New York: Basic Books, 1973), 412–453. I will cite this article as DP in the text. In his *Works and Lives: The Anthropologist as Author* (Stanford, Calif.: Stanford University Press, 1988) Geertz discusses the problem of ethnographic writing ("a hundred and fifteen years ... of asseverational prose and literary innocence is long enough (p. 24)") in essays on Levi-Strauss, Evans-Pritchard, Malinowski and Benedict, but does not subject his own ethnographic writing to critique and fails to account how ethnographic writing became part of colonial subjectivity, for anthropologist and "native" (see his discussion, pp. 132–138). The criticisms of ethnography by James Clifford can be read in critical contrast to Geertz, see his *The Predicament of Culture: Twentieth-Century Ethnography, Literature and Art* (Cambridge, Mass.: Harvard University Press, 1988). Discussion of Geertz and the fable of rapport occurs on pp. 40–41. See also, Taussig, *Nervous System.*

15. Clifford, *Predicament of Culture,* 40.

16. An anonymous reviewer of the essay queried whether my analysis at this juncture was simply my projection. Such a query is what recent work on the homosocial bond helps us to think about in a critical, political

way. In a discussion of Iago relevant to such a question Dollimore provides a helpful answer to the query, one relevant to the concerns of my analysis: "But we would be mistaken to conclude that 'repressed homosexuality' is the 'real' motivation of the homosocial bond since such a conclusion would obscure much and reveal little. Much more significant for understanding the sexual economy at work here is the way Iago's story, intentionally or not, reveals betrayal/usurpation as the typical *double* focus of masculine sexual jealousy, and a major instability in homosocial bonding. Also significant is the way Iago's story superimposes an excessive usurping masculine desire upon a betraying and unnatural female desire, confirming the culpability of both Cassio and Desdemona, usurper and betrayer, but of course hers more than his" *Sexual Dissidence,* 158. See Eve Sedgwick, *Between Men: English Literature and Male Homosocial Desire* (New York: Columbia University Press, 1985); also for a contemporary analysis of some conventions in the hyper-masculine film genre, see Sharon Willis, "Disputed Territories: Masculinity and Social Space," *Camera Obscura* 19 (1989): 5–23.

17. For a discussion of this problem of how the category of peasant has sealed off groups from a dynamic history in medieval English history, see Kathleen Biddick, "Decolonizing the English Past: Readings in Medieval Archaeology and History," *Journal of British Studies* 32 (January 1993): 1–23.

18. Spivak analyzes how such practices effect a "worlding" of the other: "He [Captain Geoffrey Birch, an assistant agent to the Governor, East India Company, 1815] is actually engaged in consolidating the self of Europe by obliging the native to cathect the space of the Other on his home ground. He is worlding *their own world,* which is far from mere uninscribed earth, anew, by obliging *them* to domesticate the alien as Master." From her article, "The Rani of Sirmur: An Essay in Reading the Archives," *History and Theory* 24, no. 3 (1985): 253.

19. Gabrielle M. Spiegel, "History, Historicism, and the Social Logic of the Text in the Middle Ages," *Speculum* 65, no. 1 (1990): 59–86; Frantzen, "Prologue," 24.

20. Spiegel, "History, Historicism and Social Logic," 85.

21. Citation in parentheses are Frantzen's words: Frantzen, "Prologue," 24.

22. Ibid., "Prologue," 24–25.

23. My invocation of orientalism produced some sharp resistance at the conference. The literature cited in this note and note 25 below makes it clear that "throwing out" the study of orientalism closes medieval studies off from active, dynamic debates in contemporary historiography. I do not think it is time to throw the study of orientalism out, but urge us to

make it more complex, to continue to historicize the process, and in so
doing raise questions about the epistemological and ontological challenges of a post-orientalist history. For selected references, that set out, re-
vise and criticize the pioneering work of Edward Said, see: Edward W.
Said, "Representing the Colonized: Anthropology's Interlocutors," *Critical
Inquiry* 15 (Winter 1989): 205–225; James Clifford, "On *Orientalism*,"
Predicament of Culture, 255–276; Timothy Mitchell, *Colonising Egypt*
(Cambridge: Cambridge University Press, 1986); Robert Young, *White Mythologies: Writing History and the West* (New York: Routledge, 1990); Gyan
Prakash, "Writing Post-Orientalist Histories of the Third World: Perspec-
tives from Indian Historiography," *Comparative Studies in Society and His-
tory* 32, no. 2 (1990): 383–408.

24. In *The Desire for Origins* Frantzen makes the important observation that "Orientalism and Anglo-Saxonism intersect at many points (p.
29)." I would broaden his intersections to include anthropology and cultural studies.

25. See also the responses to the Prakash (1990) article by Rosalind
O'Hanlon and David Washbrook, "After Orientalism: Culture, Criticism
and Politics in the Third World," *Comparative Studies in Society and History* 34, no. 1 (1992): 141–167; Dipesh Chakrabarty, "Postcoloniality and
the Artifice of History: Who Speaks for 'Indian' Pasts," *Representations* 37
(Winter 1992): 1–26. For an important feminist work of post-orientalism,
see Trinh T. Minh-ha, *Woman, Native, Other: Writing Postcoloniality and
Feminism* (Bloomington: Indiana University Press, 1989).

26. For examples of these orientalist constructions of history within
Europe, see the essays in *Nations and Narration,* ed. Homi Bhabha (New
York: Routledge, 1990) especially by Martin Thom, "Tribes within Nations:
The Ancient Germans and the History of Modern France," 23–43 and
Frantzen on Anglo-Saxonism in his *Desire for Origins.*

27. The work of Dr. Glory Dharmaraj and our conversations have in-
spired this section. Dr. Dharmaraj delivered a seminar on "Feminism, Me-
dievalism, and the Other: Postcoloniality as Critique," at the Medieval
Institute of the University of Notre Dame, November 12, 1991. See Gauri
Viswanathan, *Masks of Conquest: Literary Study and British Rule in India*
(New York: Columbia University Press, 1989) and other basic references:
D. J. Palmer, *The Rise of English Studies: An Account of the Study of the En-
glish Language and Literature from its Origins to the Making of the Oxford
School* (Oxford: Oxford University Press, 1965); Allen J. Frantzen and
Charles L. Venegoni, "The Desire for Origins: An Archaeology of Anglo-
Saxon Studies," *Style* 20, no. 2 (1986): 142–156.

28. From a report of the Early English Text Society in 1886, p. 1.
These pamphlets listed current publications of the society, reports of the

treasurer (this particular report included treasurer's accounts from 1879–1885) and a list of subscribing members for 1886. I used the volumes of the Early English Text Society in the University of Notre Dame Library. For the period from its founding to 1900, the following reports are bound in the EETS volumes: reports for 1868; 1869; 1872; 1877; 1886. I will cite these reports hereafter as *EETS Report* and year.

29. *EETS Report,* 1868, 4–5.

30. From his introductory lecture as Professor of English at Queen's College, cited in *The Rise of English Studies,* 38–39.

31. The following citation helps to shed light on this middle-class identity: "Though the Committee are sorry to terrify or disgust any one, they must say that the men they want are 'the resolute members' referred to in the last Report; men who do not think the right way to get through their work is to be afraid of it or let their stomachs turn at it; but men who know that they have a work to do, and mean to do it; men who can look 270 MSS and books in the face, and say quietly, 'Well at 9 a-year, we shall clear you off in 30 years;' who can look at £60,000 worth of work, and say, "At £1000 a-year, you're to be cut down in 60 years; and if I can manage 30 of them, my boy can settle the other 30.' The Society has a long job in hand and a heavy one; but not one that can beat men with a *will.* The Roxburghe Clube has lasted from 1812 to 1869, and has taken lately a new lease of its life. May not a Society of that Middle Class which has in great measure superseded the Upper as the mainstay of General Literature and Art, expect to do the same in the case of Antiquarian Literature?" (cited from *EETS Report,* 1868, 21).

32. *EETS Report,* 1869, 2.

33. *EETS Report,* 1877, 8. India Civil Service exams began in 1855 and English studies formed an important component (Palmer, *Rise of English Studies,* 47).

34. There were over thirty mercantile libraries founded in the United States before 1875. They were associated with the adult education movement and provided a library, reading room, lending services, and public lectures for its members. Women were admitted to mercantile libraries. The first annual report (1859) of the Brooklyn Mercantile Library lists 100 female members. These libraries were open in the evenings and collected works which were "best calculated to promote the moral and intellectual elevation of the mercantile character." (From the Philadelphia Mercantile Library, cited in William Douglas Boyd, Jr., "Books for the Young Businessmen: Mercantile Libraries in the United States, 1820–1865; doctoral dissertation, Indiana University, 1975.

35. Much work remains to be done on the politics of the Asiatic Society of Bengal. For a critical perspective, see Viswanathan, *Masks of Con-*

quest. For more apologetic texts, see O. P. Kejariwal, *The Asiatic Society of Bengal and the Discovery of India's Past, 1784–1838* (Oxford: Oxford University Press, 1988); Garland Cannon, *The Life and Mind of Oriental Jones: Sir William Jones the Father of Modern Linguistics* (New York: Cambridge University Press, 1990). For the Sanskrit Renaissance, see also Spivak, "The Rani of Sirmur," 264–265. Kejariwal and Spivak differ significantly in their approaches to the Asiatic Society and the construction of a "past" for India in the nineteenth century.

36. My paper can only gesture toward the complexities of the Sanskrit Renaissance, see Gayatri Chakravorty Spivak, "Can the Subaltern Speak?" in *Marxism and the Interpretation of Culture* (Urbana: University of Illinois Press, 1988), 299.

37. Words of the eminent Sanskrit scholar Edward FitzEdward Hall written in 1868 and cited in Kejariwal, *Asiatic Society,* p. 3; *EETS Report,* 1877, p. 1. For fascinating anecdotes of how Müller came to work on manuscripts of the *Rig Veda* at the East India Company in London and how the East India Company came to finance the publication of his work, see F. Max Müller, *My Autobiography: A Fragment* (London: Longmans, 1901): "However, I thought little of India, I only thought of the library at the East India House, a real Eldorado for an eager Sanskrit student, who had never seen such treasures before (208); also, "The Danger of Ambiguity: Friedrich Max Müller," in Maurice Olender, *The Languages of Paradise: Race, Religion, and Philology in the Nineteenth Century* (Cambridge, Mass.: Harvard University Press, 1992), 82–92.

38. Take, for example, "The Additional Analogues" by W. A. Clouston, written in Glasgow (Glasgow University Library subscribed to EETS), which appear after Frederick J. Furnivall's edition of the *Wright's Chaste Wife,* vol. 12 (1875) of the Early English Text Society publications. In those analogues Clouston cites Persian texts, a recently translated Sanskrit collection, *Katha Sarit Sagara,* trans. Professor C. H. Tawney, which, according to Clouston, just appeared in Calcutta (p. 27, n. 1). See other references (p. 32) to *Indian Fairy Tales,* publications of the *Indian Antiquary, Select Tamil Tales* (Madras, 1939).

39. Viswanathan, *Masks of Conquest,* 3.

40. Salman Rushdie, *Satanic Verses* (New York: Viking, 1988), 343.

41. Chakrabarty, "Postcoloniality," 23.

42. The version through which most undergraduates encounter Bede is the following, *A History of the English Church and People,* trans. Leo Sherley-Price and revised by R. E. Latham (Harmondsworth: Penguin Books, 1955), 38. For the ironic purposes of my imaginary meeting in the medieval institute I am not going to qualify what we might mean by "English" in the eighth century, what we might mean by "Old English" in the

twentieth century, etc. For a critical edition, see *Bede's Ecclesiastical History of the English People,* ed. by Bertram Colgrave and R. A. B. Mynors (Oxford: Clarendon Press, 1969), hereafter called Colgrave and Mynors. My allusions to Bede in this section are influenced in contesting ways by the following studies: André Crépin, "Bede and the Vernacular," in *Famulus Christi: Essays in the Commemoration of the Thirteenth Centenary of the Birth of the Venerable Bede,* ed. Gerald Bonner (London: SPCK, 1976), 170–192; Michael Lapidge, "The School of Theodore and Hadrian," *Anglo-Saxon England* 15 (1986): 45–72; Katherine O'Brien O'Keeffe, "Orality and the Developing Text of Caedmon's *Hymn,"* *Speculum* 62, no. 1 (1987): 1–20; René Derolez, "Runic Literacy among the Anglo-Saxons," in *Britain 400–600: Language and History,* ed. Alfred Bammesberger and Alfred Wollmann, *Anglistische Forschungen* 205 (1990), 397–436; Frantzen, *Desire for Origins,* 130–167; Sarah Lynn Higley, *Between Languages: The Uncooperative Text in Early Welsh and Old English Nature Poetry* (University Park, Penn.: Pennsylvania State University Press, 1993); Malcolm Godden and Michael Lapidge, *The Cambridge Companion to Old English Literature* (Cambridge: Cambridge University Press, 1991); Seth Lerer, *Literary and Power in Anglo-Saxon Literature* (Lincoln, Neb.: University of Nebraska Press, 1991); Clare A. Lees and Gillian R. Overing, "Birthing Bishops and Fathering Poets: Bede, Hild, and the Relations of Cultural Production," forthcoming in *Exemplaria.*

43. For references to the complex political project of reappropriating and refiguring Malinche (or Malintzin) among Chicana feminists, see: Norma Alarcón, "Chicana's Feminist Literature: A Re-vision through Malintzin/or Malintzin: Putting Flesh Back on the Object," *This Bridge Called My Back: Writing by Radical Women of Color,* ed. Cherríe Moraga and Gloria Anzaldúa (New York: Kitchen Table: Women of Color Press), 182–190; Gloria Anzaldúa, "La conciencia de la mestiza: Towards a New Consciousness," *Making Face, Making Soul,* ed. Gloria Anzaldúa (San Francisco: An Aunt Lute Foundation Book, 1990), 377–389; Cherríe Moraga, "From a Long Line of Vendidas: Chicanas and Feminism," in *Feminist Studies/Critical Studies,* ed. Teresa de Lauretis (Bloomington: Indiana University Press, 1986), 173–190. For a historical study of the figure of Malinche from sixteenth-century documents to contemporary Mexican feminism, see Sanra Messinger Cypess, *La Malinche in Mexican Literature: From History to Myth* (Austin: University of Texas Press, 1991). For another perspective, one that carefully avoids contemporary Chicana feminist appropriations of Malinche, see David E. Johnson, "Women, Translation, Nationalism: La Malinche and the Example of Juan García Ponce," *Arizona Quarterly* 47, no. 3 (1991): 93–116 (I am grateful to Ted Cachey for sharing this reference).

44. See D. Emily Hicks, *Border Writing: The Multidimensional Text* (Minneapolis: University of Minnesota Press, 1991).

45. Said, "Representing the Colonized," 255.

46. Homi Bhabha, "DisseminNation: Time, Narrative, and the Margins of the Modern Nation," in *Nation and Narration,* 317.

47. Anzaldúa, "La conciencia de la mestiza," 379.

Visions of Medieval Studies
in North America

Patrick J. Geary

As WE BEGIN our reflection on medieval studies, it is appropriate to remember that North Americans, in the view of Europeans, are the "other," that is, voices they perceive as situated, like our Russian, Australian, New Zealand, and Japanese colleagues, on the periphery of the geographical and perhaps sometimes intellectual world of the Middle Ages. Since no scholars currently teaching and working in Europe have been invited to participate in this collective reflection on the past and future of medieval studies, I propose to bring something of this external vision to our attention. In particular I wish to examine what, if anything, scholars believe makes the medieval scholarship of North Americans distinctive from that conducted in Europe. In other words, what is it we do, what is it that we do well, and, what distinguishes or unites us with our European colleagues?

In this examination I am much less interested in my own perceptions of medieval studies than I am in how we perceive ourselves and are perceived by European colleagues. To this end I have contacted a spectrum of Canadian and U.S. scholars in English, and French, in art history and other disciplines within medieval studies and asked them frankly what if anything they see as distinguishing the work that they and their North American colleagues do from that done in Britain and on the Continent. Not, however, being content to present the self-image of North Americans, I have also asked a number of British, French, German, Belgian, Austrian, and Italian scholars the same questions. How do they see the work done by New World medievalists? How does it fit into what they and their colleagues are doing? When they see differences, how do they account for those differences?

This, I must emphasize, was not a rigorous, formal survey. It was entirely impressionistic, relying largely on my own informal network here and abroad. Nevertheless, it has allowed me to begin to see what we do in a somewhat different light. I share these comments, which out of consideration to those I pressed for frank evaluations I keep anonymous, in the hope that they might serve as introductions to some of the issues facing North American medievalists in the last decade of the twentieth century. In particular I urge us to listen to the voices and visions from outside of North America so that we might begin to understand ourselves as others see us.

Some foreign scholars suggest that in their fields, North Americans lead the world. This is the opinion of one European musicologist, who suggests that the Germans who arrived in the U.S. after Kristallnacht not only continued to make major contributions but succeeded in training subsequent generations of American musicologists who have continued the tradition both in editing work, although generally with relatively few manuscripts consulted, and in theory. Part of the American leadership, he concedes, is by default: in Germany there are ever fewer medieval musicologists and he expects the tradition to die out altogether shortly. In France, he describes the state of medieval musicology bluntly as "misérable."

In some fields, the differences between the kinds of scholarship being done on the two sides of the Atlantic is minimal. This seems to be the case in Middle English. Today, thanks to Margaret Thatcher, it is very difficult to talk about a distinct American as opposed to British Middle English tradition: some of the very best British are here permanently or come regularly. We have something else to thank Margaret Thatcher for: the systematic destruction of British higher education that has radicalized and polarized many of the best minds in British academia, who have organized for survival around a kind of Marxist material culture approach to Middle English which has also found fertile ground in some North American literature departments and MLA panels.

If there is a difference in approaches to Middle English on the two sides of the Atlantic, perhaps it is the relative diversity and eclecticism represented in the American scene. Twenty years ago, the fight was against dominant traditions which celebrated church hierarchy, the reading of literature for power politics, or reading Middle English through Augustinian or perhaps neo-Thomist optics. This is old stuff today. And yet survivors of the intellectual history tradition jostle the new historicists, Marxists, post-modernists, and post-deconstructionists, all of whom still find themselves on panels at conferences with people who are not afraid to mock intertextuality and interdisciplinarity. It is relevant in understanding this anarchy to realize that here these intellectual traditions exist in an institutional and political atmosphere which, while threatening, is not yet Thatcherism. At the same time, one must gauge the extent to which the emergence of the new historicist tradition today, no less than the Robertsonian analysis of the 1960s, tends toward hegemony. Thus far, the general answer is that new historicists and Marxist materialists do not search for, or at least have not achieved, this hegemonic position. Still, one can ask whether for some at least, pluralism is a dirty word.

Other areas of medieval studies exist within the cracks and corners of exactly this diversity in departments of English. One is medieval Latin, once the cornerstone of medieval studies, which rarely has its own identity outside of Toronto. This tradition, which originated in the generation of Traube students including Beeson, Rand, and Charles U. Clark, has no institutional base in American universities. Instead Latinists hide out in faculties of English, philosophy, French, and even history, where they are frequently made more welcome than in departments of classics.

Some practitioners see this as a blessing. First, I am told, the dispersion of Latinists across the university functions as a kind of glue, holding together medieval vernacular literature studies. In a major university, one is never far from someone in German, English, or Romance languages who is actually a Latin philologist reminding us that vernacular literature was, for most of the thousand-year period we study, a minor genre usually written by people who did most of their writing and thinking in Latin. Second, because Latinists must do other things as well, they have remained more in touch with literary critical methodology and the like than classics ever has, "where," as one Latinist who teaches in a classics department suggests, "we're always a struggling generation behind." He concludes that "The fact that 'medieval Latin' specialists are to be found in an odd variety of departments has a negative effect on collegiality among them as a group, but a positive effect on their interaction with colleagues otherwise." The down side, he goes on to say, is that it is hard to transmit a discipline when there is no core program where one can send students for training.

One American suggested that our peculiar relationship to Latin training results from our lack of connectedness to European assumptions about this language. In Britain she contends, Latin was taught in schools in a way that implied a congruence between the British Empire and that of the Romans. The Latin of the Aeneid was somehow their Latin too. British medievalists feel comfortable with this humanistic Latinity and find it in the Renaissance of the twelfth century for example, or in the great bishop-administrators of the thirteenth. In Germany Latin is the legal language and so Germans reading medieval Latin see the juristic and constitutional implications. In France and in Italy, Latin is simply the language, for French and especially Italian *are* Latin, changed and evolved of course. Thus in France all historical inquiry is in a sense literary inquiry and writing medieval history explicitly a literary activity. But in the U.S. Latin is strange, curious, foreign, somehow not ours. It is unmoored from anything in our secular history and resonates only with our religion; but even this, since Vatican II, is gone. "All this means," she concludes, "that American medievalists visit the Middle Ages as a more utterly and profoundly foreign country than European medievalists." Small wonder that medieval Latinists, the ultimate aliens, must make their living in the American university by doing something else.

This problem of people practicing their professional interests on their own time while making their living teaching in other fields is also at the heart, I am told by one European Byzantinist, of the deep problem affecting Byzantine studies in North America. There are no jobs in Byzantine history. This is not an exaggeration. This year, one post was announced in all of North America, and the offer was subsequently canceled. The result is that North American Byzantinists, like medieval Latinists, must sell themselves as something else. Generally this is to teach western European history or possibly Greek language or history, unless they leave academe altogether for another profession.

Since there are no jobs in Byzantine, there are few teachers of Byzantine, few institutions where students can be trained to be Byzantinists, and still fewer where Byzantinists can develop the broad perspective on history in which to understand the Byzantine world. This, my European informant contends, is the basic problem of Byzantine studies in North America: undergraduates and graduate students lack the historical context within which to draw comparative frameworks for understanding Byzantium. They are too ignorant of Latin Europe, of Islam, and of the Far East. This tunnel vision cuts Byzantine culture off from its sibling cultures. Byzantium on its own is not as interesting as Byzantium in a medieval world, or Byzantine traditions compared with Chinese bureaucracy or Japanese feudalism.

Byzantine studies are seen either as a part of ethnic Greek studies or as a luxury which is among the first to go in times of austerity. And yet, within the contemporary world, the Byzantine tradition is essential if we are to understand the vast changes affecting eastern and central Europe as well as the Near East. Heavens knows that America desperately needs such knowledge. However, for the most part American Byzantinists (my informant continues) are either incapable or uninterested in addressing these broad and vital concerns which would demonstrate the connectedness of Byzantine studies to understanding the Slavic, Hellenic, and Turkic worlds of today. The tunnel vision which characterizes students going into Byzantine studies characterizes too much of the work of those who have survived in the profession, or so I am told.

The opposite of tunnel vision is seen to characterize much of other areas of medieval history, although this breadth is a two-edged sword. The negative component is that some Europeans see Americans as too far removed from the sources. As one Belgian scholar suggested, many European scholars consider that North Americans hover over the surface of their subject but fail to do the kind of exhaustive local research necessary to master thoroughly all of the documents, topography, and local history in the way that a native historian can. I am very familiar with the problem. Several years ago I struggled for months with everything from eighteenth-century local publications to World War II ordnance maps to CIA publications in an attempt to identify some 200 places in Provence and the Piedmont in an eighth-century testament. After publication, a colleague who is a native of Avignon pointed out that one village near his home that I had identified as belonging to the list had received its name only in the nineteenth century in honor of a French military hero. Had I been a native of Avignon, I would have never made such a blunder.

On the other hand, the same Belgian who points to the perception of the superficiality of American archival research suggests that Americans work comparatively, more frequently addressing the theoretical framework and broader conclusions and implications of their work than do many Europeans whose deep familiarity with local sources exists in a vacuum. He attributes this not only to the inaccessibility of sources to those of us who must do archival research in one-semester or at best one-year increments, but also to the institutional situation in which we find ourselves. First, we are forced to teach early modern and renaissance periods in our disciplines as well as medieval and thus are exposed to theoretical problems and issues raised outside of medieval perspectives. Second, we seldom can specialize on as narrow a geographical perspective as a single country in our courses.

An American writing in French history echoed this positive appreciation of the influence of the teaching system in his own work. Although he publishes exclusively on medieval France, he always teaches comparative French and English history. His knowledge of English history has made him a closet comparativist: all of his work is implicitly comparative, even though one sees only the French side of this comparison in his publications.

This broader, comparative aspect of American medieval studies and particularly medieval history is the characteristic most frequently mentioned by Americans and Europeans alike. With rare exceptions, Europeans remain tied to a local or national conception of the past. Our esteemed European colleagues whom we so much admire are in fact the counterparts to our colleagues at home who teach American civilization and whose parochialism we so much regret. Several German colleagues, commenting on the relative ignorance of North American scholarship in Germany, explained that for all their strength, many German medievalists are driven by the fear that they might have to compete not only with each other but with foreigners, and they deal with this by simply ignoring these outsiders. Thus North American, French, or British scholars seldom appear in the bibliographies of major German reference works or syntheses. When North Americans are recognized, and they give as examples John Freed's work on the Salzburg ministerials and Andrew Lewis on the Capetians, their thematic and methodological contributions to, for example, the history of the medieval nobility or the ministerialiage are ignored. These outsiders are recognized simply for providing specific regional studies, usually of areas on the margins of German scholarly interest.

In North America it is hard to ignore competing traditions. One French scholar commented that "The contrasts and confrontations formed in Europe are reflected in America. It seems to me that difference *chez vous* has a positive effect, namely that diversity is not isolated by more or less national traditions but rather is encountered within great universities. The clash of diverse attitudes is both constant and beneficial."

By no means is this European parochialism limited to political historians. Speaking of the great David Knowles, one scholar admitted that for all his learning, Knowles tended to think of Scotland and England as more similar than England and France in the Middle Ages because in the twentieth century they are part of the same national polity. A British scholar echoes the opinion that North Americans can escape this parochialism, saying that North Americans have at their disposal all the European traditions, and it is the choice and the blending of traditions that gives them such strength.

This lack of national tradition or bias is constantly emphasized by Europeans. As one British historian suggested, "American medievalists have the potential to transcend or avoid the inevitable national biases or perspectives of European scholars, since they don't have to identify with one particular European country," although he adds "many do." An Austrian concurred, saying that in his experience, Americans take a unified view of the Middle Ages while European scholars work within national if not nationalist traditions. It would be no exaggeration to say that unlike Americans, most Europeans do not do European history.

The reason that Europeans do not study European history is that great specter hovering over European medieval studies, as over all aspects of Europe's past, nationalism. If in North America, medieval studies are seen as superfluous luxuries or the retreat of those wishing to escape into a never-never land of pre-class, pre-industrial society, and if we sometimes look longingly at the central position that our counterparts play in their nations' cultural life, we must not forget that they do so at a great price. What is different in the relationship between the role of medieval studies in North America and that in Europe is that European societies have appropriated the Middle Ages as their own, have integrated it into their national and regional mythologies, and thus have created explicit but highly arbitrary links with this period. Medieval civilization means something to Europeans, but it does so because of a long and often ugly tradition of the conscious elaboration and manipulation of medieval culture which began at the end of the eighteenth century. This tradition is alive and well, fostered by a general culture which rewards medievalists and reinforces their scholarship when they operate within these tried and true traditions. This is as much a part of the European publishing industry, tourism, and economics as it is of education. To cite but a minor example, a few years ago I published a small survey of Merovingian history which, in English, is called *Before France and Germany* and which attempts to place early medieval history within a non-national context. It met with considerable scholarly and popular success in France, but the success was probably due in large part to the French title, which I only learned when I received a copy of the translation: *Naissance de la France*.

An Austrian colleague cited a more important example of the freedom of North American scholars. Since the nineteenth century, both Romance and Germanic scholars had been content to imagine that the Gothic people installed in Italy in the late fifth and sixth centuries had appropriated one-third of the arable land from Roman landowners. The sources could be read to imply this, and Germans were pleased to think that Germanic peoples had been powerful enough to carry out such a major shift of land ownership in an extraordinarily brief period. French and Italians had been pleased to accept it as well, seeing it as one more case of brutal German aggression. Walter Goffart, eschewing nationalist scholarly traditions, simply suggested that if such an enormous expropriation had taken place, there would have been a tremendous outcry that would have left some trace in the sources. From this non-ideological perspective he was able to begin elaborating a thesis of barbarian and Roman accommodation which has received wide-spread acceptance, even from Europeans.

My Austrian colleague sees this willingness to look outside of traditional approaches as a reflection of American pragmatism. Americans, he says, are pragmatists rather than ideologues. This indeed accounts for the methodological pluralism that one sees in disciplines such as Romance literature, Middle English, and history. North Americans are drawn to theory, but to the dismay of many of their theoretically oriented European colleagues, they take an enormously eclectic approach to applying theory to their work. Social and cultural anthropology, for example, have by Germans' own admission made little inroads into contemporary German historiography, but they are no more influential in North America than in certain British and French circles. The difference is that while European scholars tend to apply a single tradition of analysis, Americans are willing to mix and match from a whole spectrum of anthropological traditions. Some would dismiss this as an "anything goes" approach. Others would see it as a more pragmatic "anything that works" attitude. "The net result," as a British colleague suggests, "is originality." This, she suggests, combined with a reliance on the seminar to a greater extent than in Britain, "leads to a far more experimental approach than is possible in Europe."

This global and eclectic approach to medieval studies, if at times superficial and at other times liberating, also influences the subjects that we tackle. In Europe, both national agendas and a tradition of master-apprentice relationships maintains the questions asked and the subjects treated within safe and familiar directions. Americans tend to tackle issues that are essentially supranational, intellectual history and crusading history for example. A British scholar suggested that "Almost all of the good work [in the history of medieval philosophy] seems to come from people like Marilyn McCord Adams and Bill Courtenay." Many scholars of English literature spend as much time working on Italian, French, or Latin texts as they do on Chaucer or the Pearl Poet, which they see not at all as separate but rather as organically united.

On the other hand, some Europeans suggest that this focus of Americans leaves us more tied to elite culture, particularly in church, intellectual, and institutional history, than is today common in much of Europe. A British scholar suggests that North Americans may lead in intellectual history, literary theory, art history, and the new cultural history. On the other hand, we are often so tied to the old cultural history that we do not even understand the directions and implications of recent approaches to medieval culture being done on the continent.

Unlike our early modern colleagues, few of us outside of the Herlihy tradition practice the sorts of social, demographic, and cultural history of the inarticulate which demand intimate knowledge of masses of local archives. There have been few American contributions to the plethora of regional studies which have dominated French medieval history since the 1950s. A British social historian suggests that the lack of social history in the American tradition (obviously he is either overlooking or excluding the Raftis school at Toronto) may result from Cold War ideology or perhaps a tendency for Americans interested in society to study American society. Those who pursue medieval history do so, he suggests, with a sense that the Middle Ages has an "aura—catholic, nostalgic, faintly elitist— that makes people who choose it gravitate into intellectual/cultural fields."

One area in which Americans do excel, and in which they are seen to do so, at least by some British, Belgian, German, and French historians, is in women's history and gender studies. A British historian who admits to initial skepticism credits women's studies with "opening up to the rest of the world a field virtually discovered in America." One German historian writes that American work on women's history has become very important for German historiography, where such questions have always been marginal. This historian goes on to suggest that the very lively discussion and debate within American scholarship over the relationship among women's history, gender history, and traditional historical questions has helped German scholars avoid falling into a kind of egocentric feminist history which both avoids the integration of gender issues into more traditional historical studies and closes the possibility of new perspectives.

A number of American and European scholars emphasized the role of the unique institutional circumstances in which North American medieval scholarship develops in determining its content. First are research centers which bring together scholars from different disciplines and different national traditions on an ongoing basis. In

Europe, such interdisciplinary cooperation is not unheard of, particularly in German *Sonderforschungsbereiche,* but these are *ad hoc* programs of limited duration. As a British scholar remarked, from the British perspective, "the point about American medieval studies is that they exist. Medieval interests are not just tacked on to departments dealing with other things. There is far more integration in North America."

On the other hand, a French scholar pointed out that in spite of these institutional arrangements, research projects of a genuinely collective nature are rare. American medieval scholarship is deeply individualistic. This scholar relates the dearth of real cooperative research to an American free market approach to people, careers, and ideas, in which scholars are in constant competition for better pay, bigger grants, or a position at a more prestigious university. Small wonder that competition rather than cooperation often characterize our professional relationships.

Second, although most of us teach in disciplinary departments, a good number of us have had at least some training in interdisciplinary programs in medieval studies, a very rare phenomenon in Europe outside of Louvain. On many campuses, we are involved in medieval studies committees which emphasize horizontal orientations rather than chronological ones. Again, some European scholars encourage interdisciplinary contacts in their seminars—many of us have experienced this in the seminars of Jacques Le Goff and Georges Duby, for example—but these are individual, not institutional initiatives.

Third, through our professional organizations, including the Medieval Academy and our regional associations, we tend to listen more to scholars in other disciplines than do our European colleagues. Finally, one Austrian said, one must not forget medievalist "homecoming parties," particularly the vital socializing as well as scholarly role of Kalamazoo. He added, "some would laugh, but they would be wrong to do so."

For all of this, many American medievalists find medieval studies are curiously deracinated on this continent. This might seem simply the obvious result of not living in Europe and thus being unable to play the same cultural role for a wider society as our colleagues in England or on the continent. As a British scholar put it, "In Europe it's different because you can still touch it in some sense." Actually, this is a bit too simplistic. Europeans no more live in the Middle Ages than do Americans. In all but folkloric aspects, they live in a world no closer to the Middle Ages than our own. That peculiar complex of political, cultural, and mental traditions, prejudices, aesthetics, and comportments that developed in Europe during the Middle Ages is, for better or worse, the common heritage not simply of Europe or even the West but of contemporary world civilization. By embracing such western traditions as capitalism and technological mastery of the physical world, Japan and Korea are as much heirs of Europe's Middle Ages as are the modern societies of France and Germany. As victims of the darker side of western imperialism and racism, so too are the nations of Africa and Latin America. And so too are North Americans, less by virtue of a rapidly decreasing percentage of the population who are of European ancestry than by a common participation in the positive and negative aspects of this ambiguous heritage. As one American scholar suggests, "Although American medievalists think that medieval history is *their* history, most of them do not think of medieval history as their *national* history."

If American medievalists find themselves deracinated, it is less a result of pursuing scholarship in isolation from Europe as it is in pursuing it in isolation from our own society. One European suggested that the essential problem is the question of the place of intellectuals in our countries. The North American university campus reflects spatially the social isolation of the North American "academic." "This is," he continues, "a cultural model of the *longue durée* which goes back to the foundation of Oxford and Cambridge in the countryside around 1200, at the moment when the University of Paris was being founded in the heart of a young capital."

This isolation from our own society is real, and often by choice. And yet I think that the best North American medievalists have always fought this separation even while recognizing the fundamental difference between how Americans and Europeans pursue the Middle Ages. The best scholars have attempted to break out of the mental *cordon sanitaire* which separates academia in general and medieval studies from the rest of society. The great generation of American institutional historians, for example, while they may have made important contributions to the history of France or of England, were never really interested in the history of these or of any other nations *per se*—they were interested in the history of statecraft. Likewise, social historians such as David Herlihy have been content to pursue social structure and order in Italy, Ireland, or Scandinavia with equal enthusiasm. And in our literature departments, scholars are generally interested in language, representation, and communication at least as much as the examples of it that they find in a particular vernacular tradition or at a particular historical moment. Thus one finds that combination, so often irritating to Europeans, of American pragmatism and a taste for theory, abstraction, and generalization. Medieval studies in America is not and cannot be the same as medieval studies in Europe, because we are not Europeans (nor, one might add, are most European scholars who remain, unlike their business and industrial leaders, mired in national perspectives). However, precisely because the contemporary world is equal heir or victim of the Middle Ages, we are in a position to continue our dialogue with our European colleagues from whom we will continue to learn and who, frequently, learn from us. And for the same reason, North American medievalists are in a privileged position to dialogue with colleagues in other disciplines attempting to understand the contemporary world. These are our fundamental challenges: to recognize who we are, and what we are in a position to do uniquely and excellently.

Byzantium and Modern Medieval Studies

Michael McCormick

A BYZANTINE PERSPECTIVE on the issues placed before the Notre Dame conference on the Past and Future of Medieval Studies suggests many possible approaches. As I understood my task, at least two different questions appeared essential. First: *why* study Byzantium? And secondly, *how* should we study Byzantium? Both questions can usefully be framed on different levels. Let me distinguish three:

1. A "universal" level. Here the question of why do Byzantium is a subset of the broader one: why do history?

2. A broad "medievalist" level. If you agree medieval history is worth doing, why do Byzantium, of all things?

3. A specialist, Byzantinist level. Why ask certain questions about Byzantine history?

The first level involves daunting domains beyond my ken: philosophy, human psychology, and even dean's offices and university budgets. At this "universal" level, different answers are possible, ranging from the "utilitarian" approach of policy institutes or political science programs to more self-centered approaches. For instance, in the latter vein one might imagine a philosophical defense of history as an act of love—for the human past, for the craft, etc.—or, perhaps ever more potent, an apology for history as an act of liberation. Historical study as liberating self-understanding seems to have particular resonance of late, at least to judge by many personal statements accompanying applications to graduate studies in European history which refer to the applicants' desire to explore family roots in this nation of immigrants. Alternatively, the question could be framed in the institutional terms the organizers suggested for medieval studies in general: what is the role, contribution, and future of Byzantine studies in the modern university? The third, specialist level, has lately spawned lively if informal debate among Byzantinists, but it appears more appropriate to another venue. For now it seems most useful to focus on the second level, that of the medievalist. After the why of it, we might consider, briefly, the issue of how to study Byzantium in the context of modern medieval studies.

Perhaps the most obvious response to the question of why we should study Byzantium is the old one: Byzantium's enduring impact on the modern world, embodied, for instance, in words we have borrowed from Byzantium, words like "diaper," "boutique," or "icon."[1] Those of us who would laugh at this idea have not been watching the national evening news of Russia, which lately has featured reports on such current events as the ceremony marking the installation of an icon of the Virgin Mother of God in the women's ward of a local hospital.

Among the more recent and sophisticated versions of this classic answer, two in particular merit mention. Alexander Kazhdan of Dumbarton Oaks has argued that the opportunity Byzantium affords us to study a totalitarian civilization in the past has particular resonance for the twentieth-century human condition. The classicist J. K. Newman, on the other hand, has evoked the significance of a Christian Eurasian gateway civilization to a twenty-first–century global culture centered on the Pacific rim. But these are explanations which seek to relate Byzantium to the modern world and my brief here is the medieval one.[2]

Speaking as a western medievalist, I see three major questions: What is Byzantium? Why are Byzantine studies the poor stepchild of medieval research? And finally, why should a (western) medievalist, at whatever state of his or her career, care about Byzantium of all things?

The first question allows a brief answer: Byzantium never existed. No emperor, no subject called himself "Byzantine." It was the "Roman" empire, the emperors were Romans, as were its law, its institutions, and its citizens. It was of course not the same as the empire of Augustus, or even Constantine. But its inhabitants believed it was. Byzantium's self-image as "Greek" is a relatively late—twelfth century—development, and at least in part a response to western insistence on linguistic ethnicity as an element of self-understanding. But the society that centered around the Aegean basin and reached from Italy to Armenia was a distinctively "medieval" version of the old Roman empire.

Given that this was the medieval phase in the history of the Roman empire, or a sizable piece of that old empire, and that even your average man in the street is likely to imagine that the Roman empire was an important thing, how is it possible that Byzantium is so underdeveloped in medieval studies?

Four factors certainly contributed to this lack of interest, starting, perhaps, with ethnocentrism—modern Greece is presumed to be less important than modern France or England. Moreover Byzantine studies originated as and remained until very recently an auxiliary discipline of classics, with all the value judgments such fate entails for a post-classical civilization. Thirdly, the youth of Byzantine studies must be accounted a factor. Distinguished scholarly study of Byzantium goes back at least as far as DuCange—western medievalists may not appreciate that DuCange stands near the top of the Byzantinist pantheon for his magnificent *Glossarium* of medieval Greek and his research into Byzantine prosopography and topography. Nonetheless Byzantine studies' continuous development in western Europe really begins only at the end of the nineteenth century, a full two generations after "medieval" studies had been launched.[3] In America, of course, Byzantine studies are even younger, in only their second or third generation today, if we reckon their establishment from the time A. A. Vasiliev (1867–1953) succeeded M. I. Rostovtzeff (1870–1952) at the University of Wisconsin in Madison from 1925 to 1939.[4] And finally, the fatal flaw: Byzantine studies require one or two languages beyond the already large complement needed by western medievalists, and those languages are very difficult.

Other factors can be adduced, but I think that these four most illuminate the relatively underprivileged status of Byzantine studies in contemporary western Europe—outside of Greece—and the Americas. Of them, I personally believe the "youth" factor and the "handmaiden of classics" syndrome may be the most significant.

Given, then, that Byzantinism is a youthful, relatively underdeveloped field operating on an area as "un-European" as Italy, Croatia, Ukraine, and Turkey, why, of all things should the (western) medievalist bother with Byzantium? For simplicity's sake, I shall focus on only two key issues: Byzantium as part of the medieval world, and secondly, the methodological perspectives that that fact raises.

First and foremost, Byzantium was a "medieval" civilization by virtue of its characteristics. Obviously the chronology is right! But on a more profound level, it shares characteristics that many of us consciously or not consider to be medieval. Religion played an essential role in Byzantine social, mental, and political organization. Peasant communities and great estates dominated Byzantium's fundamentally agrarian economy. The labor of the fields was flanked by significant but, at times, peripheral commerce which culminated in the luxury trade and periodic markets or fairs. The latter were themselves often connected back to religion via the annual celebration of a saint's feast-day.[5]

Byzantium's fascination with universal monarchy is no less medieval than that of Charlemagne, Frederick II, or Dante. So also Byzantium's sociopolitical elite crystallized around the mutual dependencies and tensions between monarchy and aristocracy. In Constantinople as in the West, the late classical legacy defined high culture. Byzantium, in a word, displayed characteristics which will not appear unfamiliar to even the most parochial of "occidentalists." Byzantium can justly be reckoned a medieval civilization, no less than the German empire, Aragon, Latium, or Capetian France.

The perceptions of medieval people do not contradict this. Some of them felt comfortable enough with this culture to immigrate to Byzantium and spend the rest of their days there, from the last Lombard king of Italy to the Varangians. If I may quote an eleventh-century count of Chartres, writing to his wife:

> With great joy I arrived in the city of Constantinople. The emperor [Alexios I] has received me worthily and honorably and most affectionately, as though I were his own son, and he has enriched me with the greatest and most valuable presents, and in the entire army of God and of us, there is no duke nor count nor other powerful person in whom he places greater trust or favor than in me. In fact, my dear, his imperial highness has often recommended, and keeps recommending, that we entrust (*commendemus*) one of our sons to him. He has promised to give him so great and distinguished an *honor* that he will not hanker after our own. In truth, I tell you, to-

day there is no one like him alive on earth. . . . Your father
[William the Conqueror], my dear, though he gave out many
and great things, was almost nothing next to this man.[6]

Although in the end these warm feelings would not predominate in
the Crusaders' difficult relations with Alexios, it is worth remembering that they occurred.

Byzantium too felt itself to be a part of medieval Christendom.
Thus a ninth-century emperor stressed that Byzantine policy accorded westerners privileged status because of their common
religion.[7] And beyond the shared cultural characteristics, Byzantium was also very decidedly a part of the medieval world by its
vigorous interaction with Latin and Slavic Christendom and with the
house of Islam, although the intensity and nature of this interaction
varied over a thousand years. A few examples? In a hitherto unpublished commentary, the late Bernhard Bischoff and Michael Lapidge
have uncovered the impact that a Byzantine émigré's Antiochene
biblical training made on early Irish and Anglo-Saxon exegesis.[8] As
quintessentially "medieval" a document as the Donation of Constantine aimed among other things to claim for eighth-century clerical aristocrats of Rome the prestigious trappings of contemporary
senators in Constantinople.[9] The way in which a dying Charlemagne solemnly transmitted the imperial title to his son Louis the
Pious was obviously and explicably modeled on a ceremony staged
in Constantinople two years before.[10] Around 900, Emperor Leo VI
liked to show off his Frankish military retainers at state banquets in
Constantinople. The half-Greek Otto III needs only to be mentioned, along with the Italian merchants resident at Constantinople
or the Benedictine monastery on Mt. Athos.

Byzantine-western interaction was of course no one-way
street. Thus the western technique of cloisonné enamel appears to
have traveled eastward in the ninth century. Later, Byzantine fascination with the feudal life-style extended even to the jousts and
tournaments that replaced the ancient chariot races in the Great
Hippodrome of Constantinople, and the Byzantines avidly adapted
western courtly romances into Greek. The massive impact of the
later medieval vernaculars pervades the Greek language of the Middle Ages and of today. Even in the world of the imagination, chansons de geste like *Le voyage de Charlemagne* assumed that Charles
the Great, the quintessential "father of Europe," had traveled to
Constantinople.[11]

So the links are there, waiting only to be systematically studied as part of the broader pattern of connections among the regions of medieval Europe. But it is important, indeed essential to study Byzantium not only as the source for so-called "Byzantine influence" on the "West" or for the diffusion eastward of Latin European culture. It is also essential to study Byzantium as an integral part of the medieval world.

In Byzantium, the institutions and peoples of perhaps a third of the former Roman world developed in dialogue with—but also at some distance from—Byzantium's siblings on the other side of the Balkans. This may introduce my second main reason why medievalists—and especially North American ones—should care about Byzantinism: because Byzantium affords us the opportunity to pursue a fascinating kind of comparative history.

Here I might indulge in a more personal note about my experience of medieval history as a young American student in Belgium, since it sheds some light on differing approaches to our common enterprise. I arrived there, filled with youthful enthusiasm and unbounded ignorance, eager to study medieval history. My ideas of medieval history had been shaped by my own teachers, of course, but also and especially by long winter nights reading the house organ of North American medievalism. From *Speculum* I had learned that medievalists worked on all kinds of evidence: buildings, manuscripts, *Beowulf, Roman de la Rose,* Grosseteste, papal bulls. They did so on a European scale: *Speculum* was filled with studies about England, France, Italy, and Scandinavia. And so were our historical congresses. It seems to me that, perhaps because of our distance from Europe and our own national experience, Americans arrived early at a broader view of Europe as a useful level of historical analysis. To my surprise, the perspective at Louvain was rather different. Emphasis on the techniques went beyond even that of the Torontonian masters, and the geographic focus often approached the microscopic: the history not even of the County of Namur, but of a particular parish within the county of Namur, or of a particular monastery in Flanders. I experienced this not as disappointment, but as amazement: because in truth, as I soon learned, the evidence was there in sufficient quantity to allow, indeed to require a narrowing of the geographic focus for the standard, exhaustive *Louvaniste* approach to many periods and problems of the greatest historical import. To the methodological dictate of exhaus-

tiveness was joined the typical and natural European concern with
the archives and history of the area or country where one happened to live.

But even then European medieval history was in some sense
reacting to what one might be tempted to call a North American
model. Certainly my own teacher Léopold Genicot constantly emphasized to his students the importance of viewing specific cases
against broader geographic perspectives. In 1992, the year slated for
European unity, many of Europe's historians are rethinking the geographic categories of their work. The level of analysis has shifted
and this in two diametrically different directions.

In the first place scholarship has zeroed in on the "micro"
level: much of the defining research of our time has focused on
regions and subregions: Namurois, Mâconnais, Mittelrhein, Hamp-
shire, Latium, or Catalonia. With the kind of total history championed by Marc Bloch, specificity is the ransom of accuracy.
Paradoxically, in a second and complementary fashion, medieval
research seems to be gravitating toward a "macro-level." The regional analyses are increasingly organized into broader supra-
regional syntheses, which, by their very nature, imply a comparative approach. And the best regional analyses are prefaced or concluded by comparative appraisals of the particular case under
review. If we examine, for instance, two very similar books on medieval agrarian economic development written in the same country
and in the same tradition of historical analysis about thirty years
apart, we come to an interesting observation. Georges Duby's *Rural
Economy and Country Life in the Medieval West* was first published
in 1962. The explicit geographic frame of reference is "l'Occident
médiéval," which the subtitle further specifies as "France, England
and the Empire." The implicit and frequent standard of reference is
the Mâconnais or, to a lesser extent, a handful of other regions of
France. In the text itself, a good number of comparisons are made
with England, fewer with Germany and fewer still with Italy and
Spain. The selection of translated documents which accompanies
the text achieves a wider panorama. Now three decades later Robert Fossier's *Enfance de l'Europe* has, in some sense, redone Duby's
book, albeit on a shorter time scale.[12] Virtually every aspect of
Fossier's discussion treats differing but related patterns of socio-
economic development over at least three broad zones: the south,

including Italy, the Riviera, and Spain; the center, comprising, say, central and northern France, the Rhineland and England; and finally, the North and East: including the Celtic world, Scandinavia, eastern Germany, and the western Slavic world. Often enough, the progress of regional monographic research has allowed Fossier to multiply the zones even further. Although some still find Fossier's geographic coverage to be uneven, the expanding horizons of medieval studies are unmistakable.

My point is simple: much of the significance of the magnificent work currently being done on the micro-regional level reveals its full implications only when viewed in a macro-regional and comparative perspective. That is, an intraregional comparative approach is becoming an exciting and productive tool of historical analysis: indeed, forerunners of this kind of work have been around for several decades already, if we think for instance of Brentano's *Two Churches* or Southern's *Western Society and the Church* in the English-speaking world. And of course there is nothing new under the sun, if we think back to Petit Dutaillis or Bloch.[13] The examples would be easy to multiply. The advances of regional monographic studies now encourage, indeed oblige a wider geographic horizon of synthesis than was feasible only thirty years ago.

This then is the second compelling reason for advocating research on Byzantium as part of an integrated study of the medieval world. Here we can pursue a kind of comparative history of unique character by analyzing similar issues in a somewhat different context. For the Byzantines emerged from the same general geographical and cultural matrix as their western cousins and confronted many similar challenges. How they solved them and how those solutions differed or resembled solutions developed elsewhere in Europe deepens our understanding of both the common and the distinctive patterns of British, French, Lombard, or Hungarian history. Potential or already broached subjects of investigation spring easily to mind, like the phenomenon of classicizing cultural movements, the formation and transformations of aristocracies, the processes of deurbanization and rebirth of cities, rulership, or the problem of relations between secular and religious authority.[14]

Indeed, it is profoundly disturbing and exciting to observe that the parallels reach beyond mega-structures and movements to some of the very distinctive details of the supposedly unique development of the medieval West. Two which have already been noted elsewhere and seem to me extremely striking are the nearly simultaneous emergence of a minuscule bookscript in Latin and Greek and the emergence of family names. In the latter case, the parallel extends to the predominance of names derived from rural sites and even from castles among part of the aristocracy.[15] These examples could easily be multiplied to include, for instance, the roughly contemporaneous emergence of vernacular *chansons de geste,* or the parallel development of rhythmic poetry in Latin and Greek which supplanted the old quantitative meters of classical antiquity.

This is not to suggest that there is a direct link of cause and effect between these Byzantine and western developments. Indeed, in the case of minuscule scripts, the most convincing exploration of a causal link has been abandoned even by its author.[16] In the absence of direct causal connections, we might call these cases "structural parallels" between Byzantium and the West. The simultaneous existence of these structural parallels at the opposite ends of Christendom challenges much of what has been written about the developments in the "West."

So real historical interconnections and the opportunity for comparative vistas are two key reasons why medievalists can no more ignore Byzantium than Scandinavia, Italy, or France; Byzantine developments are no less significant than western economics, gender issues, or theology in our enterprise of exploring a total past.

But if then we, as western medievalists, should be interested in Byzantium, we must consider, however briefly, the second major issue: how to do Byzantium?

Obviously—and especially in the case of a graduate program—this should entail appointing a good Byzantinist, whose multiple competences will strengthen several different areas of a program and appeal to academic constituencies in other departments like art history, classics, Near Eastern studies, Slavic studies, comparative literature, or religion. The interdisciplinary approach Byzantine studies have inherited from their roots in classics in no way discourages such links. But in the real world of our troubled economy and budgets, this is not an option for many of us in the immediate future. Failing that, it is still possible to do something provisional but useful toward capitalizing on Byzantine research for medieval studies and to do it today.

It is true that extensive original research on Byzantium requires at least one additional language beyond the usual medievalist equipment, and Greek is notoriously complicated. But it is also true that it used to be virtually impossible to have anything but the most superficial acquaintance with the discipline because of its youth and concomitant lack of guidebooks, because of its forbidding technicity (bearded vs. non-bearded *protospatharioi!*), and because of its Greekness. There was no half way. You were either a Byzantinist, having spent years learning how to parse and accent Greek, or you abstained.

Those days are over for a number of reasons. First and foremost, the simple development of the field itself: useful monographs have proliferated in the standard western European languages on plenty of key subjects. It is now possible, for instance, to consult a fine monograph on the workings of money in the Byzantine economy as a point of comparison for similar developments in the West.[17] Why should a specialist working on, say, the monetary economy of the Low Countries and seeking a comparative perspective hesitate to consult scholarly opinion on the same problem in Byzantium any more than on Catalonia or Latium? The differences will surely be no less enlightening than the similarities.

Secondly, Byzantinists have recently accelerated their production of studies, texts, and tools which invite non-specialists to join them in considering their corner of the medieval world, for the mutual benefit of both. I have appended a short sampling of such works for your consideration, and it is largely self-explanatory. Given the notorious difficulty of late and medieval Greek even for accomplished Byzantinists, it has become virtually standard procedure to equip all new critical editions of Byzantine sources with facing translations into the modern western languages. Those of us who like to incorporate translated primary sources into our undergraduate teaching will find among Byzantine texts a treasure trove aching for comparison with similar western documents. Examples spring to mind from the chanson de geste *Digenes Akritas,* to an aristocratic will of the eleventh century or the eighth-century Farmer's Law, so similar in so many respects to the early Germanic legal codifications.[18] And there are of course plenty of Byzantine sources which directly illuminate western matters, like Anna Comnena's famous account of the First Crusade, or the letters of a Byzantine ambassador to Otto III cited in the Appendix. In a similar vein,

Dumbarton Oaks is planning a major project to translate into English the essential corpus of Byzantine saints' lives.

By way of conclusion, it may be noted that an event of historic importance in the development of Byzantine studies occurred in the spring of 1991 which is directly relevant to the issue at hand. An essential new tool has appeared in the three volumes of the *Oxford Dictionary of Byzantium*. In this, the first encyclopedic dictionary of Byzantine civilization ever published, every major source, institution, and historical phenomenon is concisely, clearly identified, explained, and supplied with bibliographical references in a way that is useful for specialists and non-specialists alike.

Nowadays, then, there is little reason for western medievalists—at the very least in their undergraduate teaching—to fail to encourage their students and themselves to consider the comparanda available in texts, conceptions, institutions, and problems from the other half of medieval Christendom. And there is a further reward for the brave. Just enough has been done in the young field of Byzantine history to make it accessible, but not yet enough to do more than scratch the surface. This makes Byzantium a scholarly gold mine. Whether our interests lie in literacy, popular religion, diet, women, urbanism, or diplomatic, pioneering issues and insights beckon the bold.

APPENDIX: A QUICK REFERENCE GUIDE
TO BYZANTINE STUDIES

1. General Introduction

A. P. Kazhdan and G. Constable. *People and Power in Byzantium: An Introduction to Modern Byzantine Studies.* Washington, D.C. 1982. Stimulating overview of the state of Byzantine studies with suggestions for future directions and western comparisons.

2. General Histories

G. Ostrogorsky. *History of the Byzantine State.* Trans. J. Hussey. 2d ed. New Brunswick, 1969. Authoritative for traditional political history.

C. Mango. *Byzantium: The Empire of New Rome*. New York, 1980.
Exciting and very different in focus from Ostrogorsky, this history
treats subjects as diverse as peoples and languages, the Byzantine
understanding of the physical universe, literature, and art.

3. Translations

Two bibliographies update and extend the material found in C. P.
Farrar and A. P. Evans, *Bibliography of English Translations from Medieval Sources* (New York, 1946), and M. A. H. Ferguson, *Bibliography of
English Translations from Medieval Sources, 1943–1967* (New York,
1974).

B. MacBain. "An Annotated Bibliography of Sources for Late Antiquity in
English Translation." *Byzantine Studies/Études byzantines* 10 (1983):
88–109 and 223–247.
E. A. Hanawalt. *An Annotated Bibliography of Byzantine Sources in English Translation*. Brookline, 1988.

In addition, most volumes in the continuing international project to
reedit all major Byzantine sources possess reliable facing translations in
western European languages. *Ca.* 40 vols. of this *Corpus fontium historiae
byzantinae* (hereafter CFHB) have been published to date, in different national subseries. Four recent examples:

Nikephoros Patriarch of Constantinople, Short History. Text, translation,
and commentary by C. Mango. CFHB 13. Washington, D.C. 1990.
One of the two main Greek historians of the seventh and eighth
centuries.
Three Byzantine Military Treatises. Text, translation and notes by George
T. Dennis. CFHB 25. Washington, D.C. 1985.
Includes a Justinianic treatise on strategy intended for the educated
citizen, and a tenth-century treatise on hit and run warfare against
the Arabs composed by a contemporary general.
The Correspondence of Leo, Metropolitan of Synada and Syncellus. Greek
text, translation and commentary by M. P. Vinson. CFHB 23. Washington, 1985. Letters of a Byzantine ambassador to Otto III.
The Letters of Ioannes Mauropous, Metropolitan of Euchaita. Greek text,
translation and commentary by A. Karpozilos. CFHB 34. Thessalon-
ica, 1990. Letter collection of an eleventh-century intellectual and
courtier.

4. General Reference

A. P. Kazhdan. Ed. *The Oxford Dictionary of Byzantium*. 3 vols. New York and Oxford, 1991.

Contains several thousand authoritative short-entries by leading specialists on every aspect of Byzantine civilization, from diet to shipping, from liturgy to individual historical sources (including western ones) on Byzantium.

NOTES

1. See for example, Franz Dölger, "Byzanz als weltgeschichtliche Potenz," in *Paraspora. 30 Aufsätze zur Geschichte, Kultur und Sprache des byzantinischen Reiches* (Ettal, 1961), 1–19, originally published in 1949; other examples in M. McCormick, "Byzantium's Role in the Formation of Early Medieval Civilization," in *Byzantium and Its Legacy* (= *Illinois Classical Studies* 12:2 [1987]): 207–220. For the probable Byzantine origin of these words, see H. and R. Kahane, "Abendland und Byzanz: [Literatur und] Sprache," in *Reallexikon der Byzantinistik* 1 (Amsterdam, 1976): 345–639, here 385–386, 379–380, 368–369 respectively.
2. A. Kazhdan and G. Constable, *People and Power in Byzantium: An Introduction to Modern Byzantine Studies* (Washington, 1982), 1–18, esp. 18ff; J. K. Newman, "Diachronic Perspectives," in *Byzantium and Its Legacy*, v–ix.
3. For an overview of the history of Byzantine scholarship, G. Ostrogorsky, *History of the Byzantine State,* trans. J. Hussey, 2d ed. (New Brunswick, 1969), 1–21.
4. On Vasiliev's career see, e.g., N. G. Garsoïan, "Vasiliev, Alexander Alexandrovich," in *Dictionary of American Biography. Supplement* 5, ed. J. A. Garraty (New York, 1977), 708–709; see on his move to Wisconsin to replace Rostovtzeff, three years his junior, G. W. Bowersock, "Rostovtzeff in Madison," *American Scholar* 55 (1985/1986): 391–400, here 398–399. One might include in the second generation, for instance, Peter Charanis, who studied with Vasiliev in the early 1930s: see A. E. Laiou, "Peter Charanis, 1908–1985," *Dumbarton Oaks Papers* 39 (1985): xiii–xv.
5. On the Byzantine saint's fair, see S. Vryonis, Jr., "The *Panegyris* of the Byzantine Saint: A Study in the Nature of a Medieval Institution, Its Origins and Fate," in *The Byzantine Saint,* ed. S. Hackel (London, 1981), 196–226.

6. H. Hagenmeyer, *Die Kreuzzugsbriefe aus den Jahren 1088–1100* (Innsbruck, 1902), 138–140, here 138–139: "Imperator uero digne et honeste et quasi filium suum me diligentissime suscepit et amplissimis ac pretiosissimis donis ditauit, et in toto Dei exercitu et nostro, non est dux neque comes neque aliqua potens persona, cui magis credat uel faueat quam mihi. Uere, mi dilecta, eius imperialis dignitas persaepe monuit et monet, ut unum ex filiis nostris ei commendemus: ipse uero tantum tamque praeclarum honorem se ei attributurum promisit, quod nostro minime inuidebit. In ueritate tibi dico, hodie talis uiuens homo non est sub caelo. . . . Nostris quoque temporibus, ut nobis uidetur, non fuit princeps uniuersa morum honestate adeo praeclarus, pater, mi dilecta, tuus multa et magna dedit, sed ad hunc paene nihil fuit." The punctuation is unsatisfactory: there should probably be a period after "praeclarus."

7. Leo VI, *Taktika* 18:77, ed. R. Vári in *A magyar Honfoglalás kútföi*, ed. G. Pauler and S. Szilágyi (Budapest, 1900), 44–45; more easily accessible in *PG* 107:672–1120, here 964C–D, where the section is numbered 18:78.

8. Bischoff and Lapidge's *editio princeps* of an Old Testament biblical commentary which draws extensively and explicitly on the teaching of Theodore of Tarsus and Canterbury is now in press in the *Corpus christianorum, series latina*.

9. *Das Constitutum Constantini* 15, ed. H. Fuhrmann, MGH Fontes iuris germanici antiqui in usum scholarum 10 (Hanover, 1968), 88–91.

10. W. Wendling, "Die Erhebung Ludwigs d. Fr. zum Mitkaiser im Jahre 813 und ihre Bedeutung für die Verfassungsgeschichte des Frankenreiches," *Frühmittelalterliche Studien* 19 (1985): 210–238, esp. 207–223.

11. Leo VI: Philotheus, *Cleterologium,* ed. N. Oikonomides, *Les listes de préséance byzantines des IXe et Xe siècles* (Paris, 1972) 177:28–32; Otto III: *Oxford Dictionary of Byzantium* [hereafter cited as *ODB*] 3 (Oxford, 1991): 1542; Amalfi: *ODB* 1:73; enamel: D. Buckton, "Byzantine Enamel and the West," *Byzantinische Forschungen* 13 (1988): 235–244; tournaments: *ODB* 1:412; romances: *ODB* 3:1804–1805. Linguistic borrowings: H. and R. Kahane, "Abendland und Byzanz," 536ff. *Voyage: ODB* 3:2187.

12. G. Duby, *Rural Economy and Country Life in the Medieval West,* trans. C. Postan (originally published with the more cumbersome but more accurate title *L'économie rurale et la vie des campagnes dans l'Occident médiéval: France, Angleterre, Empire, IXe–XIVe siècles. Essai de synthèse et perspectives de recherche*) (Paris, 1962; reprint, Columbia, S.C., 1990); R. Fossier, *Enfance de l'Europe, X^e–XIIe siècles: aspects économiques et sociaux,* Nouvelle Clio, no. 17 (Paris, 1982).

13. R. Brentano, *Two Churches: England and Italy in the Thirteenth Century,* 2d ed. (Berkeley, 1988); R. W. Southern, *Western Society and the*

Church in the Middle Ages (Harmondsworth, 1970); C. Petit-Dutaillis, *The Feudal Monarchy in France and England from the Tenth to the Thirteenth Century,* trans. E. D. Hunt (1933; London, 1936); M. Bloch, "La genèse de la seigneurie: idée d'une recherche comparée," *Annales d'histoire économique et sociale* 9 (1937): 225–227; cf. his course lectures of 1936 first published a generation later: *Seigneurie française et manoir anglais* (Paris, 1967).

14. The first of these has attracted some scholarly attention: see, e.g., B. Schimmelpfenning et al., "Renaissance/Proto-Renaissance, Renovatio/ Renewal, Rezeption. Bericht über eine Begriffs-Diskussion," in *Kontinuität und Transformation der Antike im Mittelalter,* ed. W. Erzgräber (Sigmaringen, 1989), 383–390; W. Treadgold, ed., *Renaissances before the Renaissance: Cultural Revivals of Late Antiquity and the Middle Ages* (Stanford, 1984); for a comparison of rulers' accession rituals, see J. Nelson, *Politics and Ritual in Early Medieval Europe* (London, 1986), 259–281.

15. See McCormick, "Byzantium's Role," 214–216, with bibliography. For castle names, see A. P. Kazhdan, *Sotsial'nyj sostav gospodstvuyushchego klassa Vizantii xi–xii vv.* (= The Social Structure of Byzantium's Ruling Class in the 11th and 12th centuries) (Moscow, 1974), 187. A revised Italian edition of this seminal study is now in preparation.

16. C. Mango, "La culture grecque et l'Occident au VIIIe siècle," in *I problemi dell'Occidente nel secolo VIII,* Settimane di studio del Centro italiano di studi sull'alto medioevo, no. 20 (Spoleto, 1973), 683–721, here 716–721. Cf. his "L'origine de la minuscule," in *La paléographie grecque et byzantine* (Paris, 1977), 175–179, esp. 177–178, as well as McCormick, "Byzantium's Role," 215 with n. 25.

17. M. F. Hendy, *Studies in the Byzantine Monetary Economy, c. 300–1450* (Cambridge, 1985).

18. *Digenes Akritas,* ed. and trans. J. Mavrogordato (Oxford, 1956); S. Vryonis, Jr., "The Will of a Provincial Magnate, Eustathius Boilas (1059)," *Dumbarton Oaks Papers* 11 (1957): 263–277; W. Ashburner, "The Farmer's Law," *Journal of Hellenic Studies* 30 (1910): 85–108 and 32 (1912): 68–83.

On Medieval Judaism
and Medieval Studies

JEREMY COHEN

As I PONDERED the provocative questions on the agenda for this conference, I was struck by the grouping of "Judaism, Byzantium, Islam" alongside literature, philosophy, history, the fine arts, and the like on a program devoted to the relationship between medieval studies and the various disciplines in the modern academy. Islam is a religion, Byzantium a place, Judaism a blend of religion, nationality, and ethnicity. Not one of the three is an academic discipline; yet each one generated a medieval civilization of its own which exerted a noteworthy and distinctive impact on the medieval Christian civilization of Western Europe. The Jews comprised the only non-Catholic group consistently accorded official toleration in the medieval Latin West; theirs was the culture of the medieval European minority par excellence, essential to the foundations of the majority's culture but peripheral to its priorities and aspirations.[1]

I venture the suggestion that there are informative parallels between the situation of Jewish culture in the context of medieval European Christendom and the place of medieval studies in the modern Western university. Unpopular, perceived as irrelevant and obsolete, and grounded in languages, texts, and terminologies inaccessible to the majority—such was Judaism during the Middle Ages and such is the study of the Middle Ages on many a college campus today. More instructively, though, the appreciation of medieval Judaica in the modern university reflects the peculiar traits of both the medieval (Jewish) experience and contemporary academic discourse—especially that which we commonly term "Jewish studies," *inasmuch as it derives from the encounter between*

73

them. Precisely this encounter between perspectives in Jewish cultural history strikes me as illuminating for our concerns with the modern study of the medieval; and I therefore propose to direct my attention to the medieval Jewish text, its modern academic reader, and the meaning of the former for the latter. Since both the distinctively medieval European Jewish experience and modern Jewish studies derived in large measure from the interaction of Judaism and Christianity, what follows will speak directly to my own perceptions of what I "do" as a medievalist. However much all this manifests a minority point of view, I hope that it will prove instructive for the concerns of the majority; I firmly believe that it should.

CHARACTERISTICS AND CONTOURS OF THE MEDIEVAL JEWISH EXPERIENCE

Although it commonly conveys a similar impression of cultural darkness, the term "medieval" need not and frequently does not denote the same period of time in Jewish history as it does in the history of Western civilization at large. Surveys of medieval Jewish history begin as early as 135 C.E. (the end of the Bar Kokhba rebellion in Palestine) or as late as 633 (the Arab conquest of Palestine), and they can extend to 1492 (the expulsion of the Jews from Spain), 1666 (the conversion of the messianic pretender Shabbetai Tzvi to Islam), or even 1791 (the emancipation of the Jews of France).[2] While my own research interests focus on the European Jewish experience during the Christian Middle Ages, I try in my survey courses to emphasize exemplary sociocultural phenomena and patterns of behavior rather than specific dates (or even centuries).

Medieval Jewish history differs from that which preceded it—and, in large measure, from that which followed it—on several essential grounds. First, unlike their ancient ancestors and much less so than their modern descendants, medieval Jews lived under the rule of a Christian or Muslim religious community that nurtured the ideal of a world in which no Jews remained. As hegemony over ancient Israel had passed from Assyrians, Babylonians, and Persians to Greeks, Egyptians, Syrians, Romans, and Parthians, foreign princes generally cared little that biblical religion and culture differed markedly from those of other ancient Near Eastern civilizations. So long as the Jews paid taxes and did not rebel, they enjoyed considerable leeway in regulating their own social, economic, and cultural lives. Instances of suppression of Jewish communal autonomy were strikingly few and usually resulted from a lack of Jewish cooperation with—if not outright rebellion against—the prevailing Gentile power. Anti-Judaism or anti-Semitism may have existed in antiquity, but it rarely characterized the policies of Near Eastern empires; the Seleucid Antiochus IV Epiphanes' unprecedented persecution of Judaism in the mid-160s B.C.E. was the proverbial exception that proves the rule. Medieval Christians and Muslims, however, enlarged their respective empires under the banners of religions that sought to conquer the world, and they attributed special significance to the conversion of the "people of the Book." Yet for various ideological and more practical reasons, not the least of which was their debt to Jewish traditions, both Christianity and Islam generally tolerated the existence of Jews and the practice of Judaism in their midst. In Christendom, the Jews alone routinely enjoyed such recognition; in the world of Islam they shared it with other non-pagan groups (e.g., Christians and Zoroastrians), but they more than others succeeded in making this status facilitate their survival and growth. Anomaly and ambivalence therefore typified the station and perception of Jews in medieval society. On the periphery of the non-Jewish communities in which they lived, subject to the constant enticement and hostility of the majority, Jews nevertheless fit somehow into the medieval world, and their peculiar position continually evoked the curiosity, the consternation, and/or the resentment of the Gentiles.

Second, medieval Jewish history transpired for most intents and purposes in the Diaspora; and, as historian Yitzhak Baer has noted, "in this period, Diaspora means dispersion without any visible political center."[3] Not only did the overwhelming majority of Jews live outside the land of Israel, but the experience of those who did reside in Palestine differed but little from that of communities elsewhere. To be sure, the site of the ancient Jewish commonwealths evoked the respect and reverence of medieval Jews everywhere. Some Jews always resided in the land of Israel, and the medieval Jewish community there boasted important academies, rabbis, and spokesmen. Yet in the Muslim world their stature was usually inferior to that of Babylonian rabbinic leadership; and, as the Middle Ages wore on, Babylonian Jewish institutions failed to consolidate world Jewry, either within or beyond the geographical orbit of Islam. The Jews of the Middle Ages lacked a national home, with its own Jewish polity and vernacular language, the leadership and influence of whose institutions could provide Jews worldwide with a single, unifying cultural center.

Third, in marked contrast to Jewish life today, that of the Middle Ages developed almost exclusively within the corporate framework of the organized Jewish community. The Jews of the Roman Empire received Roman citizenship in 212 C.E., and modern scholars have debated how long Jews continued to possess civic rights and responsibilities under the rule of Rome's medieval heirs. Most all concur, however, that such rights deteriorated steadily through the period; by the time medieval Christian civilization had reached the peak of its development, these rights had disappeared. The Jews were aliens. They lived outside the corporate, legal framework of the society at large, and whatever protection they enjoyed derived from their membership in the tolerated minority. Jews related to their Gentile rulers and neighbors as an alien society, paying taxes, enjoying rights and privileges, suffering discrimination, and even enduring persecution as members of such a corporate entity. No less important, Jews themselves conceived of Jewish life as viable and legitimate only within the collective of the community. Briefly put, one could not live or survive as a Jew on one's own during the Middle Ages; without acceptance by and membership in a particular Jewish community, the Jew had no status as a Jew—neither in the eyes of the Gentile authorities nor in dealing with his or her coreligionists. The *qehillah* or entity of the community accordingly stands at the hub of Jewish social and cultural history during the Middle Ages. Typified by what Walter Ullmann described as an "ascending" view of political power,[4] the small, often isolated *qehillah*—and particularly that in Christian Europe—treasured its independence and self-sufficiency. Just as it provided for all of its own social, educational, and religious services, so too did it retain primary and ultimate judicial jurisdiction for itself, along with the right to impose strict discipline on its members. The *qehillah* (plural: *qehillot*), for instance, could deny prospective newcomers permission to join its ranks, and it sought to punish most severely anyone who compromised its authority, whether by resorting voluntarily to Gentile courts or by informing against its members to non-Jewish authorities. Paradoxically, some communities actually secured from Gentile princes the right to impose capital punishment on Jews who informed against their coreligionists to those very rulers.

And finally, some of the salient features of the *Weltanschauung* of medieval Jewry warrant enumeration. At the bedrock of this collective worldview lay essential principles of biblical religion: belief in one, providential God who created the world and designed a comprehensive plan for human history within it; the divine authority of Mosaic law; the election of Israel. To these, the overwhelming majority of medieval Jews added the doctrinal legacy of the rabbis of the Talmud. They believed that alongside the biblical law given to Moses at Sinai God had revealed a tradition of interpretation which was transmitted orally from one generation of rabbinic sage to the next; that this tradition had flowered in the literature of the Talmud and Midrash; that compliance with God's will demanded of the Jew adherence to the detailed Halakhah or rabbinic law of the "oral Torah" in addition to the more general precepts of the written Torah of Moses; that the duly ordained rabbis of each generation who maintained and developed the Halakhah were in effect the sole legitimate mediators of God's will among the Jews; and that study and active observance of the dual Torah stood at the center of the distinctive, divinely ordained mission of the Jewish people. But beyond its biblical and rabbinic foundations, and no doubt as a result of the circumstances we have discussed above, the worldview of the medieval Jew normally included an obsession with *galut,* the state of being in exile, alienated from the spatial and temporal situation he deemed fully appropriate for himself and his people. Albeit in varying degrees, to be sure, medieval Jews yearned to live in a different time and a different place. Medieval Jewish culture accordingly strove above all to mitigate, if not to resolve, the frustrations and insecurities generated by the displacement of *galut,* allowing the Jew somehow to narrow the gap between his present Jewish existence and his presumed Jewish destiny.

THE MODERN STUDY OF MEDIEVAL JUDAICA

Unlike biblical and talmudic Judaism, which had long commanded the attention of Christian scholars, academic investigation of the medieval chapter in Jewish history awaited the birth of modern Jewish studies in the nineteenth century, by which time the worldview and cultural priorities of Western European Jewry had changed considerably. Jewish intellectuals had subscribed with alacrity to the European Enlightenment's vision of a new, egalitarian human society, which they believed would emancipate them from the inferior station of an alien minority. Yet the proposals for the emancipation of European Jewry from its subordinate, alien, medieval status themselves derived from an ideology of universalism in many ways no less threatening than that of medieval Christianity or Islam. "The Jews should be denied everything as a nation, but granted everything as individuals," a representative of the National Assembly had proclaimed in Revolutionary France;[5] its logic and good intentions notwithstanding, such a declaration bespoke the common assumption that emancipated Jews should willingly abandon much of that which made them different from Christians. In an illuminating essay on "Emancipation and Jewish Studies," Israeli historian Jacob Katz summarized instructively the view of the liberal camp in the Christian Enlightenment that wished to "ameliorate" the status of Jews.

> Even the moderate spokesmen had some expectations in this direction. They looked to emancipation to bring about a broadening of Jewish occupational patterns, as well as changes in what they regarded as questionable Jewish business ethics. Many were of the opinion that the anomalous status of the Jews could be reversed only by their total assimilation into the general life of the country. It was taken for granted that future Jewish generations would adopt the prevailing manners and culture, including language, of the cultures they inhabited. The governments themselves had insured this by obliging Jews either to attend public schools or to establish their own modern educational institutions. Finally, there were hints, and in some cases even official measures, pressing Jews to reform their religion. At the same time, hand in hand with the endeavors designed to effect the Jews' cultural and social integration,

there were indications that the Jews would be expected to loosen their ties with fellow Jews abroad.[6]

While one hardly ought to reduce the intricacies of modern Jewish history to a handful of sweeping generalizations, it is remarkable to what extent these anticipations have materialized. Even after the rationalist universalism of the Enlightenment had given way to the particularist, most impulsive and instinctivist ethic to Romanticism, proponents of Jewish enlightenment, or *Haskalah,* still yearned to prove to the Christian civilization of Europe that they were capable of modernization and worthy of inclusion as equals. Whether in the renunciation of blatant nationalism and ethnicity, in the redefinition of their Jewish identity according to the principles of some universal, "ethical culture," or in the reform of their religion according to standards set by modern varieties of Christianity, western Jews have ever since felt obliged to prove themselves deserving of social and political acceptance.

Yet could one maintain an edifying sense of Jewish identity at the same time? How might Judaism and Jewish culture survive so as to appear at once unobtrusive to the Christian and meaningful to the modern Jew? Influenced by the Romantic penchant for the Gothic and the arcane, by Hegelian historiosophy, and by the philological investigations of the *Volkstum* at German universities, noted Jewish scholars of the early and mid-nineteenth century sought a solution in *Wissenschaft des Judentums.* They believed that the "Science of Judaism"—the subjection of the national and traditional religious literature of the Jews to the thoroughly scientific analysis of the modern academician—would identify the essentials of Jewish experience, would demonstrate their continued relevance, and would establish their acceptability in the contemporary world. *Wissenschaft* marked the birth of modern scholarship in Jewish studies, which derived from the immediate sociocultural needs of its proponents no less than the ancient and medieval Jewish civilization which it scrutinized. In a term paper written in 1818 at the University of Berlin, blandly entitled *Etwas über die rabbinische Literatur, Wissenschaft's* prime mover Leopold Zünz formulated what still ranks as a major curricular manifesto for the academic study of Judaica: "In order to recognize and distinguish among the old and useful, the obsolete and harmful, the new and desirable, we must embark upon a considered study of the people and its political and

moral history." Secular science must accompany a thorough expertise in Judaic language and literature. The study of Judaism must
bridge the worlds of the particular and the universal.[7]

Modern Jewish studies thus emerged to justify Jewish emancipation and, at the same time, to safeguard Judaism from the perils
of emancipation; as we shall soon observe, these considerations
have borne directly on our understanding of medieval Jewish civilization. Yet no less significantly, the contemporary study of medieval Judaica also reflects the failure of the Enlightenment and
emancipation to secure for modern Jews much of the freedom and
equality which they craved. Despite the enfranchisement of most
Western European Jews between the years of the French Revolution
and the unification of Germany, anti-Semitism only increased in extent and intensity. As much as Jews sought to accommodate the expectations of the Christian intelligentsia, anti-Jewish hostility struck
out at successively deeper levels of Jewish identity: Jewish religion
and lifestyle, Jewish nationality, Jewish ethnicity, and, finally, (the
fabrication of) Jewish race. The twentieth century, whose first decades heralded the long-awaited emancipation of East European
Jewry and the rise of National Socialism, witnessed unprecedented
inhumanity in the persecution of Soviet Jews and the "final solution" of Hitler's Third Reich. From the second half of the nineteenth
century, *maskilim,* proponents of *Haskalah* or Jewish enlightenment, themselves began to question the wisdom of their worldview.
By 1871, Judah Loeb Gordon, the very enthusiast of *Haskalah* who
just several years earlier had cried to his Russian Jewish compatri-
ots, "Wake up, my people ... be a human in your travels and Jew
[only] at home," now lamented, "For whom do I toil, to what avail,
the good years wasted?" In 1883 Gordon actually responded to the
wave of anti-Jewish pogroms in Tsarist Russia on a note of support
for the nascent Zionist movement's desire to establish a Jewish national home in Israel. "Young and old," he wrote, "we all shall go."[8]
Some began to argue that not in emancipation by the non-Jewish
world but in auto-emancipation lay the solution to the modern
"Jewish question." Although few may have advocated a return to the
traditionalism or the ghetto of the Middle Ages, the ensuing rise of
Jewish nationalism that culminated in the recreation of a Jewish
polity, coupled with the ascending perception of anti-Semitism as
perpetual and insurmountable, could cast a distinctive Jewish cul-

tural history in a new, more favorable light. As we shall see, so too could it militate in the opposite direction. Alongside anti-Semitism and nationalism, the emergence of more traditionally inclined varieties of modern Judaism contributed diverse viewpoints and proponents to the academic enterprise of Jewish studies. Discoveries of long lost Judaic texts, in the famous Cairo genizah and elsewhere, have added hitherto unappreciated complexity to our understanding of medieval Jewish civilization, as have an array of methodological breakthroughs in the academic discourse of western universities—the contributions of Marx, Darwin, Freud, Weber, Lévi-Strauss, Einstein, Derrida, and so many others. To conclude rather bluntly: the composite perspective from which we study and understand the Jews of the Middle Ages has much to do with the circumstances and self-understanding of the Jews of modernity.

THE EXEMPLARY MODES OF MEDIEVAL JEWISH CULTURAL EXPRESSION

The interplay of medieval and modern cultural history in the discourse of Jewish studies underlies the regnant approaches to countless issues, questions, and sources, and we now turn to one broad area of medieval Jewish experience by way of example. Let us consider the four distinctive modes of cultural expression among Jews of Christian Europe during the high Middle Ages. First in the Rhineland and then in Northern France, Ashkenazic Jewish scholars reached unprecedented accomplishments in their pursuit of the study of Torah, written and oral alike. Rabbi Gershom ben Judah of Mainz ("the light of the exile," 960–1028) laid the groundwork for a native European tradition of talmudic scholarship, bequeathing to generations that followed him both essential textual tools and an institutional context for their study. At the same time he strove to demonstrate how the Halakhah of the late ancient rabbis could adapt to the peculiar needs and circumstances of European Jewish life. Gershom's pupils' pupil Rashi (Rabbi Solomon ben Isaac of Troyes, 1040–1105), after returning to France from his studies in the Rhineland, authored basic, introductory commentaries on most of the Hebrew Bible and Talmud, which expedited the private, individual study of these sacred texts among laymen no less than they inspired the subsequent treatises of his disciples in turn. In the realm of biblical studies, Rashi spurred the research and analysis of *peshat*, the primary intention and literal meaning of the Scripture, by a broad array of twelfth- and thirteenth-century exegetes, ranging from his relatives on the one hand to Christian scholars on the other hand. Rashi's efforts likewise gave rise to that of the Tosafists, including his grandsons Samuel and Jacob ben Meir, who used their master's interpretation of the talmudic text as a springboard for a more analytic and exhaustive opus of their own, in many ways a rabbinic incorporation of dialectical, scholastic method within a running commentary on the Talmud. For the Tosafists (named after their *Tosafot* or *additiones* to the commentary of Rashi), Torah-study undergirded effective rabbinic leadership in the *qehillot*, at the same time as it proffered medieval Jews a means to withdraw from the isolation and alienation of Christendom's Jewish minority, to find fulfillment by joining a discussion of God's word that linked many centuries of Jewish history.

Alongside the communal leadership and scholarship of the Tosafists, the twelfth and early thirteenth centuries witnessed the flowering of Ashkenazic Jewish pietism or Hasidism, whose most prominent spokesmen included Rabbi Samuel ben Kalonymos of Mainz and his son Judah, each dubbed *he-Ḥasid* ("the pious"), and Rabbi Eleazar ben Judah of Worms. Investigators have cited numerous factors to explain the appearance of this strange movement, in which observant adherents of talmudic Judaism developed a quasi-monastic lifestyle and ideology to meet their cultural needs and aspirations. German Jewish reaction against the primacy of the Northern French Tosafists perhaps fuelled dissatisfaction with the dialectic of their juridical scholarship and with the rabbinic ethos that it fostered. In the wake of the massacres of Jewish communities in the Rhineland during the First Crusade, survivors may have sought to institutionalize an ethic of *qiddush ha-Shem* (literally "sanctification of God's name," most commonly in the sense of voluntary martyrdom and self-sacrifice) that had characterized the behavior of many Ashkenazic Jews in 1096. Internal developments in esoteric Jewish theosophy and mysticism no doubt made their contribution too, as did the prevailing Christian cultural context of monastic reform and experimentation.

Closer to the Mediterranean, in Southern France and in Spain, the circulation of the philosophical and philosophical-halakhic writings of Moses Maimonides facilitated Jewish cultural creativity in a different realm, that of rationalism and metaphysics. While he himself belonged to the civilization of the Muslim world, the works of the Aristotelian Maimonides reached European Jewry just as the newly translated corpus of Aristotle's works stormed into Latin Christendom. From the final years of the twelfth century through the opening years of the fourteenth (and, in many ways, much longer still), the Jews of Europe debated vehemently over the place of rationalism and Greek science in rabbinic Judaism: how to react to contradiction between the teachings of science and revelation; in what measure to subject the precepts of Bible and Talmud to rational explanation; how much to allow principles of reason and dialectic to govern the timeless rabbinic activity of interpreting sacred texts. As the discord between rationalist and anti-rationalist camps in Provencal, Spanish, and even Northern French Jewish communities escalated, tensions overflowed into hostile controversy, propaganda, decrees of excommunication, a veritable sea of apologetic literature, and even the burning of Maimonides' books (by Christian inquisitors, at the request of anti-rationalist Jews, in Montpelier in 1232). The multi-faceted parallel with the Christian debate over Aristotle—from the appearance of his newly translated works to the variegated ecclesiastical efforts to limit their dissemination and to the condemnations of Latin Averroism in Paris and Oxford—should be obvious and instructive. In both cases, the experience of controversy, the need to take a stand on the issues of faith and reason, signaled cultural creativity and growth no less than any specific developments in the fields of philosophy and theology.

Much as the Tosafists' commitment to the scholarship of jurisprudence (and its corresponding halakhic ethos) may have struck the *Hasidim* of Ashkenaz as spiritually bankrupt, so too was the burgeoning of Maimonidean rationalism in Provence and Spain accompanied by new currents of mystical piety and theosophic reflection: those of the Kabbalah. From the nearly simultaneous appearance in late twelfth-century Provence of the kabbalistic book *Bahir* and of kabbalistic cells in which inspired visionaries communicated their insights into the world of the divine *sefirot,* the new Jewish mysticism soon made its way southwest across the Pyrenees.

Thirteenth-century Spain gave rise to the highly prolific center of kabbalistic research in Gerona, the ecstatic mysticism of Abraham Abulafia, and the crowning achievement of all—the compilation of the *Zohar* by Rabbi Moses ben Shem Tov of León and his colleagues around the end of the century. Some have linked the birth and growth of the Kabbalah to those of the dualist Cathar heresy among Christians; others have identified its origins in the penetration of essentially foreign Gnostic traditions into the mentality of rabbinic Jews. Whatever the respective merits of these theories—which are not mutually exclusive—we find compelling the suggestion of Moshe Idel, that hardly by accident did the Kabbalah take hold during the heyday of Maimonidean rationalism and in the same geographic regions.

> Kabbalah emerged in the late twelfth and early thirteenth centuries as a sort of reaction to the dismissal of earlier mystical traditions with a philosophical understanding. Kabbalah can be viewed as part of a restructuring of those aspects of rabbinic thought that were denied authority by Maimonides' system. Far from being a total innovation, historical Kabbalah represented an ongoing effort to systematize existing elements of Jewish theurgy, myth, and mysticism into a full-fledged response to the rationalistic challenge. Indeed, we can consider Kabbalah as part of a silent controversy between the rationalistic and mystical facets of Judaism.[9]

Naturally, each of these four modes of medieval Jewish culture expression—analytic textual scholarship, pietism, rationalism, and mysticism—flourished insofar as it enabled its proponents to find satisfaction as medieval Jews. Yet because they have done much to give the European Middle Ages their distinctive character in the history of Judaism, their common characteristics as a group merit further explication. All of these tendencies and outlooks emerged within the framework of the "normative" rabbinic Judaism of the age, the essentials of whose worldview we have described briefly above. At the same time, each of the four departed from classic rabbinic norms in a distinctive manner, spawning its own method for interpreting sacred texts, and thus constituting what one scholar has aptly called a "creative misreading" of revealed tradition.[10] That each one generated and responded to often vehement controversies within the Jewish community perhaps manifests the urgency of their programs, and severity of the pressures which bore upon medieval Jews to turn adverse conditions into a basis for survival and fulfillment in *galut*. Each mode of cultural expression cultivated religious perfection in its select fashion. Each engineered a means of escape—whether into a diachronically perceived community of scholars, a quasi-sectarian collective of pietistic elite, a higher world of philosophic contemplation, or a secret mystical realm of interaction with the divine—whereby its proponents might overcome the oppressive conviction of geographical and cultural displacement. Nevertheless, the scholastic discourse of the Tosafists, the monastic asceticism of the Ashkenazic *Hasidim*, the dissonant encounter between faith and reason, and the increasing popularity of theosophic and ecstatic mysticism all had important parallels in the high medieval culture of the Christian majority. Granted the still ongoing debate over direct influences (in one direction or the other), the fact remains that medieval European Jewish civilization was no less European than Jewish. It reflects instructively on the distinctive predicament of that minority: on the periphery of a society from which it had no viable exit, it necessarily sought assimilation and isolation simultaneously, molding its singular identity in the idiom of the majority.

The predicament of still another minority demands consideration here, however; for it is not only the *medieval* dialectic between Jewish and Gentile worlds which underlies the significance of these cultural pursuits in recent scholarship. As the modern study of medieval Judaism commenced, the "enlightened," universalist perspective of *Wissenschaft des Judentums* ranked Maimonidean rationalism as the healthiest, most constructive outlet for Jewish cultural creativity; highlighting those natural, scientific truths which Judaism shared with other creeds best served the needs of *maskilim* who clamored for political and social emancipation in nineteenth-century Western Europe. Medieval talmudic scholarship, to the contrary, was typically deemed overly casuistic, pietism separatist and intolerant, and, worst of all—hence the most illustrative example—the Kabbalah with its derivative messianism deviant and destructive. Among the champions of *Wissenschaft* and in many respects the father of modern Jewish historiography, the German Jew Heinrich Graetz accordingly extolled the virtues of

"Moses Maimonides with his determination to exorcise the phan-
toms of the mind,"[11] while he deplored "the insane theories of Kabbalah [which] had spread their snares and disturbed the minds, and
produced pseudo-messianic orgies that cast shame upon Judaism
even to the end of the last [i.e., eighteenth] century."[12] Albeit in a
different tenor, Graetz anticipated the aforementioned linkage between rationalism and the rise of Kabbalah elaborated by Idel, and
he bemoaned the transition from the philosophic (1040–1430) to
the rabbinic/mystical (1230–1780) stages in Jewish history. "Upon
the meridian of Judaism purified by philosophy, the dark clouds of
a current inimical to knowledge are already gathering which descend in a thick vapor of rabbinism, inaccessible to light, and a confused mysticism."[13] Graetz's programmatic proposals to define the
relevance of his monumental survey of the Jewish past betray a blatant predisposition to such summary judgments in his scholarship.

> I would only like to consider whether Judaism still has a real
> significance and value in the critically minded present, and in
> that future which may be yet more estranged from all religious
> forms, only to show that those who are deeply convinced of its
> fundamental principle and historical influence, may joyfully
> make it their vocation to hold by Judaism steadfastly, and so
> transmit it to posterity. . . . I have endeavored to prove that this
> fundamental principle must be sought for in ethical idealism
> (humanity in the highest sense of the word), and in pure ra-
> tional monotheism, adverse to all mysticism and disfigure-
> ment. I have also attempted to show that for the future of
> mankind these qualities have not yet become superfluous for
> the education and regeneration of society.[14]

Although Graetz's multi-volume *Geschichte der Juden* remains
an invaluable research tool despite the subsequent advances and
discoveries in the field, the appraisal of medieval Jewish cultural
creativity has since fluctuated drastically in response to developments both outside and within the Jewish community. The burgeoning of modern anti-Semitism, the resulting intensification of
Jewish nationalism, the Holocaust, and the establishment of a Jewish state have invariably influenced non-Jewish perceptions of the
medieval Jewish minority. And, among Jews themselves, Zionism in
its many varieties and a variegated return to religious tradition have

yielded new, potentially extreme attitudes toward diverse relics of the Jewish past. Zionist ideology and historiography has frequently tended to view most Jewish cultural experience outside the land of Israel as in some sense inauthentic, and in large measure an irrelevant (perhaps noxious) model in the forging of a nationalist consciousness for contemporary Jews. My Israeli-born and educated university students have learned little or nothing concerning the Middle Ages in high school. Similarly striking is the omission of the Middle Ages from a recent American study of the ideal of *galut,* which considers Genesis, Deuternomy, and the Talmud in its first half and jumps to Spinoza, Moses Mendelssohn, Theodore Herzl, and their successors in its second.[15] Paradoxically, however, it is the twentieth-century luminaries of the Israeli academic establishment—Yitzhak Baer, Ben Zion Dinur, Gershom Scholem, Efraim Urbach, and others—who have made inestimable contributions to the recovery and reevaluation of medieval Judaica. As a consequence, since the early days of *Wissenschaft,* the "bad press" concerning non-rationalist currents in medieval Judaism has gradually diminished. The imposing jurisprudence of the Tosafists, the searching spirituality of the Ashkenazic pietists, and the dynamic influence of mysticism on the mainstream of Jewish religious expression have all found advocates and recognition in medieval Jewish studies. More responsible than any other for the "reinstatement" of the Kabbalah, Gershom Scholem introduced his classic study of *Major Trends in Jewish Mysticism* with unabashed praise for the ideas of the thirteenth-century *Zohar* and the sixteenth-century visionary Isaac Luria—

> those forms of Jewish mysticism which have for centuries stood out in the popular mind as bearers of the final and deepest truths in Jewish thought. It is no use getting indignant over these facts, as the great historian Graetz did. . . . Their importance for the history of the Jewish people, particularly during the past four centuries, has been far too great to permit them to be ridiculed and treated as mere deviations. Perhaps, after all, there is something wrong with the popular conception of Monotheism as being opposed to the mythical; perhaps Monotheism contains room after all, on a deeper plane, for the development of mythical lore. I do not believe that all those devoted and pious spirits, practically the vast majority of Ash-

kenazic and Sephardic Jewry, ceased . . . to be Jews also in the
religious sense, only because their forms of belief appear to
be in manifest contradiction with certain modern theories of
Judaism. What is the secret of this tremendous success of Kabbalah among our people? Why did it succeed in becoming a
decisive factor in our history, shaping the life of a large proportion of Jewry over a period of centuries, while its contemporary, rational Jewish philosophy, was incapable of achieving
the spiritual hegemony after which it strove . . . ? I cannot accept the explanation . . . that persecution and decline weak-
ened the spirit of the people and made them seek refuge in
the darkness of Mysticism because they could not bear the
light of reason.[16]

I have quoted Scholem at such length because these comments at-
test to the recent conclusions of David Biale, Moshe Idel, and
others[17] that Scholem's historiography is no less grounded in his
personal ideology than that of Graetz who preceded him or, for that
matter, than that of our own generation of Jewish historians. It is
telling that the *maskil* Graetz, the Zionist Scholem, and present-day
phenomenologists like Idel (who have bravely ushered Kabbalah
into mainstream discussions of semiotics and post-structuralist
hermeneutics) all concur as to the dialectical relationship between
medieval Jewish rationalism and mysticism—but each so as to advance his or her own particular agenda for modern Jewish studies.
Just as their mutual conclusion illuminates the dynamic of medieval
Jewish cultural expression, so does their disagreement exemplify
how our assessment of the medieval Jewish experience derives
from a fusion of medieval and modern cultural horizons, *and that
these horizons share a common foundation:* the problematic situation of the minority in a world that is and is not its own.

SOME CONCLUDING REFLECTIONS

Wishing to relate the preceding discussion to the concerns of
the majority in this symposium, this modern historian of the Middle
Ages cannot resist the characteristically medieval predilection for
the homiletical. Classical Judaic sources, from late antiquity and the

Middle Ages alike, commonly projected onto the human condition at large what we have acknowledged as the defining polarities of the Jewish cultural experience throughout history. Many rabbinic homilies depict human beings as uniquely situated mid-way between angels and beasts, sharing the characteristics of both, such that they are conflicted on the one hand, but blessed with the singular capability of willfully determining their own moral character on the other. As one midrash notes, unlike the angels and the beasts, "if human beings are deserving, they may eat of two worlds [this and the next, the physical and the spiritual] . . . , but if humans are not deserving, they must render an account to God." *To eat of two worlds:* Judaism has depicted humankind as straddling a cosmic frontier between this world and the next, while the opposition and intersection of Jewish and Gentile worlds lie at the bedrock of the process whereby Jewish civilization has developed. The perils of isolation and assimilation have ever threatened Judaism; yet balancing the two has facilitated both survival and vitality.

Where might such insight lead in formulating a programmatically oriented perspective on medieval studies? First, I would suggest that the distinctive "minority" character of medieval Judaica—both in its original setting and in its modern academic investigation—highlights the need for hermeneutical awareness in what we do as medievalists. The question, it seems to me, is not simply one of equipment: languages, paleographic training, and poststructuralist criticism blended all together. Beyond that, without denigrating the independent meaning and value of past experience, we should recognize the generic parity between the cultural artifacts we study and the fruits of our scholarship; scrutinizing how men and women made history in "the olden days," as my young children refer to what I study—or "doing" medieval history—is making modern history. This speaks to the depth and inexactitude of our concerns, as well as the importance of pluralism and heterogeneity, no less in our bibliographies than in our openness to the "other" and his or her disagreement with us. I have ceased to take unmitigated pride in a student's written evaluation of twelve years ago that my course on Judaism and Christianity was "godless, offensive to Jews and Christians alike." I say I have ceased to take *unmitigated* pride in such rebuke, because the complaint still bespeaks the encouraging sense that I was an equal opportunity offender in a manner befitting the secular academy. Yet I would now view this student's criticism as a healthy challenge, to deal with the ramifications of why she (I think) reacted in this way and I in mine. I likewise recall how when interviewed for a job just a year out of graduate school, a medieval historian questioned whether I believed one had to be Jewish to teach Jewish studies. While I still would respond with an emphatic no, I no longer would argue that Jew and non-Jew can possibly teach them identically. Precisely the differences between our orientations add to an appreciation of the medieval past that concerns us.

Much the same applies to the institutional setting for our endeavors as medievalists. Among others, Jacob Neusner has written to describe the three academic environments for contemporary Jewish scholarship: institutes or faculties of Jewish studies at Israeli universities; colleges or think-tanks exclusively for Judaic scholarship, including some rabbinical seminaries; and the traditional, disciplinarily defined departments of Western universities. Although Neusner has vigorously promoted the third context, that of the American-style university, at the expense of the other two, my own experience points to different conclusions. As did my academic training, so has my recent employment involved me in all three settings: the history department of a land-grant, midwestern university; the department of Jewish history in Tel Aviv University's school of Jewish studies; and the Shalom Hartman Institute, a small, religiously concerned but pluralistic think-tank for Jewish studies in Jerusalem. The population, assets, agenda, matters of shared concern, and tenor of the conversation vary widely between the three environments, and each enriches me, differently, as a medievalist, a historian, and a student of Judaica. In the spirit of the rabbinic adage, I am fortunate to eat of several worlds, and I deem the lesson applicable to medieval studies as well. We belong among the disciplines, in centers, *and* in separate societies and institutes all at the same time—thereby developing the specific and the generic in what we do, promoting diversity in our texts, our intertexts, and our readers.

A third and final suggestion: Although nineteenth-century *Wissenschaft des Judentums* gave birth to modern Judaic scholarship, Neusner has reflected instructively on the gap between the apologetic/polemical underpinnings of the former and the ethos of the

secular university in which the latter now flourishes. One ought not
to exaggerate on this score, to be sure. Nevertheless, Jewish studies'
transition from a provincial to a universal—or perhaps from a partisan to a pluralistic—academic context has had impact both on the
field and on the university. The pluralistic sensitivities of the 1960s
and 1970s paved the way for ethnic studies to enter the college curriculum. But once the barriers had been overcome, substantive
questions remained.

> For what did the[se] new humanities offer to justify entry into
> the realm of the disciplined intellect? The mere presence of a
> new sort of human being, formerly excluded, hardly consti-
> tuted a persuasive argument. . . . What universally accessible
> human experience did the new constituencies bring to the
> campus, to measure up to the classics of human intellect that,
> all together, had constituted the old humanities . . . ? So people
> took for granted, both old and new alike, that . . . blacks would
> study what blacks had done. Jews would study Jewish studies.
> Women would study women's studies. But everyone, anyhow,
> would still study the familiar philosophy, the Shakespeare, the
> Reformation that everyone had always studied, in the ways in
> which everyone had always studied them.[18]

Meanwhile, as we all know too well, the humanities as a group have
suffered. The economy, the cultural climate, and a new generation
of students have compelled us to reevaluate within and reassert our
importance without. As such, "the easy compromise of the 1970s
has fallen away. The new humanities cannot explain themselves
within its terms. The established humanities turn out to be unable
to explain themselves any longer."[19] For Jewish studies, the tough,
existential questions endure.

Granted that the collective of medieval studies does not number among the "new," ethnically defined humanities; its texts are
generally those of the mainstream, the old humanities. But the con-
vergent identity crises of all the humanities, new and old, may
speak to our shared agenda at this conference: Why a distinct *field*
of medieval studies? Beyond the creative exposition of anachronism, what is it that medievalists do, and how do we do it, such that
we merit our own special niche in the curriculum of the contemporary university? I close, not with a neat (or rash) attempt at a so-

lution, but with a word of thanks to the organizers and editors of this discussion for prodding us to define, to focus on, and to wrestle with the questions.

NOTES

1. For the most part, I have limited the notes to the sources for the direct quotations and allusions appearing in the body of my essay. Any attempt to provide comprehensive bibliography for the synthetic, generalizing overview which follows would result in copious, oppressively lengthy, and—given the nature of this volume—ultimately unnecessary notes. Albeit to different extents, specialists and non-specialists alike should recognize that my perceptions of the field derive from the scholarly contributions of innumerable predecessors and teachers.

2. Cf. the representative course outlines collected in Ivan G. Marcus, ed., *Medieval Jewish Civilization: A Multi-Disciplinary Curriculum, Bibliographies, and Selected Syllabi* (New York, 1988).

3. Yitzhak F. Baer, *Galut,* trans. Robert Warshow (New York, 1947), 22.

4. Walter Ullmann, *A History of Political Thought: The Middle Ages* (Harmondsworth, 1970), 12 and *passim.*

5. Paul R. Mendes-Flohr and Jehuda Reinharz, eds., *The Jew in the Modern World: A Documentary History* (New York, 1980), 104.

6. Jacob Katz, *Jewish Emancipation and Self-Emancipation* (Philadelphia, 1986), 80–81.

7. Mendes-Flohr and Reinharz, *The Jew in the Modern World,* 197.

8. Judah Loeb Gordon, *Kitve Yehudah Loeb Gordon: Shirah* (Tel Aviv, 1950), 30–31; Mendes-Flohr and Reinharz, *The Jew in the Modern World,* 312–315.

9. Moshe Idel, *Kabbalah: New Perspectives* (New Haven, 1988), 253.

10. Ivan G. Marcus, *Piety and Society: The Jewish Pietists of Medieval Germany,* Etudes sur le Judaisme médiéval 10 (Leiden, 1981), 1.

11. Heinrich Graetz, *The Structure of Jewish History and Other Essays,* ed. Ismar Schorsch, Moreshet: Studies in Jewish History, Literature and Thought 3 (New York, 1975), 170.

12. Ibid., 268.

13. Ibid., 129.

14. Ibid., 289.

15. Arnold M. Eisen, *Galut: Modern Jewish Reflection on Homelessness and Homecoming* (Bloomington, Ind., 1986); in an epilogue to part

one of his monograph, Eisen devotes several pages (50–56) to a cursory glance at "several salient features of the medieval and early modern re-interpretation of galut."

16. Gershom G. Scholem, *Major Trends in Jewish Mysticism* (1941; repr., New York, 1971), 22–23.

17. See David Biale, *Gershom Scholem: Kabbalah and Counter-History,* 2nd ed. (Cambridge, Mass., 1982); Idel, *Kabbalah;* etc.

18. Jacob Neusner, *New Humanities and Academic Disciplines: The Case of Jewish Studies* (Madison, Wis., 1984), 171.

19. Ibid., 172.

Orientalism and Medieval Islamic Studies

Richard W. Bulliet

Prior to the 1950s, medieval Islamic studies was usually understood to be a major subdivision of orientalism, a separate discipline that evolved in Europe during the eighteenth and nineteenth centuries. The hallmarks of the Islamic dimension of orientalism were understood to be a dedication to the editing of texts and a primary concern for Muhammad and the Qur'an, philosophy, literature, and political history. Orientalist faculties and journals proliferated in Europe, but there were comparatively few in the United States where development of the discipline was slowed by lack of manuscripts, distance from the Middle East, and the comparative unimportance of the Islamic world in political and economic terms.

The many achievements of European orientalism laid the foundations for all subsequent work in the field. Editions of major chronicles, like al-Tabari, Ibn al-Athir, and Ibn Kathir, provided the basis for political narratives. The most important geographical texts, edited in the Bibliotheca Geographorum Arabicorum, fleshed out the image of a flourishing urban society based on manufacture and trade. Major poetry collections from the pre-Islamic period and the first three Islamic centuries, along with belletristic works from the same period, made the masterworks of Arabic literature available for translators. And the medieval European interest in Aristotelian philosophy from Arabic sources continued unabated.

Given the many thousands of manuscripts available for editing, the choices made by the European orientalists suggest their preferences and interests. Islamic religious texts, particularly post-1000, were seldom edited. Likewise, biographical dictionaries containing tens of thousands of notices concerning religious scholars received the attention more of Muslim than of European editors. Most striking, however, was the comparative paucity of editions of Persian and Turkish texts, apart from chronicles and poetry.

In choosing texts to edit, the European orientalists were implicitly setting the intellectual agenda for scholars who studied the newly available texts, most often the orientalists themselves, and interpreted them for non-orientalist readers. "Medieval Islam" thus became typified as the saga of Muhammad's life, the political history of the caliphate, the transmission of Greek philosophy to Europe via Arabic, and the early flourishing and subsequent stagnation of Arabic poetry, seen as the greatest of the arts of the Muslims. Although masses of manuscript evidence for the careers and achievements of medieval Muslim religious scholars were available, the European orientalists displayed little of the fascination with religious thought and practice so characteristic of European medievalists of the same period. Nor did they concern themselves greatly with the period after 1000, except in the context of crusader history.

After World War II, orientalism in Europe revived slowly, many orientalists choosing to emigrate to the United States where interest in Islam was still in a fledgling state. Such noted European orientalists as H. A. R. Gibb, Gustave E. Von Grunebaum, and Joseph Schacht became the leading lights at Harvard, UCLA, and Columbia respectively. The students of scholars such as these preserved the orientalist discipline into the next generation, but no American university maintained the orientalist tradition intact. Paleography, diplomatics, and text editing played only minor roles in American curricula; and no university proved able to assemble a critical mass of scholars in the orientalist tradition. Lecture courses, both by immigrant and newly trained American scholars, continued to focus on the life and career of Muhammad, the narrative history of the caliphate down to 1000, and cultural history with an emphasis on philosophy and Arabic poetry and belles lettres, but the number of scholars well enough trained to undertake editions or translations of major medieval texts remained very small.

Part of the difficulty the founding generation of European orientalists in the United States faced in trying to establish their profession was the attraction of students to a rival academic approach that was distinctively American: Middle East studies. With the financial encouragement of the U.S. government and the Ford Foundation, a few elite universities undertook to establish training programs, usually leading to the master's degree, designed to provide Middle East specialists for the diplomatic and intelligence corps and for private businesses and non-profit organizations interested in the Middle East. This was explicitly an educational response to the perceived new role of the United States as a great power with worldwide responsibilities. Moreover, the cachet of official sponsorship made it difficult for the European scholars to criticize, even when they recognized its innate shallowness.

Middle East studies was militantly interdisciplinary and usually embodied in non-departmental institutes and centers with autonomous hiring, curriculum, and degree-granting powers. Many notable European orientalists took part in and even directed these new programs. In the 1950s, Hamilton A. R. Gibb presented magisterial lectures on pre-Islam and early Islam in a course for graduate students that featured other faculty delivering slide lectures on Middle Eastern geography, lectures on Ottoman history, and lectures on modern Persian, Arab, and Turkish history. Given the wide popularity of "dog and pony show" courses in foreign area studies curricula, this may not seem surprising. But it is difficult to imagine that graduate students interested in Europe would be expected to take a course in "European History" designed along similar lines. And it is difficult to imagine European orientalists in their home universities voluntarily involving themselves in a course of such broad and superficial content.

The cleavage between medievalists in the orientalist mold and medievalists more interested in working within the parameters of Middle East studies extended into the realm of publication and granting of degrees. The former scholars identified most closely with the Islamic branch of the venerable American Oriental Society, and the latter with the newly formed Middle East Studies Association. Each organization had its respective journal which reflected its approach to the field. As for degrees, the orientalists had the upper hand as granters of the doctorate, most often within a department entitled Near Eastern Studies, Middle Eastern Languages and Cultures, or something similar. The doctoral degree did not exist in the non-departmental, master's degree–oriented world of Middle East studies. Nevertheless, those medievalists who identified with the interdisciplinary Middle East studies approach often had greater access to money and an ability to attract students who were concerned with fitting themselves for an academic marketplace which displayed little demand for orientalist skills.

Needless to say, this situation generated rivalries, both personal and general; but they were comparatively minor. No one was able to argue persuasively that the approach of medievalists of the Middle East studies persuasion was better or worse than that of orientalists in the true European mold; for, in fact, all had been trained pretty much the same way, at least through the 1960s. Orientalism maintained an intellectual domination, even among the self-identified non-orientalists, when it came to defining agendas for study. Despite the non-departmental and avowedly interdisciplinary ethos of Middle East studies and the existence of new institutions devoted to the enterprise, no intellectual breakthrough occurred to redefine the field of medieval Islamic studies.

When a breakthrough finally came at the end of the 1970s, it came, perhaps necessarily, from someone who was neither an orientalist nor a specialist in the study of the Middle East. Since the publication in 1978 of Edward Said's *Orientalism,* medieval Islamic studies have evolved rapidly and in ways that both bring into question their relation to medieval studies of Christian Europe and open up problems that European medievalists do not have to face. Both tendencies, ironically, stem from a single basic circumstance that played only a minor role in the thinking of earlier orientalists, whether European and American, namely, their personal status as non-Muslims born and educated outside the Islamic world. European medievalists study a culture and society that is situated unalterably in the past; and the past it is situated in is, for the most part, their own. By contrast, medieval Islamicists with Western cultural backgrounds study a past culture and society of which they, for the most part, are not heirs, and one that many of the world's Muslims believe still informs their daily lives. All historians intrude upon the past as outsiders, but medieval Islamicists who are not personally from a Muslim background are outsiders in both time and culture. And for the past fifteen years they have been ever more frequently made aware of that situation by the many learned and unlearned Muslims in the world who view their scholarly efforts with suspicion.

The index of the change can be seen in three books. Jean-Jacques Waardenburg published *L'Islam dans le miroir de l'occident* in 1962. In it he analyzes the lives and accomplishments of five

European orientalists: Ignaz Goldziher (1850–1921) from Hungary, Snouck Hurgronje (1857–1936) from the Netherlands, Carl Becker (1876–1933) from Germany, Duncan Black MacDonald (1863–1943) from Scotland, and Louis Massignon (1883–1962) from France. The first and last of these figures, Goldziher and Massignon, are arguably the two most important Western scholars of Islam in the twentieth century. The former, at the turn of the century, developed a synthesis of Islamic religious development that set the agenda for studies for the next two generations. He also set in motion the *Encyclopedia of Islam* project, edited by "A group of European Orientalists," that largely defined the approach and scope of medieval Islamic studies during that period. The latter, Massignon, fundamentally revised Goldziher's law and theology-centered paradigm by adding to it a profound concern for mysticism and spirituality. The other three scholars, though less influential, represented, for Waardenburg, important added perspectives on Islamic studies: observation of local custom and collaboration with colonial government (Hurgronje), philhellenic humanism (Becker), and missionary purpose (MacDonald).

Thus the five portraits collectively represent medieval Islamic studies as a religion-centered (but not therefore religious) scholarly enterprise proceeding by the method of reading texts and trying to grasp therefrom either a totalistic view of Islam or a sense of the major issues involved in its study. Though Waardenburg speaks of Becker and Goldziher in particular as taking "historical" views, his analysis (and my own appraisal) of the work of these scholars and their contemporaries concludes that the historical bent of the orientalists of that era was remarkably naive in terms of historiographical method. Language learning and text editing so consumed the preparation phase of scholars' careers that their ability to subject the data they found in the texts to sophisticated historical analysis remained poorly developed.

Yet the orientalist tradition within which these five scholars worked had a very high *esprit de corps.* Waardenburg's five subjects and their colleagues formed a closely interknit and, for the most part, mutually supportive scholarly society, as Waardenburg's biographical sketches amply show. There were no powerful factions dedicated to philosophically or methodologically opposed strategies. Blistering reviews of new publications within the group were rare. And personal feuds did not develop strong ideological content until the World War II period and later when scholars became caught up in the Nazi cataclysm or the decolonization struggles.

This sense of harmonious and cooperative labor in the name of a broadly agreed upon orientalist objective suffuses Maxime Rodinson's book *La Fascination de l'Islam* published in 1982. Reared in a Jewish working class environment, Rodinson became an atheist, a communist, and an outspoken supporter of Third World peoples struggling against European domination. In all of these ways, he is the very antithesis of Waardenburg's orientalist quintet. Yet in the two long essays from the 1970s that form the bulk of his book, Rodinson has nothing but praise and admiration for the European orientalist tradition from the time of Antoine Sylvestre de Sacy (1758–1838) onward. Today one of the more eminent senior orientalists in France, and one of the very few willing to make pronouncements on current political matters, Rodinson nevertheless refrains in this book from bringing his sharp critical skills to bear on the words and deeds of his pious, well-placed predecessors who generally felt so comfortable with their governments' imperialist policies in Muslim lands.

What lends added fascination to Rodinson's *La Fascination de l'Islam* is the introductory essay that deals with Edward Said's *Orientalism,* which was published in 1978 between the writing of Rodinson's longer essays and their collection for publication. Despite the fact that Rodinson is an ardent exponent of the pro-Palestinian political agenda that Edward Said so eloquently espouses in other works, he attacks Said briefly but ferociously by labeling his approach to orientalism "Zhdanovite." Since Stalin's friend Andrei Zhdanov, who died in 1948, was associated with militant suppression of intellectual dissent from Kremlin policies in the French communist circles Rodinson frequented prior to his expulsion from the party for intellectual deviation, Rodinson's use of this term cannot be written off lightly. In essence, he is saying that the interpretation of the European orientalist tradition expressed by Edward Said seeks to coerce readers into an unequivocal condemnation of several generations of great scholars as running dogs of imperialism.

There is no more vivid testimony to the impact of Said's analysis of orientalism than the fact that by 1987, for the English translation of his work entitled *Europe and the Mystique of Islam,*

Rodinson had deleted his criticism of Said. What in 1978 was a scholarly outsider's outrageous critique had come to be accepted as an intellectual monument that could not be casually assailed.

I do not propose here to praise, condemn, or even analyze Edward Said's proposition that the orientalist profession over the past two centuries contributed fundamentally to the creation and reification of a quasi-mythic Other, the Orient, thus wittingly or unwittingly serving and justifying European and American imperialism. Irrespective of the cogency and insight of Said's analysis, the widespread acceptance of his thesis, at least as a serious topic of study, has greatly changed the climate in which medieval Islamicists work and forced a reexamination both of the philosophical bases of that work and of relations between scholarship on medieval Islam and other academic and non-academic enterprises.

I will briefly outline the changed and changing circumstances of the profession under these headings and then draw some general conclusions about the current state and future of the field.

First, the disinclination of scholars to criticize one another's work has greatly diminished. The earlier divergence of some medievalists toward Middle East studies had established some distance between them and the more traditional orientalists, but this had been more an institutional than an intellectually critical division. Everyone knew one another in a small field, and expressing a strongly critical attitude toward a more senior scholar was a dangerous career decision for a young scholar.

By depicting the glittering tradition of kingly orientalists as a procession of malevolent nudists, Said legitimized criticism of all sorts. Some of it has been constructive, and some merely strident. Significantly, it has emanated from the Muslim scholarly community as well as from non-Muslim scholars working in the Western tradition. Classic works long viewed as scholarly landmarks, including the major writings of all of the scholars mentioned earlier in this essay, have been subjected to scathing critique. On balance, despite the bruised feelings that have resulted, this new critical climate must be adjudged a positive and stimulating reaction to Said's work.

The second area of change during the past decade and a half has been audience. Who reads the works by Islamic medievalists? Thirty years ago one would have answered, "other Islamic medievalists." Today one must add, "Muslim intellectuals concerned for their cultural tradition." The suspicion engendered by Said's broadside against orientalism, combined with the renewed political salience of Islam in the contemporary world, has produced a new and wider audience for works on medieval Islam. Where once the few Muslim students in a classroom could be expected to listen docilely to whatever was said about their religious tradition and to read the assigned books with similar credulity, today an Islamic medievalist must continually appraise his or her words in terms of the message they may be conveying to Muslim students and readers.

The negative aspects of this change of audience include, on the one hand, self-censorship to avoid offending Muslims, and, on the other, a deliberately antagonistic attitude as embodied, for example, in an introductory comment in Patricia Crone and Michael Cook's *Hagarism* (1977) that the book was written "by infidels for infidels." On the positive side, the new audience is broader, more challenging, and more critical than before, and the standards of scholarly analysis have thereby been raised. The kind of broad generalization about the nature of Islam or of Muslims that was so dear to the orientalists of a century ago now seems jejune and even insulting.

The third area of change involves the notions of humanism and faith. One product of the Enlightenment was a disposition to place reason above faith in academic endeavor. The demythologization of elements of Christian and Jewish tradition proceeded either from an animus against religion altogether, or from a desire to purify religion by applying to it the highest and most objective standards of scholarly critique. To some extent, this same impulse carried over into medieval Islamic studies where it took the form of non-Muslim scholars "demythologizing" various aspects of Islamic tradition. This was accompanied by a general dismissal of traditional Islamic scholarship, both of the medieval period and as preserved in the surviving institutions of higher Muslim education, as hopelessly subjective, noncritical, and biased by blind faith.

The last fifteen years have witnessed both a growth in the attention given to traditional Islamic scholarship and a debate on the role non-Muslim medievalists should play in analyzing the roots of Muslim faith. Christian Décobert in his important new book *Le Mendiant et le combattant. L'institution de l'islam* (1992) analyzes the "demythologizing" school of thought associated with the names of John Wansbrough, Patricia Crone, and Michael Cook as adhering to a "humanistic," anti-religious methodology. However, the question remains unresolved how to carry out medieval Islamic studies touching on fundamental articles of Muslim faith in an atmosphere of heightened religious sensitivity, international political controversy, and critical scrutiny. The problems faced by European medievalists struggling to make the thought of Hugh of St. Victor or the organization of Cistercian monasteries seem relevant to the modern world are exactly opposite from those of Islamic medievalists in the West, whose writings on law or theology are often assumed to be informed by contemporary political agendas.

A bracing critical climate, new and more diverse audiences, and a new sensitivity to the philosophical principles underlying the study of a faith community are hardly a recipe for disaster. Indeed, medieval Islamic studies can properly be considered a robust field of academic research. The study of Islamic philosophy is being pushed in new directions by fresh interest in Sufi illuminationism and Shi'ite neo-Platonism. Sufism and Shi'ism in all of their aspects are being studied as never before. Social history based on biographical dictionaries is opening up new fields of study, as is the rereading of texts from the point of view of post-structuralism or post-modernism. The traditions of the Prophet and other aspects of the Islamic religious tradition are similarly coming in for intensive study. And medieval Persian sources are finally being explored with the intensity formerly reserved for Arabic. Even in the reference area there is a burst of productivity, most notably in two massive projects initiated by Ehsan Yarshater, the translation of the chronicle of al-Tabari, and *The Encyclopaedia Iranica.*

Yet this vision of liveliness and productivity might not be universal. Traditional orientalist concerns with text editing and high culture no longer reign supreme, and that must surely displease some advocates of that approach. Moreover, looking to the future, there is every likelihood that the next generation of scholarship will confirm an already significant transformation of what has traditionally been a non-Muslim scholarly enterprise into an overwhelmingly Muslim one. From the standpoint of the Western idealization of the academy as a community of pure thought entirely isolated from religious bias, this might appear inconsequential. But it is not. One has only to read a book like Mahmud Ibrahim's *Mer-*

chant Capital and Islam (1991) to discover the discomfort and defensiveness an American-educated Muslim scholar can feel in writing about the origins of his faith from a Marxist perspective. The foraging of a common and mutually cordial scholarly enterprise among Muslim and non-Muslim medievalists, particularly including scholars trained in religious or secular institutions within the Muslim world, is a great challenge for the next generation. But it will not be achieved until the ghost of the orientalism conjured up by Edward Said is somehow laid to rest.

As one views this prospect in comparison with European medieval studies, three things stand out. First, the issue of interdisciplinary or non-departmental studies and institutions is not very important in the Islamic field. This issue was dealt with in the 1960s, and a realization was reached that changing rubrics and administrative structures has little impact unless there is an accompanying challenge to traditional thought patterns. Middle East studies as envisioned in the 1950s has now waned. Doctoral level study within disciplinary departments regained importance as the regional studies master's degree lost the cachet it once had. The intellectual currents that have led a few anthropologists and sociologists to look at medieval Islam, and a few Islamicists to interest themselves in social, economic, scientific, or technological matters flow from the general ferment of the social science disciplines rather than from the foreign area studies concept.

Second, the new salience of faith and "orientalist" bias as all-pervasive critical approaches has terminated the long apprenticeship of Islamic studies to traditional European scholarship. It is no longer possible to view Islamic studies as a simple extension eastward of techniques and attitudes derived from classical studies or medieval Christian studies. Hopefully, however, this will open the possibility of new relationships between medievalists. If studies of medieval Islam succeed in establishing their philosophical and methodological autonomy vis-à-vis medieval Europe, it should be possible for the two to relate to each other on a sounder and more challenging basis. Indeed, I eagerly look forward to the time when medieval history and society will be taught and studied as a unity, with Christianity, Judaism, and Islam all combined. But this cannot be achieved until medieval Islamic studies acquire true intellectual autonomy.

And third, the relevance of medieval Islam to a twenty-first century curriculum is not in question. The debates over Eurocentrism, canonical lists of "great" monuments of thought and letters, and the suggested necessity of shrinking Western culture to fit proportionally into a world-oriented academic enterprise will, if anything, redound to the benefit of Islamic studies. At worst, even with a full reassertion of confidence in the necessity of imbuing all students with a knowledge of our culture's medieval European roots, medieval Islamic studies will still command a place in the curriculum as the foundation stone for understanding the growing trend toward religiously based Islamic political action around the world. Ayatollah Khomeini inadvertently provided what the Cold War educationists of the 1950s sought for unsuccessfully, a rationale for studying medieval Islam and the modern Middle East in an integrated fashion. It remains to be seen whether this will lead to a new orientalism or to a meeting of Muslim and non-Muslim minds that will benefit scholarship and the world political community alike.

How the Past Is Remembered: From Antiquity to Late Antiquity, the Middle Ages, and Beyond

SABINE MACCORMACK

EACH PRESENT HAS ITS PAST. Indeed, it is possible to choose a past, along with appropriate methods of remembering it. Such choices have been made, often quite consciously, at different times. In the aftermath of a series of spectacular Christian victories over the Muslims, for example, Alfonso X of Castile and his team of compilers incorporated a variety of episodes from the Bible and the works of several Roman poets and historians into their survey of the history of Spain, the *Primera Crónica General de España* and its companion work, the *General Estoria*.[1] The deployment of these biblical and Roman sources enabled Alfonso to view the history of Christian Spain as coextensive with world history, and this project in turn underpinned his political aspirations.[2] Similarly, humanist scholars examined the classical past by way of finding in it precedents applicable to their own period,[3] while in the contemporary United States the search for visions of the past capable of articulating the aspirations of groups and individuals has become, in effect, a national passion.[4]

In this contemporary context, the history of the European Middle Ages appears to become ever more irrelevant. At the same time, universities as institutions and teachers of the traditional humanistic disciplines as individuals regularly come under fire for purportedly failing to live up to the challenge of the present; whether this is the challenge of facilitating alternative visions of the past or that of communicating a canon of knowledge or expertise to

the next generation.[5] All too often, debates surrounding these is
sues are conducted as though a canon, let us say of texts or of
knowledge and skills, were a fixed and static entity, and as though
an understanding of it were communicated only by authoritative
statement and assertion, and not also, or not principally, by a willingness to comprehend more of human experience than what is
purely personal, purely centered on the self. In this essay, therefore,
I would like to reflect on the manner in which certain individuals
have looked to classical antiquity by way of differentiating themselves from it while at the same time recognizing in the classical
past a point of departure, a relevant otherness. My purpose here is
to show that, while the classical and late antique past loomed large
throughout the Middle Ages and beyond, the reasons for the presence of that past changed with lapse of time, and with that, the vision of the past itself changed. This reality regarding the manner in
which a cultural tradition is passed on from one generation to the
next is usually overlooked in our current debates about canon, the
purpose of universities, and the nature of identity.[6] For in these debates, European ideas, be they classical, medieval, or more recent,
tend to be bunched together as a uniform and unchanging corpus,
to be either accepted or rejected *en bloc.*[7] This view, it seems to me,
is incorrect. Europe has not been unique in transmitting for centuries an ancient but continuously changing and expansive cultural
tradition.[8] It is useful to be aware, for example, that Confucianism,
and Buddhism in China and then in Japan have had an equally long
history of transmission, in the course of which those traditions also
changed, while at the same time continuing to sustain the meanings
with which their exponents endowed them.[9] In explaining the resulting relationship or tension between continuity and change, tradition and innovation, medievalists are in a position to address the
very issues that concern us today.

Indeed, scholarly engagement with issues of the day has long
motivated research into the Middle Ages, beginning in the seventeenth century and continuing to the present. Mabillon, like the
other seventeenth-century founders of the discipline, thus combined his dedication to scholarship, the study of manuscripts, of
liturgical and textual traditions, of chronology and political history with the endeavor of understanding the Catholic church as it

was in his time and with his own personal pursuit of Christian devotion.[10] Similarly, many contemporary medievalists seek to understand not just the medieval past, but also the role, whether special or not, of "the Western tradition, and especially its early stages,"[11] in the contemporary world and perhaps also in their own lives. This, at any rate, appears to be one of the concerns that underlies enquiries into medieval topics that range *inter alia* from perceptions of individuality, of feminine piety, of homosexuality, and of childhood on to the more traditional study of social organization, of representative institutions, of universities and intellectual traditions.[12]

If this kind of committed engagement with the past were not possible, it would mean that the past we study has truly died: that the historian's greatest art, which is to resurrect the dead on the written page, would be practiced on dead people to whose lives our minds and feelings would ultimately have to remain indifferent. At the same time, being in this way engaged with the past we study, we must admit that complete objectivity is not really possible in historical enquiry because the questions we ask will always be motivated in some fashion by the experience of our own present. But that does not mean that nothing can be understood, or that historical integrity must inevitably be sacrificed to contemporary relevance. The point is that we cannot claim to understand the past if we are not prepared to lend our ears to those who spoke in it and to listen to them in their own words; if we are not prepared to consider the images and objects they created within the context in which these were first meaningful or to comprehend the social and political order that produced words, images, and objects in the first place.

With this, let me turn to how specifically the tension between the exigencies of the past and those of the present has been articulated by discussing—however briefly—some episodes in the reception of Vergil's *Aeneid.* What can be learnt from these and similar episodes punctuating medieval history is that we are not the first to experience contradictions and confusions in formulating our ideas about how the past is to be understood and whether this past is worth understanding in the first place. Nor are we the first to find that the past is not static, and that it can never be quite the same for any two beholders. That does not mean, however, that the past is a fiction or personal invention to be manipulated at will.[13]

There is a further issue that I would like to highlight in examining these episodes in the reception of Vergil. This is the tension between the continuities that link us to our past and the discontinuities that separate us from it. For in examining how these continuities and discontinuities were perceived and understood by different people we can reach a greater understanding not only of them, but also of ourselves and of the dilemmas confronting us.

The classical period—let us say it extends from Homer to Marcus Aurelius, or perhaps from Homer to Constantine—spans over a millennium. It was thus a period that had its own pasts, such as the Homeric past of fifth-century Greece,[14] and the Greek past as seen by the Romans.[15] With all that, an unprecedented rupture occurred in late antiquity, a discontinuity that was perceived even by contemporaries.[16] Nonetheless, late antiquity was, in many respects, a conservative age: a time when the elites of the Roman empire sought to preserve the political and cultural legacies they had inherited—and this was true of both pagans and Christians. Ever since Gibbon, however, historians have more often viewed late antiquity as a period defined by change, by the triumph of Christianity, and by the ultimate transformation of the Roman empire into the barbarian kingdoms in the West and Byzantium in the East.[17] This tension between change and continuity is discernible in every aspect of late antique experience. In late Roman schools, grammarians and rhetors taught the classical texts,[18] but how those texts would be understood—whether conservatively or innovatively—was not entirely predictable. So it was with late antique interpretations of Vergil's *Aeneid,* which range from simple paraphrase to philological and philosophical commentary and allegorical exposition, all of which in due course exercized their influence on Vergil's subsequent readers.[19]

Among those who read Vergil in antiquity and late antiquity, the most penetrating, although also the most critical and even, at times, hostile was Augustine. As a boy and young man, Augustine loved the stories Vergil told, and the emotive experiences that could be lived and relived in reading the *Aeneid* helped to articulate his own inner life.[20] After his conversion, still deeply involved with Vergil's poetry, Augustine allegorized lines from the beloved poet in order to apply them to his now Christian experience.[21] In his maturity, however, Augustine more often chose Vergil as a spokesman for those aspects of Roman culture and the Roman past that he believed had to be rejected. Vergil's concept of selfhood and citizenship, of the way in which one belongs to one's society and has obligations towards it, his concept of the divine and of the Roman state all met with Augustine's repeated and often bitter objections.[22]

Rome, the city with an eternal destiny that Vergil's Aeneas had set out to found, was for the mature Augustine merely an example of what was amiss with political power. Rome's mission, as Vergil had stated it, was to

> implant the law of peace,
> to spare the conquered and beat down the proud.

In addition, Rome was to endure forever. To the Romans, Vergil's Jupiter had said, "I bestow an empire without end." Both propositions evoked Augustine's censure. On the one hand, he juxtaposed with Rome's history of conquest the history of the City of that God "who resists the proud and gives grace to the humble." And on the other hand, he addressed Jupiter, one of the false gods of the pagans, with derision:

> This empire that you gave, you who gave nothing: is it on earth or in heaven? It is on earth. But even if it were in heaven, "Heaven and earth shall pass away." What God has made shall pass away, and how much sooner will that city pass away which Romulus has founded.[23]

The eternal kingdom, the only valid focal point of patriotism, was the City of God, an alien and pilgrim in political society, and to this pilgrim city Augustine therefore applied Vergil's prophecy of empire without end by slightly changing the poet's wording.[24]

Augustine's rejection of Vergil's political vision was matched by his refutation of Vergil's perception of individuality, of how the soul is joined to the body. At the end of his journey through the world of the dead, Vergil's Aeneas reached the Elysian fields, where he saw the great Romans of the future. There they were, free from care and living a blessed life. How could it be, Aeneas asked while watching these sublime beings, that they would return again to a careworn existence on earth?

> Can we believe that these exalted souls return once
>   more to have a mortal body?
> What fearful yearning for the sun draws them to
>   misery?[25]

Augustine repeatedly quoted these words by way of refuting pagan
and in particular Platonist beliefs regarding the fall of the soul into
a material body, beliefs which at the same time bore on the life after
death.[26] But as a very old man, himself not far from death, Augustine perhaps remembered his past affection for the "most exalted
poet" of the pagans[27] and, returning once more to the much discussed issue, wrote in gentler, more conciliatory terms. For Vergil's
perception of the soul's desire for a body, for individuation, Augustine now thought, had in some way anticipated the Christian resurrection of the dead at the end of time when each soul would
receive its body

> in such a way as never to relinquish that possession, never to
> be parted from that body even for a brief moment.[28]

The possession of an immortal body by those who would sing the
praises of the Lord for all eternity was foreshadowed on earth, Augustine suggested to his readers, by the miracles of curing that were
performed in his own day by God and his saints: miracles in which
the terror of pain and the terror of death were transformed into the
living certainty of the resurrection of all flesh.[29]

The boundary between Christians and the great pagans of classical antiquity was not a fixed one during Augustine's lifetime. It was
not only to convert his own pagan contemporaries that Augustine
returned again and again to the classical authors. Rather, he returned to them because they formed part of his cultural universe,
the infrastructure on which his understanding of Christianity was
built. This was why, at the end of his long life, his thoughts turned
once more to the poet who had moved him so deeply in his youth.
The passion, whether of love or of hostility, was gone, but the desire, indeed the need, to explain in what way he differed from
Vergil and in what way he agreed was all the greater. One could not
become a Christian, after all, without grappling with one's own personal past, and thus with the authors whom, as Augustine pointed
out again and again, one had studied and loved when young, whom
pagan contemporaries still studied and loved.[30]

Augustine did not quite live to see the dismemberment of the Western Roman empire. Once this had occurred, however, the pagan Roman past looked very different[31]—just as, perhaps, the "Western tradition" will look very different once it will no longer be possible for us to take its continuance for granted. After the Western Roman empire had been transformed into the kingdoms of the Visigoths, Franks, Lombards, and Anglo-Saxons, it was no longer necessary to explain, as Augustine had done, what was wrong with Roman power, nor was it necessary to insist on Vergil's errors. Instead, differences between pagan and Christian philosophy could be noted without compromising the poet's authority.[32] Moreover, Vergil was not only the poet of Rome's foundation and political destiny, but also, in the Fourth Eclogue, the prophet of the birth of a messianic child, the birth, as many late antique and medieval Christians liked to think, of Jesus.[33]

Political events and the conversion of the Mediterranean world to Christianity thus conspired to empty Augustine's polemic against Vergil and against Vergil's Rome of much of its force. Imperial Rome grew into a certain continuity with the Rome of pilgrims and popes, and with Rome the center of a Christian empire. As a result, the Augustine who had written about his own inner world and about the nature of society and hence about the City of God, now captured his readers' attention more than did the Augustine who had polemicized against Vergil's Rome as described in the *Aeneid*.[34] Such was the Augustine of Dante. When thus Dante chose Vergil as a guide to his own thoughts and feelings, to hell and purgatory, the internal and external worlds that he discovered were marked by many Augustinian characteristics.[35] Vergil had described the inner movements of the soul as occurring imperceptibly, as events capable of taking place before the person in whom they occur can become fully aware of them. So it was, for example, that Dido was *infelix,* unhappy and lost in love for Aeneas, well before she became aware of it and recognized in herself "the signs of that ancient fire." The imperceptibility of the origins of emotion and decision also preoccupied Augustine,[36] and in Dante, these themes recur once more, anchored in the interpenetrating texture of his reading both of Vergil and of Augustine.[37]

At the same time, Dante's reading of Augustine did create a certain distance between himself and Vergil. For Dante, as earlier for Augustine, the prophecy of the Fourth Eclogue was not enough to include Vergil in the Christian dispensation, because according to the inscrutable justice of God, of which Augustine had written, that prophecy had illumined the path for others, even though its author could not himself perceive its import.[38] Hence, among the first souls whom Dante encountered on his descent to hell in the company of the revered poet were those of the good and noble human beings who had not been encompassed in salvation, of whom Vergil himself was one. His heart seized by sadness, Dante asked Vergil if ever anyone had left this place, to which Vergil responded that he had seen how "a mighty one, crowned with a sign of victory" had brought forth Adam, Abel, Noah, Rachel, and Jacob and many others. But Vergil at that time had not been able to recognize this "mighty one," who was Christ[39] and by the same token would not accompany Dante during the final phase of his journey, the journey through the celestial spheres.

Vergil speaks in the *Commedia* as Dante's guide and also as the poet of the *Aeneid.* The same leaves fall, the same birds fly in Dante's similes as in Vergil's, and the same figures of classical myth and history populate the verses of the two poets. Nonetheless, every one of Dante's evocations of Vergil's words, images, or characters comprises a simultaneous and deliberate distancing, reformulation, or correction.[40] For Augustine, participation in the story of Vergil's *Aeneid* had been, for the most part, a matter of confrontation and polemic that was centered on Rome and its founder Aeneas. By the early fourteenth century when Dante was writing, by contrast, lapse of time, the end of the Roman empire of antiquity and its reconstitution in Christian guise had, in some respects, brought Vergil closer. Dante thus lived with Vergil as one lives with a beloved friend whose speech patterns and thoughts penetrate and transform one's own, a friend, however, who had in the end to be left behind.

Others, meanwhile, continued to study, comment on, and even imitate the revered poet,[41] and in due course translated the *Aeneid* into vernacular languages. Among the earliest of these translations is that by Don Enrique de Villena, who also made the first translation of the *Commedia* into Castilian. Villena's prose translation of the *Aeneid,* undertaken between 1427 and 1428, was a monumental enterprise, for it came accompanied by an extensive commentary

on context and vocabulary that was drawn both from the late antique commentary of Servius and from Villena's own knowledge.
Villena sought to communicate both the meaning and the poetic
qualities of the *Aeneid,* and his rendering is full of felicitous turns
born of profound reflection on the text. This was the work of a
scholar: a man who wanted to be sure that his readers understood
as much as possible of the *Aeneid* and would be aware of what a
translation can and what it cannot give. He thus explained that he
translated not word by word but "according to the meaning and by
the word-order that sounds best," so that his readers "could taste
the fruit of Vergil's hidden doctrine." Villena's learned apparatus to
his translation served this same purpose of enhancing the reader's
understanding of the many levels, aesthetic, philosophical, and historical, of Vergil's text.[42]

Villena recognized the profound distance that separated him
and his contemporaries from Vergil's time. Indeed, in his preface,
he was at pains to point out just how long ago Vergil had lived.[43]
His approach to Vergil differed profoundly from that of Dante, because what he sought to convey was an objective understanding of
the *Aeneid,* not an understanding mediated through his own ideas
and preoccupations. Villena's enterprise was an unusual one, at any
rate for his period and in the Spanish peninsula. Most of his Castilian contemporaries were far more likely to find in classical authors
precedents for their own ideas and actions, without wishing to ask
whether their interpretation was strictly in harmony with the classical author's original intent.[44]

As everyone knows, a scholarly understanding of cultural and
chronological distance of this kind became ever more usual in the
Renaissance, during the Reformation and Counter-Reformation, and
during the seventeenth century, the period of the great classical and
patristic editions from which we still benefit.[45] But—and here is a
paradox which as a historian one must confront—more scholarly
does not inevitably mean better.

Contemporary Vergil scholars would not admit that what Villena described as Vergil's "hidden doctrine," by which he meant an
allegorical interpretation, was part and parcel of what Vergil intended to write.[46] But these allegorical interpretations, whether
freely made or whether ascribed to Vergil's original intention,
played a role of very great importance in the history of European

ideas. With this, I move on to the reception of Vergil in Spanish America. Perhaps the point I have in mind could be more significantly made by discussing the reception of Aristotle in medieval Spain and Spanish America.[47] But let me go with Vergil and also explain why I think this matter merits the attention of medievalists.

In the first place, the history and cultural history of Spain from Roman times to now has been neglected by foreign scholars for generations, if not for centuries, while Latin America tends to be studied less for its culture than for its politics and economics.[48] But European history and the history of Europe overseas are incomplete if Spain and Portugal are omitted in the manner that is customary currently. More work is thus needed in this field. Within a European framework, the transition from antiquity to the Middle Ages in Spain is worth studying in its own right, not to mention that contacts between early medieval Spain and Northern Europe are best understood if examined from both ends.[49] But as it stands, the majority of textbooks of medieval history contain summary treatments of the Iberian peninsula at best. The result is that, on the one hand, the Western Mediterranean looks deceptively Italian, and on the other, the European origins of Latin America remain next to unintelligible. In the contemporary United States, such an approach to medieval history makes little sense.

Secondly, early colonial Latin America was the heir to the late antique and the medieval legacies of Spain and Portugal. It was in Latin America that early Christian ideas about the nature of religious conversion, filtered as they had been through Spain's multicultural past, were first implemented in a systematic fashion. The results are with us still. A late antique or medieval art historian would find in Latin American religious art of the colonial period and even of today much that is strange, but also a variety of iconographies and modes of visual expression that are continuous with European antecedents.[50] Similarly, the organization of the colonial church, and the daily expression of devotion in private and public resonate with late antique and medieval antecedents, and the same can be said of secular life.[51] In Latin America, as in the late antique Mediterranean and Bede's England, pagan cult sites were turned into Christian ones. At Copacabana on Lake Titicaca, for example, the Virgin Mary has responded from the late sixteenth century until now to the needs of her worshippers, speaking with them in dreams, curing diseases, finding lost animals, mending broken marriages, and attending to all the other needs of daily life.[52] Such supernatural interventions link this ancient cult site of the Incas to the cult sites of late antique and medieval Europe, where also the Virgin and the saints remedied the pains and sorrows of human existence.[53]

At the same time, we must not hold too comfortable a view of these continuities between Europe and the Americas. Conversion in early colonial Latin America was a conflictive, violent process. It is easy at first, with a late antique and medieval background, to view the evangelization of Peru and Mexico as an organic progression to a more reasonable form of religious expression, much as many missionaries did.[54] As one missionary in Peru wrote, conversion amounted to a progression of the Incas and their former subjects toward "las Indias de la gloria," the Indies of glory.[55] But on closer inspection, such a perspective is partial at best, because it overlooks the terrible ravages that evangelization wreaked on indigenous cultures and on the indigenous social order. One is thus led to study and understand the many metamorphoses of indigenous cultures and religions within the context of a Christian and Spanish colonial state.[56] For only in this way can one grasp what evangelization and conversion amounted to in cultural and political terms. At the time in his life when Augustine reformulated his attitude to Vergil so as to find in him evidence of what should be rejected about pagan thought and letters, he was also beginning to advocate religious coercion, the intervention of the Roman state on behalf of the Catholic church, as a viable instrument to achieve doctrinal unity.[57]

Recourse to religious coercion was fundamental in the evangelization of Latin America. It was justified by appeals not only to Augustine, but also to the practice of the Visigothic and medieval church in Spain.[58] Reflection on these matters is likely to lead us to revise our understanding of conversion in the late antique Mediterranean as being infinitely more complex and problematic than is usually allowed for, and the same goes for the long drawn out conversion of Northern Europe.[59] Regarding Latin America, and regarding the position of medieval studies in a wider world, a tip of this iceberg becomes discernible if we turn once more to the reception of Vergil.

The emergence of Amerindian cultures on European intellectual horizons triggered off a slow but profound transformation in ideas about the nature of society, culture, and religion.[60] An early phase of this transformation is documented in a work that was, in effect, the first early modern comparative study of religion. This is the *Apologética Historia* of Bartolomé de Las Casas, completed in 1559.[61] In this work, Las Casas endeavored to prove that Amerindian cultural achievements matched those of Greco-Roman antiquity and of his own contemporary Europe. For this purpose, he classified Amerindian, and by implication European civilizations, according to a Thomist-Aristotelian scheme that made of cultural diversity a symphony. This symphony of cultures replaced the hierarchy, with Europe at the top and America at the bottom, that many contemporaries of Las Casas were inclined to perceive when comparing the two continents.

Discussion in the *Apologética Historia* focuses on government, social organization, education, and the arts, but the central theme is religion. Here, Las Casas argued that the indigenous people of the Americas had comprehended the fundamental ethical and philosophical truths that were also articulated in Christian teaching long before Europeans arrived in the Americas, and that Amerindian religious institutions matched, if they did not excel, those of Greece and Rome. Among the many authors, ancient, medieval, and contemporary, whom Las Casas adduced to drive home this point, Vergil was one. But it was, when we look back to earlier interpretations, Vergil with a new face. For Las Casas, like before him Italian humanist scholars whose work he had consulted,[62] read Vergil's *Aeneid* not so much as the epic of Rome's origins, but as a source that documented Roman religion, politics, and material culture. Issues that had impassioned Augustine and Dante—in what sense the political order of imperial Rome might or might not be perpetuated in a Christian society, and to what extent Vergil comprehended what was at stake in the life after death—interested Las Casas not at all. Instead, Las Casas looked to Vergil and other classical authors for information about the evolution of ancient society and of human society in general, for information also about Roman religious customs and the Roman gods, the sacrifices they had received and the rituals that had been performed in their honor.[63]

In short, Las Casas perused the text of Vergil for facts about Roman religion and society, much as a classicist in our own century might do.[64]

At the same time, however, the Vergil of Augustine and Dante, the Vergil also of Don Enrique de Villena, the poet whose verses either enshrined an essential and necessary truth or else staked out a position that had to be contradicted, also lived on in Spanish America. To explain this issue, I choose as an example the work of a seventeenth-century Augustinian Friar, Antonio de la Calancha, who wrote about Peru a history that is in some ways a counterpart to Augustine's *City of God*. Just as Augustine saw in the Roman empire no more than one of many possible contexts for the pilgrimage of the City of God in this world, so Calancha couched his story of the conversion of the Incas in a framework deeply critical of the conquering Spanish culture of which by birth he was a member. And just as Augustine viewed the relative peace that the Roman empire had brought with it as the context in which the City of God progressed on its hidden pilgrimage, so Calancha perceived in Spanish culture and political culture no more—but also no less— than an instrument of evangelization.[65]

But there are some important though subtle differences between Calancha's attitudes to politics, culture, and religion and those of Augustine. We can glimpse these differences by comparing what the two authors derived from Vergil. Calancha's Vergil, unlike Augustine's, was a universal poet whose work was to be studied in the framework of a long tradition of commentary and exegesis. Vergil possessed what Villena called *doctrina,* a quality that made his words applicable to personal and political situations anywhere. Allegory was one method, but not the only one, of identifying this *doctrina.* Where thus Augustine in his maturity quoted Vergil to highlight what was wrong with pagan religion and the Roman empire, Calancha also quoted Vergil to illustrate the errors of Inca and Andean religion. The errors of the gentiles of his own time, Calancha argued in the footsteps of Las Casas,[66] were identical to those of the gentiles of the ancient Mediterranean. But Calancha's argument was more diversified than that of Augustine. For when Calancha used Vergilian lines to describe Inca cults, he did so with a dual purpose. On the one hand, those cults were addressed to false gods. But on the other hand, they were endowed with all the splendor and dignity of the ancient world as studied by humanist scholars of the preceding two centuries. An Andean sacred site near Trujillo thus reminded Calancha of the temple to Juno that had been erected by Queen Dido of Carthage in Vergil's *Aeneid;* the myth of the oracular deity Pachacamac brought to mind ancient myths of destruction and metaphorphosis that he also found in Vergil; and the Andean culture of sacred stones was explained by reference to the Roman cult of Cybele, because these stones were revered no differently from Cybele, the Berecynthain Mother, when, in Vergil's words,

> crowned with a mural crown she is drawn on a chariot
> through the cities of Phrygia.[67]

Comparing pagan religions worldwide was fashionable in Calancha's day.[68] But more was at issue in his writing. For the Vergilian resonances he found in the Andes illustrated for him, as they had done earlier for Las Casas, not only the universality of religious error, but also the parity of Andean civilization with the civilization of Europe. Vergil's authority could thus be appealed to by way of formulating a cultural acceptance of the ancient world, and this in turn led Calancha to accept the civilization of the Incas as valid and worthy of study.

Humanist historians of the Americas by contrast found there a variety of barbarian cultures that were by definition inferior to European culture. The reason for such a verdict is that these historians looked in the Americas for precise equivalents to what they appreciated most in European culture, equivalents that not surprisingly were not there to be discovered.[69] The symphonic model of cultural diversity that was espoused by Las Casas, Calancha, and some others was more flexible, because here comparisons were constructed over a broader spectrum of periods of European history, a broader spectrum also of possible human achievement. This symphonic model constitutes one of the classical and medieval legacies of Europe in the Americas. Yet, while we may find such a model appealing in our own time, and thus approve it in the past, we must also realize that it has negative aspects. Those who in the sixteenth and seventeenth centuries viewed European and American cultures in symphonic terms tended to emphasize similarities between Europe and the Americas and to minimize differences. This meant that the particular and unique features in American cultures were all too easily discounted. The resulting ignorance of the particularities and uniqueness of American cultures in turn led to facile descriptions of the alien as exotic,[70] and these descriptions are currently much more readily decried than corrected.[71] There is, in short, no substitute to listening to the past in the words and the terms of those who were alive in it.

History is the study, one might say, of change and continuity, and these do not happen without conflict. Different visions of the past can be harmonious with each other, but often, they are conflictive. Indeed, harmony and conflict tend to be linked to each other like the two faces of a coin. This is what I have tried to illustrate by commenting, however briefly, on the late antique, medieval, and early modern reception of Vergil. My vision of medieval studies as viewed from late antiquity is of a discipline that is open to such ambiguities and uncertainties; a discipline, moreover, that is open to the shadows, as well as the highlights, of the impact of Europe on the world. What we must face is that shadows and highlights have been and will continue to be inseparable.

In our period, when communication across the globe can be taken for granted, it is easy to suppose that culture, our own culture, can be readily modified, and that our identity, whether collective or individual, is something that can be "constructed," somehow at will. We might accordingly choose to shift our attention away from the diverse legacies that we have inherited from medieval Europe to something that seems more relevant. But things are not so straightforward. It was not possible for Augustine in his maturity and old age simply to discard the pagan poet who had helped to shape his emotive vocabulary when he was young. Neither was it possible for Las Casas and Calancha to reflect on Amerindian civilizations independently of the cultural vocabulary with which they had grown up, because that vocabulary made reflection possible in the first place. We need our own culture in all its multiplicity and complexity if we are to understand other cultures, and if we are to understand ourselves. The more ample and generous we can thus make our understanding of what for good and for ill the past has bequeathed to us, that much more wisely will we be able to contemplate whatever it is that confronts us now.

NOTES

I would like to thank David Ganz and Rachel Jacoff for their comments on an earlier version of this paper.

1. R. Menéndez Pidal, "La crónica general de España que mandó componer Alfonso el Sabio," in *Estudios Literarios* (Madrid, 1920), 80–249; C. F. Fraker, "Scipio, and the Origin of Culture: The Question of Alfonso's Sources," *Dispositio* 10, no. 27 (1985): 15–27; Rosa Lida de Malkiel, "La *General Estoria*. Notes literarias y filológicas," *Romance Philology* 12 (1958–1959): 111–142, and 13 (1959–1960): 1–30; D. Eisenberg, "The *General Estoria*: Sources and Source Treatment," *Zeitschrift fur romanische Philologie* 89 (1973): 206–227.

2. See F. Rico, *Alfonso el Sabio y la "General Estoria,"* (Barcelona, 1984), esp. 101ff.; S. MacCormack, "History, Memory and Time in Golden Age Spain," *History and Memory* 4, 2, (1992): 38–68.

3. The classic work dealing with this topic is H. Baron, *The Crisis of the Early Italian Renaissance* (Princeton, 1966); for a recent commentary, see J. Bentley, *Politics and Culture in Renaissance Naples* (Princeton, 1987), 196f.

4. For an exceptionally eloquent and illuminating personal vision of the transposition of a Polish and Jewish past into an American present, see Eva Hoffman, *Lost in Translation: A Life in a New Language* (New York, 1989).

5. See now *Wild Orchids and Trotsky: Messages from American Universities,* ed. Mark Edmundson (New York, 1993).

6. Leora Auslander, "Feminist Theory and Social History: Explorations in the Politics of Identity," *Radical History Review* 54 (1992): 158–176. The dilemma of articulating identity is not confined to the present or to the United States: H. Lebovics, *True France: The Wars over Cultural Identity, 1900–1945* (Ithaca, N.Y., 1992).

7. A. Bloom, *The Closing of the American Mind: How Higher Education Has Failed Democracy and Impoverished the Souls of Today's Students* (New York, 1987).

8. R. R. Bolgar, *The Classical Heritage and its Beneficiaries: From the Carolingian Age to the End of the Renaissance* (New York, 1954) and Ernst Robert Curtius, *European Literature and the Latin Middle Ages* (Princeton, 1953) remain invaluable. Maria Rosa Lida de Malkiel commented on Curtius's omissions regarding Spain in her essay, "Perduración de la literatura antigua en occidente," *Romance Philology* 5 (1951–1952): 99–131, reprinted in her *La Tradición clasica en España* (Barcelona, 1975), 271–338. See also, in that same volume (341–397), her essay, still

worth consulting, on Gilbert Highet, *The Classical Tradition: Greek and Roman Influences on Western Literature* (Oxford, 1949).

9. W. Theodore de Bary, *East Asian Civilisations: A Dialogue in Five Stages* (Cambridge, 1988); J. M. Kitagawa, *On Understanding Japanese Religion* (Princeton, 1987).

10. Note the mingling of scholarly commentary and personal devotion in *Museum Italicum seu Collectio Veterum Scriptorum ex Bibliotecis Italicis. Eruta a D. Johanne Mabillon et D. Michaele Germain, Presbyteris et Monachis Benedictinae Cong. S. Mauri* (Paris, 1687).

11. See Van Engen's Agenda Paper, 4.

12. I merely select a few recent examples from a huge literature: John F. Benton, "Consciousness of Self and Perceptions of Individuality," in *Renaissance and Renewal in the Twelfth Century,* ed. R. L. Benson and Giles Constable (Cambridge, 1982), 263–295; Caroline Walker Bynum, *Holy Feast and Holy Fast: The Religious Significance of Food to Medieval Women* (Berkeley, 1987); John Boswell, *Christianity, Social Tolerance and Homosexuality: Gay People in Western Europe from the Beginning of the Christian Era to the Fourteenth Century* (Chicago, 1980); P. Aries, *L'enfant et al vie familiale sous l'Ançien Régime* (Paris, 1987). For work in the more traditional fields of medieval history that at the same time raises new issues, let me cite A. Funkenstein, *Theology and the Scientific Imagination from the Middle Ages to the Seventeenth Century* (Princeton, 1986); R. W. Southern, *Saint Anselm: A Portrait in a Landscape* (Cambridge, 1990). Norman F. Cantor, *Inventing the Middle Ages: The Lives, Works, and Ideas of the Great Medievalists of the Twentieth Century* (New York, 1991) presents an acerbic but informative perspective on the development of the field.

13. A Momigliano, "History in an Age of Ideologies," *American Scholar* 51 (1982): 495–507.

14. J. -P. Vernant, "*Panta kala:* from Homer to Simonides," in his *Mortals and Immortals: Collected Essays* (Princeton, 1991), 84–91; S. Weinstock, "Die platonische Homerkritik und ihre Nachwirkung," *Philologus* 82 (1926–1927): 121–153.

15. Elizabeth Rawson, *Intellectual Life in the Late Roman Republic* (Baltimore, 1985); Erich S. Gruen, *Culture and National Identity in Republican Rome* (Ithaca, N.Y., 1992), especially chapters 2 and 6; Susan E. Adcock, *Graecia Capta. The Landscapes of Roman Greece* (Cambridge, 1993).

16. Santo Mazzarino, *The End of the Ancient World* (London, 1959); Ramsay MacMullen, "Provincial Languages in the Roman Empire," in his *Changes in the Roman Empire: Essays in the Ordinary* (Princeton, 1990), 32–40. See also, M. Wes, *Das Ende des Kaisertums im Westen des römischen Reiches* (Granvenhage, 1967).

17. A. Momigliano, "After Gibbon's *Decline and Fall*," in his *Sesto contributo alla storia degli studi classici e del mondo antico,* vol. 1 (Rome, 1980), 265–284. Some recent works: Patrick J. Geary, *Before France and Germany: The Creation and Transformation of the Merovingian World* (Oxford, 1988); G. W. Bowersock, *Hellenism in Late Antiquity* (Ann Arbor, 1990); Averil Cameron, *Christianity and the Rhetoric of Empire: The Development of Christian Discourse* (Berkeley, 1991).

18. R. Kaster, *Guardians of Language: The Grammarian and Society in Late Antiquity* (Berkeley, 1988).

19. Apart from the famous commentary by Servius, there is the paraphrase by Tiberius Claudius Donatus, *Interpretationes Vergilianae,* ed. H. Georgii (Stuttgart, 1969); Macrobius's discussion of Vergil in his *Saturnalia* ed. I. Willis (Leipzig, 1963); and the Platonizing commentary of Fabius Planciades Fulgentius, *Expositio Virgilianae Continentiae,* ed. T. Agozzino and F. Zanlucci (Padua, 1972); note the excellent introduction by the editors. Domenico Comparetti, *Vergil in the Middle Ages* (New York, 1929) remains a valuable guide for the reception of Vergil. See also H. de Lubac, "Virgile philosophe et prophète," in his *Exégèse médiévale. Les quatre sens de l'Écriture,* volume II, part II (Paris, 1962), 233–262.

20. Augustine, *Confessions* 1.13.20; 1.17.27; note also Augustine's contentiousness on matters Vergilian when he was a schoolboy, *Confessions* 1.13.22

21. See especially the prayer in Augustine *De Ordine* (ed. W. M. Green, in *Corpus Christianorum, Series Latina,* vol. 29) 1.4.10, incorporating quotes from Vergil, *Aeneid* 10.875; 3.88–89; and 11.785–788.

22. Augustine, *Sermon* 105 (Migne, *Patrologia Latina* 38, col. 623), on Vergil flattering the Romans because he was "selling words" to them ("quid faciam qui Romanis verba vendebam?" Augustine has Vergil say). For the innuendo, compare Augustine, *Confessions* 9.2.2 on his resigning his position as rhetor, "ne ulteris ... bella forensia mercarentur ex ore meo." Augustine's quotations from classical Roman authors are collected in H. Hagendahl, *Augustine and the Latin Classics* (Stockholm, 1967).

23. Vergil, *Aeneid* 6.852–853, cited by Augustine, *City of God,* preface; Vergil, *Aeneid* 1.278–279, cited by Augustine, *Sermon* 105 (Migne, *Patrologia Latina* 38, cols. 622–623).

24. Augustine, *City of God* 2.29, "imperium sine fine dabit," to describe an act of the Christian God, adjusted quotation from Vergil *Aeneid* 1.279 "imperium sine fine dedi," said by Jupiter.

25. *Aeneid* 6.719–721. Translated literally, line 721 reads "what fearful yearning for the sun (holds) the wretched (souls)?"

26. Augustine, *City of God* 14.5; 21.3; *Sermon* 241.5.5 (*Patrologia Latina* 36, 1135–1136). *City of God* 22.26.

27. "nobilissimus poeta eorum," *City of God* 15.9; cf. 4.11; 10.27.

28. *City of God* 22.26.

29. *City of God* 22.7–9.

30. See, for the literary results, Michael Roberts, *The Jewelled Style: Poetry and Poetics in Late Antiquity* (Ithaca, 1989).

31. Cf. above n. 16. Also, Fedor Schneider, *Rom und Romgedanke im Mittelalater. Die geistigen Grundlagen der Renaissance* (Munich, 1929; Darmstadt, 1959); Walther Rehm, *Der Untergang Roms im Abendländischen Denken. Ein Beitrag zur Geschichte der Geschichtsschreibung und zum Dekadenzproblem* (Leipzig, 1930; Darmstadt, 1966). The issue was that reflection on Rome took place in the context of thinking about a Europe of which Rome was no longer the political center, see R. A. Markus, "Gregory the Great's Europe," *Transactions of the Royal Historical Society* 31 (1981): 21–36 (reprinted in his *From Augustine to Gregory the Great* [London, 1983]); K. Leyser, "Concepts of Europe in the Early and High Middle Ages," *Past and Present* 137 (1992): 25–47.

32. This is the approach of Fabius Planciades Fulgentius, *Expositio* (above n. 19). The work is in the form of a dialogue between Fulgentius and Vergil. To Fulgentius's objections about Vergil's ideas regarding reincarnation (*Aeneid* 6.720, the same passage Augustine had also censured, above at notes 25–28), Vergil responds amiably:

> At ille subridens: Si, inquit, inter tantas Stoicas veritates aliquid Epicureum non desipissem, paganus non essem: nullo enim omnia vera nosse contigit nisi vobis, quibus sol veritatis inluxit. Neque enim hoc pacto in tuis libris conductus narrator accessi ut id quod sentire me oportuerat disputarem, et non ea potius quae senseram lucidarem. (p. 64)

T. Aguzzino, "*Secretum quaerere veritatis.* Virgilio *vates ignarus* nella *Continentia Vergiliana,*" in *Studi classici in onore di Quintino Cataudella,* vol. 3 (Catania, 1972), 615–630.

33. Antonie Wlosok, "Zwei Beispiele frühchristlicher "Vergilrezeption": Polemik (Lact., div. inst. 5.10) und Usurpation (Or. Const. 19–21)," in *2000 Jahre Vergil. Ein Symposium. Wolfenbüttler Forschungen,* ed. Viktor Pöschl, vol. 24 (Wiesbaden, 1983), 63–86.

34. Theodor E. Mommsen, "St. Augustine and the Christian Idea of Progress: The Background to *The City of God*," in his *Medieval and Renaissance Studies,* ed. Eugene F. Rice (Ithaca, N.Y., 1959), 265–348; Amos Funkenstein, *Heilsplan und natürliche Entwicklung, Gegenwartsbestimmung im Geschichtsdenken des Mittelalters* (Munich, 1965), especially on Otto of Freising, 93–113. The perceived continuity between Roman imperial, i.e., pagan, past and Christian present is especially apparent in pilgrims' manuals, see Master Gregorius, *The Marvels of Rome,* tr. John

Osborne (Toronto, 1987); *The Marvels of Rome. Mirabilia Urbis Romae,* tr. Francis Morgan Nichols (New York, 1986).

35. See Giuseppe Mazzotta, *Dante, Poet of the Desert. History and Allegory in the Divine Comedy* (Princeton, 1979). See also John Freccero, "The Prologue Scene," in his *Dante and the Poetics of Conversion,* ed. Rachel Jacoff (Cambridge, Mass., 1986), 1–28. An important older study is Charles Till Davis, *Dante and the Idea of Rome* (Oxford, 1957).

36. *Aeneid* 1.745 "infelix Dido," said before Aeneas begins the story of Troy and his wanderings and before Dido has become conscious of her feeling for Aeneas; *Aeneid* 4.23, "agnosco veteris vestigia flammae," says Dido, confiding to her sister after she had listened to Aeneas's account of the fall of Troy and his wanderings. Dante applied this line to himself with regard to Beatrice, *Purgatorio* 30.48, see Mazotta (above n. 34), 186. In Augustine, the classic example of a decision reached before it has become conscious is his description of his conversion, *Confessions* 8.7.16 ff.; note 8.19 "illuc me abstulerat tumultus pectoris, ubi nemo impediret ardentem litem, quam mecum aggressus eram, donec exiret, qua tu sciebas, ego autem non." In the *City of God* (especially books 12–14) Augustine returned to the topic in terms of will and the origin of evil.

37. Note for example *Inferno* 30.130 ff., where Vergil reprimands Dante for thoughts and desires he has not expressed and is barely conscious of; similarly, Beatrice's reprimand in *Purgatorio* 30.55ff. See also *Inferno* 4.51 (Vergil) "che 'ntese il mio parlar coverto;" *Purgatorio* 4.1ff., on sense perception and the soul.

38. Augustine, *City of God* 10.27 on the extent and nature of Vergil's prophecy, with Dante, *Purgatorio* 22, where Statius quotes the Fourth Eclogue, on the same topic. See also *Inferno* 11.80; 101, on Aristotle's *Ethics* and *Physics* as explaining the punishments for incontinence and usury—but Aristotle himself was also in Limbo, *Inferno* 4.130ff. Pierre Courcelle, "Les exégèses Chrétiennes de la Quatrième Églogue," *Revue des Études Anciennes* 59 (1957): 294–319.

39. Dante, *Inferno* 4.52ff.; see Jeffrey T. Schnapp, *The Transfiguration of History at the Center of Dante's Paradise* (Stanford, 1986), 3 ff.

40. Leaves and birds, Vergil, *Aeneid* 6.309ff.; Dante, *Inferno* 3.109ff., with John Freccero, "Dante's Ulysses: from Epic to Novel," in his *Dante* (above n. 35), 136–151 at 141–150. On Dante's reformulations and corrections of Vergil see *The Poetry of Allusion. Virgil and Ovid in Dante's 'Commedia',* ed. Rachel Jacoff and Jeffrey Schnapp (Stanford, 1991). The essays by Robert Hollander, Michael Putnam, and Peter Hawkins in this collection are especially relevant. Earlier scholarship on Dante laid greater emphasis on the continuities between Vergil and Dante; see, for example, E. Auer-

bach, "Dante and Vergil," in his *Gesammelte Aufsätze zur romanischen Philologie* (Bern, 1967), 115–122.

41. E. Bolsiani and M. Valgimigli, *La corrispondenza poetica di Dante Alighieri e Giovanni del Virgilio* (Florence, 1963): the correspondence, in Latin, is filled with Vergilian echoes and quotes. Maria Rosa Lida de Malkiel, *Dido en La literatura española. Su retrato y defensa* (London, 1974). R. Vianello, "Su un commento Virgiliano attribuito a Nicola Trevet," *Studi Medievali* 32 (1991): 345–367, a commentary on the *Eclogues*.

42. *Traslado de latin en romance castellano dela eneyda de virgilio, la qual romanco don enrrique de villena,* Biblioteca Nacional, Madrid, MS 17975 fols. 9r–19v. Villena wanted to explain the poem both in its own right and in its tradition, thus pointing out that Vergil's Aeneas in some respects stood for Augustus, although the poem also addressed each individual reader: this was how its extraordinary influence from Vergil's own time down to Dante and the present could be explained, fol. 9v; 14 rf.. I cite from the manuscript because I have been unable to obtain the edition of Villena's *Eneida* by Pedro-Manuel Catedra, published by Humanitas in Barcelona (1985). M. Menéndez y Pelayo, *Traductores españoles de la Eneida. Apuntes bibliograficos* (Madrid, 1879) is still useful.

43. BNM MS 17975 fol. 13 r. See further on this prologue, Derek C. Carr, "Pérez de Guzman and Villena: A Polemic on Historiography," in *Hispanic Studies in Honor of Alan D. Deyermond. A North American Tribute,* ed. John S. Miletich (Madison, 1986), 57–70, citing the earlier literature.

44. Ottavio di Camillo, *El Humanismo Castellano del Siglo XV* (Valencia, 1976); see also G. Serés, "Pedro González de Mendoza y la 'Grande Iliada de Homero,'" *Boletín de la Biblioteca de Menédez y Pelayo* 65 (1989): 5–54. Villena's inclination toward looking for "Vergil's hidden doctrine" has a very long ancestry going back to antiquity, see above n. 19. Unlike Augustine and Dante, who thought that the Christian prophetic dimension of the Fourth Eclogue was unintended by Vergil (cf. above n. 38) Vergil's Platonist commentators, like later Villena, did attribute the "hidden doctrine" to Vergil's intended meaning.

45. L. D. Reynolds, *Scribes and Scholars: A Guide to the Transmission of Greek and Latin Literature* (Oxford, 1974); R. Pfeiffer, *History of Classical Scholarship from 1300 to 1850* (Oxford, 1976). For Spain, note the enormously learned and insightful Vergilian commentary by Juan Luis de la Cerda, *Aeneidos sex libri priores* and *Aeneidos sex libri posteriores* (Cologne, 1628).

46. Richard Heinze, *Virgils epische Technik* (Leipzig, 1928) has not really been replaced by more recent work. But see, from a very large literature, Philip Hardie, *Virgil's Aeneid: Cosmos and Imperium* (Oxford,

1986); W. R. Johnson, *Darkness Visible: A Study of Vergil's Aeneid* (Berkeley, 1976); and the collection of essays ed. I. McAuslan and Peter Walcot, *Virgil* (Oxford, 1990).

47. See on this topic, L. U. Hanke, *Aristotle and the American Indians: A Study on Race Prejudice in the Modern World* (Chicago, 1959) which has become a classic; A. Pagden, *The Fall of Natural Man: The American Indian and the Origins of Comparative Ethnology* (Cambridge, 1982). Both works deal with the repercussions of Aristotelian categories principally in European contexts, leaving the heuristic value of these categories with regard to Amerindian civilizations unexplored.

48. For a badly needed corrective, see Richard Morse, *New World Soundings: Culture and Ideology in the Americas* (Baltimore, 1989).

49. See J. N. Hillgarth's pioneering essays on Ireland and Spain, reprinted in his *Visigothic Spain, Byzantium and the Irish* (London, 1985) numbers 6–8; also Jacques Fontaine, "Mozarabie hispanique et monde Carolingien: les échanges culturels entre la France et l'Espagne du VIIIè au Xè siècle," *Anuario de Estudios Medievales* 13 (1983): 17–46; A. Barbero de Aguilera, "Los 'síntomas españoles' y la política religiosa de Carlomagno," *En la España medieval. Estudios dedicados al profesor D. Angel Ferrari Núñez* vol. 1 (Madrid, 1984), 87–138.

50. Teresa Gisbert, *Iconografía y mitos indígenas en el arte* (La Paz, 1980) is a pioneering study.

51. See Richard Morse, "Claims of Political Tradition," in his *New World Soundings,* 95–130.

52. S. MacCormack, "From the Sun of the Incas to the Virgin of Copacabana," *Representations* 8 (1984): 30–60.

53. Benedicta Ward, *Miracles and the Medieval Mind* (Philadelphia, 1987).

54. R. Ricard, *The Spiritual Conquest of Mexico* (Berkeley, 1986) highlights this aspect of conversion. For a very different view, Louise M. Burkhart, *The Slippery Earth: Nahua-Christian Moral Dialogue in Sixteenth-Century Mexico* (Tucson, 1989); see also, R. Trexler, "Aztec Priests for Christian Altars: The Theory and Practice of Reverence in New Spain," in his *Church and Community 1200–1600: Studies in the History of Florence and New Spain* (Rome, 1987), 469–492.

55. S. MacCormack, "Antonio de la Calancha. Un Agustino del siglo XVII en el Nuevo Mundo," *Bulletin Hispanique* 84 (1982): 60–94.

56. M. J. Sallnow, *Pilgrims of the Andes: Regional Cults in Cuzco* (Washington, D.C., 1987) is exemplary.

57. See on this thorny topic, the admirable small book by E. Lamirande, *Church, State and Toleration: An Intriguing Change of Mind in Augustine,* Augustinian Institute, Villanova University (Villanova, 1975).

58. S. MacCormack, *Religion in the Andes, Vision and Imagination in Early Colonial Peru* (Princeton, 1991), 388.

59. For a recent approach to these issues that surprises by its sheer simple-mindedness, see A. Murray, "Missionaries and Magic in Dark Age Europe," Review Article, *Past and Present* 136 (1992): 186–205. The difficulty that must be confronted is that cultural and hence religious boundaries cannot be assumed to be stable, and are thus not capable of being analyzed according to one single and continuous model. This difficult issue is treated with great success by Bruce Mannheim in his important book, *The Language of the Inca since the European Invasion* (Austin, 1990).

60. J. H. Elliott, *The Old World and the New* (Cambridge, 1970); Urs Bitterli, *Cultures in Conflict: Encounters Between Europeans and Non-European Cultures, 1492–1800* (Stanford, 1989).

61. The work was not published until the modern period, but much of its content circulated in print thanks to the extended excerpts made from it by Jerónimo Román in his *Repúblicas Del Mundo,* see S. MacCormack, *Religion in the Andes,* 245f.

62. A work that Las Casas referred to frequently was Lilius Gregorius Giraldus's influential and scholarly *De diis gentium.*

63. Apart from the many incidental references to Vergil in Bartolomé de Las Casas, *Apologética Historia,* 2 vols., ed. Edmundo O'Gorman (Mexico City, 1967), see in particular chapter 47, on pre-civilized societies; chapters 106–107, 117, 119 on the Roman gods, with citations from various Roman authors including Vergil; similarly chapters 150–152 on sacrifices.

64. See for example, P. Boyancé, "La religion des 'Georgiques' a la lumière des travaux recents," in *Aufstieg und Niedergang der römischen Welt,* ed. W. Haase vol. 31 (Berlin, 1980), 549–573; R. F. Thomas, "Tree Violation and Ambivalence in Vergil," *Transactions of the American Philological Association* 118 (1988): 261–273.

65. S. MacCormack, "Un Agustino"; see also S. MacCormack, "The Fall of the Incas. A Historiographical Dilemma," *History of European Ideas* 6 (1985): 421–445.

66. Calancha read the arguments of Las Casas as reiterated in Jerónimo Román's *Repúblicas del Mundo,* see above n. 61.

67. *Aeneid* 6.784f. with Antonio de la Calancha, *Corónica Moralizada del Orden de San Augustín en el Perú* (Barcelona, 1639) ed. I. Prado Pastor (Lima, 1974–1981), 845; see also Calancha, 833, 932, 1092 (Trujillo). Note also p. 1320f., where Calancha refers the words "casta fave Lucina" from Vergil, *Eclogue* 4.10 to a miracle-working Virgin Mary. Like Las Casas, Calancha has numerous incidental quotations of and references to Vergil and other ancient authors, which give evidence of his extensive classical reading.

68. A summary of these endeavors, focusing on the work of the Jesuits, may be found in Philip Bonanni, *Musaeum Kircherianum sive Musaeum a P. Athanasio Kierchero in collegio Romano Societatis Jesu iam primum incoeptum, nuper restitutum, auctum, descriptum ac iconibus illustratum* (Rome, 1729).

69. See for example the much translated and reprinted, very influential work of Francisco López de Gómara, *Hispania Victrix. Primera y segunda parte de la historia general de las Indias* (Madrid, 1965) which discusses Indians in a context provided by classical and Italian Renaissance historiography; as a result Gómara's information about Indians can only be used with much reserve.

70. Voltaire's *Candide* is a classic example.

71. As for instance by T. Todorov, *The Conquest of America. The Question of the Other* (New York, 1984), the difficulty being that Todorov's strictures of Spanish sixteenth-century descriptions of Amerindian cultures are of little use when it comes to describing and interpreting these cultures in their own right. The "other" thus turns out to be no more than a further reflection of self, and the author has committed the very offense he censures.

Who's Afraid of the Renaissance?

RANDOLPH STARN

A GENERATION AGO the "revolting medievalists" (as we Renaissance historians liked to say) were loudly proclaiming that what was true in the Renaissance was not new, and that what was new then was not true anyway. For better or worse, the old disputes have mostly subsided, but the relative calm is due as much perhaps to exhaustion or a sense of futility as anything else. Even today manifestos of the so-called New Medievalism in literary studies complain about condescending attitudes toward the Middle Ages. We can still read claims for the breakaway originality of the Renaissance as if this were an uncontested truth. Hostile propensities seem to be coded like some wayward genetic trait into the relations between medieval and Renaissance scholars.[1]

The fact is that our disagreements have never been any more serious than domestic quarrels—or any less serious, either, since domestic feuding is often the most knowing and wounding sort. It will hardly come as news that the concept of the Middle Age sprang from the consciousness of a few literary intellectuals, that the cultural revival they longed for presupposed an intermediate time between the ancients and the "rebirth" of antiquity they hoped to bring about.[2] In effect, the medieval and Renaissance studies were co-dependents from the start in a relationship neither party could abide—or quite do without. No doubt the greater provocation came from the Renaissance side, with its vested interest in lengthening, lowering, and lessening the middle period for the sake of a quicker, higher, and greater Renaissance, but medievalists have obviously given back as good, and as bad, as they've got.

However they get established, binary oppositions tend to play themselves out in any number of variations, and this has virtually

129

ensured that disputes over the preeminence of one period or the
other would return time and again. To be a distinct period, the Renaissance needs it shadowy medieval Other, just as the Middle Age
needs its Renaissance counterpart as a condition of being clearly
distinguished and defined. In a kind of perpetual Derridean *différ-
ance* the periodizing oppositions go on differing from and, in all
senses, deferring to one another. And since history often blunders
blurrily across clearcut lines, they can always be breached by some
awkward "exception" that serves to reopen debate. It is easy to let
some light into the Dark Ages, or to cast a medieval shadow in the
bright dawn of somebody's Renaissance.[3]

Medieval and Renaissance studies are inextricably bound together, too, by what I think of as the trinitarian orthodoxies of periodization. We cannot have a Renaissance without an intervening
death, dormancy, or decline and an original to be reborn, and we
cannot have a middle period without at least one age or epoch at
either end. One way or another, any scheme of periodization with a
Middle Age and a Renaissance requires a three-part plot, with a beginning, middle, and end or, at least, sequel. Besides, both terms
have been locked into the "drama of Western Civilization," with its
storybook succession of cultures and its "Occidentalism."[4] In this
country the periodization of history in the classroom accompanied
the professionalization of historical research beginning in the late
nineteenth century. This was one way for an increasingly fragmented profession to organize a coherent curriculum. Moreover,
specialized study of European history was justified by a mission of
general education in "our" Western values that sanctioned American outreach overseas. The stock complaints about teaching obligations conflicting with research needs have usually ignored the
awkward fact that we would not have our research projects and our
graduate seminars without our survey courses. Ironically, historians
in the new European Community have little practice expounding
"European" history as distinct from the national or local varieties
and may have to learn how to do so from us even as we become
more "multi-cultural."[5]

There are also close institutional parallels between medieval
and Renaissance studies. Both are interdisciplinary, and both have
been defined and practiced as such primarily by literary scholars
rather than, say, by historians, who tend to be oriented by method-

ological, chronological, and geographical differences rather than by cross-disciplinary interests or anxieties. To put it another way, neither medieval nor Renaissance studies is a discipline like history, art history, and musicology, or a field such as Chaucer studies or the Common Law. Nevertheless, medievalists and, to coin a no more awkward term, renaissancists of very different persuasions do come together in regional, national, and international undertakings, if sometimes only because they may not know where else to go. The Mediaeval Academy's *Speculum* and the Renaissance Society's *Renaissance Quarterly,* like the Geneva-based *Bibliothèque d'humanisme et Renaissance* and the Istituto Nazionale's *Rinascimento* edited in Florence, publish and review scholarship on virtually every sub-specialty.[6]

The learned societies, publications, and conferences do foster some sense of community of course. But as any old hand knows, the ecumenical tent is also an arena of difference, indifference, and outright hostility. Scholars of the most generous interests may find it hard to care about the latest volume in the Rolls Series or humanism in Transylvania, nor should they be expected to do so if they are not historians of England's medieval institutions or students of the Renaissance *in partibus;* for that matter, why should the specialist welcome the generalist's well-meaning but clumsy embraces? If anything, the genially eclectic range of medieval or Renaissance studies practically invites dissent from some sub-field or self-consciously "new" interpretation or approach.[7]

Still, the old battles over preeminence are, as I have said, clearly out of fashion. Recent skirmishes over alleged misrepresentations of the Middle Ages or the Renaissance have not turned into fullscale battles; there is something distracted and forgetful about them, as if much ink had not been spilled along these lines before. Meanwhile the *Journal of Medieval and Renaissance Studies,* institutional centers for same at UCLA and elsewhere, and SUNY Binghamton's series of Medieval and Renaissance Texts and Studies solicit scholarship across conventional chronological and topical boundaries. Less official, but I suspect at least as significant, testimony comes from the shelves of Moe's Bookstore in Berkeley, where Medieval and Renaissance literature run together from Abelard and Beowulf to Rabelais and Shakespeare, presumably on the principle that it's all old stuff anyway. If some scholars may be distressed by the muddle, others will be grateful for the concession of so much shelf-space.

For surely one of the most compelling reasons for the relatively peaceful relations between medievalists and renaissancists is a more or less acknowledged fear that none of us matters very much these days. It is easy to blame the usual suspects: loss of confidence in the grand narratives of progress; liberal guilt about the neglected margins of Western history; the decolonization of the non-European past; cultural amnesia and illiteracy; the sacrifice of historical studies to science, the market, technology, and political convenience, not to mention short-sighted colleagues and bottom-lining deans. All this is drearily familiar. We hear less often that the range of humanistic studies has vastly increased with these supposedly dire developments; that obsessions with the past have sprung up with the decline of modernist visions of the future; that our accounts of the European past are no longer fighting the Cold War; or that students of the humanities, of all people, should not be fazed by cultural changes and nostalgia for a mythical Golden Age. I don't remember hearing anyone say that a volume like this one, far from writing an epitaph, attests to the vitality of medieval studies.[8] Perhaps medievalists have an occupational weakness for feeling embattled, like their knights, monks, or pilgrims; renaissancists have good grounds for a kind of professional cheerfulness, except that we know a world "reborn" is bound to grow old, or to decline and fall like its ancient avatar. In any case, it is probably true to say that we have come to be more fearful of isolation and irrelevance than of one another.[9]

All this suggests, to me at least, that the time is right for freeing ourselves from the old conventions of periodization. This proposition is a radical one only in the etymological sense of going back to the roots. Considering that until at least the eighteenth century historiography was a pluralistic endeavor, constituted by a multiplicity of versions or stories of the past, sharp periodizing boundaries look like a belated innovation. Even if Petrarch did invent the "Dark Ages," he did not think he was living in a Renaissance; and while Petrarch's successors often thought of themselves as Renaissance men, they did not necessarily make clearcut distinctions when it came to actually writing history. Humanist historians found the stirrings of change in the twelfth century, Vasari's artistic *Rinascita* began with Giotto and Arnolfo di Cambio, and Erasmus could praise Benedict of Nursia and Thomas Aquinas. Methodical distinctions between one period and another were more to the taste of Enlightenment publicists, nineteenth-century philosophers, pedagogues and historians, and the authors of our textbooks.[10]

Italian history offers particularly interesting openings for chronological trespassing across medieval and Renaissance lines. Even skeptics probably will concede that if there were a Renaissance, it was significantly Italian—and then go on to point out that medieval-Renaissance distinctions are actually rather fuzzy in Italy. Jacob Burckhardt himself recognized as much by beginning the charter text of Renaissance studies with the Hohenstaufen emperors and the Italian little Caesars who imitated them. The most foward-looking Renaissance historians, such as Leonardo Bruni and Flavio Biondo, dated the revival of Italy from the rise of the medieval city-states; a sly modern variation suggests that Italy turned "medieval" only after the Sack of Rome in 1527 opened the way for the Counter-Reformation, and Spanish domination of the peninsula.[11] In any case, no area had more forms, more intensively mixed, of government, of economy, or of the Christianizing, chivalric, classicizing cultures that went into the "making of the Middle Ages," and of "Renaissance Civilization" too.

We may not all agree, of course, about the primacy of Italy or the emphasis on continuity at the expense of change. In the heyday of the "Renaissance Debate" medievalists liked to point out that there had been cultural "renascences" outside Italy, that the Italians were relatively late bloomers, and that they borrowed a great deal from France besides. That Quattrocento art simply *looked* different was one supposedly clinching renaissancist rejoinder.[12] But I am not so much interested in the old arguments here as I am in observing that Italy was as much a showplace of the long Middle Ages as of an arriving Renaissance. Most historians of Italy I know would be quite comfortable with this proposition. At least among historians, only a few true believers are left to recite the litany of Renaissance individualism, Machiavellianism, and secularism when, in the rolling Burckhardt phrases, the medieval "veil . . . of faith, illusion, and childish prepossession . . . melted into air," so that "*objective* treatment and consideration of the State and of all the things of this world" became possible and "the *subjective* side" could replace the old consciousness of self "only as a member of a race, people, party, family, or corporation—only through some general category." The dominant view for at least a generation or so has been that Renaissance Italians were caught in webs of collective identities and obligations to "party, family, or corporation," that they were preoccupied with political legitimacy, and that they were no better or worse than conventional Christians. Enthusiasm for the Renaissance has become, if anything, a nuisance or an embarrassment for many Italian Renaissance historians.[13]

I want to come back to this view, because I think it has sometimes been accepted as facilely as the hyper-Burckhardtian one used to be. The point for now is that the Italian city-states obviously did not make medieval and Renaissance history exclusively. Lombardy and the Veneto got their new-style *signori* already in the thirteenth century; Florence, capital of Renaissance culture, was something of a political dinosaur as a Renaissance republic in an age of princes. Venice made up a whole political culture by denying change, and the Roman papacy proved eminently adaptable while proclaiming unbroken succession from St. Peter. Left on their own, the Italians never lost much or threw much of anything away, either; without their German, Spanish, Austrian, French and, some would say, their Piedmontese invaders, perhaps they never would have done so. There was no one monarchy to centralize the record and no revolution to finish the job.

"All of Italy can be . . . seen as one enormous archive," proclaim the editors of the journal *Quaderni storici,* the Italian answer to the hugely influential French *Annales.*[14] Appropriately enough, what historians have been calling "microhistory" has been a self-consciously Italian counter to the long-term, structurally synthesizing "histoire totale" of the French. It seems appropriate, too, that neither this approach nor any other predominates in Italy, that there is no national historical establishment or historiographical agenda, and that the major, multi-volume national history, the Einaudi *Storia d'Italia,* is a marvelous hodgepodge of articles arranged according time, topic, or editorial whim. Not the least important reason for the variegated historiography of medieval and Renaissance Italy is that many of its leading practitioners are non-Italians from quite different professional traditions. Under these circumstances it is hardly surprising that the boundaries of periodization have not been very rigorously enforced.[15]

I can offer personal testimony about the temptations of border-crossing in Italian history. Some years ago I was investigating the environment, the incidence, institutional framework, law, and literature of exile in the history of the Italian city-states.[16] None of this stopped with the Middle Ages, or began for the convenience of Renaissance historians. I had to work over the long term, from what I thought of as "premises and vestiges" to the age of Dante and then on to the fall of the last haven of republican exiles at Montalcino near Siena in 1559. What struck me in the history of what I called the "contrary commonwealth" was two quite different configurations of attitude, theory, and practice. One pitted fiercely menacing, but generally ineffectual, partisan regimes inside most Italian towns against a self-righteous, collective opposition on the outside; the other was relatively discriminating, more "humane," but also more oppressive because exiles could be more effectively controlled by the territorial states that dominated the peninsula after the later fourteenth century. I made the divide clearer and cleaner than I would probably do now. The point would be the same though: to portray different modes of political integration and opposition, not to characterize one as medieval and the other as Renaissance, even less to argue that the Renaissance version was an improvement or progress.

In a book that has just appeared my co-author and I analyze the forms and functions of three public rooms commissioned by three regimes—republican, princely, and absolutist—over three centuries, from 1300 to 1600.[17] The book deals with the meaning of images—that is, with iconography—but it is even more concerned to show what images in context *do* by way generating subjects in all senses of the word—that is, topics, themes, individuals "subject" to experiment, and people under the authority of a given political regime. I have called this approach, in fittingly cumbersome terms, "formalist pragmatics," meaning by that to point out, among other things, that the formal means of art have instrumental effects, and vice versa. If the book works over the long term and in very different settings, this is due to the profligacy of Italy in artistic and political experiment, not because it much matters whether some phenomena were "medieval" and others "Renaissance."

Now Italian history happens to be a particularly good example of ties that bind and opportunities that beckon medieval and Renaissance studies. Obviously though, I do not think the Italian case is altogether unique. If nothing else, this line of argument should appeal to the aggrandizing instincts of everyone since it licenses medievalists to annex the Renaissance and renaissancists to gain time in the Middle Ages. But, even those who might welcome such a merger will recognize costs as well as benefits, including, for a start, this sort of corporate parlance. So what do we stand to lose? And what, if anything, can be done about it?

Both medieval and Renaissance studies and their specialized constituencies have more or less distinct traditions, institutions, canonical texts, pedagogical styles, and so forth. I suspect that many scholars would gladly bid good riddance to some of these, though we would probably not agree about which were expendable. We sometimes take on the attributes of the people we study (and vice versa); the fact is that the stock medieval roles do not appeal to me very much, and I can well imagine that, say, the persona of the Renaissance prince has limited attractions. Whether or not this is a liability or a virtue, Renaissance studies has fewer technical requirements, supposing that medievalists still do train in the languages, paleography, diplomatic, codicology, and other "auxiliary sciences" of the grand tradition of medievalism. Many Renaissance scholars are like medievalists with insufficient training, but medievalists for their part, owe some of their impressive scholarly discipline to the fact that they have so little material to work with.[18] The point here is the conservative one that we already have enough to do to keep up in our own fields without meddling in others. Frankly, I am not especially concerned about this, partly because Renaissance studies has never run a very tight ship, but also because I think that scholars are likely to go on doing what they already do anyway. Nevertheless, I can sympathsize with real or, for that matter, imagined fears of dilution and homogeneity.

I am more concerned that in consolidating medieval and Renaissance chapters in European history we may not have enough framing, focus, or plot to relate a distinctive or coherent history of Europe at all. There is some risk that histories of "Olde Europe" would become merely accumulative, antiquarian, and annalistic, or like the new ethnic republics, fiercely separatist and partisan. Histories post-modern style, where everything wrought in the past is at once indiscriminately historical and available in the present, have no anachronisms, and this would put historians out of work. Then too, the absence of overarching narratives promotes a kind of historiographical *horror vacui* and the proliferation of any number of particular tales. I don't know which prospect is more alarming: that historians will run out of new topics or that they will come up with ever more trivial ones.[19]

Having said that, as a Renaissance historian, I am professionally inoculated against claims of uniqueness for this or that historical period. I have heard such claims for "our" Renaissance all too often for all too many specious reasons. Besides, a Renaissance presumes, however fancifully, but practically by definition, connections with a distant past as well as breaks from a more immediate one. What Panofsky's virtuoso line-up of medieval "renascences" in Carolingian, Ottonian, and twelfth-century Europe goes to prove is not so much that any particular classical revival was the real thing but that classicism, and more generally pulsations of tradition and change, have recurred with some regularity over the long term in European history.[20] I have found it both liberating and instructive to think about the history of Europe over the long span (from, say, 800 or perhaps 1000 to 1789) in terms of a shifting calculus of recurrent tensions and simultaneous narratives that the old medieval-Renaissance separations tend to arrange in linear succession—for example, between sacred and profane, margin and center, hierarchy and non-hierarchy, force and prescription, and so forth.[21]

Such a scenario does not depend on a lockstep sequence of ages or dictate a direction to history or the historian. But this does not necessarily leave us adrift on a boundless historical sea. It does not mean, either, that we are condemned to the kind of revisionism that simply reproduces the categories of a conventional interpretation in reverse. I am thinking of the Oedipal ritual of Burckhardt-bashing by Renaissance historians, who point, say, to collectivities, not to individualism in Renaissance Italy, or to medieval political traditions, not to the modern state: Burckhardt upside down is still Burckhardt.[22]

The alternative I want to propose here takes genealogy as a historiographical model—a good medieval and Renaissance model, I might add, and one with as much contemporary resonance as

Foucault.[23] As a kind of historical discourse, genealogy works by shape (its "trees") and succession (its lineages). It does so, however, with reference to particular dates and events. Thus while genealogy is sequential, it also charts discontinuites, breaks, and failures; and while it figures novelty—some new family connection and a new set of genes—it also represents continuity. History constructed in genealogical terms is additive and cumulative but not necessarily confined to a preordained outcome or plot, for any genealogical telos can only be established retrospectively because it is impossible to know in advance just how the next generation will be formed or how it will turn out.

The Renaissance metaphor is itself an interesting study in genealogical history. As I have already suggested, even Panofsky's several "renascences" before his authentic Quattrocento Renaissance have come to seem too episodic to account for the persistent borrowing from antiquity over the long term. Nor has more recent research upheld Panofsky's argument for the reintegration of classical form and content at the end of the fifteenth century. The results are too complicated, contradictory, and interesting to be contained by Panofsky's climactic Renaissance synthesis.[24]

One "genealogical" aspect of this newer picture is the multiplicity and simultaneity of quite different, if more or less parallel and occasionally overlapping, lines of descent. In a standard account of the "Renaissance discovery" of antiquity Roberto Weiss admitted that "undeniably, some antiquities were known and treasured during the medieval centuries," but then insisted unrepentantly that "on the whole, they were generally appreciated in the wrong way."[25] Like all tales of triumph, the story of the "right way" is actually a narrative of exclusion. The loss of a sense of continuity and the objectification of antiquity as a remote age are prerequisites for the alleged gain of knowledge of the ancient past as such. The history of the idea of the Renaissance thus becomes the pre-history of modern archeology, classical studies, and classical philology. Other strands of medieval and Renaissance culture that called for restoration or revival get omitted or marginalized accordingly—so, for example, campaigns for religious reform; radical or reactionary social movements that looked to a mythical Golden Age; quarrels between the "ancient" and the "modern" schools of medieval theology and philosophy; or vernacular echoes of antiquity that had little or nothing to do with scholarship. The lineages of these developments—and many others—are only gradually being restored to the history of the idea of the Renaissance.[26]

As a result, we can follow many branches of affiliation and of difference. The older Renaissance debates, still paying tribute to nineteenth-century historicism, tended to treat more or less distinct activities as emanations or reflections of the spirit of an age. Whether or not spirits can have a history is a question I will gladly beg for the fact that we do have many recent histories of distinct practices, techniques, or disciplines whose project was in one way or another a "revival of antiquity." This is not to say that the *grands récits* of, say, the rise of classicism, individualism, or humanism have disappeared, though one would think that the dubious careers of such "isms" would have long since discredited them. Yet the old narratives have been complicated, qualified, and in some instances superseded by *petites histoires* of writing, collecting, and editing, or of rhetoric, historiography, and law.[27]

The history of Renaissance antiquarianism is a good example. Where Weiss presented a narrative of progress culminating in modern (i.e., nineteenth-century positivist) classical archeology, Salvatore Settis's multi-volumed, collaboratively authored series of essays on the "memory" of antiquity in Italian art branches out along many different lines. Weiss's Renaissance invented the concept of the anachronism, but we are reminded by Gisella Cantino Wataghin that Andrea Fulvio's *Antiquitates urbis* (1527), the epitome of the new Renaissance archeology, traced the antiquities of Rome from Janus to Emperor Conrad, "trying to reestablish an impossible continuity that would simply annul the intervening millennium." Far from distinguishing historical periods, "Renaissance antiquarianism does not make distinctions of principle between the pagan and Christian monuments of Rome, which appear side by side in the *Roma instaurata* of Biondo and in the works inspired by it, up to the *Antiquitates* of Fulvio...." The first map of ancient Rome (1498) was produced by Annio da Viterbo, a notorious forger of "ancient" history. One of Weiss's "Descartes of archeology," Onofrio Panvinio, proceeded from Romulus to Charles V in his book on the Capitoline tables (1556), emending his texts (as he says) where necessary and making them up (as he does not say) when they were lacking. The spoliation of the ruins of Rome was as continuous as the legislation meant to protect them.[28] As for the archeological museum, its lineage is quite indistinct in those Renaissance collections of "anticaglie" divided into "naturalia" and "artificalia" and arranged according to analogies or "sympathies."[29]

We could go on in detail. But wouldn't this only mistake the ramifications of the genealogical "tree" for the Renaissance forest? Actually, I prefer the close-up view to the hazy panorama of an essential Renaissance. From a middle-range perspective, however, we can identify coherent themes while situating them in specific settings and tracing out variously dominant, recessive, or seemingly extinct lines of historical descent. Consider what I will call the Ancient Treasure Trope.[30]

Already in late antiquity, with the contraction and defensive concentration of the population, the sepulchral city, the ruin, the buried artifact, fragment, or shard became real and imagined objects of wonder. Not only the storytellers, but also the historians, theologians, and lawyers discussed them as sources of history, holiness (or diabolical cunning), and wealth. These associations did not recede suddenly or evenly. There is plenty of evidence that Renaissance collectors valued the antique fragment for the sake of mystery, money, status, and imagination. Various motives generated particular histories around discrete, but occasionally interlinked, sites, from relics in churches, trophies in the piazza, and sculpture in the garden to the merchant or scholar's *studio,* the princely cabinet, and the dealer's shop. The specialized museum collection housed in its own space is a post-Renaissance phenomenon, and hardly an irreversible one. The multi-media, multi-purpose museums of our times have more in common with the Renaissance museum than the systematically specialized institution that emerges toward the end of the eighteenth century.[31]

No doubt the epic struggles between medievalists and renaissancists were more exciting. Peaceable kingdoms are probably boring, though we have little enough real evidence on this score either in the large world or in academe. Scholars in the humanities, we can be sure, will always find something to argue about, including the irenic kind of proposal I have just sketched out.

I do not anticipate mass conversions, in part because there is already something of the genealogist in people with historical interests. What I have been characterizing as genealogical history allows for heterogeneity and connecting linkages by foregrounding the specific instance while insisting that specifics are variously sequential; it is frankly presentist while marking lines of descent and of failed succession from the past. It is hard to imagine historians finding many surprises in that formulation. I hope to have shown that for those of us interested in the Middle Ages and the Renaissance the project I have been describing is, nevertheless, a serious alternative to the lockstep history of distinct ages of Western civilization or to history that, for being either narrowly focused or broadly synchronic, can hardly take steps at all.

In any case, I do not think there is any safe retreat into the old camps from the wholesale rethinking of academic boundaries that is still under way. Medievalists and renaissancists, so I have argued, are too thoroughly mixed up with one another for that anyway. To forget or ignore that relationship is to be condemned to repeat the old clichés, to rehearse the old binary oppositions that have long since been retired or at least called into question.

Another prospect, hardly a more appealing one, is death by inanition. It is by now as paradigmatic as anything in the old canon to claim that the assumptions sustaining the Grand Narratives of European history have changed. "Our" task is said to be interdisciplinary, multi-cultural, non-totalizing, and decentered. I take the point of the rejoinder that this agenda too will pass, but not the implication that the latest cultural fashions are too ephemeral and trivial to matter. The concerns of the larger culture clearly did matter in the past of medieval and Renaissance studies, and there is no good reason to think this will not be the case in the future. I would guess that the vitality and perhaps even viability of medieval and Renaissance studies will depend, like the future of European unity, on how responsive we are to the very real dangers of imperialism or of isolation.

NOTES

1. Wallace K. Ferguson, *The Renaissance in Historical Thought: Five Centuries of Interpretation* (Cambridge, Mass.: Riverside Press, 1948), is still the standard work; cf. William J. Bouwsma, "The Renaissance and the

Drama of Western History," *American Historical Review* 94 (1979): 1–15
(reprinted in the author's *A Usable Past: Essays in European Cultural History* [Berkeley: University of California Press, 1990], 348–365) for a subsequent loss of confidence in sharp medieval-Renaissance distinctions. For
the actual resurgence of imperial claims for the modernity of the Renaissance or of the Middle Ages, however, see, e.g., William Kerrigan and Gordon Braden, *The Idea of the Renaissance* (Baltimore and London: Johns
Hopkins University Press, 1989); Jean Delumeau, "Une histoire totale de la
Renaissance," *Journal of Medieval and Renaissance Studies* 22 (1992): 1–
13; Stephen G. Nichols, "The New Medievalism: Tradition and Discontinuity in Medieval Culture," in *The New Medievalism,* ed. Marina S. Brownlee,
Kevin Brownlee, and Stephen G. Nichols (Baltimore and London: Johns
Hopkins University Press, 1991), 1–26; and, most bluntly, Norman F. Cantor, *Inventing the Middle Ages: The Lives, Works, and Ideas of the Great
Medievalists of the Twentieth Century* (New York: William Morrow, 1991),
esp. 17–47. *Reconsidering the Renaissance,* ed. Mario Di Cesare (Binghamton, N.Y.: Medieval and Renaissance Texts and Studies, 1992) is a convenient guide to the current state of the "Renaissance question." I am
grateful to my colleagues William J. Bouwsma, Gene Brucker, and Thomas
Laqueur for reading a draft of this essay.

2. Theodor E. Mommsen, "Petrarch's Conception of the 'Dark
Ages'," *Speculum* 17 (1942): 226–242 (reprinted in the author's *Medieval
and Renaissance Studies,* ed. Eugene F. Rice, Jr. [Ithaca, N.Y.: Cornell University Press, 1959]) is the classic account; cf., Giuseppe Mazzotta, "Antiquity and the New Arts in Petrarch," in *The New Medievalism,* 46–69.

3. These dynamics are clear even in the titles of Ferguson's chapters
on "Reaction against the Burckhardtian Tradition: The Origins of the Renaissance Thrust Back into the Middle Ages" (chap. 10) and "The Revolt of
the Medievalists: The Renaissance Interpreted as Continuation of the Middle Ages" (chap. 11) of *Renaissance in Historical Thought,* 290–385. For
more recent variations, see e.g., Brigitte Cazelles and Charles Mela,
Modernité au moyen age: le défi du passé (Geneva: E. Droz, 1990), esp.
33–44; and *The Darker Vision of the Renaissance,* ed. Robert S. Kinsman
(Berkeley: University of California Press, 1974), 3–12.

4. See Bouwsma, "The Renaissance"; I am thinking here of course
of "occidentalism" as a producer and production of the cultural stereotyping analyzed in Edward Said's landmark *Orientalism* (New York: Vintage Books, 1979).

5. See Gilbert Allardyce, "The Rise and Fall of the Western Civilization Course," *American Historical Review* 87 (1982): 695–725, and the
responses by Carolyn C. Lougee, Morris Rossabi, and William F. Woehrlin,

725–731 of the same volume; cf. more generally, Peter Novick, *That Noble Dream: The "Objective Question" and the American Historical Profession* (Cambridge: Cambridge, 1988), 47–60, 310–314.

6. These Renaissance journals were all launched with programmatic claims to covering the entire field of Renaissance studies; in practice, they have reflected national interests and methodological preferences. So, e.g., the Italian case. The first issue of *La Rinascita* (1938–1944), edited by Giovanni Papini for the Istituto Nazionale di Studi sul Rinascimento, announced that the journal would publish "studi originali" and "sicure notizie" on Humanism and the Civilization of the Renaissance; the limiting proviso, fraught with the complicated politics of scholarship under the fascist regime, was that it would offer space "a tutte le teorie che oggi si affrontano nell'interpretazione del Rinascimento Italiano, purchè, si intende, esse siano sorrette da positiva base storica e si dimostrino tali da poter condurre ad una concezione obiettiva e integrale di quella che si potrebbe chiamare dopo il 'miracolo greco,' il 'miracolo italiano'" (*La Rinascita* 1 [1938]: 1–2). Defining the Renaissance as an age of synthesis, Papini saluted its "restaurazione dell'uomo senza la negazione di Dio" (ibid., 8), while insisting that this achievement was quintessentially Italian—hence the "evident errors" of those scholars, "che vorebbero togliere all'Italia il vanto, universalmente riconosciuto fin agli ultimi anni, di essere stata la sede naturale del primo e d'ogni Rinascimento" (*La Rinascita* 2 [1939]: 4); in the same article Papini went on to divide the Italian Renaissance into three distinct periods from 1304, and the birth of Petrarch, to 1564, and the death of Michelangelo. Mussolini approved the journal in 1938, promising all necessary support in the future, but by 1941 it was being accused of a "filocattolicesimo generico" by the "conservatori di una teoria, diciamo cosí, paganeggiante, immanentista e anticattolica del Rinascimento," a charge that Papini rebutted in the name of "ricerca scientifica e... discussione libera [per] la preparazione di una sintesi che tenga conto della sterminata opulenza spirituale di quell'età e dei sacri diritti del vero" (*Rinascita* 4 [1941]: 164, 168). When the Istituto Nazionale resumed publication of a journal in 1950 under the new title *Il Rinascimento* the interest in synthesis gave way to philology and erudition, a tendency that isolated Renaissance studies in Italy from the great post-war debates between Marxists and Croceans and eventually from the coming directions of economic, social, and cultural history. My thanks to Dr. Carol Staswick for her research on Renaissance studies.

7. Actually, the "new historicism" in Renaissance literary studies is quite traditional in viewing the Renaissance as a modernizing period, in which a new subjectivity was fashioned within and against aggressive in-

stitutions demanding outward conformity and inward allegiance. This is Burckhardt's "State as a Work of Art" and "Development of the Individual" revisited. For conveniently representative samplings of "new historicist" work and the debates it has generated, see, in general, *The New Historicism,* ed. H. Avram Veeser (New York and London: Routledge, 1989); and Brook Thomas, *The New Historicism and Other Old Fashioned Topics* (Princeton: Princeton University Press, 1991). When a manifesto of the "new medievalism" declares that "new medievalism has on the whole tried to avoid reading the Middle Ages onto the modern world except as a dialectical gesture of postmodernist inquiry," it makes in the latest jargon a quite conventional claim for "the unity of the Middle Ages" (*The New Medievalism,* 8).

8. All the more so because, e.g., this is but one of several recent collections of stimulating essays on the rethinking of medieval studies, among them: Lee Patterson, *Negotiating the Past: The Historical Understanding of Medieval Literature* (Madison: University of Wisconsin Press, 1987); *The New Medievalism; Speaking in Two Languages: Traditional Disciplines and Contemporary Theory in Medieval Studies,* ed. Allen J. Frantzen, SUNY Series in Medieval Studies (Albany: State University of New York Press, 1991); and *Speculum* 65:1 (1990).

9. For especially strenuous critiques of the alleged isolation of medieval and Renaissance studies, see e.g., Patterson, *Negotiating the Past,* esp. 37–39; Ronald F. E. Weissman, "Reconstructing Renaissance Sociology: The 'Chicago School' and the Study of Renaissance Society," in *Persons in Groups: Social Behavior as Identity Formation in Medieval and Renaissance Europe,* ed. Richard Trexler (Binghamton, N.Y.: Medieval and Renaissance Texts and Studies, 1985), 39–45; and Anthony Molho, "American Historians and the Italian Renaissance: An Overview," *Schifanoia* 8 (1989): 9–17.

10. The familiar claims for *the* Renaissance attitude to history, with its invention of secular periodization, anachronism, and the integral age or epoch, would surely not have seemed familiar for Renaissance historians. Unsurprisingly, late sixteenth-century interest in systematizing historical accounts and methods actually generated more historiographical variety than uniformity; even a major "methodologist" such as Jean Bodin called his treatise *Methodus ad facilem historiarum cognitionem,* with "histories" in the plural. See William J. Bouwsma, "Three Types of Historiography in Post-Renaissance Italy," *History and Theory* 4 (1965): 303–314, reprinted in Bouwsma's *A Usable Past,* 295–307; Donald R. Kelley, *Foundations of Modern Historical Scholarship* (New York: Columbia University Press, 1970); George Huppert, *The Idea of Perfect History* (Urbana: University of Illinois Press, 1970); and Timothy Hampton, *Writing from His-*

tory: The Rhetoric of Exemplarity in Renaissance Literature (Ithaca and London: Cornell University Press, 1990).

11. Denys Hay, *The Italian Renaissance in Its Historical Background* (Cambridge: Cambridge University Press, 1961), chap. 1 ("The Problem of Italian Historiography"), is still especially useful on the chronological and geographical ambiguities in the traditions of Italian historiography; for a convenient update, see Denys Hay and John Law, *Italy in the Age of the Renaissance, 1380–1530* (London and New York: Longman, 1989), 3–11. For Renaissance versions of Italian history, Eric Cochrane, *Historians and Historiography in the Italian Renaissance* (Chicago and London: University of Chicago Press, 1981) is the essential, and always provocative, guide.

12. See Ferguson, *The Renaissance in Historical Thought*, esp. 330 f.

13. The passages from Burckhardt appear in Part II of *The Civilization of the Renaissance in Italy* on "The Development of the Individual." One would have to cite practically the whole corpus of writing on Renaissance Italy in the past twenty-odd years to document the deflation of its "modernity." I noted this tendency already in 1970 in a review essay on *Florentine Studies: Politics and Society in Renaissance Italy* (London: Faber and Faber, 1968), in *Bibliothèque d'humanisme et Renaissance* 32 (1970): 682–683. It is a leitmotif of the most recent synthesis by Hay and Law, *Italy in the Age of the Renaissance;* so, e.g., in this characteristic and by now increasingly canonical formulation: "Modern historians, sometimes equipped with methodologies (and even conclusions) from the social sciences and anthropology, have eclipsed the older certainties suggested by Marx or Burckhardt: that the Renaissance saw the triumph of the bourgeoisie, or the emergence of the individual" (p. 29). For a reflective statement by a veteran Renaissance historian, I am grateful to Gene Brucker for sharing with me the text of "The Italian Renaissance and its Contemporary Relevance," his lecture at Cameron University, Lawton, Oklahoma, April 1992.

14. Quoted in *Microhistory and the Lost Peoples of Europe,* trans. Eren Branch, ed. Edward Muir and Guido Ruggiero (Baltimore and London: Johns Hopkins University Press, 1991), 2.

15. Edward Muir, "Introduction: Observing Trifles," in ibid., vii–xxviii, gives an excellent account of the rise of "microstoria" in the Italian historical profession; cf. Thomas Kuehn, "Reading Microhistory: The Example of *Giovanni and Lusanna,*" *Journal of Modern History* 61 (1989): 512–531, for a critical reading of a widely read American example of the genre. For a comparison and critique of American vis-à-vis Italian historiographical practice, see Molho, "American Historians and the Italian Renaissance," esp. 16–17; cf. John M. Najemy, "Linguaggi storiografici sulla Firenze rinascimentale," *Rivista storica italiana* 97 (1985): 102–159.

16. Randolph Starn, *Contrary Commonwealth: The Theme of Exile in Medieval and Renaissance Italy* (Berkeley: University of California Press, 1982).

17. Randolph Starn and Loren Partridge, *Arts of Power: Three Halls of State in Italy, 1300–1600* (Berkeley: University of California Press, 1992).

18. So while medievalists have such standard cumulative manuals as Gray Boyce Cowan, *The Literature of Medieval History, 1930 to 1975,* 5 vols. (New York: Kraus, 1981) or R. C. Van Caeneghen, *Guide to the Study of Medieval History* (Amsterdam: North Holland, 1978), Renaissance historians make do with scattered specialized bibliographies and such relatively slight guides as *A Concise Encyclopedia of the Italian Renaissance,* ed. J. R. Hale (London: Thames and Hudson, 1981).

19. Hayden White, "The Question of Narrative in Contemporary Historical Theory," in his *The Content of the Form: Narrative Discourse and Historical Representation* (Baltimore and London: Johns Hopkins University Press, 1987), 26–57, is a good guide by a major participant to an extensive, and often heated, discussion of the uses and abuses of historical narrative.

20. Erwin Panofsky, *Renaissance and Renascences in Western Art* (New York: Harper and Row, 1969); see too Roberto S. Lopez, *The Three Ages of the Italian Renaissance* (Charlottesville: University of Virginia Press, 1970).

21. On the theory and practice of such an approach in general: *Post-Structuralism and the Question of History,* ed. Derek Attridge, Geoff Bennington, and Robert Young (Cambridge: Cambridge University Press, 1987); *Writing Culture: The Poetics and Politics of Ethnography,* ed. James Clifford and George E. Marcus (Berkeley: University of California Press, 1986); and *The New Cultural History,* ed. Lynn Hunt (Berkeley: University of California Press, 1989). For a recent attempt, not wholly successful, to show the diversity of Renaissance culture across a range of contexts, see *The Renaissance in National Context,* ed. Roy Porter and Mikulas Teich (Cambridge: Cambridge University Press, 1992).

22. See e.g., the works cited in n. 13 above.

23. Michel Foucault, "Nietzsche, Genealogy, History," in *Michel Foucault: Language, Counter-Memory, Practice: Selected Essays and Interviews,* ed. Paul Bouchard (Ithaca, N.Y.: Cornell University Press, 1977), 27–49; cf. the analysis by Herbert Dreyfus and Paul Rabinow, *Michel Foucault: Beyond Structuralism and Hermeneutics,* 2d ed. (Berkeley: University of California Press, 1989), 104–118. The most recent and fully developed application I know is Eilean Hooper-Greenhill, *Museums and the Shaping of Knowledge* (London and New York: Routledge, 1992).

24. Particularly suggestive, I think, in a vast literature: *Memoria dell'antico nell'arte italiana,* ed. Salvatore Settis, I: *L'uso dei classici,* II: *I generi e i temi ritrovati,* III: *Dalla tradizione all'archeologia* (Turin: Giulio Einaudi Editore, 1984–1986); Thomas M. Greene, *The Light in Troy: Imitation and Discovery in Renaissance Poetry* (New Haven and London: Yale University Press, 1982); David Quint, *Origin and Originality in Renaissance Literature: Versions of the Source* (New Haven and London: Yale University Press, 1983); Hampton, *Writing from History.*

25. Roberto Weiss, *The Renaissance Discovery of Classical Antiquity* (London: Oxford University Press, 1969).

26. See Michael Greenhalgh, *"Ipsa ruina docet*: l'uso dell'antico nel Medioevo," in *Memoria dell'antico,* I, 115–67; Salvatore Settis, "Continuità, distanza, conoscenza. Tre usi dell'antico," in ibid., III, 375–486; and Patricia Fortini Brown, "Fragments of Historical Awareness: Medieval and Renaissance Perceptions of Antiquity" (paper read at the Annual Meeting of the Renaissance Society of America, Columbia University, 1988).

27. So, e.g., William J. Courtenay, Charles Trinkaus, Heiko Oberman, and Neil W. Gilbert, "Ancients and Moderns: A Symposium," *Journal of the History of Ideas* 48 (1987): 3–50; Anthony Grafton and Lisa Jardine, *From Humanism to Humanities: Education and the Liberal Arts in Fifteenth-Century and Sixteenth-Century Europe* (Cambridge, Mass.: Harvard University Press, 1986); Armando Petrucci, *La descrizione del manoscritto: Storia, problemi modelli* (Rome: La Nuova Italia Scientifica, 1984); Donald R. Kelley, *Foundations of Modern Historical Scholarship: Language, Law, and History in the French Renaissance* (New York: Columbia University Press, 1970); Paula Findlen, "The Museum: Its Classical Etymology and Renaissance Genealogy," *Journal of the History of Collections* 1 (1989): 59–78; and especially *Memoria dell'antico.*

28. The foregoing examples and quotations are from Gisella Cantino Wataghin, "Il rapporto con l'antico fra mito, arte e ricerca," in *Memoria dell'antico,* I, 195, 197, and 206.

29. Claudio Franzoni, " 'Rimembranze d'infinite cose.' Le collezioni rinascimentali di antichita," in ibid., I, 343.

30. Michael Greenhalgh, *"Ipsa ruina docet*: l'uso dell'antico nel Medioevo," in *Memoria dell'antico,* I, 115–167, is richly informative on this theme and its variations.

31. See the full discussion of historical comparisons in Hooper-Greenhill, *Museums,* 191–215.

Medieval Philosophy of the Future!

Mark D. Jordan

You may already have recognized that I take my title from Nietzsche. More precisely, I adapt it from Wilamowitz-Moellendorff at the instance of Nietzsche. *Zukunftsphilologie!* was the mocking title of the pamphlet in which Wilamowitz attacked Nietzsche's *Birth of Tragedy* as unscholarly, as a betrayal of the high standards of philological science that Nietzsche was presumed to profess.[1] Wilamowitz later claimed that his pamphlet drove Nietzsche from the field.

> The violence done [by Nietzsche] to historical facts and all philological method was clear as daylight, and impelled me to fight for my threatened science.... Boyish as much of [the] work in question is, with [its] conclusion I hit the bull's eye. [Nietzsche] did what I called him to do, gave up his teaching office and science, and became the prophet of a non-religious religion and an unphilosophical philosophy.[2]

Wilamowitz rather overestimated his talents as a polemicist—not to say, his talents as a reader of philosophy. Nietzsche's pretext for resigning from Basel was bad health, but his motive seems to have been a new conviction of how futile it would be to continue trying to write thoughtfully for audiences of scholars. In any case, Nietzsche hardly recanted his desire to combat what passed for the interpretation of ancient texts. And the subtitle of *Beyond Good and Evil,* that last panel in his triptych of masterworks, would be "Prelude to a Philosophy of the Future." From which my own exclamatory title.

The quarrel between Nietzsche and Wilamowitz could be pertinent to our topic for many reasons. My chief reason for recalling it is to raise a question about our motives for studying the history of philosophy, a question that Nietzsche might be said to have pa-tented in several of his *Untimely Observations*. By 'motives' I do not mean to refer—at least, not immediately—to the psychological forces alleged to explain why any individual chooses life as a scholar of medieval philosophy. Nietzsche would have a great deal to say about that too, of course, as he became increasingly distrust-ful of any attempt to segregate personal secrets, the "human, all-too-human" springs of action, from the professedly dispassionate claims of institutional purpose. Still Nietzsche began by analyzing, as I mean to analyze in a different case, the institutional motives that authorize, justify, and direct the common undertaking of an aca-demic field.

One learns from observation—and reads in Nietzsche—that academic practitioners of the history of philosophy are all too likely to be unreflective—unphilosophical—about their share in institu-tional motives. There is much to reflect on. Public motives can be examined for a variety of characteristics, among them coherence, persuasiveness, practicability, longevity, sincerity. The characteris-tics are not always connected. Many long-lived research programs have been justified by appeal to motives that were incoherent but persuasive, or sincere but impracticable. I continue to hope, pi-ously, that the most illuminating studies of medieval philosophy will be motivated by reasons that are coherent, persuasive, practi-cable, and sincere. Hence I value the analysis of motives.

Analysis is particularly necessary in this case because of mod-ern philosophy's unhappy relation to its own past. One dogma embodied in the canon of modern philosophy taught that true phi-losophy ought to begin by rejecting all that had gone before in a disdainful act of Cartesian patricide. The murder was bungled, of course, as Gilson demonstrated so elegantly in his catalogue of me-dieval borrowings by Descartes himself. More recently, the dogma has begun to loosen its grip. Yet the underlying view of philosophy as essentially unhistorical persists in many departments, and there is still too little sustained reflection on philosophical motives for studying the history of philosophy.[3]

I put the question in this way rather than as a question about philosophical scholarship within "medieval studies" because I re-gard "medieval studies" as a floating coalition of conversations, re-search projects, and lobbying efforts rather than as a curricular unity. I mean no invidious distinction between disciplines and non-disciplines. Each academic "discipline" is an adventitious unity improvised amid particular circumstances. Some are older than others, some pretend to be much older than they are. I do not want to debate whether "medieval studies" is a "discipline," but rather to note that it has not succeeded in gaining much control over curricula, which is to say, over degrees and appointments. Scholars of medieval philosophy are trained and oriented within the academic guild of philosophy, however much they depend on scholars studying medieval matter claimed by other disciplines.[4]

I will proceed, then, in a vaguely Nietzschean manner, to sketch some motives, secular and sacred, that have driven modern studies of what is called medieval Latin "philosophy."[5] Nietzsche, you will remember, proposed in one of his most famous essays that historiography could be exemplary, antiquarian, or critical.[6] The trichotomy was meant to be provocative rather than precise. We would certainly need a richer division to catalogue the motives that have so far animated modern histories of medieval philosophy. But I have neither the learning nor the space for a catalogue. Let me turn instead to a single, emblematic text, from which I hope to elicit motives that can be recognized in a host of histories. Each of these institutional motives seems to me now to have lost credibility.

1. SECULAR MOTIVES

The inauguration of the modern study of medieval philosophy is often discovered in Hauréau's *De la philosophie scolastique* (1850). The date will serve as well as any, and the prize-winning monograph is a good vantage point from which to survey what is in fact a complicated and much more extended genealogy.[7] Hauréau wrote in response to a competition sponsored by the Parisian Academy for Moral and Political Sciences. The competition called for a critical examination of Scholastic philosophy, which it understood to be the philosophy cultivated—or invented—at Paris between the introduction of the new Aristotle and the fall of Constantinople.[8] The explicitly patriotic exercise was to extract from the national past what might be useful to modern secular philosophy, and chiefly such principles, procedures, or results as were discoverable in the controversy over universals.

Just in the terms of the competition there figure disparate motivations. There is, first, most obviously, a nationalist impulse. Scholastic philosophy is stipulatively defined as French—indeed, as Parisian. The definition is not an aberration. Two decades earlier, Cousin had published some works of Abelard with the sub-title, "in aid of the history of scholastic philosophy in France."[9] Moreover, and more famously, Cousin offered Abelard as the necessarily French precursor to the necessarily French Descartes.[10] In one overwrought passage, Cousin notices that both Abelard and Descartes were from Brittany, "whose inhabitants are distinguished by such a lively sentiment of independence and such a strong personality."[11]

The nationalist impulse was by no means confined to France. John of Salisbury's works were published at Oxford beginning in 1848, with a dedication to Cousin.[12] Alexander Nequam's *De naturis rerum* appeared in 1863 in the Rolls Series, and several British editions of Roger Bacon were underway before the first World War.[13] Indeed, the whole of Bacon's *Opus majus* was available in English (Oxford, 1928) barely a decade after the whole of Aquinas's *Summa* was translated into English for the very first time (1912–1917). *Les Philosophes Belges* was inaugurated in 1901 with Giles of Lessines. Within a dozen years or so it would yield editions of Godfrey of Fontaines, Siger of Courtrai, and Guibert of Tournai, as well as the revised version of Mandonnet's book on Siger of Brabant.[14] Medievalists owe much to the national rivalries of the nineteenth century and to the fantasies about regional character that accompanied them.

The rules of the Academy's competition call, in second place, for a "critical" examination of medieval philosophy. The choice of words is not casual. It alludes to that monument of Enlightenment historiography, Jacob Brucker's *Historia critica philosophiae a mundi incunabulis*. Brucker had served the *Encyclopédie* as guide to the philosophical illusions of the past,[15] and so he continued to fix patterns for historiography. Brucker devotes a considerable space in the *Historia critica* to the exposition of "scholastic philosophy," that is, of Latin philosophy from the eleventh through the sixteenth centuries. He then concludes with a bilious judgment and a list of "general observations" that is a syllabus of errors.[16] Similar judgments and similar lists can be found in the *Encyclopédie*.[17] Now the motive of critical appropriation is a little diluted in the rules for the Academy's competition, which look for some utility, other than purgation, in the study of medieval philosophy.[18] Indeed, the judges of the competition seem to view the historical inquiry as a way of despoiling the Egyptians. Durable goods—logical principles, procedures, results—are transferred from their unjust possessors among the clerical dead to the liberated and living children of modernity. In this the Academicians recall the most influential project of early modern historiography in philosophy.

The project is formulated in Francis Bacon, accomplished in Thomas Stanley's *History of Philosophy* (London, 1655–1662).[19] Stanley surveys the ancient history of philosophy in order to teach his readers how to avoid old errors and how to appreciate justly their own progress beyond them. He is moved both by a universal curiosity and an impulse towards legislation. Neither motive took Stanley into the Middle Ages, but others among Stanley's precursors and successors were moved by them to look beyond antiquity. The motive of universal erudition goes back beyond Stanley to the first inclusions of medieval authors in modern tables and bibliographies of philosophy—to the philosophical portions of Gesner's *Bibliotheca universalis* (1548), to the *Bibliotheca philosophorum* of Johann Jacob Frisius (1592), and so on.[20] It may also be said to animate such relatively sympathetic treatments of medieval authors as Launoy's *Liber de varia Aristotelis fortuna* (Paris, 1653), which narrates Parisian Peripateticism from 1209 to 1624, and Georg Horn's *Historia philosophica* (Leiden, 1655), which treats of medieval philosophy and even Renaissance Scholasticism in two of its seven books.

Universal curiosity is often qualified—say, by notions of Christian orthodoxy. The Zwinglian Frisius stops his list of the "Church Fathers" in the 1140s, because Christian writers after that point are too remote from the Gospel and too near the papacy. Curiosity will also be qualified by the pedagogical uses to which its erudition will be put. The learning of Renaissance bibliographers and polyhistors was taken up into any number of different narratives of progress, Stanley's being only the first strong story told about these incidents.

Brucker's story is different, as are the stories in his near contemporaries Tiedemann[21] and Buonafede,[22] or in Tennemann[23] and Hegel.[24] The taste for erudition must be subsumed by some didactic project in order to construct a narrative or even so much as a topical bibliography.

None of the secular institutional motives so far mentioned remains justifiable. Some are now simply not persuasive, and so the question of their justification does not arise. Others seem still to be capable of animating scholarship, but they are incoherent and impracticable. Their apparent vigor is a kind of automatic writing.

The motive of nationalism is easiest to set aside. It does not count for much among historians of philosophy in Western Europe, much less in an increasingly emancipated North America. We continue to see philosophical texts in national series, but these now seem not so much acts of patriotism as polite fictions for funding agencies.[25]

The motive of Enlightened criticism looks at first more robust than nationalism. While no one would quite subscribe to the wording of the Academy's confident call to appropriate procedures, principles, and results, a number of scholars, especially in English-speaking departments, do seem to be moved by a desire to make the medievals immediate interlocutors for current debates. Even authors who are somewhat skeptical of this desire find themselves responding to it. Thus John Marenbon, who offers very cogent criticisms of the "modern analytical approach" to medieval philosophy, nonetheless feels compelled to justify his choice of topics with an eye to hitting on questions "closely related to those which interest philosophers today."[26] Such a principle of selection is open to the most obvious complaints that it is hermeneutically unsophisticated, historically ill-informed, and philosophically violent—in short, that it is incoherent.

There remain the intertwined secular motives of universal erudition and the didactic uses of history. Many scholars still see themselves as writing histories of philosophy. These are usually no longer universal histories, to be sure, but histories of particular traditions, figures, themes, or fields. Because our notions of history are still dictated by the masters of the nineteenth century, particular histories are almost invariably strong narratives. As strong narratives, they must suppress one of the essential features of the philosophical texts that they pretend to recollect—I mean, the pedagogy embodied in the rhetorical forms of the originals. Leaving aside, then, all issues of translation, intellectual causality, and anachronistic imposition, every narrative history of philosophy becomes incoherent so far as it unthinkingly supplants the narratives of the original texts. This is nowhere more apparent than in the very choice to write a history of medieval "philosophy," as if the presupposition of a separable or autonomous philosophy were at all congruent with the pedagogies in the majority of medieval Latin texts. When the Academy asked for a history of "scholastic philosophy," it asked its contestants to tell stories that could not be the stories of the medieval texts that were supposed to be their protagonists.

I conclude, then, that none of the Academy's motives for the modern history of medieval philosophy retains its cogency. Other motives have appeared since the nineteenth century, of course, though most are variations or inversions of motives registered by the Academy. The patronizing appropriation of medieval results is inverted as an anti-modern polemic—say, in Leo Strauss's critique of modern political philosophy. Such polemics are waged on behalf of the ancients. Medieval authors figure in them either as the weak offspring of antiquity or the confused forerunners of modernity. For this motive, the interesting quarrel is just between moderns and ancients.

Something similar has happened when medieval authors are introduced into general discussions of philosophy or philosophical topics. They appear as middle figures in every sense—transitional, secondary, compromised. They appear thus in Heidegger's narratives of decline, with an exception only for Eckhart.[27] Even in less contentious renderings of the "great conversation," medieval thinkers are squeezed between ancients and moderns. The omnivorous Jaspers, for example, manages to count Augustine, Anselm, and Thomas among "the great philosophers," but he allots them less than a tenth of his time and then gives more than half of the allotment to Augustine.[28]

Another reversed motive can be seen, interestingly enough, in the history of logic, where close study revealed that medieval logical texts were actually bearers of lessons since lost. Ernest Moody praises the study of medieval logic for supplying something needed by contemporary logicians.[29] More systematically, several generations of scholars—including Bochénski, Henry, Jolivet, Kretzmann, Pinborg, de Rijk, Roos, Spade—have worked to recover lessons from various parts of medieval logic. Their discoveries have been remarkable, but their public motives often remain too much conditioned by the defensive reversal of the old project of appropriation.

In short, we have yet to find coherent secular motives for an institutional program of the study of medieval philosophy.

2. ECCLESIASTICAL MOTIVES

Having traced wider and wider circles around the motives stated in the Academy's competition, I must now notice its deliberate, if fretful exclusion of theological concerns. The exclusion is only the symptom of a prejudice that continues to have its effects.

Most scholars concede the importance to medieval historiography of the ecclesiastical program of neo-Thomism. The concessions are often grudging. They carry with them suspicions about the merit of the program—say, suspicions about the motives of the encyclical *Aeterni patris*. One form of suspicion current among Catholics goes something like this: A desire to find plausible justifications for the reaction of Catholic thought after the French Revolution and Romanticism led certain theologians to return to Thomas. Their project was secured institutionally when one of their number was elevated to the papacy. As Leo XIII, he set about issuing proclamations and establishing schools that produced an enormous neo-Scholastic industry. From which we have lately been saved by Vatican II.

This myth distorts many things. It omits, for example, the continuous teaching of medieval texts from the fifteenth century right up to the nineteenth. Important parts of medieval philosophy and theology were taught as living doctrines—that is, were re-read, meditated, re-configured—in Catholic institutions throughout modern times. Such teaching was not known or not counted as serious by secular historiography, or by northern European believers, but it was as present in the universities as Cartesianism or Kantianism.[30] One thinks immediately of Cajetan and the school at Salamanca from Vitoria to Bañez; of Toledo, Bellarmino, and Suarez among the Jesuits; of the unified curricula produced by the two

groups of Carmelite professors, the "Complutenses" and the "Sal-
manticenses." During the eighteenth century, when Scholasticism is
supposed to have been utterly extinguished, there were flourishing
and sophisticated debates, in Mediterranean Europe and almost every country of Latin America, that were recognizably continuations
of medieval debates.[31] Indeed, in April 1757, rather more than a
century before *Aeterni patris,* the Dominican Master General Juan
Tomás de Boxadors issued an encyclical letter on the study of
Thomas that was still read in every Dominican house of study, at
the start of every school year, well into this century.[32]

Another omission from the myth of *Aeterni patris* goes in the
opposite direction. It is the omission of the rigorously thoughtful
and learnedly attentive readings to which the new Thomism gave
rise. Neo-Thomism is painted as unhistorical or anti-historical ideology. Perhaps it was so in the aggregate. Yet it produced in many
particular minds a passion for rigorous historical study.

Let me take the obvious figures. Heinrich Denifle, to whom
we owe the *Chartularium universitatis Parisiensis* among many
other works, was educated entirely within the Dominican order—at
the *studium* in Graz, then at the Minerva and Saint-Maximin.[33] His
early interests included the relations of Scholasticism to the *devotio
moderna.* Franz Ehrle, the reformer of manuscript studies at the
Vatican Library, followed the parallel path for a Jesuit—at Munster,
Maria Laach, and Ditton Hall. One of his first publications was an
appreciation of *Aeterni patris.* He undertook his years of manuscript work in order to write a history of Scholasticism.[34] Clemens
Baeumker was introduced to medieval philosophy in the diocesan
academy of Paderborn by a dévoté of John of St-Thomas.[35] This
same Baeumker would found the *Beiträge* in 1891 on a conviction
of the indispensability of original sources to the understanding of
medieval philosophy. Finally, an exacting, historical exegesis of
Aquinas was pioneered at the Dominican house of Le Saulchoir, under the direction of Gardeil, Mandonnet, Sertillanges, and Lem-
monyer—all of whom had been educated and encouraged by the
Order.[36] Where would the historical study of medieval philosophy
be without these labors, which were explicitly and institutionally
motived by the project of neo-Scholasticism?

It is all the sadder to have to admit, then, that the best motives of neo-Scholasticism have now lost any ecclesiastical force.

They were not incoherent. They were rendered unpersuasive by external upheavals. Perhaps no monolithic neo-Thomism or neo-Scholasticism could have survived much past 1965 in any case. We will not know this, because reflective and historically responsible projects in medieval thought have often been rejected out of hand since Vatican II. One can point to many circumstances: the revolutionary ideology that required an *abolitio memoriae;* the discrimination against speculative interests in the religious orders; their heavy losses of academic talent; and so on. As Mary Gordon wrote a few years back, "no bookish 27-year-old in our day would be in the least tempted by the Church of Rome."[37] However many the circumstances, the result has been to render the best ecclesiastical motives for the study of medieval thought institutionally unwelcome in their old homes.

What about new homes? Outside the dialectic of neo-Thomism and its rivals, some Catholic theologians tried to engage medieval texts as living interlocutors. Obvious examples would be De Lubac on scriptural exegesis and Von Balthasar on "clerical styles" of theology. But even before the Council the movement of *ressourcement* played itself out among Catholics as a contest between the patristic and the Scholastico-Tridentine. (Not coincidentally, this opposition resembles that between ancients and moderns as understood by Nietzsche or Heidegger.) Some Anglican and Protestant thinkers have been drawn to medieval figures. The attraction has been episodic. Barth insists on the importance of Anselm for this entire theological corpus,[38] and Austin Farrer was long engaged by Aquinas. But Anglican and Protestant theologians have not studied the Middle Ages with anything like the interest they spent on the patristic period, much less with anything like the results of Catholic neo-Thomism.

Since neo-Thomism was more a movement in philosophy than in theology, one might look next for religious motives among university teachers of philosophy. In the larger circles of Western academic philosophy, which Anglophones have persisted in calling "Continental," it is hard to see where religious motives have led to any sustained dialogue with medieval thinking. There was early in the century something like a Romantic interest in pre-modern versions of revealed religion. The early Benjamin claimed some inspiration from medieval sources for his views on language.[39] But religious motivation has led "Continental" philosophy's large-scale engagements with the medievals only under the impulse of neo-Thomism—as in Maréchal, Rahner, Coreth.

If English-speaking circles in philosophy were slower to re-learn religion, there is now a widely diffused analytic "philosophy of religion." There can be no doubt here about either the genuine-ness of the religious motivation or the rich harvest of scholarship that has come from it. One can ask whether analytic "philosophy of religion" offers a coherent institutional motive for the study of me-dieval philosophy as such. I would argue that it does not. The in-coherence is due partly to habits, such as the anti-historical bias in English-speaking philosophy. Too much philosophy of religion is still written in an astonishing historical vacuum. The most persis-tent topics in the history of dogma are treated as if no one had heard of them before 1960. A larger difficulty arises from analysts' understandings of "philosophy," which are divorced from anything like what the medievals understood as "theology." The very phrase "philosophy of religion" betrays this difficulty. It discloses a self-understanding much different from that of most medieval Latin texts, except perhaps some of the condemned propositions in Bishop Tempier's list of 1277. How could a Christian teacher avoid seeing the notion of a "philosophy of religion" as anything other than an inversion of the proper relation between philosophy and religion? There is, of course, a medieval Christian theology of phi-losophy. It is a diagnosis of the condition of the human mind under paganism. But a "philosophy of religion"—that must sound to me-dieval ears like the revenge of Porphyry.

Perhaps analytic departments of philosophy offer the best home for religious motives in English-speaking universities. There may be no better place for an American Christian or Jew to study medieval philosophy. To reach this conclusion would also be to conclude that there can now be no coherent institutional place-ment of that study.

3. MOTIVES FOR THE FUTURE

If the secular and ecclesiastical motives for the modern study of medieval thought are full of difficulties, we might expect the study to dissipate. In fact, we are awash in the academic study of medieval philosophy. The bibliographies are twice or three times what they were in the hey-day of neo-Thomism. Indeed, one often imagines that there are today more students of thirteenth-century thought than there were in the thirteenth century. How can this be if the most prominent institutional motives are unpersuasive or incoherent or impracticable? Have alternatives already been found?

They have not. We labor now, not under a regime of reflective motives, but under a regime of market forces. The causes for the growth in the academic study of medieval philosophy are the causes of academic "over-production" in all humanistic disciplines. There are many such causes. Some are reactions to the growth and diversification of institutions, with a predictable strain on theoretical consensus and a predictable turn to quantitative measures. Other causes arise from the failure to think about epochal changes in our technologies for handling texts. Machine-searchable bibliographies and whole-text databases—to take two obvious examples—are terrible temptations to accelerate the pace of scholarly production. Still other causes of "over-production" can be identified as institutional compensations for a tacitly shared lack of conviction. It is easier to do more of the same than to justify what one is doing, as it is easier to repeat mechanical activities than to discover reflective ones.

I mention these things not only to answer the objection that the quantity of current scholarship must arise from some new intellectual motive, but also to suggest that we will not easily be able to find or make new public motives. The institutional causes of "over-production" cannot be stopped by individual scholars or even by disciplinary groupings of scholars. Nor will we attain significant curricular reform of any scope and duration. Fortunately, our academic institutions are sufficiently porous to admit many contradictory activities. Having no curricula, they host fragments of innumerable curricula. An astonishing variety of personal motivations can find expression, including personal re-invigorations of some of the older institutional motives. There is much that is noble and edifying in these personal choices. Indeed, we could help ourselves, our colleagues, and our students by being more candid on occasion about why we choose our scholarly lives, if we still do choose them. But between the intractable institutional motives and the partly articulable private ones, there is a middle space that philosophy has always considered decisive—the space of persuasion to undertake philosophy, the space of philosophic teaching.

It is very difficult to teach medieval texts so that they become occasions for thought rather than for condescension or ironizing. We should not hesitate to admit, then, that the teaching of the history of medieval philosophy has often been unphilosophical. (The same admission should be made for the whole history of philosophy and for academic philosophy generally.) Help for teaching comes not only from living teachers, but also from the pedagogies enacted in the texts of philosophy that we read. In them too we can discover convincing and coherent motives for the study of medieval philosophy.

From its beginnings in the West, the question about motives for studying philosophy has been a question *for* philosophy. On many ancient accounts, the only acceptable motive is a passion for wisdom. This passion finds its origin and only analogue in erotic desire. Only an erotic madness is strong enough to free one from the civic entrapments that otherwise distract the talented. It was the great philosophic audacity of early Christian authors to recognize that philosophic projects of persuasion by *eros* could be transmuted into something of service to the Gospel. Yet erotic persuasion is not easily domesticated within guilds and programs for guild-licensing. Perhaps that is one reason why universities as such—I mean, as opposed to *didaskaleia, studia,* academies, coffee-houses, and Norwegian huts—have never been particularly hospitable to philosophy.

In the interstices of our modern universities we are permitted to read philosophic texts. Their pedagogies attempt to instill in us a properly philosophic *eros.* Some texts do so quite obviously. The Greek and Roman works called protreptics or exhortations to philosophy are records of persuasion. More importantly, if less obviously, there is hardly a work of ancient philosophy worth reading that does not enact such persuasion. Transmuted forms of this persuasion to the most desirable intelligibility are seen in the rhetoric of the medieval works we call philosophical and theological. In the strange and dissonant voices of the medieval texts—their rhetorical structures, their pedagogies—we hear the offer of the best motives for reading them, which is to say, of the best motives in them. The main chance of our chaotic situation is to let those voices speak without being silenced by something tediously familiar—by the drone of our most recent debates, by reductive historical narratives, or by any of a dozen ventriloquisms. Our task is to invent ways of teaching and writing about medieval persuasions to speculation that are not tedious betrayals of speculation.

I have no recipe for these ways of writing and teaching. To confess this is one privilege of the prophetic mode. I do continue to draw encouragement from Nietzsche. While Wilamowitz plodded on through his very scholarly monographs, Nietzsche reworked the aphorism into a supple and provocative 'imitation' of the persuasive discourse of Greek philosophy. Perhaps we could begin to do the same if we thought about our writings as replies to the acts of persuasion in our medieval interlocutors' writings. Perhaps we could conceive our teaching—whenever we do still conceive teaching—as gestures of persuasion in response to theirs. Of course, we cannot begin to do any of this until we refuse to treat as self-evident the public or private motives for our ceaseless scholarship.

NOTES

1. For the debate between Nietzsche and Wilamowitz-Moellendorff, see most recently William Musgrave Calder III, "The Wilamowitz-Nietzsche Struggle: New Documents and a Re-appraisal," *Nietzsche-Studien* 12 (1983): 214–254; Jaap Mansfeld, "The Wilamowitz-Nietzsche Struggle: Another New Document and Some Further Comments," *Nietzsche-Studien* 15 (1986): 41–58; and the remarks by William Arrowsmith in his introduction to the translation of Nietzsche, "We Classicists," *Unmodern Observations,* ed. Arrowsmith (New Haven, Conn.: Yale University Press, 1990), 309–312.

2. Ulrich von Wilamowitz-Moellendorff, *My Recollections: 1848–1914,* trans. G. C. Richards (London: Chatto & Windus, 1930), 151–152.

3. For descriptions and diagnoses of the prevailing prejudices against history, see *History and Anti-History in Philosophy,* ed. T. Z. Lavine and V. Tejera (Dordrecht: Kluwer, 1989), 1–31, and *La philosophie et son histoire,* ed. Jules Vuillemin (Paris: Odile Jacob, 1990), 17–136.

4. Even Gilson, who came out of a strongly interdisciplinary conversation at Strasbourg and who went on to conceive in Toronto the most coherent curriculum in medieval studies, continued to speak of himself as

"a philosopher" and to situate his work within the academic discourse of philosophy. The history of Gilson's Institute seems to an outsider to have been driven largely by the rivalries of the modern disciplines rather than by any ideal of a unified and hierarchical "medieval" wisdom.

5. From this point forward, I will drop the quotation marks around the word 'philosophy', but it should be understood that I am using the term under erasure. Most prevailing notions about the academic discipline called 'philosophy' cannot be used as a way of dividing medieval discourse. I must also warn that I confine my remarks to the study of medieval Latin thought. This study has, in any case, very often set the agenda for the study of Islamic, Jewish, and Byzantine thought. I would be happy to be told that my melancholy accounting of motives no longer applies outside of Latin philosophy, but I would also want to be shown what alternate motives have been found.

6. Nietzsche, "History in the Service and Disservice of Life," in *Unmodern Observations,* 95 and thereafter.

7. Little has been written about the fate of medieval authors under modern philosophy. One detailed and informative study is John Inglis, "Aquinas and the Historiography of Medieval Philosophy: A Reevaluation," Doctoral dissertation, University of Kentucky, 1993. Inglis argues persuasively for the role of the anti-skeptical projects of Joseph Kleutgen and Albert Stöckl in the constitution of the modern history of medieval philosophy.

8. Barthélemy Hauréau, *De la philosophie scolastique* (Paris: Pagnerre, 1850), 1:i–ii.

9. Victor Cousin, *Ouvrages inédites d'Abélard, pour servir à l'histoire de la philosophie scolastique en France* (Paris: Imprimerie Royale, 1836). In the same years (the winter of 1838–39), Charles de Rémusat was declaiming parts of a five-act *Abélard* to enthusiastic salon audiences. See the remarks of his son in the preface to *Abélard, drame inédit* (Paris: Calmann Lévy, 1877), v. Within the decade, the elder de Rémusat would publish his *Abélard, sa vie, sa philosophie et sa théologie* (Paris: LaGrange, 1845).

10. Cousin, *Ouvrages inédites,* iv: ". . . de sorte que la France a donné à la fois à l'Europe la scolastique au XIIᵉ siècle par Abélard, et au commence du XVIIᵉ, dans Descartes, le destructeur de cette même scolastique et le père de la philosophie moderne. Et il n'y a point là d'inconséquence; car le même esprit qui avait élevé l'enseignement religieux ordinaire à cette forme systématique et rationnelle qu'on appelle la scolastique, pouvait seul surpasser cette forme même et produire la philosophie proprement dite."

11. Cousin, *Ouvrages inédites,* iv.

12. John of Salisbury, *Opera omnia* 1, ed. J. A. Giles (Oxford: J. H. Parker, 1848). The dedication begins, "To Victor Cousin, in whom are united the nobility of mind which ought to characterize a peer of France. . . ."

13. By Bridges, Williams, and Norgate (1897–1900), by Steele (1905–1940), and by Rashdall (1911).

14. See volumes 1–2 and 8–9 of the series, all produced by 1914.

15. The debt is acknowledged explicitly and in response to criticism by an "Avertissement" at the head of the second volume. See *Encyclopédie ou dictionnaire raisonné des sciences, des arts et des métiers* (Paris, 1751–1765) 2:iv.

16. See the section "De natura, indole et modo philosophiae scholasticae" in Brucker, *Historia critica philosophiae . . .*, 2d ed. (Leipzig: Haeredes Weidemanni & Reicherri, 1767) 3:869f. As a summary judgment, consider the following: "Qui itaque his deliciis amplioribus frui cupit, illi ipsa philosophorum Scholasticorum praecipuorum[,] v.g. Alberti M.[,] Thomae, Scoti, Occami et similium, scripta adeunda sunt, quae de omnibus philosophiae partibus relinquerunt. Quae qui nunquam inspexit, nulla ratione comprehendet, quam profunda philosophiae omnis labe correpta sit, et quam marcidi eius vultus compareant, quae spectra lemuresque in hos veritatis campos irrepserint, quantumque inde vera philosophandi ratio damnum passa sit" (3:870).

17. See the article "Scolastiques," 14:770b–777b, with the charges at 777a–b.

18. Hauréau, *Philosophie scolastique* 1:ii: "[Les concurrents] s'appliqueront à dégager et à mettre en lumière ce qui, soit parmi les principes, soit parmi les procédés, soit parmi les résultats que nous a légués la Philosophie Scolastique, pourrait encore être mis à profit par la philosophie de notre temps."

19. See Bacon, *De dignitate et augmentis scientiarum* 2.4 and 3.5. Stanley cites Bacon explicitly in the *History of Philosophy: Containing the Lives, Opinions, Actions and Discourses of the Philosophers of Every Sect*, 2nd ed. (London: Thomas Basset, 1687), 490. Even where Stanley does not cite him, Bacon seems to inspire the *History*'s project.

20. For the bibliographies, see Michael Jasenas, *A History of the Bibliography of Philosophy* (Hildesheim and New York: Georg Olms, 1973), 16–41. The *Tabula compendiosa* published by Morellius in 1547 encompasses only ancient philosophy.

21. Dietrich Tiedemann, *Geist der speculativen Philosophie* (Marburg, 1791–1797). On Tiedemann's handling of medieval philosophy, see M. Longo, "L'immagine della scolastica tra 'tempo bui' e idea di progresso: Il contributo di D. Tiedemann," in *Itinerari e prospettive del personalismo:*

Scritti in onore di Giovanni Giulietti (Milan: Ist. Propaganda Libraria, 1986), 429–455.

22. "Agatopisto Cromaziona" (= Appiano Buonafede), *Della istoria e della indole di ogni filosofia* (Lucca: G. Riccomini, 1766–1781). On Buonafede's treatment of medieval texts, see Gregorio Piaia, *Vestigia philosophorum* (Rimini: Maggioli, 1983), 223–229.

23. See Wilhelm Gottlieb Tennemann, *Grundriss der Geshichte der Philosophie*, ed. A Wendt, 3d ed. (1820), §§233–267. The allocation of space in the *Grundriss* is noteworthy: ancient philosophy, 47%; medieval, 11%; modern (Renaissance through the young Hegel), 42%. Note also the invocation of Tennemann by Hauréau, *Philosophie scolastique* 1:2. Hauréau counts among his contemporary authorities not only Tennemann, but Brucker, Cousin, de Rémusat, and Rousselot. Among Humanist scholars, he cites Horn and Launoy.

24. For the Berlin lectures of 1825–1826, see Georg W. F. Hegel, *Vorlesungen über die Geschichte der Philosophie, 4: Philosophie des Mittelalters und der neueren Zeit*, ed. Pierre Garniron and Walter Jaeschke (Hamburg: Felix Meiner, 1986), 10–45 (for patristic, Islamic, Jewish, and medieval Latin authors). For Hegel's judgment on the "external" or captive character of medieval philosophy, see especially pp. 30–31. He gives medieval philosophy less than a third the space he gives to the period from Bacon to Schelling, less than a tenth what he gives to ancient philosophy.

25. Thus we have the recently inaugurated corpus of medieval German philosophers, an edition of Henry of Ghent that is still underwritten in part by the Belgian government, and Robert Grosseteste and Robert Kilwardby appearing among the *Auctores Britannici Medii Aevi*. The changed political circumstances of central Europe may well produce new bodies of patriotic scholarship, but I cannot see that they will reinvigorate the whole discipline.

26. John Marenbon, *Later Medieval Philosophy (1150–1350)* (London and New York: Routledge & Kegan Paul, 1987), 2, to which compare the criticisms on pp. 85–89.

27. I mean the middle and later Heidegger, of course. The situation is rather different in Heidegger's early work on a ps-Scotistic treatise. He there makes the central issue in the historiography of medieval philosophy to be the issue of discerning essential philosophical problems in medieval texts. See Martin Heidegger, *Die Kategorien und Bedeutungslehre des Duns Scotus*, as in his *Frühe Schriften* (Frankfurt a. M.: Vittorio Klostermann, 1972), 135–148.

28. Karl Jaspers, *Die grossen Philosophen* 1 (Munich: R. Piper, 1957) and *Die grossen Philosophen: Nachlass* 1, ed. Hans Saner (Munich: R. Piper,

1981). Augustine, Anselm, and Aquinas receive 124 pages out of 1,635. A few other medieval figures appear among the fragments published in *Nachlass* 2.

29. Ernest A. Moody, "The Medieval Contribution to Logic," reprinted in *Studies in Medieval Philosophy, Science and Logic* (Berkeley: University of California Press, 1975), 371–392, at pp. 389–390.

30. Judgments of discontinuity continue to appear even in learned and sympathetic historians. See, for example, Gerald A. McCool, *Nineteenth-Century Scholasticism: The Search for a Unitary Method* (New York: Fordham University Press, 1989), 27–30.

31. There is no adequate history of Scholasticism after Trent, though many scholars have wished for one. Partial and preliminary surveys of some of the hundreds of figures and texts to be treated by such a history can be had in Leonard A. Kennedy, *A Catalogue of Thomists, 1270–1900* (Houston: Center for Thomistic Studies, University of St. Thomas, 1987), and Walter B. Redmond, *Bibliography of the Philosophy in the Iberian Colonies of America* (The Hague: M. Nijhoff, 1972).

32. See Daniel-Antonin Mortier, *Histoire des maîtres généraux de L'Ordre de prêcheurs* (Paris: Picara, 1903–1920) 7:392–393.

33. Martin Grabmann, "Heinrich Denifle O.P. und Kardinal Franz Ehrle S.J.," *Philosophisches Jahrbuch* 56 (1946): 9–26, at pp. 9–10.

34. Ibid., 16–17.

35. Augustine A. Bogdanski, *The Significance of Clemens Baeumker in Neo-Scholastic Philosophy* (Milwaukee: Marquette University Press, 1942), 38–40. Note also Baeumker's encounter with Tennemann's *Grundriss* (p. 41). Baeumker himself contributed some autobiographical remarks to Raymond Schmidt, *Die deutsche Philosophie der Gegenwart in Selbstdarstellungen* (Leipzig: Felix Meiner, 1921) 2:25–56.

36. For a summary recollection of the historical project at Le Saulchoir before 1920, see M.-D. Chenu, "Regard sur cinquante ans de vie religieuse," in *L'hommage différé au Père Chenu* (Paris: du Cerf, 1990), 259–268, at pp. 261–263. The more famous memoir is obviously Chenu's "Une école de théologie, le Saulchoir" (1937), reprinted in Giuseppe Alberigo et al., *Une école de théologie, le Saulchoir* (Paris: du Cerf, 1985).

37. From her review of Richard Gilman's *Faith, Sex, and Mystery*, in *New York Times Book Review*, January 18, 1987, p. 27.

38. Karl Barth, *Fides quaerens intellectum: Anselms Beweis der Existenz Gottes in Zusammenhang seines theologischen Programms*, 2d ed. (Zollikon: Evangelischer Verlag, 1958), 10.

39. See Benjamin's "On the Program of the Coming Philosophy" and Bernd Witte, *Walter Benjamin: An Intellectual Biography* (Detroit: Wayne State University Press, 1991), 42–43.

The Future of the Study
of Medieval Christianity

E. Ann Matter

It WILL NOT BE DIFFICULT for any of us to recognize that the past two decades have brought about big changes in the way scholars interpret the Middle Ages. Periodization gives us some obvious examples: we now tend to think of medieval Christianity as bounded by the Late Antique world and the Early Modern period, rather than by the Roman Empire and the Reformation. This is not simply a shift in terminology—it represents an important conceptual change from categories of periodization based on political and institutional history to a view of historical periods as gradually developing cultural self-definitions. And, although the Dark Ages die hard (a student once complained because I did not tell him exactly where they are), at least we do not get too many books about them (wherever they are) anymore. Instead, we have fine studies of neglected topics in early medieval history, such as Barbara Kreutz's *Before the Normans* and John Cavadini's *The Last Christology of the West* on the Spanish Adoptionist controversy.[1]

There has also been a change of consciousness taking place in scholarship about the Christian tradition. Although complete objectivity about one's assumptions is difficult, if not impossible, late twentieth-century scholars struggle to take account of their own intellectual, religious, and political biases. The result has been the framing of new questions about ignored (or scorned) topics: the Gnostics, the Anabaptists, early scholasticism, Carolingian theology, medieval biblical exegesis.

Contemporary medievalists are also very flexible, combining technical expertise with far-ranging and theoretical concerns.

There is, for example, quite a thriving industry these days in Carolingian studies, but it does not necessarily require permanent residence in the ninth century. Indeed, many of us move comfortably between chronological periods and conceptual problems. Perhaps it has always been the case that medievalists developed multiple skills in order to deal, even at the introductory level, with such an enormous chronological span. After all, none of us can afford to know and teach about only one century. But I think that our generation has developed a sort of multiple competence, that is, many medievalists actually *specialize* in more than one figure or area. Often this is because a scholar is chasing an idea or a symbolic complex of images through many centuries, as in recent work on heresy, apocalypticism, and mysticism.[2] As one moves from period to period, especially in the process of becoming acquainted with the languages, sources, and secondary literature of different periods and regions, one can gain new insight into the assumptions and difficulties of a completely different area of research. Nothing made me more aware of the fragility of fragmentary manuscript evidence, the sort of problem Carolingianists deal with often, than working my way through a (relatively modest) collection of archival material from seventeenth-century Pavia. At the end of each day, as I dug myself out from under a pile of documents, I would wonder what kinds of records had originally been kept in a Carolingian monastery, and where the fragmentary texts I had studied might have fit in the whole. I experienced this new type of research as a cross-fertilization. I have had delightful conversations about this experience, often at a historiographical, or even a theoretical level, with colleagues who work in widely varying disciplines and time periods. This experience has helped me to take seriously the challenge to understand my own theoretical assumptions, as well as those of the objects of my study.

Connections between medievalists, especially through conferences, especially the annual Congress of the Institute for Medieval Studies of Western Michigan University, have further encouraged this cross-fertilization by exchanging information, ideas, and approaches at a heretofore unprecedented rate. The explosion in information technology has brought us into contact through electronic bulletin boards, even as it has made it possible to gain easier access to and better manipulate our sources. Just the fact of having large parts of the *Corpus Christianorum* series, or soon the *Patrologia Latina* on CD-ROM is a luxury that would have been unimaginable twenty years ago.[3] One prognosis of the future that I can offer with very little trouble is that the concept of the appropriate technology of medieval studies will change radically; our innovative luxuries (such as data bases of medieval text series) will seem like basic necessities, as basic as we now find the xerox machine that was such a jealously guarded luxury when I was an undergraduate.

It would be interesting to reflect theoretically on the differences in intellectual creativity that these changes will create, both beneficial and problematic. It is important at least to note that the ability to retrieve vast amounts of information quickly does not ensure sophisticated analysis of that material. But I have offered these thoughts as examples of how twentieth-century scholarship in general has changed and is changing and will now concentrate on specific instances of how this situation has influenced the history of Christianity. If it is true that contemporary medievalists are interested in unexplored territory, are multi-disciplinary, technologically sophisticated, and theoretically self-aware, what impact has this had on the way the Christian Middle Ages are understood and taught?

As a means of approaching this question, I would like to look at three multi-volume enterprises in Christian history that stand as emblems of the conception of the field. One of these, Adolf von Harnack's *History of Dogma,* is a monument of German scholarship from the turn of the twentieth century, while the other two, Jaroslav Pelikan's *The Christian Tradition* and Bernard McGinn's *The Presence of God: A History of Western Christian Mysticism,* represent the perspectives of American scholars in the last quarter of this century; in fact, McGinn's project is still underway.[4] In spite of the obvious (and great) differences between these series, they are all three alike in the fact that they treat vast chronological sweeps of time (from the first to the twentieth centuries of the Common Era) in a synthetic way, with a specific aspect of Christianity in mind. It is in the approach, in the view of Christianity that inspires each series of books, that I see evidence of the great changes that have taken place in the study of Christianity over the past century.

Harnack wrote a history of dogmatic teachings of the institutional church from the first to the sixteenth century. His interpretation of Christian dogma, the officially proclaimed beliefs of the Christian community as mediated by the ecclesiastical hierarchy, was overtly informed by his Lutheran background. His tolerance for traditions and structures he found corrupt or decadent was slight.[5] Pelikan's work is a history of Christian *doctrine*, of what the church believes, confesses, and teaches in every age. Pelikan quotes a phrase of the fifth-century monk Vincent of Lérins: "ubique, semper, ab omnibus," that is, what is believed everywhere, always, and by all, as a guide to what a historian might consider "the church" in each historical context.[6] McGinn has by far the widest and most comprehensive view of Christianity. Even though his subject matter might seem at first glance the most restricted of the three, his approach to the Christian tradition takes into account whole continents of experience and discourse the other two books do not find interesting: affective spirituality, liturgical theology, women's experience. Of the three authors, McGinn is most likely to take seriously the beliefs of Christian thinkers outside the official realm of orthodoxy.

These changes are not just the result of the personal preferences of three great scholars, but reflect a shift of focus in the study of Christianity. This shift of focus came about partly because of the broad changes I have already discussed: a loosening of sectarian demands on scholarship (both Pelikan and McGinn attempt evenhandedness in their treatment of varieties of Christian expression), a cross-disciplinary focus, and the accessibility of new texts in new, technologically advanced forms, which make the study of the Christian tradition much easier. But I also think these changes, especially the changes reflected in McGinn's project, are the result of some more specific trends in twentieth-century scholarship about medieval Christianity. I would like to consider several of these new historical enterprises.

The first example has to do with the history of Christian women, an area in which I have witnessed a revolution. When I was an undergraduate, there was very little interest in women's history, even very little concept of medieval women as a subject of investigation. One excuse given for this situation was that there was so little evidence available. Certainly, women's voices were muted: the original sources were badly edited (if at all), English translations were woefully inadequate, both technically and conceptually. Although it could be argued that this was the case with most medieval texts in the 1960s, and is, lamentably, still the case with too many, the difficulty of finding good critical editions of works by even very important literate women (Hildegard of Bingen, Gertrude the Great) is compounded by the number of other textual problems. Many works, for example, were conceived by medieval women thinkers, but mediated into print by others, male and female (the writings of Elisabeth of Schönau, Mechtilde of Hackeborn, Angela of Foligno, Catherine of Siena, Margery Kempe). In the early 1970s, there was hardly anything to get one started. Perhaps in consequence, secondary scholarship, with a few notable exceptions such as the works of Lina Eckstein, Mary Jeremy Finnegan, Herbert Grundmann, and Eileen Powers, limited itself to stereotypes about women's roles.[7]

Obviously, part of the etiology of this situation is the assumption that women's voices and experiences were not as important as men's. It was, after all, men who attended the medieval universities, who fought the Crusades, who were the authors of medieval theology and literature. This seems especially true if the definition of medieval theology and literature is limited to the works that shaped the official world of the medieval hierarchy, a male construction. The reconstruction of women's roles in the medieval church, begun under the influence of feminist historiography, had led to an understanding of women's contribution to the discourse of medieval Christianity. Several scholars have contributed to this enterprise: Caroline Bynum, Penelope Johnson, Jo Ann McNamara, Susan Stuard, Suzanne Wemple.[8] The research of these and many others has allowed us to paint a new picture of medieval Christianity, a picture that is not fixated on the official acts of the hierarchical elite, but makes a more honest attempt to consider the religious experience of the wider Christian community. This new perspective on Christian history helps us to see some traditional elements of piety, for example, the passion of Christ, in a new light. Bynum explains the fact that women were leaders in the medieval spirituality of the *imitatio Christi*, and especially that women predominated among stigmatists, with a complex analysis of the role and symbolism of the female body in medieval religious practice. When Bynum says "women mystics often simply became the flesh of Christ, because their flesh could do what his could do: bleed, feed, die and give life to others,"[9] she gives evidence of a dramatic shift in the foreground and background of medieval Christianity. We find ourselves in a new landscape.

And when we look closely at the new landscape, we see a number of medieval *men* who were also insufficiently accounted for, or interpreted only as deviants from the consensus. The last two decades have witnessed a revival of intellectual interest in Christian spiritual traditions, orthodox and heterodox, elite and popular. The Paulist Press series *Classics of Western Spirituality* began in 1978 with the writings of Julian of Norwich and continues to produce several volumes a year.[10] Because so much of our evidence for women in medieval Christian culture fits into this broad definition of spirituality, the two movements of historical rediscovery have strengthened and complemented one another. Mystics, prophets, and spiritual leaders, male and female, are now a part of the portrait of medieval Christianity, even part of the portrait of the medieval Church. We now have the resources, both primary and secondary, for a whole new story about medieval Christianity. To borrow a term from Hans Robert Jauss, we are creating a new "horizon of expectations."[11] Because of this new horizon of expectations Bernard McGinn can visualize a comprehensive treatment of Western mysticism, in contrast to the specifically Christian, systematic, and theological focus of Evelyn Underhill's classic study of mysticism.[12]

A wider perception of the traditions of medieval spirituality has helped us to conceive a broader understanding of medieval theology. This is particularly clear in work that is currently underway: Eileen Kearney, for example, argues that Peter Abelard's letters of spiritual counsel to Heloise are as much his theology as the *Sic et Non;* and the work of Marcia Colish is showing us Peter Lombard as more than just formal innovation. As we begin to understand the internal coherence and intellectual context of the Lombard's thought, perhaps the use of the *Sentences* as a school text up to the sixteenth century will seem less of a curiosity. Then, perhaps, we will see that the curiosity has been the idea that scholars from Albert the Great to Calvin gained the degree of *magister* by writing a commentary on a text which had no philosophical or theological merit.[13]

As a final example, consider the changing conception of biblical exegesis as a part of medieval theology. The point has been made clearly enough that when Beryl Smalley began work on what became *The Study of the Bible in the Middle Ages,* she received little encouragement.[14] Smalley herself even ended her career writing about preachers and historians, rather than the monastic and canonical exegetes that were the subject of her first book. And, in retrospect, even Smalley's conception of the study of the Bible in the Middle Ages seems limited to the search for the literal sense at the School (rather than the Abbey) of Saint-Victor in Paris. Yet Smalley has left a legacy which, combined with the greater freedom in the posing of questions enjoyed by medievalists of the 1980s and 1990s, has inspired scholarship in several fields of study: history (Margaret Gibson), literature (Ann Astell), religion (Grover Zinn, myself).[15] Finally, some of the important treatises have been edited, and we can work with critical texts of the exegesis of Rupert of Deutz, Bernard of Clairvaux, and Andrew of Saint-Victor.[16] But we still have no critical editions of the exegesis of Honorius Augustodunensis (Honorius of Regensburg), Haimo or Remigius of Auxerre, or Hrabanus Maurus.

Burton Van Name Edwards has been editing the exegesis of the School of Auxerre for the *Corpus Christianorum* series,[17] but the biblical interpretations of Hrabanus Maurus are still rather *terra incognita,* a land not even deemed worthy of exploration. Of course, Hrabanus wove his interpretations together from the exegesis of his predecessors, but in doing so, he made a synthesis that was both all his own and enthusiastically received. Both the sources and the transmission of Hrabanus's exegesis are mines of information about the theological concerns of medieval and early modern Christianity. What other explanation can we give to the prominent position of these treatises in Suger's library at Saint-Denis, or to the fact that they were in print by the mid-sixteenth century?

But the most influential and, lamentably, the least understood realm of medieval exegesis is the *Glossa ordinaria.* This standardized running gloss to the Bible was one of Beryl Smalley's interests and has been studied by several other scholars, including Christopher De Hamel.[18] We have made some progress in our understanding of the *Glossa:* Smalley complained that "the myth of Walafrid Strabo's authorship dies hard, since it is preserved in bibliographies and library catalogues"[19] but it has finally died, even in dictionaries and encyclopedias. We know that the *Glossa* was not written all at once, that it treats different books of the Bible very differently, and that it took shape, or at least parts of it did, between Paris and Laon in the early twelfth century.

Scholarship on the *Glossa ordinaria* has headed almost exclusively in one direction. The tendency has been to think of the *Glossa* as a school text, and consequently look to thirteenth-century Paris for its classical form. But little has been understood of the form that circulated widely in schools of monks and canons which did not become part of the university movement. We know that the *Glossa ordinaria* was copied and read throughout France, Southern Germany, Austria, and parts of Spain and Italy, and yet most of the scholarship on the *Glossa* has focused on Paris. A joint effort by John Cavadini, Karlfried Froehlich, Mark Zier, and myself is taking a broader view of this problem. We are studying the structure, sources, and proliferation of the *Glossa ordinaria,* focusing on the *Glossa* in its earliest distinguishable stage. Of course, as a widely used schoolbook, the *Glossa ordinaria* underwent a process of change, especially notable in the manuscripts from the university world in Paris. We understand that many scholars are most interested in the later, scholastic, form of the *Glossa ordinaria;* by concentrating on the earliest stage, we hope to provide important background that studies of the later *Glossa* would need to orient and define their own textual limits.

As a first step, Gibson and Froehlich have made available a facsimile edition of the earliest printed version of the *Glossa*, the version printed by Adolph Rusch of Strassburg in 1480/81, the printed version of the *Glossa* closest to the mid-twelfth–century coalescence of the text.[20] Our ultimate goal is to produce a morphology of the gloss given to each biblical text, and to compile a hand-list of manuscripts of the *Glossa ordinaria* to each book of the Bible. And we plan to make this information available in computerized form as well as hard copy, in a database which can be searched for many different fields: book of the Bible, date, country, monastic order or canonical congregation, and so on. This material will give us, for the first time, information about the sources and structure of each book of the *Glossa.* It will help us determine how the work developed as a whole, to the point that it could be printed as a complete commentary on the whole Bible. And, the thing that intrigues me the most, it will show us who read it. These will be crucial resources for the long-overdue production of critical editions of individual books of the *Glossa ordinaria*. Because of the conception of the *Glossa* as an important object of study and the technological resources needed to create the database, this project could not even have been conceived twenty years ago.

What is the future of the study of Christian history? It is an exciting prospect, but faces some notable challenges. Future students of medieval Christianity will be much broader in their focus, both chronologically and conceptually; they will be less dogmatic and more open to trends and influences from different levels of society and different religious traditions, including (although I have not spoken of them here) Judaism and Islam; expanded technological resources will enable them to manipulate texts with a speed and sophistication we can scarcely imagine. At least, this is a vision of what the study of medieval Christianity can become if we can preserve an academic context which is open to innovation, and if we can secure resources needed to incorporate new technology. These are the goals for which we need to work within our own institutions, particularly facing down the raging tide of debate about what is "politically correct." The examples of new medieval scholarship I have given, for example, could be attacked by either side of the "p.c. debate": as both breaking prized preconceptions and as dwelling on the irrelevant. We should take care not to let this debate impede us from the things we think, from our position *in medias res,* most important.

We will have to fight for our part of the resources of the future academic world, but we should not base our fight on orthodoxy or antiquarianism. We have a good deal more to offer. Medievalists have not been known as the most innovative group of scholars, and the study of religion has always had to assert itself against sectarian preferences and definitions. Nevertheless, scholars of medieval Christianity are taking up ambitious, far-reaching research projects which will continue the notable shifts in our historical "horizon of expectation." This is neither paradox nor happenstance.

NOTES

1. Barbara Kreutz, *Before the Normans: Southern Italy in the Ninth and Tenth Centuries* (Philadelphia: University of Pennsylvania Press, 1991);

John C. Cavadini, *The Last Christology of the West: Adoptionism in Spain and Gaul* (Philadelphia: University of Pennsylvania Press, 1993).

2. For example, Robert E. Lerner, *The Age of Adversity, The Fourteenth Century* (New York: Cornell University Press, 1968), *The Heresy of the Free Spirit in the Later Middle Ages* (Berkeley: University of California Press, 1972; rpt. Notre Dame, Ind.: University of Notre Dame Press); *The Powers of Prophecy: The Cedar of Lebanon Vision from the Mongol Onslaught to the Dawn of the Enlightenment* (Berkeley: University of California Press, 1983); *Weissagugen Über die Päpste: Vat. Ross. 374 enstanden um 1500* (Zürich: Belser Verlag, 1985). Bernard McGinn. *Visions of the End: Apocalyptic Traditions in the Middle Ages* (New York: Columbia University Press, 1979); editor and translator. *Apocalyptic Spirituality* (New York: Paulist Press, 1979); *The Calabrian Abbot: Joachim of Fiore in the History of Western Thought* (New York: Macmillan, 1985); editor, with John Meyendorff, in collaboration with Jean Leclercq, *Christian Spirituality: Origins to the Twelfth Century* (New York: Crossroads, 1985); *The Foundations of Western Mysticism: Origins to the Fifth Century*, vol. 1 of *The Presence of God: A History of Western Christian Mysticism* (Chicago: University of Chicago Press, 1991).

3. *Cetedoc Library of Christian Latin Texts on CD-ROM* (Turnhout: Brepols, 1991–), *The Patrologia Latina Database* (Alexander, Va.: Chadwyck-Healey, 1992–). Both projects are available at least in preliminary form, and will be revised, updated, and completed in the next few years.

4. Adolph von Harnack, *History of Dogma,* 7 vols. (1885, translated from the third German edition of 1893 by Neil Buchanan, 1894, reprinted New York: Dover, 1961) "First Part: Introductory Division, Book I: The Preparation, Book II: The Laying of the Foundations," "Second Part: The Development of Ecclesiastical Dogma, Book I: A History of the Development of Dogma as the Doctrine of the God-Man on the Basis of Natural Theology, Book II: Expansion and Remodelling of Dogma into a Doctrine of Sin, Grace, and Means of Grace on the Basis of the Church. Book III: The Threefold Issue of the History of Dogma." Jaroslav J. Pelikan, *The Christian Tradition* (Chicago: University of Chicago Press); vol. 1 *The Emergence of the Catholic Tradition (100–600)* (1971), vol. 2 *The Spirit of Eastern Christendom (600–1700)* (1974), vol. 3 *The Growth of Medieval Theology (600–1300)* (1978), vol. 4 *Reformation of Church and Dogma (1300–1700)* (1984), vol. 5 *Christian Doctrine and Modern Culture (since 1700)* (1989). Bernard McGinn, *The Presence of God: A History of Western Christian Mysticism:* vol. 1, *The Foundations of Western Mysticism* (New York: Crossroad, 1991), vol. 2, *The Development of Western Mysticism,* vol. 3, *The Flowering of Western Mysticism,* vol. 4, *The Crisis of Western Mysticism,* all forthcoming from Crossroad.

176 *E. Ann Matter*

5. For example, see Harnack's treatment of medieval mysticism in his chapter "The History of Piety," Second Part, Book II, vol. VI, pp. 97f.

6. Vincent of Lérins, *Commonitory* 2.3, Pelikan, vol. 1, p. 333, and *passim.*

7. Lina Eckenstein, *Woman under Monasticism* (Cambridge: Cambridge University Press, 1896). Mary Jeremy Finnegan, O.P., *Scholars and Mystics* (Chicago: Regnery, 1962), reprinted in a new edition as *The Women of Helfta: Scholars and Mystics* (Athens, Ga.: University of Georgia Press, 1991). Herbert Grundmann, *Religiöse Bewegungen im Mittelalter: Untersuchungen über die geschichtlichen Zusammenhänge zwischen der Ketzerei, den Bettelorden, und der religiösen Frauenbewegung in 12. und 13. Jahrhundert* (1935; reprint, with additions, Hildesheim: Olms, 1961). Eileen Power, *Medieval English Nunneries c. 1275 to 1535* (Cambridge: Cambridge University Press, 1922); *Medieval Women,* posthumously edited by M. M. Postan (Cambridge: Cambridge University Press, 1975).

8. Caroline Walker Bynum, *Jesus as Mother: Studies in the Spirituality of the High Middle Ages* (Berkeley: University of California Press, 1982); *Holy Feast and Holy Fast: The Religious Significance of Food to Medieval Women* (Berkeley: University of California Press, 1987); *Fragmentation and Redemption: Essays on Gender and the Human Body in Medieval Religion* (New York: Zone Books, 1991). Jo Ann McNamara, *A New Song: Celibate Women in the First Three Christian Centuries* (New York: Haworth Press, 1983); co-editor with Barbara J. Harris, *Women and the Structure of Society: Selected Research From the Fifth Berkshire Conference* (Durham, N.C.: Duke University Press, 1984); editor and translator, with John E. Halborg and E. Gordon Whatley, *Sainted Women of the Dark Ages* (Durham, N.C.: Duke University Press, 1992). Penelope D. Johnson, *Equal in Monastic Profession: Religious Women in Medieval France* (Chicago: University of Chicago Press, 1991); Susan Mosher Stuard, editor, *Women in Medieval Society* (Philadelphia: University of Pennsylvania Press, 1976); editor, *Women in Medieval History and Historiography* (Philadelphia: University of Pennsylvania Press, 1987). Suzanne Fonay Wemple, *Women in Frankish Society: Marriage and the Cloister 500 to 900* (Philadelphia: University of Pennsylvania Press, 1985).

9. Caroline Walker Bynum, "The Female Body and Religious Practice in the Later Middle Ages," in *Fragmentation and Redemption,* 222.

10. Julian of Norwich, *Showings* (New York: Paulist Press, 1978).

11. Hans Robert Jauss, *Toward an Aesthetic of Reception,* trans. Timothy Bahti (Minneapolis: University of Minnesota Press, 1982) xii and *passim.*

12. Evelyn Underhill, *Mysticism* (1910, 12th ed., 1930, reprint New York: Image Doubleday, 1990).

13. The *Sentences* of Peter Lombard are finally being considered as serious and influential theology thanks to the work of Marcia L. Colish. See her article in this volume.

14. Beryl Smalley, *The Study of the Bible in the Middle Ages* (Oxford: Basil Blackwell, 1952; Notre Dame, Ind.: University of Notre Dame Press, 1964/1978; 3rd ed. revised Oxford, 1983). For the reception of Smalley's book, see R. W. Southern, "Beryl Smalley and the Place of the Bible in Medieval Studies, 1927–84," in *The Bible in the Medieval World: Essays in Memory of Beryl Smalley*, ed. Katherine Walsh and Diana Wood (Oxford: Basil Blackwell, 1985), 1–16.

15. Margaret T. Gibson, *Lanfranc of Bec* (Oxford: Clarendon Press, 1978). Ann Astell, *The Song of Songs in the Middle Ages* (Ithaca: Cornell University Press, 1990).Grover A. Zinn, editor and translator, *Richard of Saint-Victor, The Twelve Patriarchs, The Mystical Ark, Book Three of the Trinity* (New York: Paulist Press, 1979). E. Ann Matter, *The Voice of My Beloved: The Song of Songs in Western Medieval Christianity* (Philadelphia: University of Pennsylvania Press, 1990).

16. Rupert of Deutz, *Liber de divinis officiis*, CCCM 7 (1967); *Commentaria in evangelium S. Johannis*, CCCM 9 (1969); *De sancta trinitate et operibus eius*, CCCM 21–22–23–24 (1971–72); *Commentaria in canticum canticorum*, CCCM 26 (1974); *De gloria et honore filii hominis, super Matheum*, CCCM 29 (1979), all edited by R. Haacke. Bernard of Clairvaux, *Sancti Bernardi opera*, ed. J. Leclercq, C. H. Talbot, H. M. Rochais (Rome: Editiones Cistercienses, 1957–). Andrew of Saint-Victor, *Expositio super heptateuchum*, ed. C. Lohr, R. Berndt, CCCM 53 (1986), *Expositio super Danielem*, ed. M. Zier, CCCM 53F (1990), *Expositiones historicae in Libros Salomonis*, ed. R. Berndt, CCCM 53B (1991), *Expositio in Ezechielem*, ed. M. A. Signer, CCCM 53E (1991).

17. The unpublished commentary on Genesis of Remigius of Auxerre edited by Edwards is forthcoming in the CCCM, another Genesis commentary published in the PL under the name of Remigius is in the final stages of preparation. Edwards is now beginning a critical edition of the influential commentary on the Song of Songs by Haimo of Auxerre.

18. C. F. R. De Hamel, *Glossed Books of the Bible and the Origins of the Paris Booktrade* (Suffolk: D. S. Brewer, 1984).

19. Smalley, *The Study of the Bible*, 57.

20. *Biblia Latina Cum Glossa Ordinaria: Facsimile Reprint of the Editio Princeps Adolph Rusch of Strassburg 1480/81,* ed. Karlfried Froehlich and Margaret Gibson (Turnhout: Brepols, 1992), see especially the preface, v–xxvi.

On Dispelling the Malaise in Scholastic Theology

Joseph Wawrykow

THE RECENT CONFERENCE on the Past and Future of Medieval Studies offered further evidence of the precarious standing of the scholarly study of scholastic theology. The Conference covered much, probing the prospects of a whole range of the disciplines that are contained under the heading "Medieval Studies." The study of scholastic theology, however, was conspicuous by its absence. No session, not even a paper, contemplated the future shape that the study of the scholastic theologies of the Middle Ages might take, a point that was noted by Mark Jordan with regret in his presentation on medieval philosophy. The sense of exclusion was magnified by the comments in passing of another speaker, who in fact reported scholastic theology "dead," offering this comment as a salutary warning to those who might become complaisant about their own disciplines. That declaration is overstated, but perfectly understandable. "Vigorous," "thriving," "engaging," are hardly the terms that spring to mind as I contemplate my discipline; it is easy to see how the casual observer might miss the occasional spasms of scholarly activity. By almost any standard that might be used to gauge the vitality of a discipline—the number of its practitioners, the venues and quantities of publication—scholastic theology is found wanting. The entire discipline seems sunk in a deep and extended lethargy, and the ambitious would probably be well advised to seek their careers elsewhere.

Some may wish to dispute this dreary characterization, or at least may be puzzled by it. Are things really this dismal? The temptation to ascribe a greater health to the study of scholastic theology may be especially strong at a university such as Notre Dame, graced as it is by numerous specialists in medieval philosophy. We are prone to lump "philosophy" and "theology" together—we do this in our graduate curriculum; the Institute even sponsors a journal that links the two. And, the close connection is warranted by medieval practice: the "scholastic" studied by the historian of philosophy and by the historian of theology is often one and the same; among the skills acquired by the scholastic theologian are those which we would term "philosophical."[1] Yet, the distinction that informs Jordan's comment at the Conference still holds good. While closely related, the two disciplines are not identical, and their differences should be respected. Without denying areas of overlap, the student of scholastic theology is likely to be interested in different topics, and success in handling these topics presupposes a different training—in the history of reflections on the central issues of Christian faith, certainly, but more generally in the history of Christianity as well.[2] Accordingly, the vigor of the one discipline should not be attributed to the other. The vitality of medieval philosophy— exhibited not least in the host of genuine disagreements among its students about goals and methods—remains but an aspiration for its theological counterpart.

The profile of scholastic theology remains imperfectly sketched, however, when viewed solely in relation to medieval philosophy. We shall go a long way towards giving greater definition to this discipline by locating scholastic theology in two additional settings; in doing so, the principal sources of its malaise will come to the fore. The first setting is fairly obvious. Few could doubt that the massive shifts in Catholic theology in the aftermath of the Second Vatican Council have had profound implications for work in scholastic theology. The years after the Council saw the rise of a multiplicity of theologies, many of which challenged the neo-scholastic successors of the medievals for their supposed insularity and inwardness and preoccupation with the arcane.[3] Similarly, the religious orders most inclined before the Council to preserve the medieval scholastic flame have more recently themselves fallen into hard times. Many of the developments in contemporary Catholic theology are in fact personally appealing: I am not inclined to bemoan an increased prominence for the laity in theological work, and certainly welcome the greater sensitivity to the dispossessed and the powerless evident in some of these newer theological forms. Yet, another feature of recent Catholic theology *is* distressing and speaks directly to our present topic. Not only was the neo-scholasticism that ruled before the Council discredited and rejected; practitioners of the new theologies in many cases became hardened to the possibilities of the past, finding it difficult, if not impossible, to distinguish the neo-scholastics from the great medieval theologians. The first, exuberant reaction against scholastic theology in its neo-scholastic guise was undoubtedly necessary, not only to create a space for the new theological explorations but, in some cases at least, to exorcise the demons of the seminary past. But the resulting caricature of the Middle Ages and of medieval thought that still finds currency in some important Catholic theological circles has by now become tiresome. Even a cursory sampling of recent theological offerings finds confident, if poorly supported, assertions of the lack of imagination and creativity in medieval theological writing, of the divorce between theological work and religious experience, of the decentering of Christ and the concomitant deficient renderings of God and of the human person, of the over-fondness among the medievals for natural theology at the expense of genuine Christian concerns, of the excessively legalistic, juridical cast of scholastic versions of divine-human relations.[4] Nurtured in an environment of such hostility and incomprehension, it is little wonder that a new generation of theologians has been in no great hurry to embrace scholastic theology.

Prevailing trends in the "history of Christianity" have similarly dampened enthusiasm for scholastic theology. The "history of Christianity" is multi-faceted, a region of scholarly discourse that is broad in its ambitions. In terms of time, it runs from the close of the New Testament period through to the present; it also embraces both a wide variety of materials—liturgical, institutional, spiritual, intellectual, even artistic—and an impressive array of methodological approaches, as is proper given the breadth of its materials. In principle, no single kind of subject matter should predominate, *or* be excluded; the complexity of even religious existence would seem to demand complementarity in subject matter and approach in the study of a given period. Unfortunately, actual practice falls short of this expectation. In a word, historians of medieval Christianity have tended to neglect thought and the cognitive, and often look askance at those who are still preoccupied by intellectual history and, especially, the history of theology (including scholastic theology).[5] Indeed, this lack of interest cuts across the board. Not only have scholastic theologians been moved safely to the margins; scholars who specialize in the spiritual writings which have enjoyed great prominence in recent research would themselves seem to delight in ignoring the apparent dogmatic content of these favored medieval authors. This blindness to their theological literacy and technical sophistication, I would add, has undoubtedly impoverished our understanding of these spiritual authors, both female and male.

Yet, the marginalization of medieval thinkers and of the conceptual dimensions of medieval Christianity need not be final. The inattentiveness to intellectual matters plaguing historians of medieval Christianity is not theoretically grounded, as if due to some reasoned and well-articulated theory of religion that would justify or necessitate the rejection of thinking and thought in the consideration of medieval Christianity. Rather, it seems to have emerged from a vague sense that in contrast to the cognitive, the affective can somehow be more readily and reliably apprehended across time— an offshoot, no doubt, of the thoroughly modern notion that feeling is more authentic and transparent than thought. Already there are indications of discomfort with this assumption, and of an enhanced awareness of the need to be more attentive to the connections between belief and practice. As one example, I would cite the recent work of Miri Rubin;[6] Rubin has found it impossible to consider the medieval feast of Corpus Christi without at the same time exploring its intellectual underpinnings, including scholastic reflections on the eucharist. Rubin's work offers considerable solace and inspiration, arguably presaging the more secure integration of scholastic theology into modern renderings of the Middle Ages.

Other signs of hope dot the landscape; together, they lead me to believe that the future of the study of scholastic theology, while not brilliant, may be considerably brighter. While undoubtedly few in number, people continue to be attracted to the discipline, and their work shows not only courage but considerable variety, from the editing of hitherto obscured authors to fresh appraisals of issues of theological style and content.[7] Indeed, recent decades (the darkest years) have even seen marked advances in our understanding of

late medieval scholastic theology, due especially to the work of
Heiko Oberman and his disciples. Similarly, Roman Catholic theologians never completely abandoned the Middle Ages. Even after
the Council, a solid corps of important Catholic theologians, both
in America and abroad, continued to learn from the medievals, often incorporating the legitimate concerns and insights of the new
styles of theologizing into their reappropriation of the medieval
past.[8] And, there is growing recognition in Catholic circles that the
flight from the past that has characterized some recent theologies
may have been too precipitous. At the Catholic Theological Society
of America, the principal association of Catholic theologians in this
country, the repeated call in recent years for renewed attention to
the Catholic past has resulted in the inauguration last year of work-
shops in patristic and medieval theology, to be held annually.[9] Finally, it is with special interest that I note the emergence into
prominence on the American scene of the "Yale school," ecumen-
ically minded, mostly Protestant theologians with varying degrees
of affiliation with one of the east-coast universities. The work of
such thinkers as Kathryn Tanner offers eloquent testimony to the
continued creative possibilities of scholastic theology.[10] In fact, before the openly avowed debt of the "Yale theologians" to the great
scholastics, it is tempting to extend one of Weisheipl's predictions:
the coming renewal not only of Thomas-studies but of scholastic
theology in general may occur at the *secular* university.[11]

But, while confident that it does have a future, it is by no
means immediately evident what form the study of scholastic theology should take. To suggest how its changing circumstances
might best be met in working out of the malaise, I would thus like
to conclude by indicating three areas of research that might prove
especially promising, drawing both on my own research agenda
and the work of the more progressive scholars in the field.[12] I am
aware, of course, that in the end, such lists are meaningful only in
the execution, not the enumeration, and so I will keep these suggestions tantalizingly brief.[13]

First, research must squarely address the daunting challenges
that confront modern readers of scholastic theology. Reading the
scholastics is no easy task, and readers can become bewildered before the different literary forms and strategies adopted by scholastic
authors. This puzzlement, I would think, is in no small measure re-

sponsible for a pronounced tendency to treat scholastic texts as if they were but simple repositories of discrete propositions, to focus merely on what might be called the "content" of these writings. This, however, is to miss much, to miss the skill with which the scholastics have constructed their works and shaped their analyses. Thus, in our orientations to scholastic theology, even greater attention must be given to the literary features of scholastic works—to the suitability of scholastic techniques to scholastic ambitions, for example; to their talent in appropriating, while transforming, earlier authorities; to the entire range of their literary production.[14] Included in the latter will be the concentrated effort, already well underway, to retrieve those scholastic genres that have suffered because of the preference of earlier generations for the *Summa* and the *Sentence*-collections as *the* scholastic forms. Here, in fact, research into scholastic theology dovetails neatly with one of the hot topics in the "history of Christianity," the uses and reception of the Bible. While this audience hardly needs reminding, thirty percent of the extant work of Thomas Aquinas, for example, is cast in the form of biblical commentary.[15]

Second, closer explorations of the connections between scholastic theology and religious context, broadly construed, would seem well in order. Naturally, scholars will continue to ask about the ways in which the liturgical, institutional, and social practices of the scholastics themselves have informed their theological work. But, there should also be more systematic investigations into the relations between scholastics and other circles of Christians. Despite the best efforts of scholars such as Boyle,[16] we still have the unfortunate tendency of keeping the different forms of Christian life in the Middle Ages firmly segregated.[17] It would be especially valuable, however, to consider more thoroughly the interactions of scholastics and the religious women studied by Bynum and others; I would suspect that these encounters were at least as formative for the scholastics as for their female interlocutors.

Finally, there is the related matter of consistency and authenticity.[18] It remains useful to characterize the project of high medieval scholastic theology in terms of "faith seeking understanding." Surely one prominent aspect of the "search" is the attempt to show the connections between the major Christian beliefs about God and Christ and world, to make patent how one belief presupposes and leads to others.[19] But, the search for understanding would seem to be more inclusive, extending to the relations between beliefs, on the one hand, and attitudes, proposals for action, and actions, on the other. In our reading of the scholastics, we will want to follow their reflections on Christian behavior. According to scholastic authors, how do specific Christian beliefs generate and provide warrant for particular attitudes and actions? Especially compelling here will be the difficult cases, where medieval Christians invoked crucial Christian beliefs to justify attitudes and actions that we find abhorrent.[20] This exploration will proceed on at least two levels. We will want to ask about the *inevitability* of such behavior, about the extent to which it is due to specifically Christian beliefs, at least in their medieval and scholastic forms. But, we will also inquire about scholastic *awareness* of the possible dissonance between such action and their most profound Christian convictions, gaining in this regard a more nuanced measure of the reflective capacities of these authors.

NOTES

1. See P. Glorieux, "L'enseignement au moyen âge. Techniques et méthodes en usage à la Faculté de Théologie de Paris au XIIIe siècle," *Archives d'histoire doctrinale et littéraire du moyen âge* 43 (1968): 65–186.

2. Without wanting to overstate the case, the differences between scholars of medieval "philosophy" and of "theology" may roughly correspond to the different formalities according to which a philosopher and a theologian in the Middle Ages proceeded. In the words of Aquinas, the master in sacred doctrine (the theologian) will consider in the light of revelation "God and all things in relation to God" (that is, as revealed in relation to their beginning and their end). See *Summa theologiae* I q. 1, a. 3 ad 1. The philosophical disciplines, which in Aquinas are autonomous, can be employed in the course of this consideration; see *ST* I q. 1, a. 5 ad 2 and a. 6 ad 2. The more recent rise of "philosophy of religion" would tend to blur the distinction.

3. By necessity, my text undoubtedly simplifies a much more complex situation, in which a variety of theologies, not all of which are aptly styled "neo-scholastic," flourished before the Council.

4. The summary in the text offers an idealized summary of commonly voiced criticisms of medieval theology and religion. For the sug-

gestion that medieval scholastics were insufficiently schooled in spiritual matters, see, for example, J. Giles Milhaven, "A Medieval Lesson on Bodily Knowing: Women's Experience and Men's Thought," *Journal of the American Academy of Religion* 57 (1989): 341–372. Concern about a possibly excessive "legalism" in medieval sacramental thought surfaces in B. Cooke, *The Distancing of God: The Ambiguity of Symbol in History and Theology* (Minneapolis: Fortress Press, 1990); see, e.g., 160, 164. In some cases, closer reflection on the negative judgments about the Middle Ages made in passing may, in fact, prove useful, stimulating consideration of how these charges might best be met. To John Thiel's random comments about a supposed deficiency among the medievals in imagination and creativity, comments that pepper his *Imagination and Authority: Theological Authorship in the Modern Tradition* (Minneapolis: Fortress Press, 1991), one might refer to the strategies of different medieval authors in constructing their works, as well as to their use of authorities; I return briefly to these matters below in the text, in the discussion of the need for greater attention to the literary and pedagogical features of scholastic work. A similar approach might be taken to Michael Buckley's suggestion, in *At the Origins of Modern Atheism* (New Haven: Yale University Press, 1987), 55, that the way that Thomas structured the *Summa theologiae,* placing Christ in the Third Part and so safely removed from the consideration of God in *ST* I, may have prepared for the rise of modern atheism. For a first rejoinder to Buckley, see N. Lash, "When Did the Theologians Lose Interest in Theology?" in *Theology and Dialogue: Essays in Conversation with George Lindbeck,* ed. Bruce D. Marshall (Notre Dame, Ind.: University of Notre Dame Press, 1990), 131–147.

5. In support of this contention, I would simply note that the History of Christianity section of the American Academy of Religion has not proved hospitable in recent years to medievalists whose primary interests lie in ideas and the conceptual dimensions of medieval Christianity.

6. Miri Rubin, *Corpus Christi: The Eucharist in Late Medieval Culture* (Cambridge: Cambridge University Press, 1991).

7. I consider issues of style and content below in the text. Our understanding of the latter part of the thirteenth century will without doubt be modified through the efforts of the team of scholars, coordinated by Raymond Macken, currently preparing the *Opera omnia* of Henry of Ghent (Leuven: University Press, 1979).

8. The ethical teaching of Thomas Aquinas has continued to fascinate Catholic moral theologians. For intriguing work in philosophical theology, see David B. Burrell, *Aquinas, God, and Action* (Notre Dame, Ind.: University of Notre Dame Press, 1979), and, *Knowing the Unknowable God: Ibn-Sina, Maimonides, Aquinas* (Notre Dame, Ind.: University of Notre

Dame Press, 1986). C.-J. Pinto de Oliveria, O.P., "Saint Thomas, le Concile et la théologie contemporaine," *Nova et Vetera* 56 (1981): 161–185, has attempted to bring Aquinas directly into dialogue with contemporary theologies.

9. See in this regard Walter H. Principe's 1991 Presidential Address, "Catholic Theology and the Retrieval of Its Intellectual Tradition: Problems and Possibilities," with responses by Mary Ann Donovan and Matthew L. Lamb, in the *Proceedings of the Forty-Sixth Annual Convention* of the Catholic Theological Society of America (Atlanta, June 12–15, 1991), vol. 46, pp. 75ff.

10. Tanner, schooled as well in contemporary philosophical and social scientific debates, has thus far published two books, each of which shows an attentive reading of Aquinas: *God and Creation in Christian Theology: Tyranny or Empowerment?* (New York: Blackwell, 1988), and *The Politics of God: Christian Theologies and Social Justice* (Minneapolis: Fortress Press, 1992). My debt to the latter will be apparent in the discussion below on the third area of future research in scholastic theology. *The Politics of God* was discussed at the Workshop in Medieval Theology at the 1993 convention of the Catholic Theological Society of America (San Antonio); my report on the Workshop will appear in the *Proceedings of the Forty-Eighth Annual Convention* (forthcoming). Formative of the "Yale School" is George Lindbeck's *The Nature of Doctrine: Religion and Theology in a Postliberal Age* (Philadelphia: Westminster Press, 1984). For a discussion of this book, see the symposium in *Thomist* 49 (1985), which includes articles by William C. Placher, Colman O'Neill, James J. Buckley, and David Tracy. For the subsequent claim about Lindbeck's dependence on Aquinas, see Bruce D. Marshall, "Aquinas as Postliberal Theologian," *Thomist* 53 (1989): 353–402, along with F. J. Crosson's "Reconsidering Aquinas as a Postliberal Theologian" and Marshall's rejoinder, "Thomas, Thomisms and Truth," in *Thomist* 56 (1992): 481–524. Crosson has returned to the matter in "Rejoinder to Bruce Marshall," *Thomist* 57 (1993): 299–303. Interestingly enough, it is among the theologians of the "Yale School" that the works of Burrell mentioned above in note 8, with their attentiveness to divine transcendence and the limitations and possibilities of language in speaking of God, have received perhaps their warmest reception.

11. The forecast of the reinvigorated interest in Thomas-studies at the secular university is made in James A. Weisheipl, *Friar Thomas d'Aquino: His Life, Thought and Works* (Washington, D.C.: Catholic University of America Press, 1983), x.

12. Older readers will recognize that the following areas of research were anticipated in significant ways by such great historians as M.-D.

Chenu and Y. Congar. Among the works of Chenu that might be noted here are: *La théologie au douzième siècle* (Paris: J. Vrin, 1957) and *Introduction à l'étude de saint Thomas d'Aquin* (Montreal: Institut d'études médiévales, 1974). For a handy collection of some of Congar's articles, see *Thomas d'Aquin: sa vision de théologie et de l'Eglise* (London: Variorum Reprints, 1984).

13. A fourth, more inclusive task might be appended. There is no single satisfactory introduction to the study of medieval scholastic theology that might orient newcomers to the different genres of scholastic literature and indicate the principal topics of research as well as possibly fruitful new directions. The outstanding introduction of A. M. Landgraf, *Introduction à l'histoire de la littérature théologique de la scholastique naissante* (Montreal: Institut d'études médiévales, 1973) would need to be extended to cover the later Middle Ages; the still useful *Introduction to Patristic and Medieval Theology* (Toronto: Pontifical Institute of Mediaeval Studies, 1982; 2nd edition) prepared by Walter H. Principe, circulates in samizdat form, and similarly would require updating to include the results of newer research on the late thirteenth century, as well as on the later Middle Ages. Fortunately, information on current research is readily available through such standard bibliographical guides as *Medioevo Latino* (Spoleto: Centro Italiano di Studi Sull'Alto Medioevo, 1979ff.) and *International Medieval Bibliography* (Leeds, 1967ff.).

14. See, for example, my forthcoming article, "Luther and the Spirituality of Thomas Aquinas," *Consensus* (1993), in which I enumerate the tasks that Thomas has pursued in the construction of the treatise on the eucharist in the *Summa theologiae* (III q. 73–83); the recent volume co-edited by Mark D. Jordan and Kent Emery, Jr., *Ad Litteram: Authoritative Texts and Their Medieval Readers* (Notre Dame, Ind.: University of Notre Dame Press, 1992); and, the comments in Jordan's "The Alleged Aristotelianism of Thomas Aquinas," Etienne Gilson Series 15 (Toronto: Pontifical Institute of Mediaeval Studies, 1992), 21ff. For an orientation to some scholastic genres, see *Les Genres littéraires dans les sources théologiques et philosophiques médiévales* (Louvain-La-Neuve: University Press, 1982).

15. The figure of thirty percent is suggested by R. G. Kennedy, "Thomas Aquinas and the Literal Sense of Scripture," Doctoral dissertation, University of Notre Dame, 1985, p. 3. The most ambitious examination of the various medieval uses of the Bible remains *Le Moyen Age et la Bible*, ed. P. Riché and Guy Lobrichon (Paris: Beauchesne, 1984).

16. See, for example, the articles by Leonard E. Boyle, "The Quodlibets of St. Thomas and Pastoral Care," and "The *Summa confessorum* of John of Freiburg and the Popularization of the Moral Teaching of St.

Thomas and Some of his Contemporaries," reprinted in his *Pastoral Care, Clerical Education and Canon Law, 1200–1400* (London: Variorum Reprints, 1981).

17. Recall in this regard that the same Dominican (Thomas of Cantimpré) who wrote *Lives* of Lutgard of Aywières and other women who figure prominently in recent research on thirteenth-century spirituality, also studied under Albert the Great. An interesting fourteenth-century conjunction is provided by the correspondence of Henry of Nördlingen and Margaret Ebner; especially intriguing is his recommendation to her in 1345 to purchase the *Summa theologiae,* entire, of Thomas Aquinas (cited in the Introduction by Margot Schmidt and Leonard P. Hindsley to *Margaret Ebner: Major Works,* translated and edited by Leonard P. Hindsley [New York: Paulist Press, 1993], p. 19). One medium of contact between mendicant scholastic writers and women religious in the high Middle Ages is the *fratres communes* charged with preaching and pastoral work. On the importance of some of these women for mendicants responsible for pastoral work, see John Coakley, "Friars as Confidants of Holy Women in Medieval Dominican Hagiography," in *Images of Sainthood in Medieval Europe,* ed. R. Blumenfeld-Kosinski and T. Szell (Ithaca, N.Y.: Cornell University Press, 1991), 222–246. For an orientation to the production of women's spiritual writings, see Ursula Peters, *Religiöse Erfahrung al literarisches Faktum: Zur Vorgeschichte und Genese frauenmystischer Texte des 13. und 14. Jahrhunderts* (Tübingen: Max Niemeyer Verlag, 1988).

18. In addition to Kathryn Tanner, *The Politics of God,* I have been inspired in the following by William A. Christian, Sr., *Doctrines of Religious Communities: A Philosophical Study* (New Haven: Yale University Press, 1987), which examines the doctrines "governing" the derivation and evaluation of primary doctrines.

19. For example, in his *Cur Deus Homo,* Anselm of Canterbury is especially concerned to show the connections between the affirmation of the incarnation and the ascription of various attributes to God. See, as well, Thomas Aquinas, *Summa theologiae* I q. 1, a. 8, corpus, for what amounts to the same proposal, advanced in his analysis of the place of argument in sacred doctrine.

20. For example, on occasion Christians seemed to have justified anti-Semitic attitudes and behavior on christological and eucharistic grounds. The increased attention to the crucified Christ in high medieval writings, both "spiritual" and scholastic, would seem to militate against such behavior. At first glance, it would seem inappropriate (sinful) to employ a belief in the Christ who dies because of sin and in order to overcome sin in a sinful way. It thus would be legitimate to ask whether

theorists of the eucharist were aware of the incompatibility. Of course, even if they are and argue on christological and eucharistic grounds against such behavior, it would remain to be shown that their analyses had the desired effect. It may be that their musings, as is the case for later intellectuals, were of import only for themselves.

Intellectual History

Marcia L. Colish

WHEN I ACCEPTED THE ASSIGNMENT of reflecting on the past and future of medieval studies in the field of intellectual history, the first question I asked myself was "How far back into the scholarly past do I need to go?" In response to that question, I decided that, for practical purposes, I could start in the mid-1950s. And this, not just because it was the point when I myself embraced the calling, but because, at that time, the main currents of historiography that had animated this field from the late nineteenth century through the high tide of the "revolt of the medievalists"[1] were still flowing unabated. In charting these waters I will not attempt to log a full bibliography but will merely allude or refer to authors or titles, when I do so, in a purely emblematic way. In the nature of the case, I will also sail into the territorial waters of other disciplines; for, by definition, intellectual history comprehends a wide range of cultural artifacts and phenomena.

To shift to another metaphor, the show that was playing in the theater of medieval intellectual history when I first brought my lifetime season ticket had been on the boards for some time. The score had several *Leitmotifs*, sometimes voiced by themselves and sometimes sung polyphonically. Two of the most prominent were what I will call the conduit thesis[2] and the bundle-of-sources thesis.[3] Alone or together, they lent themselves both to the genetic fallacy, to a relentless Gallocentricity,[4] to a proleptic reading of medieval thought,[5] to an emphasis on indigenous medieval cultures,[6] or on the Christian tradition,[7] or on the classical tradition,[8] or on—yes— the grand theme of synthesis involving some or all of the above,[9] as the force driving the libretto. Whatever the permutations of the plot, and whichever of these casting directors supplied the *Helden-*

190

tenors, the goal was to justify the Middle Ages as a Good Thing in opposition to the Petrarchan "Dark Ages" model, as preserved by supercilious modern classicists, rationalists, Catholicism-bashers, and neo-Burckhardtians.

Proponents of what I have called the conduit thesis implicitly analogized medieval intellectual history to a water main. While sometimes this water main became a bottleneck, constricted by the build-up of foreign matter on its inner circumference, at other times it was unclogged by the efforts of cultural rotorooters working as the agents of successive mini-Renaissances. Even acknowledging their activities, the function of the conduit was still held to be essentially passive. The role of the thinkers performing their successive salvage operations was to keep the channel open, so that some highly prized tradition or other, a tradition pre-medieval in origin and one that was destined to flourish again in the post-medieval era, could make its perilous way through the medieval centuries as intact as might be. At worst, the conduit, if clogged, could delay or retard that flow. At best, it could speed it up and prevent the material passing through it from being contaminated. But, as proponents of this thesis argued, if medieval thinkers played an essentially passive role in functioning collectively as a conduit, their role was also a positive one, in that they kept the valued tradition alive and available. The conduit could thus also be viewed as a conveyer belt. The medieval thinkers who kept this belt moving saw to it that the pre-medieval goods on the belt, wrapped in sanitary plastic film, were delivered to the modern age, untouched by human hands.

As for the bundle-of-sources approach, its practitioners, while they viewed medieval thinkers in a less passive light, concurred with the proponents of the conduit thesis in deemphasizing their originality. It was largely in this part of the landscape that the genetic fallacy took root and flourished. Thinkers, and even selected portions of their works, were studied, and judged worthy of pats or pans, in terms of the richness of their appeal to their pre-medieval sources. Whether it was the purity with which they reflected their Christianity, their Celtic or Germanic origins, or their classicism, the brute presence of these sources in the works of medieval authors was the issue targeted. The tracking down of allusions and quotations, in a florid and erudite display of *Quellenforschung,* was

the basic research technique of practitioners of this version of medieval studies. The notion that it might be desirable to consider
what use the thinker in question had actually made of his sources,
or whether he was making deliberate choices among them, and if
so, why, or whether he was achieving anything new or different
thereby, rarely obtruded. If the researcher happened to be a
standard-bearer in the revolt of the medievalists, chances were that
he would tackle this assignment from the standpoint of the classical
bias, toting up the number of people in privileged centuries like the
ninth or the twelfth who could think like Plato and write like Cic-
ero. In any event, recourse to the parallel column mode of scholarship, rather than to an integral analysis of the applications made
by medieval authors of their materials, was the prevailing strategy of
this group.

Having mentioned privileged centuries, it is of course necessary for me to recall one of the most famous of such past readings
of medieval intellectual history, the one which saw the thirteenth as
the greatest of centuries.[10] In this treatment of medieval intellectual
history, a host of different, and even rival, outlooks could be combined. Whether the heroic prototypes were mystics, philosophers,
sculptors, or poets, and whether the climactic moment saw the hero
receiving the stigmata, Aristotelianizing Christian theology in a Parisian lecture hall, consolidating papal power, consigning worldly
popes to hell, or combining heaven and earth on the façades of
Gothic cathedrals, the thirteenth century had something for almost
everyone, be he a romantic, an aesthete, a rationalist, a supraration-
alist, a defender of the sublimity of Catholicism, or a critic anato-
mizing the stresses and strains in the fabric of high medieval
Christianity.[11] Either way, the thirteenth century was the apex of
high medieval thought. Everything before the thirteenth century
regarded as having been important at all was deemed to have been
important insofar as it had led up to the researcher's chosen high
point in that century. Phenomena that could not be pressed into the
Procrustean bed of that story line were either marginalized or ignored, whatever their appeal may have been to medieval thinkers
themselves. And, since medieval intellectual history was thought to
have reached its apex by the end of the thirteenth century, if it
moved in any direction at all after that time, there was only one

direction in which it could go—downward. Hence, the numerous appeals to the medieval synthesis and its disintegration. Whether the chief index of synthesis was Dante, Aquinas, or Chartres cathedral, the achievement it represented could not be improved on, and the thirteenth, greatest of centuries was followed inevitably by a fourteenth century conceived of and castigated as a period of decline.

While these older interpretations can still, alas, be found in some of the textbooks medievalists feel constrained to assign to undergraduates, the scholarship of the past several decades has offered some salutary correctives, even if the motives inspiring them have occasionally reflected agendas that are more culture-specific to the late twentieth century than to the Middle Ages itself. Three main changes stand out here. The first, and, in my view, the most important, springs from a convergence of the interests of philosophers trained in the Anglo-American school of logical positivism and its offshoots and the dethronement of the neo-Thomists of the strict observance in the post–Vatican II Catholic world. It has led to a highly fruitful exploration of the thought of the later medieval scholastics. New editions and major studies are making it increasingly possible for us to map the contours of late medieval speculative thought, in all its manifestation—philosophy, theology, political thought, and the history of science. Much still remains to be done here, but the new agenda is firmly in place.[12] In addition, the interest in the history of logic stimulated by this wave of scholarship has inspired researchers to make important new discoveries in the earlier period, from the Carolingian age to the twelfth century.[13] A second major force that has opened up new vistas in medieval intellectual history of late has been the interest in women's studies. This concern has animated research into a wide range of fields, notably literary studies, theology, and the popular religious culture of the Middle Ages.[14] This last point is connected with a third fresh perspective, the application to medieval culture of insights from anthropology, sociology,[15] semiology,[16] and other neighboring disciplines accenting the importance of a period's implicit as well as its explicit values and systems of meaning. Intellectual historians of the Middle Ages have begun to draw on these modes of analysis in investigating the structures and models that informed medieval thinkers and the relations between elite cultures and popular cultures, the ways in which they interacted, and the areas in which they failed to interact.

This, then, represents the main outlines of the past and present of medieval intellectual history, as I see them. As a historian, I feel a constitutional disinclination to prognosticate about the future. But, in the effort to fulfill this part of my assignment, I will pull out my crystal ball and attempt to overcome my instinctive discomfort with futurology. Let me work my way into this task by posing the following question, as a heuristic device: the future of medieval intellectual history in relation to what? The quiddities I have in mind here are the periods of history that flank the Middle Ages on either side. They seem to offer plausible *comparanda*. For, like the Middle Ages itself, both classical antiquity and the Renaissance and Reformation present some of the same obstacles to researchers and impose some of the same requirements, requirements which it is probably going to be increasingly difficult for the generation of scholars who come after us to meet. Let me mention a few of them. First, and most obviously, there is the problem of languages. The decline of instruction in classical Latin and in the modern European languages is something we can all deplore. So is the relative scarcity of centers of instruction in medieval Latin, in paleography, diplomatics, and textual criticism. These basic tools of the trade will continue to have to be acquired. And, this process is likely to entail much *labor improbus,* much inconvenience, and much academic delay for our successors. I would be happy to be able to report that our colleagues in classics see themselves as responsible for teaching medieval Latin and the mechanics of textual transmission, even for the purpose of tracking the *Nachleben* of the "good" authors in their own discipline. Alas, such is all too rarely the case.

Equally problematic are the next two deficiencies which we face increasingly in medieval intellectual history, deficiencies that are just as acute for our colleagues in Renaissance and Reformation history. Not only are otherwise well-read people totally uncatechized nowadays, irrespective of their religious beliefs if any; they are also woefully ignorant of the classical tradition. I think it fair to say that most intellectual historians have by now shed the tendentious confessional motives that formerly drove the study of the religions of medieval and early modern Europeans, and that the Panofskian quest for a Renaissance classicism reappropriated in a state of chemical purity has been exposed for the illusion that it is.[17] Still, even when purged of these extravagances and blind spots, the intellectual history of the Middle Ages quite simply has to be able to take account of the Christian and classical traditions, in themselves and in their interactions, both with each other and with the Germanic and Celtic legacies. Medievalists of the future, I predict, will be increasingly poorly equipped to do so. Those of us who teach the subject today are all too painfully aware of how little we can take for granted in these areas on the part of our students. Here, we stand in precisely the same position of disadvantage as the Renaissance and Reformation scholars. At the same time, we are better off than they are. For one thing, no one seriously doubts the existence of the Middle Ages, or regards its intellectual history as an elitist nostalgia trip or as a nefarious effort on the part of bureaucrats of church and state to undermine popular culture. Further, the tendency to view the shift from the Middle Ages to the period immediately following it as gradual, or evolutionary, and not as cataclysmic, puts the Renaissance and Reformation historians increasingly in our debt. Finally, unlike medievalists, historians of the Renaissance and Reformation are still obsessed with conceptualizing their subject in terms of modernity, however they choose to define that term. In an age when not only modernism but postmodernism have become *passé,* that obsession can make for a lot of wasted energy, not to say false consciousness, a temptation which we, as medievalists, are better positioned to be able to resist.

This thought leads me to the fourth and final issue which I think is likely to affect our endeavors in the future. Again, it is an area in which we can gain a better sense of our own position by locating ourselves vis-à-vis our colleagues in adjacent fields of history. This issue is the vexed question of "political correctness." The form it has tended to take is twofold, at least as it impinges, or is likely to impinge, on intellectual history. The first is the form of reductionistic populism, or history from the bottom up as history *tout court,* whether of Marxoid derivation or not. If pushed to its ultimate extremes, this perspective on history would regard intellectual history as such as suspect, or as politically incorrect, since it includes, inevitably, the study of elites; it deals with express, conscious, and literate thought, thought produced by thinkers who are, preponderantly, dead white males, a lot of whom are clerics, to boot. Since it is not possible to expunge all thinkers matching this description from the canon of medieval intellectual history, the worm's-eye view of politically correct historiography would seek to delegitimize this subdivision of history altogether.

Now, I do think that medieval intellectual history is in some danger from this quarter; but it is less seriously affected than the Renaissance and Reformation. For, the ideological turf on which this battle has largely been fought is located primarily in the period immediately following the Middle Ages. In turn, this is the case simply because enough material, in enough density, is available starting in that period to make possible the solid documentation of a distinct popular culture. Medievalists, thus far, have shown greater open-mindedness and less dogmatism in handling this issue. They have been able to show both the trickle down of elite culture into popular culture, the percolation up from popular culture to elite culture, the crossovers in all directions and the areas in which people in all cultural registers share the same beliefs and values, as well as the areas in which people inhabiting different cultural modes or registers march simultaneously to decidedly different drummers, picking and choosing with their different kinds of selectivity from the menu before them. It is my hope that medieval intellectual historians will continue to resist the temptation to politicize their work or to turn history into grist for the mills of metahistory. The battle lines, in Renaissance and Reformation historiography, are too hard and fast and have been drawn for too long to make it as easy for our colleagues in these fields to reclaim the territory that they have abandoned, or that has been usurped from under their feet, by the populist reductionists. It is up to us as medievalists to hold our ground, keeping in mind the long view and the short attention span of twentieth-century intellectual trend-setters.

The second form in which political correctness presents a real and likely threat to our enterprise, and here we stand shoulder to shoulder with the classicists and the Renaissance and Reformation historians alike, is in its attacks on the fearsome "E-word," namely (dare I speak its name?) European civilization itself. In support of "cultural diversity" or "non-Western studies," or whatever the local buzz-word is, some voices in our current academic establishment are calling for a dismantling or "decentering" of the curriculum in history, as in other areas of the humanities, depressing the attention accorded to Europe. This is an attack which I do not think we are going to be able to avoid, or to deflect. And, unlike the shifting fads in cultural criticism or literary theory, which appear to have all the durability of the hula hoop, I predict that, in the light of this form of political correctness, it will not be possible for medieval intellectual historians, and other Europeanists, to conduct business as usual, while sitting out this dance. Too much academic politics is at stake, of the type likely to leave blood on the floor resulting from major surgery, not to say scar tissue, imposed on basic curricula and staffing patterns.

If this prediction is correct, what should we do about it? In response, I can only offer my own prescription, medicine that some colleagues may not be disposed to take. I think we should offer a new story line for medieval intellectual history. It should be the story of how a European tradition was formed in the first place, out of the interactions among indigenes and the bearers of cultural traditions that came, originally, from outside of the European landmass. We may need to remind our hearers and readers that the Germanic peoples started out in Asia, and that Judaism, Christianity, and Islam arose in the Near East. These cultures, and not just Greece and Rome, provided both the substance and the transformative power that made medieval Europe into a great world civilization. It was, moreover, the only civilization we know, under the heading of a "premodern" or "traditional" civilization, that developed real mechanisms for the internal criticism of its own constituent traditions, and the innovations that they stimulated, so that this traditional society made of its past is not a sterile or static cultural icon but a catalyst, promoting change and modernization from within. I think that we should tell our story this way, not only because it may be expedient to do so, in the coming academic climate, or as a defense that takes the form of an attack on the enemy's own citadel. Rather, I think that we should tell the story of medieval intellectual history this way because none of the old story lines make sense any more, and because we need to place our subject on a wider and a more comparative canvas, explaining why Europe forged ahead while sister civilizations which had many of the same options and opportunities and which outpaced Europe in the early

Middle Ages, sister civilizations such as medieval Islam and Byzantium, did not produce a Renaissance, a Reformation, or a Scientific Revolution. We need, I think, to tell the story this way in order for it to make sense to ourselves, as well as to others, whether those others are hostile or well disposed. And so, in conclusion, I think that the charge of Eurocentrism can best be met by showing how European thinkers in the Middle Ages drew on their manifold cultural legacies, some originally European and some extra-European, deployed them creatively, and made them agencies of change, in ways that continue to affect the post-medieval world, European and non-European alike. In short, the charge, on the part of the politically correct, that we as Europeanists are too monocular, should be read as a challenge, and one that medieval intellectual history is ready and able to meet.

NOTES

1. The term was coined by Wallace K. Ferguson, *The Renaissance in Historical Thought* (Boston, 1948), chap. 11.

2. Two good examples of this approach are the series of volumes by Henry Osborne Taylor, *Ancient Ideals: A Study of Intellectual and Spiritual Growth from Earliest Times to the Establishment of Christianity*, 2 vols. (New York, 1896); idem, *The Emergence of Christian Culture in the West: The Classical Heritage of the Early Middle Ages* (New York, 1958); idem, *The Mediaeval Mind: A History of the Development of Thought and Emotion in the Middle Ages*, 4th ed., 2 vols. (Cambridge, Mass., 1959) and R. R. Bolgar, *The Classical Tradition and Its Beneficiaries* (Cambridge, 1958), the latter with "Renaissances" built in and the former without them. A similar approach emphasizing the contrast between mini-revivals of the classics in the Middle Ages and their "true" revivals in a "chemically pure form" in the Italian Renaissance is offered by Erwin Panofsky, *Renaissance and Renascences in Western Art* (New York, 1969). The quotation is on p. 202. A parallel treatment of literature has been offered by L. D. Reynolds and N. G. Wilson, *Scribes and Scholars: A Guide to the Transmission of Greek and Latin Literature*, 2nd ed. (Oxford, 1974); likewise, accenting philosophy, is Michael Haren, *The Western Intellectual Tradition from Antiquity to the Thirteenth Century* (New York, 1985); and accenting political thought is John B. Morrall, *Political Thought in Medieval Times* (Toronto, 1980).

3. This approach is found most widely in the history of literature. See, for instance, the seminal work by Ernst Robert Curtius, *European Literature and the Latin Middle Ages,* trans. Willard Trask (Princeton, 1990).

4. A notable example, suggesting the *longue durée* of this mode of medievalism, is Jacques Paul, *Histoire intellectuelle de l'Occident médiévale* (Paris, 1973).

5. See Francis C. Oakley, *The Medieval Experience* (Toronto, 1988) who emphasizes medieval contributions to modern institutions, modern thought, and even to modern discontents in such diverse fields as political theory, scientific discovery, and romantic love.

6. George Burton Adams, *Constitutional History of England,* ed. Robert L. Schuyler (New York, 1934) represents a widespread tendency to trace parliamentary government to the "myth of the free Saxon," a view held by other scholars who look to the Germanic legacy for the origins of modern political theory and practice in this regard.

7. At issue here may be Roman Catholic triumphalism, as in the case of Henri Daniel-Rops, *Cathedral and Crusade: Studies of the Medieval Church, 1050–1350* (London, 1957) or a more generic insistence on the pervasiveness of Christianity as the most important defining force in medieval thought, as with Betsey B. Price, *Medieval Thought: An Introduction* (Cambridge, Mass., 1992). Few scholars writing in either of these veins take account of the fact that "Christianization" meant different things to different people in the Middle Ages.

8. The references to Bolgar, Panofsky, Reynolds and Wilson, Haren, and Morrall, cited in note 2 above, and the reference to Curtius, cited in note 3 above, are pertinent here as well.

9. An extremely influential proponent of the synthesis between classical philosophy and Christian theology as the main theme of medieval intellectual history is Étienne Gilson. Nowhere in his vast *oeuvre* is this thesis developed more systematically than in his *Reason and Revelation in the Middle Ages* (New York, 1938). Extending this idea to art history as well as philosophy is Erwin Panofsky, *Gothic Architecture and Scholasticism* (New York, 1957); Henry Osborne Taylor applies it to literature as well in his chapter on Dante as the "medieval synthesis," *Mediaeval Mind* 2:555–589.

10. This phrase goes back to James J. Walsh, *The Thirteenth, Greatest of Centuries* (New York, 1913). In the history of scholasticism, leading proponents of this view have included Étienne Gilson, *History of Christian Philosophy in the Middle Ages* (New York, 1955) and Fernand van Steenberghen, *La philosophie au XIIIe siècle* (Louvain, 1966), although these two scholars disagreed on other points. The same outlook is still present in

David Knowles, *Evolution of Medieval Thought,* rev. ed. (New York, 1988). Church historians such as Daniel-Rops, cited in note 7 above, and art historians such as Panofsky and admirers of Dante such as Taylor, as cited in note 9 above, can also be included here.

11. Classic among the critics of medieval Christianity, or of Roman Catholicism in general, are such authors as Henry Charles Lea, *A History of Auricular Confession and Indulgences in the Latin Church* (New York, 1968); idem, *The History of Sacerdotal Celibacy in the Christian Church,* 3rd rev. ed. (New York, 1957); idem, *The Ordeal,* ed. Arthur E. Howland and Edward Peters (Philadelphia, 1973); idem, *The Inquisition of the Middle Ages* (New York, 1961); idem, *Materials for a History of Witchcraft,* ed. Arthur E. Howland and George Lincoln Burr (Philadelphia, 1939); idem, *Superstition and Force,* 2nd rev. ed. (Philadelphia, 1870); idem, *Studies in Church History* (Philadelphia, 1883); and George G. Coulton, *Five Centuries of Religion,* 4 vols. (Cambridge, 1923–50); idem, *The Inquisition* (New York, 1929); idem, *Inquisition and Liberty* (Boston, 1959).

12. A selection of important recent studies treating later scholasticism in a positive light would include Marilyn McCord Adams, *William Ockham,* 2 vols. (Notre Dame, 1987); Allan B. Wolter, *The Philosophical Theology of John Duns Scotus,* ed. Marilyn McCord Adams (Ithaca, 1990); and Heiko A. Oberman, *The Harvest of Medieval Theology: Gabriel Biel and Late Medieval Nominalism* (Cambridge, Mass., 1963). We have also begun to witness the emergence of post–neo-Thomist Aquinas scholarship, as in Mark D. Jordan, *Ordering Wisdom: The Hierarchy of Philosophical Discourses in Aquinas* (Notre Dame, 1986). For political theory accenting the contributions of late medieval thinkers, see, for instance, Arthur S. McGrade, *The Political Thought of William of Ockham: Personal and Institutional Principles* (Cambridge, 1974) and Francis C. Oakley, *The Political Thought of Pierre d'Ailly* (New Haven, 1964); for the history of science, see David C. Lindberg, *The Beginnings of Western Science: The European Scientific Tradition in Philosophical, Religious, and Institutional Context, 600 B.C. to A.D. 1450* (Chicago, 1992); and Edward Grant, *Physical Science in the Middle Ages* (New York, 1971). With regard to the history of logic, E. J. Ashworth, *The Tradition of Medieval Logic and Speculative Grammar from Anselm to the End of the Seventeenth Century: A Bibliography from 1836 Onwards* (Toronto, 1975) provides guidance to the recent scholarship to date of publication; see also the surveys by I. M. Bochenski, *A History of Formal Logic,* ed. and trans. Ivo Thomas (Notre Dame, 1961) and Philotheus Boehner, *Medieval Logic: An Outline of Its Development from 1250 to c. 1400* (Manchester, 1952). The contributors to Norman Kretzmann et al., ed., *The Cambridge History of Later Medieval Philosophy* (Cambridge, 1988), emphasize the history of logic.

13. Good examples are John Marenbon, *From the Circle of Alcuin to the School of Auxerre: Logic, Theology and Philosophy in the Early Middle Ages* (Cambridge, 1981); Jean Jolivet, *Godescalc d'Orbais et la Trinité: Le méthode de la théologie à l'époque carolingienne* (Paris, 1958); Marcia L. Colish, "Carolingian Debates over *Nihil* and *Tenebrae:* A Study in Theological Method," *Speculum* 59 (October 1984): 757–795. On the twelfth century, see, for instance, L. M. De Rijk, *Logica Modernorum: A Contribution to the History of Early Terminist Logic,* 2 vols. (Assen, 1967); Mariateresa Beonio-Brocchieri, *The Logic of Abelard,* trans. Simon Pleasance (Dordrecht, 1969); and the collected papers on nominalism in the twelfth century in *Vivarium* 30 (May 1992).

14. A seminal study in the field of literature has been Peter Dronke, *Women Writers of the Middle Ages: A Critical Study of Texts from Perpetua (d. 203) to Marguerite Porete (d. 1310)* (Cambridge, 1984). A good guide to recent scholarship on women in medieval religion is provided by John Nicholas and Lillian Thomas Shank, ed., *Medieval Religious Women,* 3 vols., Cistercian Studies Series, 71, 72, 113 (Kalamazoo, Mich., 1984–92). Outstanding individual studies include Barbara Newman, *Sister of Wisdom: St. Hildegard's Theology of the Feminine* (Berkeley, 1987); Caroline Walker Bynum, *Jesus as Mother: Studies in the Spirituality of the High Middle Ages* (Berkeley, 1982), esp. part 5, "Women Mystics in the Thirteenth Century: The Case of the Nuns of Helfta," pp. 170–262; eadem, *Holy Feast and Holy Fast: The Religious Significance of Food to Medieval Women* (Berkeley, 1987). Among the good recent studies on women in monasticism are Penelope D. Johnson, *Equal in Monastic Profession: Religious Women in Medieval France* (Chicago, 1991) and Sharon K. Elkins, *Holy Women of Twelfth-Century England* (Chapel Hill, 1988).

15. Seminal here are the studies of political ritual by Marc Bloch, *The Royal Touch: Monarchy and Miracles in France and England,* trans. J. E. Anderson (New York, 1989) and Ernst H. Kantorowicz, *Laudes regiae: A Study in Liturgical Acclamations and Medieval Ruler Worship* (Berkeley, 1946). More recent exponents of this approach have shifted the focus from political theology to religious behavior more generally, from the motives for patronizing monasteries to the cult of saints to sacramental ritual. Under the first of these headings, good examples include Barbara H. Rosenwein, *Rhinosceros Bound: Cluny in the Tenth Century* (Philadelphia, 1982) and eadem, *To Be the Neighbor of St. Peter: The Social Meaning of Cluny's Property, 909–1049* (Ithaca, 1989), where the social construction of patronage receives more finely nuanced and less reductionistic treatment; Steven D. White, *Custom, Kinship, and Gifts to Saints: The laudatio parentum in Western France, 1050–1150* (Chapel Hill, 1988). On the cult of saints, the anthropological or sociological approach is well represented by

Sharon Farmer, *Communities of St. Martin: Legend and Ritual in Medieval Tours* (Ithaca, 1991) and Jean-Claude Schmitt, *The Holy Greyhound: Guinefort, Healer of Children since the Thirteenth Century,* trans. Martin Thomas (Cambridge, 1983). For an analogous treatment of sacramental behavior we may contrast Miri Rubin, *Corpus Christi: The Eucharist in Late Medieval Culture* (Cambridge, 1991), who views Eucharistic ritual from a purely behavioral perspective, ignoring the religious significance it had for practitioners, with Gary Macy, *Theologies of the Eucharist in the Early Scholastic Period: A Study of the Salvific Function of the Sacrament according to the Theologians, c. 1080–c. 1220* (Oxford, 1984), who shows how popular devotion and scholastic theology mesh in the period studied, leading to a new consensus on this sacrament and on its spiritual importance for both groups. One may also contrast Rubin with Bynum, *Holy Feast and Holy Fast,* who factors gender as well as anthropological models into her analysis of female Eucharistic devotion without reducing religious experience to social scientific descriptive categories. These two latter scholars, along with others, such as Aron Gurevich, *Medieval Popular Culture: Problems of Perception and Belief,* trans. Janos M. Bak and Paul A. Hollingsworth (Cambridge, 1988), and his more recent collection of essays, *Historical Anthropology of the Middle Ages,* ed. Jana Howlett (Chicago, 1992), have emphasized the interaction and interpenetration of learned and popular culture in the Middle Ages, especially as it concerns religious life.

    16. The seminal studies in this area are Marie-Dominique Chenu, "Grammaire et théologie aux douzième siècle," *Archives d'histoire doctrinale et littéraire du moyen âge* 10 (1935): 5–28 and Martin Grabmann, "Die geschichtliche Entwicklung der mittelalterlichen Sprachphilosophie und Sprachlogik," in *Mélanges Joseph de Ghellinck* (Gembloux, 1951) 2:421–434. The best general overview from the next generation is Jan Pinborg, *Die Entwicklung der Sprachtheorie im Mittelalter,* Beiträge zur Geschichte der Philosophie und Theologie des Mittelalters, n.F. 2:2 (Münster, 1967). Good examples of the application of semiotic analysis to particular medieval thinkers and problems include Marcia L. Colish, *The Mirror of Language: A Study in the Medieval Theory of Knowledge,* 2nd rev. ed. (Lincoln, Neb., 1983); Gillian R. Evans, *The Language and Logic of the Bible,* 2 vols. (Cambridge, 1984–85); Jean Jolivet, *Arts du langage et théologie chez Abélard,* 2nd ed. (Paris, 1982); Katherine H. Tachau, *Vision and Certitude in the Age of Ockham: Optics, Epistemology, and the Foundations of Semantics,* Studien und Texte zur Geistesgeschichte des Mittelalters, ed. Albert Zimmerman (Leiden, 1988).

    17. For the range of current approaches to the classics in medieval intellectual history, see Aldo S. Bernardo and Saul Levin, ed., *The Classics*

in the Middle Ages, Papers of the 20th Annual Conference of the Center for Medieval and Early Renaissance Studies (Binghamton, N.Y., 1990). The state of the art in the non-tendentious and ecumenical treatment of medieval Christian thought is represented by Jaroslav Pelikan, *The Christian Tradition: A History of the Development of Doctrine,* vols. 1–4 (Chicago, 1971–84).

On the Field

ROBERTA FRANK

The wind blows south, the wind blows north, round and round it goes
and returns full circle.

Ecclesiastes 1:6

IT IS—OR SHOULD BE—second-nature for medievalists to take
long views, to see ourselves on one arc of a circle around which we
have been revolving for many centuries.[1] In the 1970s, a distinguished Anglo-Saxonist was asked to give a talk about the crisis in
English studies; he put particular emphasis on the Norman Conquest. At the end of William L'Isle's "Preface" to *A Saxon Treatise
concerning the Old and New Testament* (1623), a rather plaintive
King Alfred looks down from heaven and laments that his country-
men can no longer be bothered to read his Old English writings or
language: "That all should be lost, all forgot, all grow out of knowledge and remembrance," he mourns, "what negligence, what in-
gratitude is this?"[2] Political correctness runs in cycles: the author of
the Declaration of Independence from Great Britain was this nation's first and most fervent campaigner for the study of Old
English;[3] in America today a statue of King Alfred raises hackles.[4]
Wars between ancients and moderns, the mutual recriminations of
grammarians and dialecticians, of "antiquarians" and "men of taste
and imagination," of scholars and critics, of literary historians and
theorists have been going on for some time now.[5] The pendulum
seems to move back and forth in the course of a single century, al-
ternating between periods that emphasize text, product, and historical reconstruction and those that emphasize world, process, and
aesthetic reliving, between eras for which understanding is primarily verbal or philological and those for which it is fundamentally
psychological or philosophical. Scholars not in perfect "sync" with
their particular historical moment dedicate themselves either to re-

204

placing "antiquarianism" with various forms of cultural criticism, or to eliminating the errors, fabrications, and myths that others have spent their lives circulating. Everyone keeps busy.[6]

Or so we hope. Scholarship is a fragile thing and, like civil liberties and order, can be destroyed. The works of art we teach are ours by chance: the poem, the painting, the historical treatise could very well not be there. The creator of a great text endured much loneliness, toil, and suffering in its making, gambling on immortality and not always winning. Links untended snap, the lineaments of the past whirl away and vanish. Humanists in North America have always thought of themselves as working outside the prevailing ethos; medievalists are used to living in a time and place that does not quite know what to make of them. Our fellow citizens are enmeshed in the bustling, brash, brazen present. If given a free vote, the great majority would elect baseball over *Beowulf* or Madonna over Hildegard of Bingen. A writer, they say, is the product of his or her society, as a noodle is the product of a noodle machine. Language and documents look back, science looks forward: the world prefers the Utopia ahead to the Arcadia behind. But as the past retreats, the future, too, departs, leaving in its wake a momentary yawn, the grinning, glittering new and now.[7]

My own subject—Germanic philology in a broad sense—has a long and luminous tradition: rigorous, precise, learned, comprehensive, and, yes, interdisciplinary before the word.[8] The first generation of vernacular philologists saw their task as the study of medieval culture in all its richness: literary history, criticism, and aesthetics, folklore, mythology, history, numismatics, textual criticism, paleography, the visual arts, music, medicine, law, lexicography, linguistics, semantics, onomastics, dialectology, and all the rest.[9] The brothers Grimm were not mere "proofreaders" and "teachers of reading and writing" (as Nietzsche dismissively defined philologists in 1874).[10] But today philosophy (the mode that ponders "what it means to us") is again high on fortune's wheel and philology (or "what it may have meant to them") is low. Anglo-Saxonists and Nordicists look around and see their subject scorned, assailed, and rooted up, healthy programs and departments axed by provosts desperate to cut costs. Old philologists are rarely replaced unless they have managed to secure external bequests for a successor. The prognosis for Copenhagen's Old Norse dictionary is not encouraging; the premier project in my field, Toronto's *Dictionary of Old English,* is slowly starving to death. The tap that flowed so generously in the 1960s—that sudden, quick-fix influx of funds—is now a thin resentful trickle. And highly trained and devoted people whose whole lives and careers have centered on making a monument to last the centuries have become disposable—like Kleenex. This is humane scholarship, the good life, in an estranged and sadly mutilated form.

As more places in and out of the university ask insistently for money, each humanities field must launch ever more passionate and persuasive defenses on its own behalf. The rhetoric of crisis is attractive and easy to master, even though, some will remind us, "in a world full of sin and misery what happens in the arts departments of universities rarely deserves the name of crisis."[11] The word itself is related etymologically to the idea of "choice"; a crisis calls for discriminations and new moves, admonitions and exhortations:[12] if we just pull up our socks and reform ourselves, do this and not that, we'll get ahead, win friends, stay in front, gain power overnight, be first at the public trough (or at least a little closer to the head of the line). Fellow medievalists, make a few, simple, cost-free gestures: portray your subject as a battlefield in which important principles are being attacked and defended; trash the monolithic and homogeneous; historicize, contextualize, pluralize, and by all means interdisciplinize; highlight the contingent, provisional, variable, tentative, and shifting;[13] insist that everything, including modernity, did not suddenly begin in the Renaissance. Do something. In a Marx brothers movie Groucho becomes the owner of a hotel and tells his staff to change at once the numbers on all the rooms. "Ah, but what confusion," exclaims his assistant. Groucho replies: "Ah, but what fun!" It is cheering to think that action is possible, that remedies exist.

A surprising number of curricular debates find their way into the mainstream press. Clearly someone cares. Valentine Cunningham's widely reported broadside against compulsory Anglo-Saxon in the Oxford English course generated concern, rallied support from those who saw humanist ideals being undermined, and reinforced the edifice he was trying to topple.[14] The big and much publicized growth area in modern literary studies has been theory: departments that "do it" grow bigger and broader, have more specialties and specialists, texts and concentrations, including, of course, theory itself. The spectacle of middle-aged scholars agonizing in public about the openness of their closures is a small price to pay for such success. Stephen G. Nichols, editor of the symposium on "The New Philology" in the award-winning issue of *Speculum* in January 1990, perceives a consensus that "medieval philology has been marginalized by contemporary cognitive methodologies, on the one side, while within the discipline itself, a very limited, and by now grossly anachronistic conception of it remains far too current."[15] In one stroke, he sweeps cobwebs and dead wood away, and confirms the importance and potential vitality of his discipline, expands its borders, and creates new, useful work for its membership. We trust that deans, directors, and granting agencies will interpret such discussions correctly, as a sign of renewal, of healthy ferment, and not as the frenzied swarming of ants around a jam jar.

John Van Engen has asked us to reflect collectively on our enterprise, to project a rationale for medieval studies based on our own research and teaching. The proceedings of this conference will be the sum of our individual myths about why we have chosen our peculiar profession, this life of learning that all of us here are engaged in fostering. Samuel Johnson stressed the element of chance: men and women are directed in their choice of subject "not by an ascendant planet or predominating humour, but by the first book which they read, some early conversation which they heard, or some accident which excited ardour and emulation."[16] The early poetry of northwest Europe was attractive to me largely because of its darkness and our ignorance, the unknowable unknowns as well as the knowable ones. To our ordinary modern questions about chronology, authorial styles, literary indebtedness, schools, genres, patronage, performance, transmission, theme and structure, even beginnings and endings, these compositions—not entirely oral in style, not entirely fixed in text—seemed to give no intelligible or adequate answer. Studying languages and materials (all those hard -graphies, -tics, and -ologies) was fun. So was learning from solemn editors that word *X* was either the name of a legendary Norse sea-king, a six-month-old bear, the knob at the top of a ship's mast, or an interjection signaling intense disgust. This was the company I wanted to keep. Plowing through some thirty-six hundred books and articles about Saul Bellow or the twenty-five thousand works produced since the late 1780s on the true meaning of *Hamlet* seemed and still seems to me less meaningful and productive: the idea of humanistic research in medieval studies, as in classics, was not a fabrication, a euphemism for the secondary, for parasitic metatexts. It was clear early on that approaches to matters of interpretation had changed over the long course of Anglo-Saxon and Old Norse scholarship; in time I grew to appreciate that this body of intellectual endeavor and achievement had relevance to ours and was still of interest to us, even when, or especially when, in error.[17] The process of understanding is, I learned, cumulative: a long, distinguished tradition of textual and historical scholarship reaching back into the sixteenth and seventeenth centuries, a tradition to which nothing human was alien. We should not have to apologize for studying a one-thousand-year chunk of the Western intellectual and artistic tradition that still casts its light and shadow on us and on other great world traditions. There need not be a vocational argument for studying early medieval poetry. There is no vocational case for cherry-blossoms. You want that splendor in your mind if you can get it.

Our usual generalist ploys, developed to convince the public that preservation of culture is a good thing, that medieval studies can enhance their lives, are not wrong, just oddly reversible, like an all-purpose raincoat. The Arnoldian, or traditionalist, stresses the improving effects of studying the best that has been thought and said between 500 and 1500; the subversive, or revisionist, notes the destabilizing effects on society of an imaginative literature that posits alternatives to the way things are today; and the practical, or politically committed, hints at relevance by observing that the medieval texts we explicate were governed by social forces similar to those operating in our own lives. But reverse the coat and you find that some historical periods—the 1760s, for example—were quite convinced of the deleterious effects of studying the literary classics;[18] that works of the imagination, by providing psychic escape-hatches, are inherently stabilizing; and that the medieval texts we expound were governed by social forces dissimilar and even repugnant to those operative today. Rain or shine you win, but the public supporting your work is unimpressed.

My own rationale for research and teaching in medieval studies falls under four interrelated headings: history (sometimes called "politics of difference"); courtesy (or "pluralistic pluralism"); love of the word (in contemporanese, "cultural hermeneutics"); and wisdom (for which I could not find a modern equivalent).

HISTORY

Our world is addicted to the present, to contemporary concerns, contemporary heroes, and contemporary buzz-words, to parochialism and provincialism. The genius of the age is that of journalism: everything is daily, everything is shredded at close of day. Television celebrates the "now." Nostalgia (lit. "homesickness") is out, amnesia is in. Decades are named and characterized (e.g., "The Greed Decade") before they are over; home decorators advise clients: "In the 1980s, when we were harder and meaner, glossy surfaces with sharp edges were what counted socially...."[19] Things are supposed to wear out, the old junked and the new put on the shelf. The greatest gift we can give students, trapped in this present, is a sense of history, a passion for the past in all its complex, layered depth.

The literature I teach is largely anonymous, often incomplete, and usually undated and undatable. It is contingent, like human beings. Each text comes from and is formed by its own historical moment: we may not know the date of composition, but we can be sure that no one speaking or writing in any other time and place would do so in exactly that way. The fact that we cannot say when *Beowulf* was composed does not mean that the poem could have arisen in any Anglo-Saxon century. Speakers at this conference come in different sizes and shapes, genders, races, classes, sexual orientations, and so on, but there is one "difference" we lack: we are contemporaries (loosely defined), which means that everything we say can later be "placed": country and decade, certainly, and, if the interpreter is skilled, even region and year. As the scholars of the past now seem, so shall we become. Being occasional, belonging to our time and place, is unavoidable. Let us show our students that the stylish optics of recent theory are not only easy to see through and to use, but can, like granny glasses, sharpen even middle-aged sights, and pick out unexpected contours and dimensions even in fields as intensively worked over as our own. But we must also tell them, preferably by example, that scholarship builds for the future, not the present; that we are long-distance runners, not sprinters; that flimsy reconstructions may glitter for a while but do not endure; that the scholar's real audience is not yet born.

COURTESY

Reading an old poem is, to borrow an image from George Steiner, like receiving a guest or stranger from a distant land.[20] (Compulsory Old English means that your visitor has his foot in the door.) Comprehension requires attention, tact, and discretion. You presume—an initial act of trust—that communication, however approximate, will be possible. You try to make sense of the stranger's words, his particular idiom, grammar, gestures, and images. What does this word really mean? Why does he pronounce it this way here and that way there? Does he have to skew syntax with such relish? Why does he address you directly on certain occasions and not others? Where is this guest coming from? What preceding and surrounding world gives context to his utterances? You must show tender solicitude for the tiniest hints and fragments of your visitor's vanished past, their extraction, cataloging, restoring, and conserving. So what if there are things about him you will never understand: you never fully know your parents or children either. Your visitor is forever changed by your interrogation, and you are not the same person after the encounter as you were before. Learning to read a medieval text in this way soon reveals to students that comprehension and preservation are mutually dependent activities, that we miss much in our daily lives by being ignorant of someone else's culture or language, an awareness not confined to the European and Anglo-American tradition.

LOVE OF THE WORD

As modest philologists rather than cultural prophets, teachers of Old English give many undergraduate and graduate students their first introduction to the parts of speech (yes, that *is* an adjective, Jason) and to historical semantics, to the notion that words, those unstable, unnatural counters, change meaning over time. We show them that form can be functional, that rhymes and meters are living architecture, arks for crossing the sea of centuries. Pleasure in style is now a suspect posture: how boring we are and how bored with ourselves we seem. Robert Gates recently explained to the Senate confirmation committee about his flagging memory: "I have to admit to you that when I left C.I.A. in 1989 . . . I did a major data dump."[21] Alliterative perhaps, but not uplifting.

The close reading of difficult texts trains the ear to hear what people are really saying; doing so with intensity, especially when young, produces a mind capable of stretching itself, of responding to the sounds and magic of words. Some Old English and much Old Norse verse is highly complex, agonistic, and devious. Poets compete with each other in recreating tradition, and their poetry tests the audience: nothing easy, manipulable, contemptible, or sloppy here, just an integrity on both sides that sells itself neither cheaply nor casually. Perhaps minds exposed to this kind of art will be less likely to join the growing ranks of those who consider their own deeply felt convictions reason enough for refusing to read this or that work, answering scorn with scorn.

WISDOM

A portion of the early medieval verse I teach falls into the category known as "wisdom poetry." These poems insist that, although life is hard and sad, it is essential to keep up the side, to remain fully human. So Solomon in the Old English *Solomon and Saturn II* rebukes his interlocutor: "It is a wretched and despairing person who keeps harping on his misery."[22] Such an attitude informs Winston Churchill's commencement address at his old school, Harrow, after World War II. He got to his feet and said to the graduating class: "Nevah give up!" and sat down.[23] An article in the *Guardian* (July 18, 1991) reporting the attack on compulsory Old English at Oxford elicited a letter the following week (July 24) from one Alan Hindle of Bingley, a graduate of the Oxford English course some thirty years earlier. He offered a moving personal testimony to the public usefulness of reading early medieval poetry:

> When I went to Oxford to read English the Anglo-Saxon paper seemed to me a chore, the price one paid for being allowed to

spend time on literature already known and loved. Then I was given the Anglo-Saxon poem "The Wanderer" to study and not only my attitude to the course but my whole internal life was changed. Whoever wrote that poem had tuned into my moments of despair, to my regret for the passage of time, to the ultimate isolation of one's existence. I learned the poem by heart (the expression is an appropriate one) and have recited it in periods of insomnia and depression. This might make me sound like a morbid recluse but I don't think I am. My record of public activities would stand comparison with most people.

He concluded: "All I am offering is an affirmation of the value of a culture that has enabled me to lead a relatively useful life since I graduated."[24]

As teachers, as preservers and transmitters of medieval texts, we can choose the works most likely to stir the minds and imagination of our students, voices from the past that will be wise guides, lasting sources of consolation and illumination. (So Wordsworth vowed at the end of *The Prelude:* "What we have loved/Others will love, and we will teach them how."[25]) And as philologists, as people who read texts slowly and searchingly, we, too, shall perceive in these voices the shape of our own hopeless passion, of a windswept "grey brother"[26] embarked with his craft on a quest that will not end until solid ground is sighted, and that therefore never ends.

Medieval texts do not obviously intrude on the scholarly concerns of the present. Tell a modern cultural historian that Old English poetry has something to say about alienation, and you get an embarrassed shrug diluted by apathy. Clearly the wrong sort of alienation. Our field is also estranged from its own past. With each successive generation, references to the writings of scholars who worked prior to the latest "illumination" become rarer, replaced "by reverential footnotes to the ideas of an instantly canonical list of theoretical *moderni.*"[27] We are told that medieval studies as we know it was invented in the mid- to late-1960s, around the time that the writers making this claim were themselves bright-eyed graduate students. In positing a founding moment that coincides with our own, then isolating trends and talking up the long-term implications of current work, we are able to write obliquely about ourselves, pointing to our spark-proof rubbing together of dry sticks as a *momentum aere perennius.* There also is pleasure in portraying the end of our field as coinciding with our withdrawal from it. The constant threat of disintegration, of a legacy we are always about to lose, hangs over our profession, ever grimmer and graver at century's close. A simple change of name—"earlier modern studies" perhaps—is unlikely to save us; nor will strict abstinence from anthropological paradigms, semiotics, and textuality effect a cure. For the 1990s, belief in ourselves, in our dedicated subcommunity, in the worth, health, and coherence of the enterprise we are fostering, seems to me a better agenda than any hunt for miracle drugs. The poetry I teach does not have a future tense; with perseverance, medievalists may.

NOTES

1. 'Medievalist' referring to people like ourselves is first documented in 1874, the same year that 'cocaine' and 'lawn-tennis' entered the language: *The Oxford English Dictionary,* ed. James A. H. Murray et al. (Oxford, 1884–1928), s.v. *mediaevalist.* Oscar Bloch and Walther von Wartburg, eds. *Dictionnaire étymologique de la langue française,* 4th ed. (Paris, 1964), give 1867 as the first date for *médiéviste,* a word already in Émile Littré, ed. *Dictionnaire de la langue française* (Paris, 1868), fascicule 17. According to Paul Guérin, *Dictionnaire des dictionnaires,* 2nd ed. (Paris, 1892), it replaced *moyenâgiste,* used by Balzac in 1841 and current chiefly in that decade. Goethe had earlier poked fun at contemporary *Mittelältler:* see Jacob Grimm and Wilhelm Grimm, *Deutsches Wörterbuch,* ed. Moriz Heyne (Leipzig, 1885), s.v. For later derogatory uses of 'medieval' and 'medievalist', see Fred C. Robinson, "Medieval, *the* Middle Ages," *Speculum* 59 (1984): 745–756. The many ways of saying 'the Middle Ages' from the sixteenth century on are surveyed by Jürgen Voss, *Das Mittelalter im historischen Denken Frankreichs: Untersuchungen zur Geschichte des Mittelalterbegriffes und der Mittelalterbewertung von der zweiten Hälfte des 16. bis zur Mitte des 19. Jahrhunderts,* Veröffentlichungen des historischen Instituts der Universität Mannheim (Munich, 1972), esp. 9–21 and 390–419 ("Tabellarische Übersicht der Belege für 'Mittelalter' ").

2. "The Complaint of a Saxon King," par. 20 in "Preface" to *A Saxon Treatise concerning the Old and New Testament, Written about... (700 yeares agoe) by Aelfricus Abbas* (London, 1623). The book was reissued with a different title-page as *Divers Ancient Monuments in the Saxon Tongue. Written seven hundred yeares agoe shewing that both in the Old*

and New Testament, the Lords Prayer, and the Creede, were then used in the Mother Tongue . . . (London, 1638). See Rosemund Tuve, "Ancients, Moderns, and Saxons," *English Literary History* 6 (1939): 165–190.

3. Thomas Jefferson, *An Essay towards Facilitating Instruction in the Anglo-Saxon and Modern Dialects of the English Language,* written in 1798 and published in 1851 by the University of Virginia. See Stanley R. Hauer, "Thomas Jefferson and the Anglo-Saxon Language," *PMLA* 98 (1983): 879–898.

4. For the story see Karl Morrison's essay "On the Statue" in this volume.

5. The complaints of Plato and Isocrates against the ancient sophists, John of Salisbury's twelfth-century denunciation of some "modernist" he calls Cornificius, Renaissance humanists' criticism of late Scholastic educational practice, and Joseph Ritson's tirades against the trendiness and immorality of such contemporaries as Percy and Warton have a close-knit continuity—and relevance to current debates.

6. Árni Magnússon (1663–1730) described the scholarly divisions of his own day in similar terms: *Árni Magnússon, Levned og Skrifter,* ed. Finnur Jónsson (Copenhagen, 1930), I, 24; cited Jón Helgason, *Handritaspjall* (Reykjavík, 1957), 113.

7. On a disappearing past and future and the preeminence of the *now* in the publishing industry, see the eloquent observations of Octavio Paz, "Who Reads Poetry?" *Partisan Review* 4 (1991): 597–619.

8. 'Interdisciplinary' was probably born in New York City in the mid-1920s, most likely at the corner of 42nd and Madison where the Social Science Research Council was located. The first citation that I have been able to find is a statement made on Monday evening, August 30, 1926, by Professor Robert Sessions Woodworth (1869–1962), and printed in the proceedings of the *SSRC Hanover Conference* (Dartmouth College, August 23–September 2, 1926), II, 445. See R. Frank, " 'Interdisciplinary': The First Half-Century" in *Words for Robert Burchfield's Sixty-Fifth Birthday,* ed. E. G. Stanley and T. F. Hoad (Cambridge, 1988), 91–101. Although *Collins English Dictionary* states that the term 'philology', first recorded in English in 1614, is "no longer in scholarly use," in recent years there has been a number of attempts to define the art, its methods, history, and purpose: see, for example, the thoughtful contributions to *On Philology,* ed. J. Ziolkowski (University Park, Penn., 1990), prev. pub. in *Comparative Literature Studies* 27, no. 1 (1990).

9. The model for this broad conception was classical philology, well established in Germany by the time Jacob Grimm and Karl Lachmann came along. On this prelapsarian phase, when the various subfields were not yet estranged, see Karl Stackmann, "Die klassische Philologie und die

Anfänge der Germanistik" in *Philologie und Hermeneutik im 19. Jahrhundert. Zur Geschichte und Methodologie der Geisteswissenschaften,* ed. Hellmut Flashar et al. (Göttingen, 1979), 240–259; also the excellent essay by Elaine C. Tennant, "Old Philology, New Historicism, and the Study of German Literature" in *Lesarten: Méthodologies nouvelles et textes anciens,* ed. Alexander Schwarz (Bern, 1990), 153–177. On Jacob Grimm in particular, see Ulrich Wyss, *Die wilde Philologie: Jacob Grimm und der Historismus* (Munich, 1979). On the wide-ranging interests of early Anglo-Saxonists, see esp. E. G. Stanley, "The Scholarly Recovery of the Significance of Anglo-Saxon Records in Prose and Verse: A New Bibliography," *Anglo-Saxon England* 9 (1981): 223–262; reprinted in his *A Collection of Papers with Emphasis on Old English Literature* (Toronto, 1987). There is a comprehensive bibliography of scholarship on the development of Anglo-Saxon studies in *Anglo-Saxon Scholarship: The First Three Centuries,* ed. Carl T. Berkhout and Milton McC. Gatch (Kalamazoo, Mich., 1982), 183–192. See also Stanley B. Greenfield and Fred C. Robinson, *A Bibliography of Publications on Old English Literature to the End of 1972* (Toronto, 1980), 72–76 (items 801A–872); and Allen J. Frantzen, *Desire for Origins: New Language, Old English, and Teaching the Tradition* (New Brunswick, N.J., 1990). On the eighteenth-century founders of Old French literary scholarship, see, e.g., Lionel Gossman, *Medievalism and the Ideologies of Enlightenment: The World and Work of La Curne de Sainte-Palaye* (Baltimore, 1968), and Geoffrey J. Wilson, *A Medievalist in the Eighteenth Century: Le Grand d'Aussy and the Fabliaux ou Contes* (The Hague, 1975).

10. Friedrich Nietzsche, "Wir Philologen," *Unzeitgemässe Betrachtungen* (Munich, 1964), 407: "Der Lese- und Schreiblehrer und der Korrektor sind die ersten Typen des Philologen." Cited by Tennant, p. 153.

11. Graham Hough, reviewing *Criticism in the University* in *London Review of Books,* October 17, 1985.

12. See Reinhart Koselleck, *Kritik und Krise* (Frankfurt, 1959), 196–198.

13. Most of the verbs and adjectives in this sentence come from Cornel West, "The New Cultural Politics of Difference" in *Out There: Marginalization and Contemporary Culture,* ed. Russell Ferguson et al. (Cambridge, Mass., 1990), 19–36; cited by Arnold Rampersad, "Values Old and New," *Profession 91* (Modern Language Association of America, 1991): 10–14.

14. Cunningham's position was outlined in *Oxford Magazine* Fourth Week, Trinity Term 1991, 10, in *Guardian* (July 18, 1991) 23, and, under the heading "The Future of Old English," in *Times Literary Supplement* (August 30, 1991), 11, along with a response by J. A. Burrow; for a bibliography

of the controversy, see now Peter Jackson, "The Future of Old English: A Personal Essay," *Old English Newsletter* 25, no. 3 (Spring 1992): 24–28.

15. *Speculum* 65 (1990): 1.

16. *Lives of the Poets,* ed. G. B. Hill (Oxford, 1905), III, 174.

17. For a demonstration of what can be discovered by looking at the history of scholarship as a history of error, see E. G. Stanley, *The Search for Anglo-Saxon Paganism* (Cambridge, 1975).

18. See, for example, Edward Young, *Conjectures on Original Composition* (London, 1759); William Duff, *An Essay of Original Genius and its Various Modes of Exertion in Philosophy and the Fine Arts, Particularly in Poetry* (London, 1767).

19. Quoted from a recent (autumn 1991) issue of the *Globe and Mail* (Toronto).

20. George Steiner, *Real Presences* (Chicago, 1989), 155–178.

21. *The New Yorker* (November 4, 1991), 35.

22. Lines 352–53; text in Elliott Van Kirk Dobbie, ed. *The Anglo-Saxon Minor Poems,* Anglo-Saxon Poetic Records 6 (New York, 1942), 43.

23. Anecdote told by Maynard Mack, "The Life of Learning," *ACLS Newsletter* 34, nos. 1–2 (1983): 2.

24. Reprinted in *Times Literary Supplement,* August 30, 1991, 12.

25. *The Prelude, or Growth of a Poet's Mind,* ed. Ernest de Selincourt (London, 1926), Book XIV, lines 446–447 (6th ed., 1850); Book XIII, lines 444–445 (1st ed., 1805–6), has a slightly different reading: "and we may teach them how."

26. Jorge Luis Borges addresses his nameless Anglo-Saxon counterpart as "grey brother" in "To a Saxon Poet": *Selected Poems 1923–1967,* ed. Norman Thomas di Giovanni (London, 1972), 238; a second poem by Borges with the same name, p. 176.

27. Ross G. Arthur, "On Editing Sexually Offensive Old French Texts" in *The Politics of Editing Medieval Texts,* ed. R. Frank (New York, 1993), 19.

Teaching Medieval Studies:
The York Experience

DEREK PEARSALL

'MEDIEVAL STUDIES,' as I understand the term, and as I shall use it in this essay, is a name given to the practice of interdisciplinary teaching and research in the areas of study relating to the chronological Middle Ages (A.D. 500–1500) in the West. I should make it clear that this is a descriptive, not a prescriptive, definition: it is a description of teaching and scholarly practice that I have been engaged in for many years, and the definition came to me quite naturally and needed no effort of formulation, given the customary usage that has grown familiar to me. But, as I say, it is not a prescriptive definition. The emphasis on the interdisciplinary nature of "medieval studies" is central to what I understand to be useful about the term, but I am aware that the term may be more loosely or differently employed to refer to any study of any single aspect of the Middle Ages. I am content also to recognize that there may be historical and political reasons why other people might wish to avoid the necessarily arbitrary limitation of time-span, or any strict definition of "the West," or indeed any concentration on the West as such. Their reasons, however, are not mine, and I do not speak of them further.

In 1968 there was established at the University of York, in England, a Centre for Medieval Studies. It was the first such center in Britain, and its ambitions were initially modest. It was essentially an umbrella organization to oversee the teaching of a one-year master's degree in medieval studies in which the disciplines of literature, history, and art history were designed to be integrated. This master's program was the brain-child of the late Elizabeth Salter,

217

and it was her inspired teaching as well as the inspired example of her own unique ability, in her teaching and in her scholarship, to transcend the boundaries of the three disciplines that conceived the Centre for Medieval Studies, brought it into existence, and made it a success.[1] This personal inspiration and example, which to me is inseparable from everything that is truly worthwhile in the life of institutions, academic and otherwise, often found itself sitting uncomfortably with the bureaucratic procedures of university departments. This may seem strange, given that the University of York was only founded in 1963, but it was surprising how quickly creativity and innovation had to start making their way against the language of tradition, precedent, and constraint.

The Centre for Medieval Studies began therefore as a group of teachers who were interested in the prospect of interdisciplinary graduate work. The teachers were from the departments of English, history, and art history. Their teaching formed the core of the course, to which were added Latin and paleography, taught as compulsory ancillary courses but not examined. In the early years, there were so few students that the courses were more or less built around them, but as numbers increased the teaching was concentrated in a series of options, and students applied for admission to a particular option. Over the years, the options varied. There was always an attempt to ensure that the three basic disciplines, to which archaeology was added later, were represented, but the amount of attention given to each varied.

There was an Anglo-French option, which dealt with relations between England and France during the fourteenth century—political, military, literary, and artistic. This option was perhaps one of the best examples of the successfully interdisciplinary nature of medieval studies; indeed, the subject seemed to require to be studied in such a way. Froissart, for instance, was a central figure who was the legitimate property of both historians and literary scholars, and the exclusive property of neither, and there were many occasions when the convergence of the three disciplines needed no special demonstration. For a time in the late 1350s, when King John of France was maintained in luxurious captivity in England and gathered around himself French poets like Gace de la Buigne as well as Parisian illuminators and book-makers, the French court was actually resident in England.

The option on Anglo-Saxon England also had a powerful claim that interdisciplinary study was not only interesting but essential in terms, for instance, of the nature of the monastic culture that sponsored the great reflourishing of alliterative poetry in the tenth century, or the vision of history that provided the subject-matter of *Beowulf.* In that poem, too, there are allusions to art and artifacts for which archaeology, as in its analysis of the findings at Sutton Hoo, provides the explanatory evidence, enigmatic though that evidence may be.

But the central options, taken by the majority of students, whose numbers were reaching twenty to twenty-five per year in the mid-1970s, were "The Age of Richard II" and "The Late Medieval City of York." The latter worked with excellent economy, uniting in the fifteenth century the study of the rise and flourishing of a northern industrial city with the study of the stained glass for which the new wealth helped to provide patrons and the cycle of mystery plays which were socially important, not least as a means for articulating the new and more significant powers of the merchant oligarchy. The presence of the medieval city as part of the daily experience of students, the opportunity to view medieval buildings, sculpture, and stained glass at first-hand, the triennial performance of the York Cycle of Mystery Plays, were all part of the special stimulus of the course. The embracing discipline—since I think that all interdisciplinary study has to be basically in terms of or under the aegis of one discipline or another—was history, and the course was taught principally by historians with collaboration from literary scholars and art historians.

The other option, and always the one that found most recruits, was "The Age of Richard II." The combination of a great reflowering of English poetry, a court culture that in part sponsored it, a court art and architecture that to some extent matched it in elegance and splendor was extremely attractive. Here the embracing discipline was literature, and the presence among the writers studied not only of Chaucer and Gower but also of the *Gawain*-poet and Langland gave the opportunity to reach outwards into provincial or non-metropolitan culture as well as downwards into those deeper levels of social dissent and disturbance where *Piers Plowman* and the Peasants' Revolt stand in such suggestive relation. Historians were closely involved in the teaching of this course, and there were many joint seminars on such topics as the patterns of patronage that prevailed in court and aristocratic households as also on the social and economic changes that helped to produce a literature of protest. The study of art, of court style and the "International Style" could be conveniently staged to reach its climax in the inspection of John Thornton's great East Window in York Minster. The option remains the most popular one at York, where the Centre for Medieval Studies maintains a vigorous existence, though there have been changes in the shape of the courses with the arrival of new teaching staff.

Much of the teaching was done jointly, sometimes with two people involved, sometimes with three. For the teacher, if not always for the student, this was the most valuable and most interesting part of the whole enterprise, seeing and learning in detail and in depth what it was like to be a historian or an art historian, what was the nature of their approach to a subject, how they thought about things. I suppose it was the same for them, though the impression I always got, no doubt mistakenly, was that I was learning how they did things but they already knew how I did things, and that anyway there was not much to know. One of the problems of managing medieval studies at York, and it may be a common experience, was that the students mostly came from English departments, while the framework of study was almost inevitably, it seemed, historical. There is a tendency for certain kinds of material and documentary evidence to assume a primary importance, and the demand for this kind of evidence can often frustrate or silence legitimate and useful hypothesis, which is what literary study mostly consists of. It is often very difficult for a literary scholar to answer the question, Where is your evidence? without pointing to the literary text and saying, rather lamely, "It's there." But the history of Lollardy in the fifteenth century, recently superbly rewritten by Anne Hudson, is perhaps an example of what a great historian like K. B. McFarlane was trained to miss, and what it took a textual scholar to uncover.[2]

These are memories of teaching and working in the field of medieval studies in a British university. Though framed in the context of autobiography, they are intended as a chapter, or at least a short paragraph, in the history of medieval studies, and in a moment I shall try to draw some generalizations from them. First I want to indulge a little further in reminiscence. When I took up my present appointment at Harvard in 1985, it was not my expectation that I would be doing there exactly what I had been doing at York. For one thing, the departments of English and history, close cooperation between which had been the foundation of medieval studies at York, were at Harvard, though no larger, much more entrenched in traditional and constraining practice. There was no dialogue concerning practice in the teaching of medieval subjects, no machinery to facilitate such dialogue, and little except formal, albeit genial contact between teachers in the two disciplines. The graduate program in the two departments were powerfully driven by the needs of examinations, theses, and job-applications, and these left little time for that broadening of horizons which was possible with master's or beginning doctoral students at York. There was a difference, too, in the preparedness of students for such broadening. Early specialization in English schools and universities, though it has numerous drawbacks, means that undergraduates have, at the end of their degree program, a reasonable command of their discipline of study, which they have normally concentrated on exclusively, and quite intensively, for the three years of their undergraduate career. This is less true with American students.

There is at Harvard, to be sure, a theoretical facility for the teaching of an interdisciplinary version of medieval studies in the program in "History and Literature." But this program does little more than administer a menu of courses taught by members of the parent departments, and there are only occasional ventures into joint courses or joint teaching. It is different in this respect from the program in "American Civilization," which might be thought to provide a model for an undergraduate program in medieval studies, but which is not helpful as an analogy because it handles a range of materials with which an undergraduate can legitimately be expected to have a greater familiarity.

Though there were thus many disincentives to trying to continue the York experiment at Harvard, it was not easy for me to abandon completely what had been good and successful teaching practices. So I proposed an undergraduate course in "The Age of Richard II" in the "Core" or General Education program, anticipating that my students would be much excited at the prospect of studying such a dramatic period in the history of England and its culture. The first inkling that I had that all might not be as I expected was a polite note from the relevant Core course committee suggesting that, while the course was very attractive, it might be a good idea to include a date in the title. Harvard students, I was told, would be able to deduce from the title that there had once been a Richard I, but where Richard II had once been Richard II of, or when, would be beyond the limits of their knowledge. So it proved: and indeed how else could it have been? The students were enormously enthusiastic, and they very much appreciated the films I was able to show, *The Name of the Rose, The Return of Martin Gayre, Monty Python and the Holy Grail,* Pasolini's *Canterbury Tales*—some of them with a relevance to the subject matter of the course that even I cannot recall at this distance of time—but it was all a mistake. It was improper to expect that students would be able to make connections between subjects of which they knew, and could be properly expected to know, virtually nothing.

Let me now try to draw a few generalizations from these experiences. There are three levels, it might be suggested, at which one could talk of the pursuit of medieval studies as an academic discipline.

The first is at the undergraduate level. The practicability of introducing successful interdisciplinary programs in medieval studies at the undergraduate level seems limited. Students' knowledge of even one area of study is so precarious that others can only be brought in at a superficial level and this may well involve more compromises than are acceptable. There are, of course, many opportunities for a broadening of perspective in the teaching of a particular medieval topic, and it would be the assumption of most teachers of medieval literature that their subject necessarily embraces some understanding of history, religion, social, and economic practice and the "mentalities" of the past, as well as language and literary genre and tradition. Every student of medieval literature, on this assumption, is a beginning student in medieval studies. There is also room for some version of popularized medievalism, whether this takes the form of simple propaganda for one's subject or whether it takes the form of a more sophisticated critique of the crudities and misconceptions of popular medievalism. Discussion of a medieval film, whether the film is to be taken seriously or not, provides a first chance to tackle some important questions of cultural difference.

The second level at which one could speak of interdisciplinary medieval studies as a viable academic pursuit is the graduate level. This is where students have enough knowledge of at least one area of study to make some intelligent connections with other areas of study. The interdisciplinary approach, however, is most successful when organized on a synchronic basis, so that those connections can be historically firmly grounded in the social, economic, and cultural life of a particular period, the more precisely defined the better. (I do not talk here or anywhere about comparative literature as an aspect of medieval studies, since it seems to me to have its own rationale and hardly to be interdisciplinary.) The subjects chosen for interdisciplinary study must also be intrinsically closely related or capable of being so related. Linguistics, for instance, would have sat very ill in the York master's options I was outlining, and attempts to incorporate linguistics, with the best will in the world, did not work. As a corollary of this, it follows that the course of study must be carefully planned and focused. The alternatives are the kinds of courses that were put on in some of the centers for medieval studies that sprang up in England in the early 1970s, perhaps partly in an attempt to repeat the York experiment.[3] In these centers, the characteristic practice was to solicit course-offerings from all teachers who had any connection with the Middle Ages, and then to organize these courses or course "modules" into a "menu" or series of menus from which students, constrained by certain principles of choice, would select a certain number of items. Students customarily did their best to build a coherent rationale, or at least an edible meal, out of these offerings, but were often frustrated in the absence of the necessary planning by their teachers, and ended up with some peculiar combinations of subjects.

All of this has to do with preliminary graduate study—the year or two years of study for the master's degree. It was not the practice at York to encourage students to take their doctorates in medieval studies, though of course it was hoped that their research would reap the benefit of their being better informed about related disciplines. There was certainly a tendency for students, when they were choosing their thesis topics, to return to the stronghold of their own subject, in which they had had their primary training and with which they felt inwardly confident. Again, there were institutional pressures at work: as no one needs reminding, students with doctorates in medieval studies are not readily employable and have always to give artificial prominence to one element or another in their training in order to attract the attention of a major department.

This brings me to the third level at which medieval studies might be said to have an existence, that is, in the research and scholarly activities of the individual scholar, whether or not within some institution devoted to the teaching of medieval studies. Here it seems to me that the tendency is for scholars, like senior graduate students, to remain principally the practitioners of their own discipline of study. I notice that Patterson, at the end of his recent excellent book on *Chaucer and the Subject of History,* remarks with characteristic frankness that his practice as a literary scholar is continually to remind himself to "think socially" (or, as one might rephrase it, "only historicize").[4] The fact that it is a mental procedure consciously invoked indicates that it is something added to the customary practice of reading literary texts. V. A. Kolve has not described his own practice in equivalent terms ("think in images"), but he might acknowledge that this is what he, as a literary scholar, does, and does with conspicuous success.[5]

For myself, I try to see everything I read from the Middle Ages in the light of what I have learnt about medieval history, medieval painting, medieval social, religious, and political practices and ideas, as well as about related literatures, but I remain someone who thinks about "literature" as a special case of art and communication, and not an undiffentiated form of "text." I have come across art historians who can work with confidence, as Michael Camille does, among both literary texts and historical documents, but they are rare.[6] I have also come across literary scholars who can "do" history with the kind of confidence that makes one think they must have been trained as historians—Richard Firth Green comes to mind as an excellent example[7]—but I do not think I know any historians who have a "literary" understanding of a literary text or who would think it respectable to divulge the fact if they had.

We may all of us exist to some extent within the "prison-house" of our own discipline and of our own academic language.

This is maybe inevitable: the danger is that we may get to like it too much, or become unaware that there are other prison-houses nearby. The value of interdisciplinary study is the opening of the mind to the possibility of other approaches, other ways of thinking, and it may be that this opening of the mind is no more than the further expression of the desire for "the other" that made us all medievalists in the first place. This openness seems to me valuable in a special way, and perhaps uniquely valuable in the study of the Middle Ages, where the intrinsic "otherness" of the subject demands that every possible angle of vision be explored. I am aware, though, that the interdisciplinary agenda has its own historical origins and limitations, and that the future of medieval studies may have as much to do with the finding of new focal centers of study as with the interlocking or superimposing of traditionally independent disciplines.

At least one of these focal centers of study has, in fact, a long history. It is the idea of Latinity, of Latin culture, learning, and theology, especially theology, as the universal medieval discipline to which all others are radially related. It may be that the Centre for Medieval Studies at the University of Toronto, with its close association with the Pontifical Institute of Medieval Studies, derives some of its special eminence from the putting into practice of this idea of the Middle Ages. To work with the Latin writing and culture of the Middle Ages is to be at the center of the intellectual traditions of the West, and we have Curtius to tell us so, as well as large numbers of volumes of Migne, Medieval Institutes supported by religious foundations and orders, and D. W. Robertson. The value of such study is unquestionable, as is the quantity of it that remains to be done, but the claim of such study to be in a special way central and privileged needs to be questioned. The idea that the idiosyncratic and historically specific forms of discourse developed in the Middle Ages to reinforce the teaching of Christian doctrine and to ensure the preservation of a clerical monopoly on learning should be the lens through which we view the Middle Ages is like continuing to read Russian history and culture through the eyes of Soviet historians.

This may now seem like ancient history; present-day graduate students raise their eyebrows in surprise that views so simplistic should ever have gained such wide currency. Perhaps a more potent claim to interdisciplinary centrality is being made now by that form of interpretative discourse that proclaims its own decenteredness, that claims that everything is a text, including history, and that texts are all there are. Interpretation is everything, and interpretation, especially the notion of the impossibility of definitive interpretation, collapses all the disciplines together in a common indecipherability. Here, one might think, is a new basis for medieval studies.

So I thought, myself, when I was preparing a paper on "Image and Event in the Peasants' Revolt of 1381" on the occasion of the sixth centenary of that momentous event.[8] Having been accustomed for a long time to talking about the Peasants' Revolt, the world it exploded out of, and the literary responses it provoked, I became enamoured of the idea that the barriers between history and literature might be shown to be not just surmountable but nonexistent if I concentrated on the hermeneutics of the Revolt. I had picked up some ideas about the subjectivity of history and the illusion of objective reality from R. G. Collingwood, Karl Popper, and Thomas Kuhn, and I found they worked very nicely with the convenient selection of documents of the revolt so ably collected, edited, and translated by Barrie Dobson.[9] It was not at all difficult to demonstrate that chroniclers wrote not about what happened but about what they wished to believe, or wished others to believe, happened. Froissart, conscious of the poor light in which the upper classes had shown themselves during the Revolt, even produced a story in which Sir Robert Salle, faced with thousands of peasant insurgents, fights a heroic single-handed battle against them, nobly rebuking them and accounting for twelve of them with his sword before being borne down by sheer weight of numbers.[10] The whole episode appears to be a complete fabrication, though whether Froissart would have seen it in such a crude light is doubtful. For him it is what ought to have happened and therefore as valid as what might be recorded as having happened. His circumstances are similar to those of the ninth-century hagiographer Agnellus of Ravenna, writing an introduction to the *Liber Pontificalis Ecclesiae Ravennae*.[11] He explains that nothing is known of the lives of some of the saints whose stories he tells, and so he has assigned them appropriate biographies. The lives they are described as having led, that is, have the potential for being just as edifying as the lives they may have actually led (if indeed they existed). In fact, the invented lives are probably more edifying and therefore by that definition more "true," doctrinally and historically.

Examining the chronicles of the Peasants' Revolt more closely, I was able to show, at least to my own satisfaction, that there was a narrative appropriateness to key events that was surely the product of literary invention. It was the narrative appropriate to the subject that demanded that Archbishop Sudbury, praying in the chapel of the Tower of London, should have got to just that point in the Litany which says "Omnes sancti orate pro nobis" when he was dragged to his death from his place of refuge. It was the same narrative that demanded that Wat Tyler, at his meeting with Richard II at Smith-field, should call for a jug of ale and rinse his mouth out with it and spit it out villainously, thus parodying the ceremonies of courtesy performed by chivalric commanders before their armies (he may, of course, have been aware, in reality, of the requirements of this narrative). Any event that seemed fitting or appropriate was to be seen as invented for that purpose; authentic-sounding details, like the old chair that the clerk stands on to read out Richard's charter of manumission, are no more than the very familiar literary device of authenticating realism. The chronicle narrative is to be treated, it will be seen, as a literary text surviving in several witnesses: agreement, in a series of chronicle accounts, is not cumulative evidence of "what happened" but only evidence of derivation from a single witness; anything obviously appropriate and predictable is to be dismissed as an easy reading. Chronicles being what they are, there are no hard readings: so, no history, only texts.

Even historical records of the most routine and apparently un-politicized kind are doubtful witnesses to "what happened." The municipal record that tells of how certain aldermen opened the gates of the city of London to the rebels turns out to be a fabrication inserted in the record during the factional disputes of the early 1380s in order to bring discredit upon those same aldermen.[12] The only historical records which can be relied upon for objective veracity are those that no one has a reason for writing. And such records, of course, will tend to remain unwritten.

At the end of the investigation I realized that I was in a blind alley. What I was saying was accurate but useless. Demonstrations of the necessarily indeterminate nature of the meaning of texts, literary and historical, have their philosophical and political point, but they are of little use to either literary or historical understanding. In the case of the Peasants' Revolt, investigation must rely on the traditional sifting of the documentary evidence, perhaps enlightened by the recognition that all witnesses have very good reasons for not telling the truth, but recognizing too that this "truth" can only be talked about if there is an assumption of an objective historical reality: "something happened."

At the time at which I was writing, Michel Foucault was beginning to have a wider influence upon literary theorists and cultural historians. I did not recognize this importance at the time, and it is not clear to me now that he would have resolved my dilemma about the Peasants' Revolt, but he is clearly the most significant of the many influences that have gone into the making of the movement in literary and cultural studies known as the "new historicism." It might be argued that this is a new form of interdisciplinary centralization such as I have been talking about, a way of integrating not only literature and history in their traditional senses, but also texts of all kinds having to do with the social, economic, and cultural lives of people in the past, including those to do with medicine, schooling, law, etiquette, criminology, cartography—to take only a few examples. The "new historicism" is regarded still by most medieval historians as a fad of literary scholars, a technology for raiding history and bringing back exotic-sounding evidence for Foucauldian interpretations of literary texts; and many traditional literary scholars dismiss the "new historicism" as mere political allegoricism of a deradicalized kind. But the broadening of horizons of literary study that has taken place is irreversible, just as is the movement in historical study towards those aspects of social, cultural, and domestic history traditionally neglected in the concentration on political and military narrative. What is happening, it seems, is that the traditional boundaries of the subjects are being redrawn, so that in the future there will be no need for strenuous searching after successful interdisciplinary programs, since the separate disciplines will have become indistinguishable within a general multicultural diversity. The definition of "medieval studies" I gave at the beginning of this essay will then become history.

NOTES

1. Those who are not familiar with Elizabeth Salter's work in the field of medieval literature, art, and history, will welcome the following brief note of her principal writings: "Medieval Poetry and the Visual Arts," *Essays and Studies* 22 (1969): 16–32; "*Piers Plowman* and the Visual Arts," in *Encounters: Essays in Literature and the Visual Arts,* ed. John Dixon Hunt (London: Studio Vista, 1971), 11–27; "The Timeliness of *Wynnere and Wastoure,*" *Medium Aevum* 47 (1978): 40–65; "*A Complaint against Blacksmiths,*" *Literature and History* 5 (1979): 194–215; *Landscapes and Seasons of the Medieval World* (London: Elek, 1973), chapters 2, 3, and 4; *English and International: Studies in the Literature, Art and Patronage of Medieval England,* ed. Derek Pearsall and Nicolette Zeeman (Cambridge University Press, 1988).

2. Anne Hudson, *The Premature Reformation: Wycliffite Texts and Lollard History* (Oxford University Press, 1988). For the earlier narrative of Lollard history, see K. B. McFarlane, *John Wycliffe and the Beginnings of English Nonconformity* (Macmillan, 1953).

3. It would not be difficult to see in the foundation of these various centers the influence of larger economic, institutional, and demographic factors. (Some would argue that economic factors are always dominant in such institutional changes as I have described, but I would resist this in the case of York, where the innovation was the product of the vision and skill of one person.) There was the fear among individual medieval teachers that their subject was becoming increasingly marginalized, for various reasons, including the more effective operation of consumer choice, and the consequent desire to find security in banding together in larger umbrella organizations. There was also a response to more naked economic pressures. Overseas students were put on an independent fee-paying basis in England in the 1970s (fees more than quadrupled over a period of four years) and departments teaching popular subjects such as English and history were encouraged (and that may be a mild word to use) to maximize their disposable non-government income by attracting students from what were then rich countries, such as the United States. Medieval studies, as a subject that possessed a special attractiveness to students from countries without a visible medieval heritage, was an obvious choice for such courses, and the result was the putting on of some hastily improvised courses with little real academic respectability.

4. Lee Patterson, *Chaucer and the Subject of History* (Madison: University of Wisconsin Press, 1991), 423.

5. V. A. Kolve, *Chaucer and the Imagery of Narrative: The First Five Canterbury Tales* (Stanford University Press, 1984).

6. Michael Camille's two books are *The Gothic Idol: Ideology and Image-making in Medieval Art* (Cambridge University Press, 1989), and *Image on the Edge: The Margins of Medieval Art* (Cambridge, Mass.: Harvard University Press, 1992), but many of his shorter pieces are specially valuable for the connections they make between art, history, and literature, notably "The Book of Signs: Writing and Visual Difference in Gothic Manuscript Illumination," *Word and Image* 1 (1985): 133–148; "Seeing and Reading: Some Visual Implications of Medieval Literacy and Illiteracy," *Art History* 8 (1985): 26–49; "Labouring for the Lord: The Ploughman and the Social Order in the Luttrell Psalter," *Art History* 10 (1987): 423–454.

7. Richard Firth Green's *Poets and Princepleasers: Literature and the English Court in the Late Middle Ages* was published in 1980 (University of Toronto Press); his new book on literature and law in the fourteenth century is eagerly awaited.

8. Published as "Interpretative Models for the Peasants' Revolt," in *Hermeneutics and Medieval Culture,* ed. Patrick J. Gallacher and Helen Damico (Albany: State University of New York Press, 1989), 63–70.

9. R. B. Dobson, *The Peasants' Revolt of 1381* (London, Macmillan, 1970; 2nd edition, 1983).

10. Ibid., 261–264.

11. "Where I could not uncover a story or determine what sort of life they led . . . I have, with the assistance of God through your prayers, made up a life for them. And I believe no deception is involved, for they were chaste and almsgiving preachers and procurers of men's souls for God. And if any among you should wonder how I was able to create the likeness I have drawn, you should know that a picture taught me. . . ." Quoted (with parallel instances) in James W. Earl, "The Typological Structure of *Andreas,*" in *Old English Literature in Context: Ten Essays* ed. John D. Niles (Cambridge and Totowa, N.J.: D.S. Brewer and Rowman and Littlefield, 1980), 66–89 (p. 70); originally cited from the *Monumenta Germaniae Historica: Scriptores Rerum Langobardicarum,* ed. G. Waitz (Hanover, 1878), 297, by Charles Jones, *Saints' Lives and Chronicles in Early England* (Ithaca, N.Y.: Cornell University Press, 1947), 63.

12. See Dobson, *The Peasants' Revolt,* 161 (Sudbury); 165 (Wat Tyler); 160 (the old chair); 212–226 (the aldermen).

The Return to Philology

LEE PATTERSON

I WANT HERE to promote not novelty but restoration. To be sure, the very term philology conjures up visions of an older, sterner pedagogy, of the rote learning of linguistic detail, a positivist belief in factoids, a dismissal of interpretation as mere opinion, a celebration of the past for its very pastness, a contempt for innovation—in sum, a conservatism bristling with resentful indignation and shored up with a Luddite contempt for the brave new world of the contemporary academy. Fortunately, however, "The Return to Philology" is also the title of an essay by Paul de Man, which provides me with a pretext, both *for* my comments and *of* theoretical sophistication. De Man's essay was published in the *Times Literary Supplement* in December 1982, appearing as part of a symposium called "Professing Literature," which is also the title that Gerald Graff was to apply five years later to his institutional history.[1] Recycling seems to be endemic to discussions of this sort, and I do not myself claim originality. Nor in fact did de Man, who took as *his* pretext an essay by Walter Jackson Bate on "The Crisis in English Studies" that had just appeared in *Harvard Magazine*.[2] And while Bate's jeremiad has its own honorable genealogy, it expresses the central issues with such pertinence for the question of philology that it can serve as a starting point on a brief itinerary that will return us to Graff, then to de Man, and finally deliver us to my assigned topic, the crisis of medieval studies.[3]

Bate's account posited as the central, justifying element of literary studies what he called "the great Renaissance concept of *litterae humaniores*," the "body of ideals in humane letters" that has a "moral and educative effect on human character" (47–48). He saw this idea of literature as a coherent criticism of life as under threat

231

by academic specialization. The initial form this specialization took
was "above all, philology—the study of words historically—
[which] achieved a stranglehold on English studies from the 1880s
to the 1940s." According to Professor Bate,

> If you took a Ph.D. here [at Harvard] in English as late as the
> 1930s, you were suddenly shoved—with grammars written in
> German—into Anglo-Saxon, and Middle Scots, *plus* Old Norse
> (Icelandic), Gothic, Old French, and so on. . . . William Allan
> Neilson, the famous president of Smith College, had been a
> professor of English here for years. Forgivably, he stated that
> the Egyptians took only five weeks to make a mummy, but the
> Harvard English Department took five years. (49)

To be sure, Bate's account hardly stopped there. He acknowledged
that philology had lost its stranglehold, that there were moments
when "the Renaissance ideal . . . was at least given lip service" (50),
that some of the newer methodologies had virtues. But the damage
had been done. Specialization has Balkanized the Republic of Letters, cutting it off from life: literature had lost "its massive centrality
and human relevance" by means of "successive stages of special-
ism, leading to [the] intellectual emptiness" of deconstruction. And
the first of these specializations had been the deadening philology
by which, at the turn of the century, English studies had tried to pro-
fessionalize itself, to establish itself as more than "mere chatter
about Shelley."[4]

Bate's essay came in for more than its share of criticism, much
of it deserved.[5] But it told a story that remains widespread in the
profession, as Graff's *Professing Literature* both documents and itself exemplifies. At virtually every stage in Graff's history, those
who seek to affirm the relevance of literature to life are thwarted by
narrow philologists with their "endless memorization and recita-
tion of grammatical and etymological peculiarities" (28) and their
"Gradgrindian recitations" (31). And often these intellectual wars
had real institutional consequences: the humanist Irving Babbit felt
that his career at Harvard had been blocked by the arch-philologist
G. L. Kittredge, Dean R. K. Root—another Chaucerian—found the
presence of R. P. Blackmur at Princeton such a "desecration" that
he sought to exclude him from the faculty, and A. G. Kennedy,
an Anglo-Saxonist who was chairman at Stanford, for many years

forced Yvor Winters to teach freshman composition.[6] And even when philology withered away as a serious intellectual force, its retrograde habits were continued by pedantic historical scholars who sneered at mere critics.

The story that Bate and Graff tell—although to very different purposes—is hardly unique to American educational institutions. In 1581 the Dutch humanist Justus Lipsius claimed that he had rescued scholarship from a deadening pedantry. "I was the first or the only one in my time," he boasted, "to make literary scholarship serve true wisdom. I made philology into philosophy." What made Lipsius's remark telling was that it contained an allusion to a similar comment made a millennium and a half earlier. In one of his epistles Seneca had complained that the teacher of literature was now less a philosopher than a philologist or grammarian (*philologum aut grammaticum*):

> All study of philosophy and all reading should be applied to the idea of living the happy life, . . . we should not hunt out archaic or far-fetched words and eccentric metaphors and figures of speech, but . . . we should seek precepts which will help us, utterances of courage and spirit which may at once be turned into facts.[7]

The war between philological pedantry and literary philosophy is virtually conterminous with Western culture itself. It begins with Plato and the sophists, continues throughout antiquity and the Renaissance, reemerges in the German universities of the Enlightenment with the heady triumphs of Friedrich-August Wolf and Herder, and comes to some kind of crescendo in the inflammatory exchanges between Nietzsche and Wilamowitz-Moellendorf. It is a war implicated in the very term philology. On the one hand the term signifies an almost mystical *Kulturgeschichte:* Wilamowitz-Moellendorf said that "the task of scholarship is to bring the dead world to life," to provide a "pure, beatific contemplation of something we have come to understand in all its truth and beauty."[8] Yet it also conjures up a narrow positivism: Walter W. Skeat, the great nineteenth-century editor of Langland and Chaucer, referred to philology as "strictly historical methods . . . [whose] appeal lies to the facts; and the facts . . . are accurate quotations, with exact references, from all available authors."[9]

The passage between the narrow and the broad has never been easy or self-evident. Philologists have never been able to explain very successfully the larger human concerns their scholarship has served. Usually they have assumed that the accurate knowledge of linguistic and historical details was a value *per se* that did not require further justification. Or they have spoken in rather misty terms of what Hegel called the presence of the absolute spirit inhabiting the alphabet. Whenever these theories have been elaborated they have often turned out to be either politically embarrassing or intellectually inadequate: on one side, the potentially racist Aryanism of Max Müller in the middle decades of the nineteenth century, on the other, a century later, Erich Auerbach's last ditch effort to reinvoke an integral humanism against the fractures of modernity.[10] The fact is, philology has rarely been able to escape pedantry. Leo Spitzer, who was one of the few able to make the transition, has described with wit and poignancy how his initial passion for French culture was almost crushed by the "meaningless industriousness" imposed upon him by the great philologists Wilhelm Meyer-Lübke and Philipp August Becker.[11]

It might easily appear to a contemporary observer, however, that these battles are literally ancient history, or shortly on the way to becoming so. For while Professor Bate would doubtless not approve of the form it has taken, his humanist commitment to the idea that literature is valuable because it teaches truths about life is now an almost unchallenged orthodoxy. Regardless of which side of the canon wars they fight on, all participants agree that literature is crucial to civil life, that there *are* politically correct ways to teach, that nothing less than national identity is at stake. For Bate's old humanism art was valuable because it presented central human truths in an aesthetically powerful form; for the new humanism of the multiculturalist it is valuable because it provides a privileged vehicle for the appreciation of culturally determined identities. And the current debate has asserted the relevance of educational practice to social policy to a degree beyond the sophist's wildest dreams. These are heady days for academics: literary critics appear on television with such frequency that we might as well be in Paris. It seems clear, then, that the generalists have won the war between literature-as-life and literature-as-mere-literature, and that philology—with its insistence on the primacy of the textual—can finally be consigned to the dustheap of history.

Yet history also teaches us that we have heard proclamations of victory before, so perhaps skepticism is in order—the kind of skepticism that Paul de Man expressed when he called for a return to philology. The central target of de Man's criticism, both here and throughout his work, was what Christopher Norris has called "aesthetic ideology." This is the belief that art can unify the antinomies of sensuous experience and abstract intellection, that its ordered forms can regulate the disarray of life in order to provide us with "a dangerous (because immensely seductive) vision of how society might turn out if it could only achieve the state of ordered perfection envisaged by the poets and philosophers."[12] For de Man, what stands between us and the enticements of a programmatic literature—or a programmatic literary criticism—is language. If the goal of reading is to arrive at a hermeneutically sealed understanding that absorbs all aberrations,[13] then for de Man "the question is precisely whether a literary text is *about* that which it describes, represents, or states."[14]

In his essay on "The Return to Philology" de Man set against "the didactics of literature"—whether practiced by Bate's humanism or, as we now witness it, by the politics of multiculturalism—not theory in its high priori mode but what he called "mere reading." His exemplary instance was another Harvard institution, Reuben Brower's famous Humanities 6 course called "The Interpretation of Literature." According to de Man, this course required students

> not to say anything that was not derived from the text they were considering. They were not to make any statements that they could not support by a specific use of language that actually occurred in the text. They were asked, in other words, to begin by reading texts closely as texts and not to move at once into the general context of human experience or history, ... not to hide their non-understanding behind the screen of received ideas that often passes, in literary instruction, for humanistic knowledge.[15]

The effect of this "attention to the philological or rhetorical devices of language," according to de Man, was "to transform critical discourse in a manner that would appear deeply subversive to those who think of the teaching of literature as a substitute for the teaching of theology, ethics, psychology, or intellectual history" (24)—

or, we might add, politics. Thus, he concludes, "the turn to theory occurred as a return to philology, to an examination of the structure of language *prior to the meaning it produces*" (24, emphasis added). If philology is, as Roman Jakobson said, "the art of reading slowly," then it stands not in opposition to theory—as is too easily assumed—but as its central, constitutive element.[16] In de Man's formulation, philology functions as what he elsewhere calls "negative knowledge," the knowledge that "it is not . . . certain that literature is a reliable source of information about anything."[17] Or to put the matter more gently, the "reading in slow motion" that Brower taught ought to temper some of the more urgent claims currently being made on both sides of the political spectrum about the efficacy of literary study to social change.[18]

While we can hardly identify philology with deconstruction (as does de Man), it is true that both focus a peculiar intensity upon the text *as text,* that is, "prior to the meaning it produces."[19] Philology's willingness to defer interpretation has always been one of the things that has most irritated its critics. It seems to take a perverse delight in piling up facts without ever quite settling on their significance—facts, moreover, that too often seem to have little to do with the text at all.[20] But this patient tenacity has sometimes had considerable effect. Like deconstruction, philology has often functioned as an *Ideologiekritik*. Several instances are well known: Lorenzo Valla's unmasking of the Donation of Constantine; Wolf's deconstruction of the *Iliad* (which inspired Karl Lachmann to apply a similar analysis to the *Nibelungenleid,* one of romantic Germany's sacred texts); and the textual criticism that definitively deconstructed the most sacred of all Western books—the Bible—in the eighteenth and nineteenth centuries. There are less familiar examples as well. When Joseph Scaliger painstakingly worked out the chronology of pre-classical history, he ended up demonstrating, almost without quite noticing and probably without meaning to, that the Bible did not contain all human history. And Richard Bentley's famous *Epistola ad Millium* was not simply a philological tour de force by a brilliant young classicist but an attack upon those who sought to prove that the teachings of the Greeks could be reconciled with Christianity.[21] Profound ideological issues were at the center of this dry-as-dust philology, and continue to be. In his bracing book *Flawed Texts and Verbal Icons,* Hershel Parker demonstrates that the textual elements that critics have forged into a seamless unity were in fact generated by ill-informed editors and inattentive authors; and John Burrow has recently cast grave doubt upon the meaningfulness of the fragmentary nature of so many of Chaucer's poems—a lack of closure that appeals to our postmodernist sensibility but may well be nothing more than accident.[22] In short, philology at its most relentlessly skeptical forces us to reconsider received truths that turn out to be not so true after all.

While medieval studies cannot simply be identified with philology, the connection is both unavoidable and productive. Medieval studies has always defined itself institutionally by its commitment to the austere rigor of the philological sciences. Not only mastery of often obscure and always dead languages, but an entire panoply of *wissenschaftliche* practices—including codicology, paleography, diplomatics, and even archaeology—has been required of the aspiring medievalist. Medievalists are not educated, they are trained; and once initiated into the guild (given a concrete form in the Medieval Academy) they seem to disappear from the view of their collegial peers. The isolation of medievalists from the mainstream of humanistic study is an oft-remarked phenomenon that needs little demonstration. Equally obvious is the lack of interest in medieval studies of the vast majority of humanists, for whom both medieval studies and the Middle Ages remain *terra incognita*. In part this sequestration is a function of the defensive self-enclosure of medieval studies itself; in larger part, however, it derives from the role that the Middle Ages, as both historical object and disciplinary subject, has played in the development of modern thought.

As I have argued elsewhere, in the *grand récit* by which the Western historical consciousness has organized its past the Middle Ages has typically functioned as the all-purpose other.[23] According to this master narrative, the Renaissance is to be identified with modernity, the Middle Ages with premodernity; indeed, recent disciplinary discourse has replaced the term Renaissance with the more politically canny "early modern." According to this scheme, the Renaissance is where the modern world begins, while the Middle Ages, as the name with which the Renaissance endowed it declares, is a millennium of middleness, a space that serves simply to hold apart the first beginning of Antiquity and the rebeginning of the Renaissance. And ever since the Renaissance, medieval premoder-

nity has with few exceptions been experienced by modernity as
"Gothic"—exotic, obscure, difficult, strange, alien. The synonyms
offered for "medieval" by Roget's *College Thesaurus* are feudal,
knightly, courtly, antiquated, old-fashioned, out-dated, quaint.

Not surprisingly, then, those who devote their scholarly lives
to the study of this premodernity are stigmatized with an equivalent
obsolescence. As we have seen, both Bate and Graff, for all their
differences, identify those who have in the past resisted the engagement of literary study with modern life as medieval philologists.
And as every medievalist will testify, these attitudes continue in
force in the contemporary academy, where medieval studies is seen
as a refuge for those unwilling or unable to confront the demands
of contemporary intellectual life. In the *Speculum* essay I argued
this point by reference to recent accounts of subjectivity offered by
Renaissance literary critics—excuse me, by early modernists.[24]
Here I will offer only two, all-too-characteristic anecdotes from my
own experience. One is the comment of a colleague in film studies
on a visiting medievalist: "He's so interesting—and for a medievalist, too." The other is the remark of another colleague—a self-
designated cultural critic and "public intellectual"—at an oral exam
as she glanced over the list of secondary works on which the medievalist graduate student was to be questioned: "Well, I can see
from the titles that not much is happening in medieval studies."

It would not be entirely wrong to ascribe these comments—
and believe me, every medievalist can produce a similar list—to
simple ignorance. But neither would that be an adequate account.
For if medieval philology is the past that had to be rejected for the
brave new world of academic relevance to emerge, then there is an
act of Oedipal violence at work here, a violence that witnesses to
insecurities that the contemporary academy, for all its bravado, has
not been able fully to repress. The academy's current legitimation
crisis is for the most part understood as a function of the changing
demography of American society. But it is also, and I think more
profoundly, an effect of a crisis of modernity, what Weber called disenchantment. Weber meant by this term a loss of belief not simply
in divine sanctions but in the power of the intellect itself, in the
value of knowledge. He argued that while science shows that the
intellect "can, in principle, master all things by calculation," it also
undercuts the intellect by showing that "we cannot learn the mean-

ing of the world from the results of its analysis."[25] We may be able to control and manipulate reality, but we cannot understand it, in the sense of understanding either its purpose or the values that ought to guide our actions. Not so long ago people believed that conceptual analysis could teach virtuous behavior, that knowledge could bring wisdom. But even to propose such a possibility now is to solicit not just disbelief but accusations of hegemonic ambition. If the intellect is the cause of disenchantment, it is also its victim.

In the academy this disenchantment has given rise to a secular eschatologism that asserts that intellectual work is justified by the social transformations it effects. But medieval studies—like philology—resists this kind of justification and always has: in the struggle to reconcile cultural understanding with linguistic rectitude, philology has never been able to turn itself into philosophy, nor to divest itself of pedantry. But perhaps we ought to ask ourselves whether the attack on philology is not really an attack upon ourselves, whether we are not really just throwing out victims in the hope that the wolves will allow the rest of us to continue unmolested.

I want to suggest, in other words, that the uselessness of philology—its indefensible unjustifiability—scandalizes contemporary literary studies because it represents its *own* greatest fear: that the whole enterprise *cannot* be justified in terms of social effectiveness. If social transformation is our goal, then is teaching Toni Morrison really more effective than teaching Chaucer, especially when compared with a *direct* involvement with social problems? It is my own hunch that direct social activism is probably of more importance than most of the things we do in our classrooms and certainly than all of the things we do in our studies. Is it not possible, in other words, that the institutional neglect of medieval studies derives in some measure from a guilty conscience? That the medievalist is an awkward reminder that the social changes so many support and desire will require something other than intellectual work?

If these are unpersuasive words coming from a medievalist, let me cite a more acceptable source. "As writers, teachers, or intellectuals," writes Henry Louis Gates,

> most of us would like to claim greater efficacy for our labors than we're entitled to. These days, literary criticism likes to think of itself as "war by other means." But it should start to wonder: Have its victories come too easily? The recent turn

toward politics and history in literary studies has turned the
analysis of texts into a marionette theater of the political, to
which we bring all the passions of our real-world commitments. And that's why it is sometimes necessary to remind
ourselves of the distance from the classroom to the streets. Academic critics write essays, "readings" of literature, where the
bad guys (for example, racism or patriarchy) lose, where the
forces of oppression are subverted by the boundless powers
of irony and allegory that no prison can contain, and we glow
with hard-won triumph. We pay homage to the marginalized
and demonized, and it feels almost like we've righted a real-
world injustice. I always think about the folktale about the fellow who killed seven with one blow.[26]

For Paul de Man philology is subversive of received ideas because
it requires a level of linguistic attention that undoes overconfident
totalizations, "the screen of received ideas that often passes, in literary instruction, for humanistic knowledge." It is my suggestion
that medieval studies offers a similar challenge to the contemporary academy. Certainly its attentiveness to historical difference and
its maintenance of unfashionable scholarly practices set it in opposition to current academic trends. But its most profound challenge,
I believe, lies in its recognition that the work of the intellect cannot
find justification in a world elsewhere. Knowledge, it declares, is
finally its own warrant, and its value must remain a hostage to
the future.

If this analysis has any validity, then certain consequences follow. Medievalists have responded to their isolation from the mainstream in two ways. In the past, they have exploited it by ensconcing
themselves in specially funded programs, institutes, and centers.
The short-sightedness of this practice has now become evident: as
funding has dried up, medievalists' self-imposed segregation has
rendered them all too vulnerable to costcutting. Who will grant
precious funds to a program that proclaims its splendid isolation
from other humanists, especially when isolation is seen as intellectual backwardness? More recently, then, medievalists have been
careful to demonstrate that they share the same interests as their
colleagues. Their books and articles bristle with the current theoretical terminology, and disciplinary self-scrutiny has become as
vigorous a cottage industry in medieval studies as elsewhere. Here

are titles of some of the sessions at the 1992 Medieval Congress at
Kalamazoo: "Geoffrey Chaucer: Politics, Gender, and Social Con-
text," "Gendering Arthur," "Malory and Gender," "Silence, Conflict
and Resistance in the Postcolonial Classroom," "Spectacle and
Power," "*Piers Plowman* and Contemporary Theory," "Rape in the
Middle Ages," "Medievalist Feminists in the Academy," "The Self-
Understanding of Medieval Studies Today," "Essentialism and Gender Analysis," "Poststructuralism and Medieval Thought," "Feminist
Patristics and the *Pearl* Poet," " 'Pastism,' 'Presentism,' Theory:
Roundtable on Judith Butler's *Gender Trouble*," "Multiculturalism
and the Medieval Enterprise," "The Politics of Studying the Past: Reshaping the Field of Pre-Modern Studies in the Post-Colonial
World." To be sure, these sessions coexisted with, for instance,
three sessions on "The Medieval Fiddle," (which is an instrument,
not an accounting technique) and three on "Manuscript Sources of
Medieval Medicine." But no one can accuse contemporary medievalists, and especially the younger generation, of not trying to get
up to theoretical speed. If the wholesale adoption of the critical language and political concerns of other areas of literary studies will
save the Middle Ages as an object of study, then there seems little
to fear.

But what exactly is being saved? Despite the laudable energy
and inventiveness of much of this recent work, it remains true that
medieval *otherness*, the historical and disciplinary *difference* that
the Middle Ages and medieval studies have represented in the Western cultural consciousness and in the contemporary American
academy, remains under threat. If the only way that the Middle Ages
can survive is by being absorbed into a homogeneous field of disciplinary uniformity, if it must divest itself of much of what makes it
displeasing and even offensive to current academic fashion, then it
will have won a Pyrrhic victory. Here is the hardest case: is there no
place in the contemporary academy for the medieval fiddle? Can
we not foster those who seek to know the manuscript sources of
medieval medicine as well as those versed in the theory of post-
colonialism? To substitute one kind of routine for another seems
hardly to be an advance.

What I am suggesting, then, is that universities must find room
for a philologically oriented medieval studies not despite but
because of its intractable penchant for pedantry, its *Sitzfleisch*, its

fascination with the difficult, the obscure, and the esoteric. Nor must that room be a dusty closet into which only the theoretically backward and critically obtuse are hidden away. Graff has sensibly argued that English departments must "teach the conflicts" by including within their programs the ideological struggles that are agitating the profession as a whole.[27] This means that just as graduate students specializing in the Middle Ages must not be allowed to avoid theoretically informed courses in the later periods, so too must students of later literature be encouraged and even required to come to terms with both the literature and the critical practices that prevail in medieval studies. In curricular terms this entails a renewed commitment to distribution requirements. For instance, perhaps it is time to rediscover a largely forgotten part of the disciplinary history of English departments, Anglo-Saxon. While a required course in the subject has almost entirely disappeared from the graduate curriculum, some departments do allow Anglo-Saxon to fulfill at least part of the foreign language requirement. Given what I suspect is the ineffectiveness of most language requirements, this seems a good idea. It not only brings students into contact with the sources of the dominant language of their culture but with one of the most truly multicultural societies of Western history, where Celts, Romans, Germans, Scandinavians and finally Normans interacted in unpredictable ways. And yet this is multiculturalism with a difference, not the least being the role of Christianity. If as contemporary critics never tire of reminding us, difference must be protected at all costs, then it is time for an unapologetically different medieval studies to be rescued from the oblivion into which it is slipping.

NOTES

1. "The Return to Philology," a contribution to "Professing Literature: A Symposium of the Study of English," *Times Literary Supplement* 4158, 10 December 1982, 1355–56; reprinted in *Resistance to Theory* (Minneapolis: University of Minnesota Press, 1986), 21–26; Gerald Graff, *Professing Literature: An Institutional History* (Chicago: University of Chicago Press, 1987).

2. Walter Jackson Bate, "The Crisis in English Studies," *Harvard Magazine* (September-October 1982): 46–53.

3. In beginning with Bate's essay I am following the example of a number of the contributors to a conference called "What is Philology?" held at Harvard in March 1988 and published first as an issue of *Comparative Literary Studies* 27 (1990) and then as a book, *On Philology*, ed. Jan Ziolkowski (University Park: Pennsylvania State University Press, 1990). Ziolkowski points out that during the conference more references were made to Bate's article than to any other (11, n. 5).

4. This famous phrase was uttered by E. A. Freeman, Professor of Modern (i.e., medieval) History at Oxford, during the debate about the introduction of English studies into the university.

5. For a particularly sharp attack, see Stanley Fish, *Doing What Comes Naturally* (Durham: Duke University Press, 1990), 202–14.

6. Graff, *Professing Literature*, 88, 153.

7. Seneca, *Epistolae Morales*, ed. and trans. Richard M. Gummere (London: William Heinemann, 1962) 3.253. Lipsius's remark and its Senecan context are discussed in Anthony Grafton's splendid *Defenders of the Text: The Tradition of Scholarship in an Age of Science, 1450–1800* (Harvard: Harvard University Press, 1991), 39–40.

8. Ulrich von Wilamowitz-Moellendorf, *History of Classical Scholarship*, trans. Alan Harris (London: Oxford University Press, 1981), 1.

9. For Skeat, see Graff, 75.

10. On Müller, see J. W. Burrow, "The Uses of Philology in Victorian England," in *Ideas and Institutions of Victorian Britain: Essays in Honour of George Kitson Clark*, ed. Robert Robson (New York: Barnes and Noble, 1967), 180–204, and Hans Aarslef, *The Study of Language in England: 1780–1860* (Minneapolis: University of Minnesota Press, 1983); on Auerbach, Paul Bové, *Intellectuals in Power: A Genealogy of Critical Humanism* (New York: Columbia University Press, 1986).

11. "Linguistics and Literary History," in *Representative Essays*, ed. Alban K. Forcione, Herbert Lindenberger, and Madeline Sutherland (Stanford: Stanford University Press, 1988), 3–7.

12. Christopher Norris, *What's Wrong with Postmodernism: Critical Theory and the Ends of Philosophy* (Baltimore: Johns Hopkins University Press, 1990), 17. For an extended analysis of de Man's work in these terms, see Norris, *Paul de Man: Deconstruction and the Critique of Aesthetic Ideology* (London: Routledge, 1988), especially 28–64.

13. *Resistance to Theory*, 56.

14. Paul de Man, *Allegories of Reading: Figural Language in Rousseau, Nietzsche, Rilke and Proust* (New Haven: Yale University Press, 1979), 57.

15. *Resistance to Theory*, 23. A very similar description of the course has recently been given by Richard Poirier in "Hum 6, or Reading before

Theory," *Raritan Review* 9 (1990): 14–31, although Poirier seems unhappy with de Man's account (19–20).

16. For Jakobson's definition, see Calvert Watkins, "What Is Philology?" in *On Philology,* 25. For a similar argument, also drawing on de Man's essay, see Barbara Johnson, "Philology: What Is at Stake?" in *On Philology,* 26–30, and Jonathan Culler's "Anti-Foundational Philology," in the same volume (49–52).

17. *Resistance to Theory,* 10–11.

18. For Brower's definition, see Poirier, "Hum 6," 22.

19. De Man's identification is objected to by Poirier in "Hum 6," 19–20. Interestingly, textual criticism enshrines this deferral of interpretation in a now discredited dictum: *recensio sine interpretatio.*

20. In *Defenders of the Text,* Grafton describes a hilarious parody of contemporary classical education produced in 1908 by Ludwig Havatny. Here is the comment Havatny ascribes to the Professor of Greek on a scene in Plato's *Protagoras:* "As you see, gentlemen, the porter shut the gate [on Socrates and his companions]. At this passage anyone would be struck by the question of how this gate was constructed, and also by the important, still unsolved problem of door-shutting in antiquity" (cited, 214).

21. For discussions of Scaliger and Bentley, see Grafton, *Defenders of the Text,* 104–44, 12–21.

22. Hershel Parker, *Flawed Texts and Verbal Icons: Literary Authority in American Fiction* (Evanston: Northwestern University Press, 1984); John Burrow, "Poems Without Endings," *Studies in the Age of Chaucer* 13 (1991): 17–37.

23. See "On the Margin: Postmodernism, Ironic History, and Medieval Studies," *Speculum* 65 (1990):87–108, from which this paragraph is derived (92).

24. See also the splendid essay by David Aers, "A Whisper in the Ear of Early Modernists; or, Reflections on Literary Critics Writing the 'History of the Subject'" in Aers, ed., *Culture and History 1350–1600: Essays on English Communities, Identities and Writing* (London: Harvester Wheatsheaf, 1992), 177–202.

25. Cited by Rogers Brubaker, *The Limits of Rationality: An Essay on the Social and Moral Thought of Max Weber* (London: Allen and Unwin, 1984), 80.

26. Henry Louis Gates, "The Master's Pieces: On Canon Formation and the African-American Tradition," *SAQ* 89 (1990–91), 90–91.

27. *Professing Literature,* 1–15, 247–62.

Our Colleagues, Ourselves

JUDITH M. BENNETT

I WISH TO EVOKE two themes by the title of my presentation. First, the title speaks to the critical need for medievalists to reach out to our colleagues in other fields, to interest them in medieval scholarship, and to engage them in intellectual discussion. In other words, although medieval historians (like myself) should certainly maintain "lateral" associations with medievalists working in literature, art history, and other disciplines, we must pay more attention to "vertical" communication with historians working in other times and places.[1] We must, quite simply, make our work more relevant to our non-medievalist colleagues. Second, the title also evokes the exemplary role of feminist scholarship in this endeavor (for it echoes the 1971 feminist classic *Our Bodies, Ourselves*).[2] Feminist medievalists have certainly not met all the challenges of talking with our non-medievalist colleagues (and we are certainly not the only medievalists coping with such challenges), but we have made some progress and learned some lessons that are, I think, generally useful for all medievalists. In using feminist scholarship as my example, I will not be undertaking either a description or a defense of feminist medieval studies; I take it as a given that all of us recognize that there are hundreds of medievalists today who productively bring their feminist politics, in some form or another, to their research.[3] Yet, since neither collegial relevance nor feminist politics are decidedly popular among the general population of medievalists, I want to begin by claiming a lineage within medieval studies for both relevant scholarship and feminist scholarship. For as I look toward a medieval studies in the twenty-first century that engages wider audiences and encourages feminist scholars, I am anticipating the fulfillment of traditions within medieval studies

that were not new in the 1970s or 1980s but that instead date back
to the nineteenth-century origins of our field. So, let me begin to
talk about our future by considering our past.

The traditions of medieval studies that I claim as my own—as
a feminist medievalist trying to write for wider audiences—have, it
is true, found little place in our histories of medieval studies in
North America. As it has been set out for us by Fred Norris Robinson, S. Harrison Thomson, and William Courtenay, the story of the
development of medieval studies is a straightforward one: from the
late nineteenth century, a group of men, most of whom were teaching at Ivy League universities, began to focus their research and
teaching upon medieval literature, law, and history.[4] Working within
a positivist tradition, these men pursued medieval studies as a science, and working in a newly industrialized world, these men were
also largely motivated by a "rejection of the modern in favor of the
medieval."[5] In the 1920s, medieval studies in North America came
of age, with the founding of the Medieval Academy, the inauguration
of the journal *Speculum,* and the establishment of what would become the Pontifical Institute of Mediaeval Studies in Toronto. Since
these auspicious beginnings, we have developed into a field with
numerous journals, numerous conferences, and numerous centers
for the interdisciplinary study of the Middle Ages.

This is a reasonable history, but it overlooks (or perhaps
suppresses) two crucial currents in the development of medieval
studies. First, medieval studies boasts a long and distinguished alternative tradition, a self-critical tradition whose proponents have
bewailed the formation of a medieval studies community within
which we turn away from the modern world and speak only with
ourselves. In opposition to the "enclave" mentality so common in
medieval studies, some medievalists have always tried to create a
medieval studies that is engaged with the modern world—addressing modern issues and modern audiences, addressing our colleagues as well as ourselves. I can illustrate this tradition best with
a source that might surprise you: *Speculum,* which has long published articles highly critical of a medievalism that celebrates the
unmodern, the arcane, and the irrelevant. Lee Patterson's "On the
Margin" is the most recent of these articles, but it is by no means
the first.[6] In 1941, nearly fifty years before Patterson's critique,

Charles McIlwain sought quite explicitly to make the Middle Ages relevant in the modern world. Speaking movingly of the "cruelty and human savagery" of events in Europe, McIlwain tried to draw from these events new ideas about constitutional development in the Middle Ages.[7] A little over a decade later, Edgar Johnson went further, ridiculing medievalists who saw virtue in being "unstained by the sin of contemporaneity." Advocating a medieval studies addressed at a wide (even "newstand") audience, Johnson advised that we should "abandon for the moment our programs of esoteric research, and devote ourselves to a rewriting of mediaeval history that will help solve the major problems of the day."[8] Two years later, Barnaby Keeney published perhaps the harshest of these *Speculum* critiques. Speaking of humanities scholars in general and medievalists in particular, he promised:

> I shall bewail their preoccupation with the obscure and curse their avoidance of things that are important and therefore interesting. I shall point with scorn to their contempt for intelligibility, for communication to lay audiences, and for their lack of interest in synthesis, and pity them for their general desiccation.[9]

These men, of course, did not and do not speak for all medievalists, past or present. But they do speak for some medievalists, and what they have said exemplifies a long tradition within medieval studies of scholarship that is engaged with the present world in terms of both subjects and audiences. I have traced this tradition in the pages of *Speculum,* but it has existed in practice as well as theory—in the work, for example, of such celebrated medievalists as Eileen Power, Marc Bloch, and Rodney Hilton.[10] Many medievalists still aspire to the "noble dream" of objective research; many still believe it correct to avoid all connection between present-day concerns and scholarly work; many still write solely for fellow medievalists. Yet theirs is not the only tradition of medieval studies, not even perhaps the most eminent tradition of medieval studies. For decades, distinguished medievalists have embraced other ideals, seeking to deal actively with the ways in which the past impinges on the present *and* the ways in which the present impinges on the past. Medieval studies, in short, boasts a proud heritage of medievalists who have sought not only engagement between the past and the present but also fruitful dialogue between medievalists and our colleagues in other disciplines.

The second lacuna in our standard history is that it has forgotten the women. In looking back on our history, Robinson, Thomson, and Courtenay have examined the activities of such men as Henry Adams, Henry Charles Lea, Francis James Child, E. K. Rand, Charles Homer Haskins, George Lyman Kittredge, and Charles Gross. They have seldom thought—as I wish to suggest that we must—of Nellie Neilson, Bertha Putnam, Helen Jane Waddell, Hope Emily Allen, Cornelia Catlin Coulter, Helen Maud Cam, and the many other female scholars who have been part of medieval studies from its very beginnings.[11] If we remember these women and re-place them in our history, we will see medieval studies in a new way—as a field that accepted and accommodated female scholars exceptionally early, *and* as a field that has also long embraced both feminists and feminist scholarship.[12] In 1893, Florence Buckstaff published a study of married women's property rights in Anglo-Saxon and Anglo-Norman law; two years later Elizabeth Dixon examined women in the crafts of thirteenth-century Paris; and since then, female and male medievalists, generation after generation, have produced a now rich scholarship on medieval women.[13]

What, then, do these traditions of a more relevant and more feminist medieval studies have to say about our current situation as medievalists and our prospects for the future? Today, of course, medieval studies is in crisis. Budgets are getting cut, positions are being lost, our scholarship is being ignored by both classicists and modernists, and even at Oxford, the study of Anglo-Saxon is suddenly being deemed unnecessary. We often blame our "philistine" colleagues for this situation, but I think we should blame ourselves—for we have too often turned away from our disciplines, ignored our colleagues, and addressed only other medievalists. Small wonder, then, if others ignore us and fail to appreciate our work. This failure of collegial appreciation constitutes a serious threat to the survival of medieval studies; no matter how much joy and pleasure we take from our work and impart to our students, we *need* the support of our colleagues. We certainly need the intellectual stimulation they offer, but we also quite simply need their advocacy within the university. If non-medievalists appreciate medieval studies and the scholarly perspectives it provides, they will read our scholarship, support our programs, and retain our positions. Today, we lack this appreciation; for our future, we must acquire it.

Remembering our past is critical to achieving this future. If we see the history of medieval studies as including scholars who have sought wider audiences and scholars who have undertaken feminist work, we can find our way to a better future. We can build upon these as-yet underappreciated traditions to make our work more accessible, more relevant, and more interesting to more people. And we can also build upon these traditions to turn the obstacles now facing medieval studies into bridges for our future. I can best illustrate this opportunity to transform apparent problems into real possibilities by discussing how feminist medievalists are now tackling three of the challenges raised in John Van Engen's initial essay for this conference: multiculturalism, the denial of scholarly "objectivity," and interdisciplinarity.[14]

Multiculturalism can seem to pose a real threat to medieval studies. As Van Engen put it, "If Europe becomes one block alongside several others (Africa, Asia, etc.), does any place remain in the university for the study of Early Europe?"[15] Feminist medieval studies answers this question with a resounding "yes," for medievalists have much to learn from the concept of multiculturalism and much to contribute to its further study. What can we learn from multiculturalism? This new interest in multiculturalism reminds us of what we tell our students every term: that the medieval world was a multicultural world, a "medieval synthesis" of Greco-Roman, Germanic, and Christian traditions and peoples. Multiculturalism gives a new meaning to this old concept of a "medieval synthesis" at the same time that it makes us more alert to still other influences in medieval life—Jews and Muslims as well as Christians, popular cultures as well as elite cultures, Africa and Asia as well as Europe, women as well as men. For feminist medievalists, the exploration of this variety has mostly focused on uncovering the specific cultures and activities of women (as, for example, in Susan Groag Bell's study of medieval women book owners or Caroline Bynum's studies of female mysticism), but we are just at the beginning of what promises to develop into a much richer and more nuanced view of a multicultural Middle Ages.[16]

250 *Judith M. Bennett*

What can we as medievalists contribute to the study of multi-culturalism? We can offer a chronological perspective, a perspective that serves as a crucial counterweight to the presentmindedness of much multicultural scholarship. The editors of the special issue of *Signs* on medieval women argued this point strongly, reminding feminist scholars that "A fully multicultural feminism that lacks a history before 1750 is as impoverished as a feminism that attends to historical differences but lacks a multicultural appreciation."[17] One example how feminist medievalists have provided an important chronological perspective comes from debates about the low work-ing status of women in our own times; by documenting remarkable similarities between the working lives of medieval women and modern women, feminist medievalists have been able to suggest that neither capitalism or industrialism can be held responsible for the low status of working women in the 1990s.[18] The medieval West is not, to be sure, the only chronological perspective important in modern scholarship, but because it is a relatively well-documented and well-studied past, it is currently a critical chronological per-spective.[19] Medievalists, in short, have nothing to fear and every-thing to gain from multiculturalism; in its theory, it helps us to enhance further our understandings of the complexity of medieval societies and cultures, and in its modern focus, it provides us with an important role as chroniclers of the very diverse and multicul-tural Western past.

Van Engen also raised questions about the challenges posed by our modernist colleagues who "have swung decidedly toward the interpretive mode and highlighted the subjectivity inevitably present in all interpretation."[20] Feminist scholarship on the Middle Ages suggests that this rejection of the possibility that a scholar can cast an "innocent eye" upon the past provides more opportunity than challenge for our futures as medievalists. First, by questioning the thoroughness and objectivity of past scholars, feminists are add-ing in substantial ways to our corpus of information about the Mid-dle Ages. For example, in the 1950s, David Knowles excused himself from the charge of ignoring nuns in his multi-volume study of En-glish monasticism by claiming that "In truth, intimate or detailed records of the nunneries are almost entirely wanting over the whole period between *c.* 1200 and the Dissolution."[21] Janet Burton, Sharon Elkins, Marilyn Oliva, and Sally Thompson (among others) are now finding in the archives what Knowles dismissed as unfindable.[22] What happened in this specific instance has been duplicated in dozens of different areas of medieval studies; information about women that scholars once proclaimed simply irretrievable has been sought out, recovered, and reported by feminist scholars. Second, feminist scholars are also challenging old interpretations and providing new ways of seeing familiar things. Suzanne Wemple and Jo Ann McNamara (among others) have questioned the very periodization of the Middle Ages, suggesting that the so-called high Middle Ages were not, in fact, a high point for women at all.[23] Caroline Bynum has read well-known texts about and by medieval mystics in startlingly new ways.[24] Kathryn Gravdal has reread encounters between knights and shepherdesses in French pastoral poetry, emphasizing rape where other critics have emphasized playful sex.[25] Third, feminist medievalists are also creating our own interpretive agendas, independent of the traditional problems and discussions of medieval studies. E. Jane Burns has tackled the problem of women's speech in medieval literature; Susan Mosher Stuard has argued that the twelfth and thirteenth centuries brought a new notion of "gender" to Europeans (a notion that stressed differences over similarities); and in my own work on alewives, I have tried to examine how misogynistic ideas might have had very real and very negative effects on women's work.[26] In brief, the activities of feminist medievalists suggest that our postmodern recognition of the inevitable situatedness of every scholar (and his or her scholarship) is a boon rather than a threat; by throwing off the veneer of objectivity, we have been able to add new information to medieval studies, to answer old questions in new ways, and even to create entirely new research agendas. In the process, of course, feminist medievalists have also attracted new students, stimulated new archival work, and provoked new discussions: just what medieval studies needs.

Finally, Van Engen has also asked whether medievalists have "paid anything more than lip service to the notion of interdisciplinary or cross-disciplinary studies?"[27] For feminist medievalists, the challenge of interdisciplinary studies is particularly complex (since we must remain attentive to medieval studies, women's studies, and our own disciplines) and also particularly compelling (since feminist scholars embrace interdisciplinarity as a matter of both principle and practicality).[28] We have not entirely succeeded at interdisciplinary work (who ever has?), but we have made important steps toward a more interdisciplinary view of women and gender in the Middle Ages. In making those steps, we have focused, first, more on collaboration than on individual efforts. For example, in recent issues of the *Medieval Feminist Newsletter,* an extended and many-voiced discussion of interdisciplinary work has implicitly rejected the "celebration of single authorship" so critical to modern scholarship, assuming that greater interdisciplinarity will be achieved by feminist medievalists working *together* on common projects.[29] We already have many examples of the fruitfulness of such collaborations: the work of Kathleen Ashley and Pamela Sheingorn on St. Anne as a cultural symbol; the study of *Three Medieval Views of Women* by Gloria K. Fiero, Wendy Pfeffer, and Mathé Allain; and even institutional collaborations such as the Barnard project on Women's Religious Life and Communities, 500–1500.[30] Second, in working toward greater interdisciplinarity, feminist medievalists are also focusing upon *common questions.* Hence, Linda Lomperis has suggested that the key to interdisciplinary work by feminist medievalists rests in the development of research projects that transcend the disciplines: projects about feminist consciousness in the Middle Ages, about medieval women in the arts, about medieval sexuality and sexual practices, or about female agency in medieval Europe.[31] Common questions such as these do not ensure common approaches, common answers, or even comprehensible discussions, but they are at least a beginning. Third, in working toward interdisciplinary views of gender and women in the Middle Ages, feminist medievalists have not been using "medieval studies" to create a refuge from other scholars but instead have readily welcomed the ideas, theories, and lessons of our non-medievalist colleagues. The questions posed by Lomperis are very telling in this regard, for they are questions that not only allow both historical and cultural perspectives (thereby producing interdisciplinary work within medieval studies) but also derive from broader discourses among feminist scholars (thereby contributing to the interdisciplinary projects of women's studies). In this sense, one interdisciplinary program (medieval studies) is enriched by another (women's studies), taking from it questions, problems, and tools that then stimulate further research about the Middle Ages. Interdisciplinary work is perhaps always an impossible ideal, but in striving for that ideal, feminist medievalists are talking with each other more effectively *and* talking with their colleagues in other fields more effectively.

In engaging productively with multiculturalism, postmodern ideas about subjectivity, and the challenges of interdisciplinary studies, feminist medievalists are doing what all medievalists need to be doing. In the twenty-first century, universities and the intellectual inquiries nurtured within their walls will be very different from the settings that have produced and supported medieval studies during the past century. If we respond to these changes with fear and loathing, our field will suffer a lingering death at the hands of our indifferent colleagues. Yet if we not only view these changes as opportunities but also actively participate in their creation, medieval studies will thrive as a critical and appreciated part of academic life. Medieval studies can have an essential role in the universities of the twenty-first century, but it is a role that requires medievalists to engage directly with the discourses and concerns of our colleagues in other fields.

My hopes for medieval studies in the twenty-first century, then, build on long traditions of a medieval scholarship that is (on the one hand) engaged and relevant, and (on the other hand) feminist. We need to work together as medievalists specializing in literature or law or history or philosophy because we learn more about the Middle Ages if we work together. But we must not only talk among ourselves, we must not withdraw into an arcane medievalism that informs and delights only ourselves. As modern people, we must engage with the modern world, and as academics, we must first seek that engagement with our colleagues working on Nazi Germany or the twentieth-century American South or postcolonial Latin America. Our colleagues, ourselves: they have much to teach us, and we have much to teach them.

NOTES

At the time that I was writing this essay, I had just completed an essay on "Medievalism and Feminism" for *Speculum* 68, no. 2 (April 1993). Although the two essays offer very different arguments, this latter essay does draw upon subjects discussed at greater length in the *Speculum* article. It also contains (especially in the footnotes) some material taken directly from the *Speculum* piece.

1. I have taken the idea of "vertical" and "lateral" associations from William J. Courtenay, "The Virgin and the Dynamo: The Growth of Medieval Studies in North America 1870–1930," *Medieval Studies in North America,* ed. Francis G. Gentry and Christopher Kleinhenz (Kalamazoo, Mich., 1982), 15.

2. Boston Women's Health Collective, *Our Bodies, Ourselves* (New York, 1971).

3. These matters are discussed at length in my essay on "Medievalism and Feminism" prepared for a special issue of *Speculum* in 1993.

4. F. N. Robinson, "Anniversary Reflections," *Speculum* 25 (1950): 491–501; S. Harrison Thomson, "The Growth of a Discipline: Medieval Studies in America," in *Perspectives in Medieval History,* ed. Katherine Fischer Drew and Floyd Seyward Lear (Chicago, 1963), 1–18; Courtenay, "The Virgin and the Dynamo." I have not included Norman E. Cantor's new *Inventing the Middle Ages* (New York, 1991) for several reasons: it deals with medievalists, not medieval studies; it focuses mostly on scholars from Europe, not North America; and it provides a series of rather idiosyncratic and personal essays, not an attempt at a definitive history of the field.

5. Courtenay, "The Virgin and the Dynamo," 11.

6. Lee Patterson, "On the Margin: Postmodernism, Ironic History, and Medieval Studies," *Speculum* 65 (1990): 87–108.

7. McIlwain also argued that our interpretations of the Middle Ages "will be affected by our temperament, our traditions, and our peculiar studies." C. H. McIlwain, "Mediaeval Institutions in the Modern World," *Speculum* 16 (1941): 275–283.

8. E. N. Johnson, "American Medievalists and Today," *Speculum* 28 (1953): 844–854.

9. Barnaby C. Keeney, "A Dead Horse Flogged Again," *Speculum* 30 (1955): 606–611.

10. Patterson has also noted in "On the Margin" that medieval studies includes a tradition of scholars whose political commitments have enhanced their scholarship. Patterson's examples are of politically motivated " 'old philologists' like Erich Auerbach, Leo Spitzer, and Ernst Robert Curtius" (p. 107). As all these examples suggest, explorations of the connectedness between the medieval past and the modern present are perhaps more common among European medievalists than among medievalists working in North America. One possible explanation for this phenomenon is the power of the ideal of objectivity among American historians. See Peter Novick, *That Noble Dream: The "Objectivity Question" and the American Historical Profession* (New York, 1988).

I would like to emphasize that what distinguishes marxist, progressive and feminist scholars from other seemingly apolitical medievalists is merely that we are more explicit about our politics. If we agree with Eleanor Searle that "any individual scholar's sense of configuration and of significance will depend strongly on his/her world view," we must accept that all of us bring viewpoints with political import to our work. See her presidential address, "Possible History," *Speculum* 61 (1986): 779–786. As Allan Pred recently put it, "Through their selection of categories and emphases even the most vehement opponents of theory-informed historical inquiry cannot avoid building their scholarship upon an implicit theory of how the world works in a given setting." See his *Place, Practice and Structure: Social and Spatial Transformation in Southern Sweden: 1750–1850* (Totowa, N.J., 1986), 2. My thanks to Kären Wigen for bringing this book to my attention.

11. In an essay that details the work of dozens of male medievalists, Thomson mentions two women (Nellie Neilson and Edith Rickert), both very briefly. Courtenay notes that honors bestowed upon Neilson and Cornelia Catlin Coulter by the Medieval Academy recognized women's "importance and contribution to medieval studies" (p. 19), but beyond this token recognition, he says nothing about either the nature of women's importance or the extent of their contributions to the field. Norman F. Cantor in his *Inventing the Middle Ages* includes only one woman (Eileen Power) in his discussion, and she is treated in a section on "the dissenters, the eccentrics, the nonconformists" (quote from p. 376). For information on some of these early female medievalists, see: Margaret Hastings and Elisabeth G. Kimball, "Two Distinguished Medievalists—Nellie Neilson and Bertha Putnam," *Journal of British Studies 18* (1979): 142–159; Susan Mosher Stuard, "A New Dimension? North American Scholars Contribute Their Perspective," in her edited volume *Women in Medieval History and Historiography* (Philadelphia, 1987), 81–99; and John C. Hirsh, *Hope Emily Allen: Medieval Scholarship and Feminism* (Norman, Okla., 1988).

12. Because of the early prominence of women in medieval studies, it probably is no accident that the first female president of the American Historical Association was a medievalist (Nellie Neilson in 1943). As Hastings and Kimball have noted in their essay, women like Neilson and Putnam were "[n]ot feminists in the meaning of the current women's movement," but they were feminists in their own way. Hence, Neilson criticized the restrictions that faced female scholars, and she, together with Putnam, inspired some 200 graduates of Mount Holyoke to earn advanced degrees in history or related subjects. Indeed, some of these female medievalists were even recognized as feminists by their contemporaries. For example, Putnam (who completed her doctorate on the statute of labourers at Columbia in 1908) was remembered fondly by Austin Evans, Joseph Strayer,

and William Dunham as a "one of the first and most stalwart of the feminist pioneers to promote English mediaeval history in the United States." See *Speculum* 35 (1960): 522–523.

13. Florence Griswold Buckstaff, "Married Women's Property in Anglo-Saxon and Anglo-Norman Law," *Annals of the American Academy of Political and Social Sciences* 4 (1893–4): 233–264; E. Dixon, "Craftswomen in the Livre des Métiers," *Economic Journal* 5 (1895): 209–228. I would like to add four caveats. First, no direct equation links all women to all feminist scholars, but certainly feminist scholarship is a type of work particularly associated with women and particularly important to us. Some men have made very important contributions to the study of medieval women; see especially the work of David Herlihy, Joel Rosenthal, Stanley Chojnacki, and P. J. P. Goldberg. Second, all work on women is not necessarily feminist work, but the two are often equated. See, for example, the discussion of this issue by Ellen DuBois and her coauthors in *Feminist Scholarship: Kindling in the Groves of Academe* (Urbana, Ill., 1987). This broad equation between "research on women" and "feminist research" might be particularly pertinent to medieval studies because the antipathy of many medievalists toward the study of women has two clear results: (1) any study of women is *ipso facto* deemed feminist and (2) any scholar who undertakes such a project often has necessarily developed some feminist consciousness. Third, the sorts of feminist ideas that are brought to the study of medieval women are as broad (and changing) as feminism itself. In other words, there is no single "feminist line" on the Middle Ages. Fourth, feminist scholarship is today branching out beyond the study of women to the study of gender, men, sexualities, masculinity and femininity, and a host of other related topics. All of these matters are treated at greater length in my "Medievalism and Feminism."

14. See John Van Engen's Agenda Paper.

15. Ibid., 4.

16. Susan Groag Bell, "Medieval Women Book Owners: Arbiters of Lay Piety and Ambassadors of Culture," *Signs* 7 (1982): 742–768; Caroline Bynum, *Holy Feast and Holy Fast* (Berkeley, 1987).

17. *Signs* 14 (1989): 260.

18. Judith M. Bennett, "History that Stands Still: Women's Work in the European Past," *Feminist Studies* 14 (1988): 269–283, and "Medieval Women, Modern Women: Across the Great Divide," in *Culture and History, 1350–1600,* ed. David Aers (New York, 1992), 147–175. For an example of the influence of these arguments upon modern historians, see Katrina Honeyman and Jordan Goodman, "Women's Work, Gender Conflict, and Labour Markets in Europe, 1500–1900," *Economic History Review,* 2nd series, 44 (1991): 608–628.

19. I would like to emphasize that I do not subscribe to the view repeated several times at the conference that the Middle Ages is especially important as *the* original civilization of modern U.S. culture. In my view, modern U.S. culture derives from many past civilizations, of which the European Middle Ages is only one.

20. Van Engen, Agenda Paper, 4.

21. David Knowles, *The Religious Orders in England,* vol. II: *The End of the Middle Ages* (Cambridge, 1955), viii. In the extensive bibliographies found in all three volumes of this work, Knowles never cites Eileen Power's *Medieval English Nunneries* (Cambridge, 1922).

22. Janet Burton, *The Yorkshire Nunneries in the Twelfth and Thirteenth Centuries* (York, Borthwick Paper no. 56, 1979); Sharon K. Elkins, *Holy Women of Twelfth-Century England* (Chapel Hill, 1988); Marilyn Oliva, "The Convent and the Community in the Diocese of Norwich From 1350 to 1540," Doctoral dissertation, Fordham University, 1991; and Sally Thompson, *Women Religious: The Founding of English Nunneries after the Norman Conquest* (Oxford, 1991).

23. An early argument of this position is Jo Ann McNamara and Suzanne Wemple, "The Power of Women through the Family in Medieval Europe, 500–1100," *Feminist Studies* 1 (1973): 126–141. For a more recent statement, see David Herlihy, *Opera Muliebria: Women and Work in Medieval Europe* (New York, 1990).

24. Bynum, *Holy Feast and Holy Fast.*

25. Kathryn Gravdal, *Ravishing Maidens: Writing Rape in Medieval French Literature and Law* (Philadelphia, 1991).

26. E. Jane Burns, *Bodytalk: When Women Speak in Old French Literature* (Philadelphia, 1993); Susan Stuard, "The Dominion of Gender: Women's Fortunes in the High Middle Ages," in *Becoming Visible: Women in European History,* ed. Renate Bridenthal, Claudia Koonz, and Susan Stuard, 2nd edition (New York, 1987), 153–174; Judith M. Bennett, "Misogyny, Popular Culture, and Women's Work," *History Workshop Journal* 31 (1991): 166–188.

27. Van Engen, Agenda Paper, 4.

28. Feminist medievalists are highly motivated toward interdisciplinary work because our research topics often cross disciplinary boundaries (e.g., marriage, sexuality), our archives and texts require especially innovative methods, and of course, our feminist politics encourage us to work cooperatively with other scholars. In addition, the marginalization of feminist scholarship within medieval studies might have also encouraged greater cooperation among scholars in this "outcast" group.

29. Linda Lomperis, "Collaborative Work in Literature and History: What Literary Scholars Want from Historians," *Medieval Feminist Newslet-*

ter 9 (1990): 2–5. See also responses by Sharon Farmer in 10 (1990), and further discussions by Monica Green, Kathleen Ashley, Wendy Pfeffer, Ruth Mazo Karras, and Thelma Fenster in 11 (1991). The quote about single authorship is from Fenster, p. 12. The *Medieval Feminist Newsletter,* a publication of six years' standing with more than 300 subscribers, can be ordered from Thelma Fenster, Medieval Studies Center, Fordham University, Bronx, N.Y. 10458 ($15 for a two-year subscription in the U.S.).

    30. Kathleen Ashley and Pamela Sheingorn, *Interpreting Cultural Symbols: St. Anne in Late Medieval Society* (Athens, Ga., 1990); Gloria K. Fiero, Wendy Pfeffer, and Mathé Allain, eds., *Three Medieval Views of Women* (New Haven, Conn., 1989); Mary M. McLaughlin, "Looking for Medieval Women: An Interim Report on the Project 'Women's Religious Life and Communities, A.D. 500–1500'," *Medieval Prosopography* 8 (1987): 61–91.

    31. Lomperis, "Collaborative Work."

Saving Medieval History; Or,
The New Crusade

WILLIAM CHESTER JORDAN

THE UNDERLYING PRESUPPOSITION in a conference such as this is that as medievalists (or as medieval historians) we have a great deal to fear. It seems to me that the object of our fears takes three forms. Many of us see a threat in the recurrent mood swings in academic life: one year quantification is fashionable, another year the history of marginality; one year may see the history of the U.S. Civil War attract hordes of students, the next, the Vietnam War. I do not believe we can do very much about these mood swings. Interest in history, among both students and faculty, let alone the public at large, has often been faddish and contingent on factors that are unpredictable. To this extent, we sometimes benefit from the fads—and as I will try to show later, we might try to benefit from them more.

A second—and superficially more serious—fear, but one closely related to that of these mood swings is apprehension over "political" bias in intellectual inquiry. This, I take it, is conjured up in the odd word "pluriformity," a word, I am informed, borrowed from the specialized language of medieval philosophy and used, in the present context, to characterize the pressures on traditional studies from the defenders and entrepreneurs of various new methods and objects of analysis.[1] The world, and our country specifically, are made up of many little worlds, each striving to recover or invent its identity. In these struggles for identity, some traditionalists feel left out because the most vocal (and to them the most insidious) pluriformists regard the content of traditional work or the methods by which it is undertaken as racist or sexist or imperialist.

259

There are those, moreover, among the conservatives within the field who see the "real" enemy as the enemy within, those who have been trained as traditional medievalists or who have benefitted from the academy and who now, in supposed comfort and safety, turn against the "tradition" that makes their professional lives possible, stripping away its supposed objectivity and holding it up as a lie—sometimes implying that it was a conscious, deliberate lie. To say that, like mood swings, this kind of criticism and its reactionary response will have their own history—more intense and successful at some times, faint and unsuccessful at others—is not to say that they are trivial; but, again, more on this later.

The third and final object of our fear is the increase in knowledge in history and the expanding areas of inquiry across the scholarly spectrum. The truth is that there *are* more areas of legitimate historical inquiry now than yesterday. Problems largely ignored in the past—questions of sexuality, gender, race—may be said to have a *prima facie* right to be addressed now. But these are not the only new areas of inquiry. For example, most teachers who would have said ten or twenty years ago that the 1960s were too recent to study regard that decade, at the present time, as a perfectly reasonable focus for courses and students' work. Many traditional historians, not just medievalists, also see the growth in prestige of new fields outside of history—molecular biology, for example, or computer and information science—as still one more nail in the coffin of traditional subjects and modes of inquiry. If faddish philistinism is one threat and certain vague but ominous "moral" values seem at risk or are a threat from the enemy within, the very existence of our field appears imperiled by the growth of new fields that administrators want to pour money into in order to increase their prestige and the prestige of their institutions. To the perennial risk that most of the money will go to athletics is added the fear that what is left will go to big science and big—perhaps, even stupid—social science.

"Faith," Saint James said, "without works is dead." I have no desire to be a crude but faithful conservative who goes down with the traditional ship, content that in the end someday, somewhere, someone will say, "he told us so." On the other hand, I have no desire to ally myself with those who would gild our discipline with the false pieties of what has come to be called "political correctness": the kind that would prefer, for example, work on the political leadership of Ghengis Khan, as opposed to Charlemagne, since the khan was a person of color. I propose, rather, two things: first, to take seriously the opportunities offered by the liveliness of current debate and the assertive call for new theories, new methods, new contexts, and new subjects of inquiry within our discipline; and second, to exploit as we have singularly failed to exploit in the past, the deep commitment I perceive among Americans to learn about the Middle Ages—traditionally conceived or otherwise.

I would argue that the changing character of prevailing interests has deeply enriched scholarship and, to some extent, teaching. Without denying for a moment that many of these issues were treated with grace and erudition by earlier scholars, I would be willing to assert that the last two decades have seen a genuine transformation in our understanding of a number of issues in the history of the Middle Ages. Work on sex and gender would not have been stimulated without the variety of feminist movements we have lived through and continue to live through. Here I would only mention a few of the collected studies which demonstrate the richness of the harvest: *The Marriage Bargain: Women and Dowries in European History,* ed. M. Kaplan (New York, 1985); *Women and Work in Pre-Industrial England,* ed. L. Charles and L. Duffin (London, 1985); *Women and Work in Pre-Industrial Europe,* ed. B. Hanawalt (Bloomington, 1986); *Women and Power in the Middle Ages,* ed. M. Erler and M. Kowaleski (Athens, Ga., and London, 1988).

Much, perhaps most of the work on Jewish-Christian relations, on the position of heretics in medieval society, on the status of children, and on popular culture would also not have been undertaken without the heightened sensitivity to minorities and alternative cultures that was a characteristic feature of the 1960s and 1970s in political life in the United States. At last, the insights gleaned from the major body of this scholarship are being integrated into what might be called old-fashioned analyses of power: did it matter that feudal states ignored or denied the public role of marginal groups? Did personal relations across ethnic and confessional lines have any success in deflecting the power of strong institutions—the familiar old duo of church and state—when these institutions concentrated their resources to root out heresy or humiliate Jews? If we can ask whether women had a renaissance, can we not also ask whether Jews had a renaissance of the twelfth century? Such questions challenge our research techniques (how do we answer them?) and our scholarly paradigms (why should we?). But they seem to me to be interesting *prima facie,* and I would recommend, among many others, the following works for your consideration. Besides the seminal study of marginality in Paris of Bronislaw Geremek, a work deeply colored by the author's reading of cultural anthropology,[2] there is of course Robert Moore's stimulating book, *The Formation of a Persecuting Society* (Oxford, 1987). Specifically on the Jews I would suggest Maurice Kriegel's *Les Juifs à la fin du Moyen Age* (Paris, 1979) and Gavin Langmuir's book of collected essays, *Toward a Definition of Antisemitism* (Berkeley, 1990), as well as his ruminative look at the origin and persistence of anti-Semitism, *History, Religion, and Antisemitism* (Berkeley, 1990).

Let me say immediately that I have difficulties with all these works. Moore argues far too often from silence at a number of critical points, and he does not always wear his theoretical raiment, derived from historical sociology, as lightly as he should.[3] Kriegel's application of the word "caste" to the position of the Jews in southern European society in the Middle Ages is problematic.[4] And Gavin Langmuir, I believe, frequently slips into over-interpretation and over-argument; old and poorly digested theory on occasion hangs like an ominous shade above many of his otherwise most penetrating observations.[5] But for all my misgivings, all these authors grapple with fundamentally important problems and show how valuable it can be to employ a range of critical theory to explicate knotty issues.

The skeptic who grants that these few works are tolerable might still insist that far too many bad articles and books, with a great deal of jargon and misapplied, misunderstood, or fundamentally unnecessary theory have been produced in the effort to do feminist history or subaltern history or whatever. Granted, but this should hardly persuade serious scholars to ignore theory or refrain from using as much of its specialized language as is needed to write economically on the issues they are exploring. Sometimes ordinary language cannot accommodate new ideas efficiently . "Some Guidelines for Readers Evaluating Submissions," published by the editors of *Exemplaria* in its maiden issue, put the matter nicely, if paradoxically:

> Intelligibility, we recognize, is sometimes achieved only at the expense of "clarity," and difficulty of style is often a prerequisite of intelligibility; but we also hope that, for example, interested undergraduates browsing in periodical rooms can pick up *Exemplaria* and grasp the ideas at stake in any given article we publish.[6]

In any case, we can assuredly do no worse than most medievalists did a half century ago. There was less jargon borrowed from other disciplines then, but a painfully large number of bad, alternately craven and hubristic articles appeared in the first thirty years of *Speculum*. It is true that this *oeuvre* of a half century ago seems quaint now and the bad prose and weak arguments almost endearing in such a context. But imagine what it must have been like in the middle of the Great Depression, say 1935, to get the latest issue of *Speculum,* open it and read Alexander Haggerty Krappe's pontifications on the "inductive laws" for doing comparative medieval literary study.[7] Pompous in places, jargony in others, suffocatingly whiggish everywhere, and with not one new idea and no new data, the article must have struck the best young medievalists of the time with despair: "this is what gets published in *Speculum.* Aargh!" But that was hardly an argument against doing comparative literary studies.

Perceptive observers of the time made the point. C. W. David, in the same volume of *Speculum* in which Krappe's article appeared, wrote a stunning description of the masterly achievements of the greatest American medievalists in the half century from 1884 to 1934.[8] But he was quick to add that "whatever be thought about our achievement in mediaeval history, we have surely achieved mediocrity" as well.

> ... it is easy in fixing attention on the best of our work, to overlook much that is drab and dull and uninspired. It cannot be denied that much of our scholarship lacks richness of background and that we often write badly; indeed that many of us are less interested in literary excellence than we should be. It is perhaps for this reason that, outside the classroom, our in-

fluence has been less than it ought to have been, and that we have failed to create a wider interest in our subject among the reading public. . . . But it is well to remember that mediocrity is not confined to America alone.[9]

He cautioned his readers that "much remains to do." And he chided them with the reminder that "our vision is . . . unfortunately limited by tradition. We have too long been accustomed to regard the Middle Ages almost exclusively from the classical, the western Christian, and the European standpoints."[10] A modern "multiculturalist" could not have expressed the point better.

Nevertheless, when we turn to the methodological issues that the reliance on borrowed jargon evokes in our own day, the tendency is for many of us to feel imposed upon. It used to be social thinkers, like Gramsci and Geertz, now it is literary critics and self-professed cultural critics who are described as the culprits, force-feeding us with their gobbledygook (helped along, of course, by the turncoats, the enemy within). Yet, if it is true that many medievalists claim inspiration from Foucault, and Derrida, and Lacan, and de Certeau, and a host of others more or less familiar, many of the theorists found their inspiration in the analytic and descriptive studies that even the most staid traditionalist would praise (or at least would find hard to denounce as utter trash). The obvious example—though very old now—is Kantorowicz's *King's Two Bodies,* to which Clifford Geertz attributes "a major influence on the direction" of one of his own most provocative works, *Negara: The Theater State in Nineteenth-Century Bali.*[11]

Moroever, some social scientists continue to read medieval studies, benefit from them, and cite them. Here is the voice of a sociologist constructing a theory of an "ideal society" in a recent issue of the journal, *American Behavioral Scientist:*

> . . . a sociologist would ask what the effective possibilities for implementation of a normative order were before trying to establish that order as an ideal. Indeed, it is unlikely for a moral ideal to emerge or survive where there is no imaginable forum in which the wrongs it identifies could be punished or the rights vindicated. One example is the transformation of moral discourse in feudal Europe with the rise of court life. Bloch (1975) argued that only when feudal courts succeeded in establishing their effective political authority, making pos-

sible appeal to a law 'above' the power of contending parties, did deepened conceptions of moral selfhood and of moral guilt or intention as part of criminal responsibility develop in Western law.[12]

I do not say that R. Howard Bloch would necessarily agree with this sociological reading of his work, but it seems pretty clear at least that his work has been read and admired by one sociologist. To pursue this theme, even a quick perusal of some of the most up-to-date work on Third World issues will also show the pervading influence of medievalists—non-traditional and, more often, traditional medievalists. The preference for the work of traditional medieval historians may be because politics and economic relations of production still loom large in studies of Third World societies. People working on power in largely non-literate historical societies (like those of the Middle Ages) are producing volumes that seem to speak directly (and in a certain sense, because of their historical remoteness, disinterestedly) to Third World specialists. Ricardo Godoy found inspiration and valuable insights for his work on agricultural labor and development policy in the present rural society of Andean Peru in the studies of Bruce Campbell, one of the leading historians of medieval English rural society.[13] Walter Zenner, an anthropologist specializing in middleman minorities in Third World countries, seems to have seen parallels, to some extent, with the Jewish moneylenders in thirteenth-century France on whom I have published.[14] In work I have done on women and credit in pre-industrial societies, I had to read widely in economic and social anthropology and development studies.[15] My reading has convinced me that the scholarly commerce between medieval history and modern Third World history is likely to go on and deepen in the decade ahead.

In general, then, we ought to take seriously the possibilities of new discoveries and new insights that arise out of the cacophony of academic culture presently besetting us and we ought to recognize that the much-besieged traditional historical study of the Middle Ages remains vigorous and is having an impact on many other disciplines, especially those related to colonial, neo-colonial, and Third World areas of study.

My second point is that we ought to exploit the deep well of interest in many parts of American society to learn about the Middle

Ages. Perhaps a conference like this one is not the precisely appropriate forum to discuss this, but if it is not discussed here, it is not
likely to be discussed anywhere. So, if at some level it might be
preferable to use the remainder of this essay as an opportunity to
address the scholarship, shape, and direction of my particular field,
at another it is at least useful to explore the broader, non-scholarly
world of medieval enthusiasms, which ought to provide a large potential audience for serious medieval studies. For it is useless to
have a field without an audience.

Of course, we ordinarily think of our audience as the university—other scholars and "motivated" college students (the motivated being preciously defined, often enough, as those interested in
taking our own courses). It is these students that many of us are
most concerned about losing as a result of the perceived shift in
academic culture to pluriformity. But these "motivated" and "traditional" college students (dwindling in number as some think) have
not come to their interest in the Middle Ages from reading scholarly
books (and did not do so in the mythical "good old days" either, as
C. W. David pointedly reminded his readers in 1935).[16] Interested
students come from a wider "popular culture" eager to drink in
something about the Middle Ages. Though routinely ignored by
professional medievalists, the public this culture serves needs our
attention. And if they get it, that can only translate into stronger enrollments (and all the moral value that some people think comes
from studying the Middle Ages). How do I know that the deep well
of interest is out there? I checked.

It almost goes without saying that popular novels and movies,
which adults read or go to, frequently evoke the Middle Ages. Some
evoke them better than others; some, like the novel, *The Sheriff of
Nottingham* by Richard Kluger, that has recently appeared, struggle
hard, if with indifferent success, for historical accuracy.[17] Some are
pure fantasy, marking the setting of the Middle Ages with only the
most obvious signposts. But the continued popularity of the genres
bespeaks the persistent fascination of adults with the Middle Ages
which they learned to love as children.

Children are still literally besieged by images of the Middle
Ages today: popular books such as Mitsumasa Anno's *Anno's Medieval World* (1980) which makes medieval science come alive and Jonathan Hunt's *Illuminations* (1989) which, as one reviewer puts it,

uses the alphabet as a framework to explore the medieval age. Each letter introduces a term that is explained in an illuminated paragraph and illustrated with a . . . line-and-wash drawing. Alchemy, Black Death, Coat of Arms, Dragon, and Excalibur typify Hunt's word choices.[18]

One can add to these books the impressive series by David Macaulay—*Cathedral* (1973), for example, and *Castle* (1977)—that create captivating imaginary worlds of medieval buildings and structures. The trade journal, *Booklist,* in any issue will usually list a handful of new books on the Middle Ages—fiction and nonfiction—for children: a scanning of recent issues noted two works by Sarah Howarth, *Medieval People* and *Medieval Places* (both 1992); a children's medieval atlas by John Briquebec, *The Middle Ages* (1990); and a pop-up book for tots, Gillian Osband's *Castles* (1991).[19]

Cartoons, with poetic license, routinely invoke the Middle Ages. In "Young Robin Hood" which one can see on Sunday morning where I live, a recent episode showed villagers starving. Hagala, the sorceress from Sherwood Swamp, found it hard to get her magic to work to remedy the situation, so Robin Hood and his band of merry men played a few tricks to restore her confidence in the power of her magic. When evil Prince John sees her do some of her magic, he seizes her because he wants her to get rid of King Richard's ghost which has been troubling his sleep. Happily, Robin Hood and his friends, with the aid of Maid Marian, rescue Hagala from Nottingham Castle (in the process helping themselves to some of the prince's ill-gotten gold). Leaving Marian behind, Robin, in a delicious bit of anachronism, laments to us all that "parting is such sweet sorrow."[20]

We may carp at such silliness, denounce the anachronisms and the errors, pontificate that the Middle Ages ought not to be presented as mere fantasy. The fact remains that, however distorted the images, the interest is there: in castles, in kings and queens and magic (of which there was plenty in the *real* Middle Ages). Why does this obvious entertainment interest not translate into widespread serious interest in college? The answer, I believe, lies at least partly in the influence of the schools. Every child who enjoys the fantasies of the Middle Ages and whose interest may even be sharpened in a more technical way by good popular books like those of

David Macaulay is likely to be turned off by some of the insipid material that is taught in grades kindergarten through twelfth. It is not the teachers whom I blame; it is very much the books.

To be sure, a full analysis of the pedagogical situation with regard to the teaching of the Middle Ages in the schools would requite a great deal more space than I can give it here. Moreover, it would require the kind of expertise and mastery of studies of educational experience and theory that I do not possess. The impressions that a scholar and parent such as I have received from the material I know about may very well be skewed. Nevertheless, it seems a commonplace that humanistic education in the schools is suffering. The observations I offer here are neither a diagnosis of the illness nor a prognosis for the future. I intend rather to raise a few questions and make a few suggestions about the dimensions of the problem that faces us as medievalists. All of my remarks are tentative and, therefore, subject to systematic revision.

If it is a commonplace that the textbooks that transmit knowledge of the Middle Ages (and history in general) to pupils in grades K–12 are unimpressive, we must ask why this is so. How many active scholars serve on the committees that oversee the writing or adoption of textbooks for public schools? Does our professional organization lobby anyone—publishers, state boards of education—to see that serious, active scholars have an input into the creation or supervision of school texts? One vibrant accurate paragraph on castle building or chivalric orders in the Middle Ages in one of the books used in the California or Texas system would do more to sharpen children's interest in the Middle Ages than much of the verbiage in bland, boring, flat social studies books does now.

Does our professional organization (or should it) look into the possibility of videos (not just talking heads) for K–12 which could bring accuracy about the Middle Ages into the classroom and, if done right, some pleasure with it? A whole nation of children is learning about the Civil War from the Ken Burns series. It can now learn about the Renaissance thanks to the historic fifteen-year effort of one of my colleagues at Princeton, Theodore Rabb. Should our professional organization look into the possibility of National Endowment for the Humanities or National Endowment for the Arts backing for an enterprise that could bring the Middle Ages into the elementary school classroom in a similar way—*with some flair?* (I do not mean, by the way, the kind of videos now being produced at the University of Toronto, which, however they are assessed as art or for their other merits, concentrate on particular texts and have a professorial sheen to the marketing. I am talking about something that can reach young hearts.)

The American Council of Learned Societies (ACLS), that most staid, sober-minded, and scholarly umbrella group, has seen the light on these issues. Humanistic scholarship—whether theory intoxicated or not—cannot survive or at least be vigorous if scholars rarely think about what happens in the schools. Consequently, ACLS has launched a full-scale study (with major foundation support) of the K–12 curriculum, what sorts of changes can and should be made in it, and what pedagogical methods are appropriate for transmitting the content of the humanities curriculum. This undertaking, fortunately, will involve real scholars (not only specialists from schools of education, but active humanistic scholars) who will also go into school districts, work directly with school teachers, and then go—with those same teachers—to test some of the projects and proposals that come out of the formal study. This will take place in school districts in Los Angeles, Minneapolis, San Diego, and Brookline, Massachusetts, for starters, and six to eight more districts distributed geographically and ethnically over the next three or four years. The difficulties in arranging this, I should point out, were considerable: teachers' unions are understandably suspicious of another study of their members' alleged failures by people who never enter a city classroom, but the gifted leadership of this project has managed to work even with the teachers' unions. Would it not be appropriate for our professional organization to engage in a serious study of how the Middle Ages is taught and how it can be improved at the K–12 level, if not as part of this project (since donors have their own priorities that must rightly be respected), at least in some serious manner?[21]

Let me add also that the ACLS has entered what look to be successful negotiations with Scribners/Macmillans for the "Junior Dictionary of the Middle Ages," which will be a children's version of *The Dictionary of the Middle Ages* whose publication has recently reached conclusion.[22] Is it not part of our responsibility, when this project is announced, to lobby for the purchase of this tool for elementary and high school libraries? And is it not our professional organization that should articulate the utility of such a tool for K–12 students?

Let me end on a cautionary note. I have tried to paint a picture
of the challenges and possibilities that face us as medievalists. I believe that there are significant opportunities before us. Of course,
the new crusade will hardly win us Jerusalem. Many public school
textbooks will continue to be bland or inaccurate or both. I have
my doubts whether our professional organization, whatever its best
interests, will think it has the resources (or even the resources to
apply for the resources) to look into some of the issues I have
raised. After our best efforts, I am sure that there will still be three
thousand colleges out there with bone-headed administrators who
could not care less about introducing an honors course in the Middle Ages into their curriculums when they can spend money on a
media event like a debate on political correctness. There will still
be people who argue that the study of the European past is a dis-
traction for people of color—and its imposition a kind of neo-
colonial power-trip for the Establishment. Fine. We do not have to
give up, let alone go around stupidly praising the European past for
achievements it never made or ignoring its treacheries and false
promises. I still would argue that there are small battles to be won
here and there and that, by winning them, we will be in a better
position to protect and nourish whatever there is about medieval
studies that is worth protecting and nourishing. The real problem is
the discourse among ourselves: the intemperate language, the an-
ger, the paranoia of seeing fellow scholars as political enemies. I
may not like this or that new "—ism" or this or that old tradition.
Nevertheless, it would be terribly destructive of all aspects of our
project and, what is more important, destructive of our moral universe, if we were to end up turning scholarly squabbles, serious as
they may occasionally be, into the kind of civil war that, a generation from now, will be considered the cause, not the result, of any
supposed collapse of our enterprise.

NOTES

Some of the research for this paper (the tracking down of popular books,
comic strips, cartoons, movies, television programs, and toys with medieval themes) was carried out by Victoria, John, Clare, and Lorna Jordan,
whom I wish to thank. The data which they accumulated I have had to use
sparingly.

1. The word appears in the agenda paper, "The Past and Future of Medieval Studies," for this conference. For example, on p. 4 of that paper, potential participants are informed that, "The humanities departments of universities have been overwhelmed by a sense of the pluriformity of human experience." And they are asked to address whether an "emphasis upon the pluriformity of medieval experience [will] do more justice to the sources and satisfy those who judge the Middle Ages as uniform and hence uniformly uninteresting."

2. *Les Marginaux parisiens aux XIVᵉ et XVᵉ siècles* (Paris, 1976).

3. For various critical responses to Moore's work, see the reviews of Michael Clanchy, Bernard Bachrach, and James Given in *TLS*, September 11, 1987, p. 990; *Choice* 25 (1988): 1740; and *American Historical Review* 94 (1989): 1071, respectively.

4. Another critique appears in Noël Coulet's " 'Juif intouchable' et interdits alimentaires," an essay in *Exclus et systèmes d'exclusion dans la littérature et la civilisation médiévales* (Aix-en-Provence and Paris, 1978).

5. I have discussed Langmuir's books in two reviews *American Historical Review* 97 (1992): 838–839, and *English Historical Review* (forthcoming).

6. *Exemplaria: A Journal of Theory in Medieval and Renaissance Studies* 1 (1989): 226.

7. A. H. Krappe, "Mediaeval Literature and the Comparative Method" *Speculum* 10 (1935): 270–276.

8. "American Historiography of the Middle Ages, 1884–1934," *Speculum* 10 (1935): 121–137.

9. David, "American Historiography," 136–137.

10. Ibid., 127, 137.

11. Ernst H. Kantorowicz, *The King's Two Bodies: A Study in Medieval Political Theology* (Princeton, 1957); Clifford Geertz, *Negara: The Theater State in Nineteenth-Century Bali* (Princeton, 1980), 236.

12. Ann Swidler, "The Ideal Society," *American Behavioral Scientist* 34 (1991): 567.

13. Ricardo Godoy, "The Evolution of Common-Field Agriculture in the Andes: A Hypothesis," *Comparative Studies in Society and History* 33 (1991): 395–414.

14. Walter Zenner, *Minorities in the Middle: A Cross-Cultural Analysis* (Albany, 1991), 173.

15. William Jordan, *Women and Credit in Pre-Industrial and Developing Societies* (Philadelphia, 1993).

16. David, "American Historiography," 137.

17. Richard Kluger, *The Sheriff of Nottingham* (Viking Penguin, 1992).

18. *Booklist*, 15 September 1989.

19. I have not seen, let alone read all these books. My point is merely that the production of such titles seems to be steady and in no danger of abating.

20. The program appears on WPIX (Channel 11), an independent station operating out of New York.

21. My discussion of the ACLS project is based on a description paper issued in December 1991, "The ACLS Elementary and Secondary School Curriculum Development Project."

22. There have also been suggestions for one or more supplementary volumes to the original series in order to cover subjects omitted in the original project. Negotiations continue.

On the Statue

KARL F. MORRISON

OUR TRAINING MAKES US expert at "unpacking" and reading the entrails of symbols. Not long ago, Alfred University, in New York State, was in need of a single emblem; for each department had its own. A common emblem, it was felt, would produce unity throughout the institution. The university was named for Alfred the Great, a scholar and patron of scholars. It had recently acquired a statue of the king as a young warrior. What could have been more natural, some proposed, than to take the statue as an emblem of the whole university, expressing, as the sculptor intended, "the virtues of leadership, scholarship, and faith"?[1]

The nature of symbols opens them to diverse readings. More than half the students in a random survey (53%) found Alfred an inappropriate symbol, since he was male, Caucasian, western European (a DWEM, or dead, white, European male), and, besides, a king. He embodied anti-democratic practices, if not ideals, of a departed culture, alien to pluralism. No objection appears to have been raised to the king's militarism, plainly alluded to by the statue. A minority (32%) favored adoption; a smaller minority (15%) registered no opinion.

Without knowing how, or whether, this controversy may be settled, I take it as my point of departure. The multiplicity of emblems (to each department its own), the wistful aspiration of at least part of the professorate for commonality if only emblematic, the submission of the matter to survey among none of the gold or silver citizens in the Republic (or even of the brass or iron ones), and the predominant mistrust of universities expressed in current political discourse (including debates in state legislatures) all bear on our appointed subject. I stress that this hostility is directed against

273

King Alfred the Great, sculpture by William Underhill; photograph by Pamela S. Link. *Coll.* Alfred University. Used by kind permission of William Underhill, Pamela S. Link, and Alfred University.

both the support of some kinds of research and teaching here (in North America) and now (at the end of the twentieth century) and the subjects that we hold up for reflection: namely, the class structure of early medieval society and its impelling values, aspirations, and achievements. When one people or age rejects another for its virtues, even the least chance of sympathy is excluded. The idealized, naturalistic style of the statue expresses abiding sympathies of several kinds, one of which is that with a noble and enduring, though now beleaguered, cultural heritage. Another sympathy is less explicit, but more humane. The statue portrays a standing figure. Its posture charitably omits allusion to the piles which made Alfred's life hell on horseback.

To my mind, the subject of our discussion is stated in political terms. The *quaestio* for debate appears to be whether medieval studies, abounding in good itself, diffuses its goodness, or benefits, to other segments of the academic curriculum. Given the leanness of these years, such a *quaestio* can only imply a claim for fiscal support. One is put in mind of Newman's claim for including theology in university instruction.[2] I am convinced that there are pitfalls in the *quaestio* as posed.

The architects of this *conversazione* have followed common usage by referring to "medieval studies" in the singular, as something that stands somehow apart from "other disciplines." By locating "it" in "the modern university," they also express a general assumption that "medieval studies" can be conveyed from teacher to student.

However, these are not the only possible answers to the Platonic questions, whether something is one or many, and whether it can be taught. Indisputably, each method and branch of study has its own history, as becomes readily apparent when students of art, canon law, science and technology, music, and political constitutions compare notes. Many fields have their own collegial associations, journals, and reference tools, and, in the departmental dovecotes of most universities, they nestle beneath the wings of different parental disciplines.

There, as the careers of history and philosophy illustrate, they have found very different forms of nurture. Insofar as a subject is its history (just as texts and readings of texts may be constituted by transmission) the case for retaining medieval studies as a grammatically singular subject would appear uncertain. Vastly more uncertain is what may be meant when "medieval studies" is personified, as in the statement, "Medieval studies did such-and-such." Correspondingly, the question whether what is called medieval studies can be taught remains open. What is, after all, called "medieval studies"? Whether it, or they, can be taught in "the modern university" is yet another question. A new university of Cyprus is now being established along thoroughly western administrative and pedagogical lines. There is room for Byzantine history, above all in its Cypriote aspects. But none of the fields represented at this conference figures, at least, in the initial stages of organization. The studies under review have quite another configuration in Japanese universities.

One recognizes that the portrait peering out from the phrase "the modern university" is not abstract but verisimilar, one endowed with distinctly North American features. Even so, North American universities (and colleges) are so various that no single phrenology can be assumed. Should we include the New School for Social Research, "a university that cherishes the provocative"? During the current term, the New School offers only one course in medieval subjects (specifically in art history) among "several thousands."[3]

It is often good to ask exactly what made a question thinkable to a particular person at one time. For every question is constructed on armatures of the past and has the power to shape answers and future questions that repeat the same pattern concentrically, like a nautilus shell. One can hardly avoid running in this kind of hermeneutic or (more properly) vicious circle if we consider medieval studies singular, rather than plural, and locate it in the curricular and administrative framework of a generalized figure of a North American university in the present day.

Through the years, early coordinates of this Archimedean point have guided auditors of what are called medieval studies. The resulting summaries are, on the whole, pointillist compositions, papers delivered at conferences at which individual scholars profess an invisible, intangible, and ineffable commonality, while they schematize the categorically discrete anatomies of their own fields.[4]

The auditors presupposed, not only that the ventures called medieval studies would be pursued in (and defined by) the context of a North American university, but that even the legitimation of that venture could, and must, be wrenched from professorial corporations. The struggle to establish, sustain, and propagate those studies, characterized as "the revolt of the medievalists,"[5] took place in university libraries and committee rooms, and its vindication in that setting has never been entirely and everywhere secure. Those earlier audits—many of them written in a period of abundance when universities in North America were ramifying and proliferating—frequently strike an apologetic, and even a polemical, tone. There is also, occasionally, a note of exasperation, especially at the continued use of the adjective "medieval" as a pejorative term, re-enforced, to be sure, by associations that Nazis drew between themselves and great epochs in German history.[6]

These arguments for studying medieval culture differed from ones set forth by much earlier scholars, before the emergence of modern universities and historical professions. Our concern is not with those distant explorers of what were, as yet, relatively unknown continents of human experience. However, it may be helpful to invoke the name of Montesquieu (1689–1755) in order to give some measure of change. His *Spirit of the Laws* (1748) fell as a flame into the tinderbox of revolutionary political thought. His study of Germanic institutions formed an important part of his argument that systems of law expressed national characters, which were formed through time by circumstance and experience that continually changed and that could be deliberately changed for the better once human minds were enlightened.

With a cautious regard for royal censors, Montesquieu looked to early Germanic government as an ideally mixed form of constitution, securing both the privileges of nobility and clergy and the civil liberty of the people. This order, with its general regard for human happiness (in freedom) was corrupted in the age of chivalry. But Montesquieu persisted in his study for twenty years, and published it in the hope of assisting "human beings to be cured of their prejudices." Montesquieu had in mind recovery, not from "ignorance of particular matters, but from ignorance of self": that is, of one's own nature (preface).

"It is in seeking to instruct human beings," he wrote, "that one can put into practice the general virtue which comprehends the love of all." He did not lose heart in the ebbs and flows of his long, elusive work when he found what passed for truth only to lose it in the light of subsequent investigations. For, as he surveyed studies on related subjects written throughout Europe, he did not feel alone in his inventive powers. "And I too am a painter," he concluded. "This I have said with Correggio" (preface).

Writing half a century later, in the shadow of the Terror, Condorcet (1743–1794) drew a contrasting assessment of the Middle Ages. And still, while he lamented the decline of human intellect after Julian the Apostate's death, and the ascendancy of "priestly tyranny and military despotism," Condorcet found in the same age the abolition of domestic slavery and the origins of "the rights of man," of which ancient peoples neither had, nor could have had, any conception. In "the eternal chain of human destiny," the spirit of liberty and the progress of moral sentiments that it inspired moved thereby with renewed vigor advancing virtue, happiness, and love of the human race (*L'Esquisse d'un tableau historique des progrès de l'esprit humain*).

Of course, the Enlightenment produced many interpretations other than those of Montesquieu and Condorcet. My point is simply that, even as *philosophes* modeled their ideal human states of virtue, love, and happiness on "heavenly cities" set forth by medieval theologians and generally taught to the *philosophes* while they were children in the schools of religious orders, they also incorporated elements of medieval history in their ideas of historical progress.[7] For Montesquieu, incorporating them was part of the exercise of self-knowledge and recognition.

This exercise long continued to animate commitments such as were expressed in the Gothic revival, beginning in the eighteenth century and continuing into the twentieth, and in related investigations, for example, in the study of Thomist theology and vernacular languages and literatures. Under the colors of nationalism, self-knowledge was commonly recognized as a motive for the study of constitutional history, as it was, for example, in the conclusion of Pollock and Maitland's *History of English Law* where a handful of lawyers at Westminster in Bracton's day were characterized as "making right and wrong for us and for our children" in Britain and in "kingless commonwealths on the other shore of the Atlantic Ocean."[8] Self-knowledge in a different key warranted the observation (1965) "that monasticism has been principally studied by those

who are personally involved in it, and has been on the whole neglected by disinterested secular historians."[9]

Rendering account of "the growth of... medieval studies in
America" (1963), S. Harrison Thomson expressed a related commitment when he said: "The Middle Ages are early American history
and they should be so presented."[10]

These self-seeking appropriations of bygone eras were intended to legitimate the present by establishing its tried and proven
value in the long course of human events. But the appropriators
were also seeking their own futures in the vigor, durability, and
rightness of their antecedents. This is explicit in Maitland's reference to generations yet unborn. The extrapolation of a glorious,
perhaps even an imperial, future for themselves from the European
past enticed North American scholars during the late nineteenth
and early twentieth centuries, expressing as they were the needs
of social orders which, in their dominance, were both recent
and imperiled.

It would be wrong not even to suggest other motives. For example, by his own account, H. O. Taylor wrote out of a passion of
religious inwardness, combining individuality and fellow feeling.
He found his thinking expressed in the idea (set forth also by Augustine) of all human lives as notes in a cosmic song. Taylor
thought God the singer, and he couched his ideas by conflating two
meditations by Guigo of La Grande Chartreuse (c. 1083–1137):
"Easy is the way to God, since it advances by laying off burdens....
Thou hast been clinging to one syllable of a great song and art troubled when that wisest Singer proceeds in His singing. For the syllable which alone thou wast loving is withdrawn from thee, and
others succeed in order. He does not sing to thee alone, nor to thy
will, but His."[11]

From the beginning, in the European Enlightenment, medieval studies were motivated, *inter alia,* by varied impulses of self-
knowledge, which, of course, could include knowing the Other,
friend or foe. These impulses, as well as zeal for accuracy, led to the
"revolt of the medievalists," the object of which was to transfer the
beneficent achievements of the Renaissance, from the fifteenth to
earlier centuries, thereby expunging reproaches such as Condorcet
had poured upon them. What Curtius called "the phenomenon of
American medievalism" was perhaps among the clearest demon-

strations of the connection between medieval studies and self-knowledge because it came so suddenly, beginning in the 1870s from antecedents in literature, architecture, and the visual arts.

"The American conquest of the Middle Ages" did not initiate, but rather followed, public imagination.[12] The susceptibility of that imagination to change is evident, not only in the origins of medieval studies, but in the decisive change from German to French (or, better, Anglo-Belgian-French) patterns imposed upon them by the shift in public sentiments before and during World War I, a change readily illustrated by comparing two works by Henry Adams: *Essays in Anglo-Saxon Law* (1876), a collection of studies by Adams and three students in his seminar at Harvard, and *Mont-Saint-Michel and Chartres* (1912).

Adams's career is instructive. He resembled Montesquieu and Condorcet in that his excursions into medieval culture were remote from his main interests and occupations. Like them (and like H. O. Taylor, whom he taught at Harvard), he possessed private wealth that gave him privilege, leisure, and independence. Yet, unlike them, he lived, taught, and studied in a university, only to abandon his career, disenchanted by what he called the "idiocies" of university life. (Following where Adams led, Taylor abandoned teaching after two years at Columbia.) He withdrew increasingly from society into a cocoon of his own exotic design. Like many books published in its era, *Essays in Anglo-Saxon Law,* the fruit of Adams's studies in Germany and one of the first monuments of seminar instruction in the United States, is now crumbling into dust. Verdant in reprintings, *Mont-Saint-Michel and Chartres,* a work of his old age, was, quite consciously, an essay in self-discovery and absorption, a pendant to *The Education of Henry Adams.* It was an escapist, self-indulgent witness to social alienation, written as a personal memoir and, at first, published only for private distribution. Adams released it to the general public with a characteristic mixture of coyness and scorn.

Yet, when we consider the milestones in the career of American medievalism during the last century, none compares in lasting public appeal with this idiosyncratic testament, written outside academic precincts. In the absence of translations, one can also conclude that even *Mont-Saint-Michel and Chartre's* appeal has linguistic and perhaps national boundaries. By accident, *Mont-*

Saint-Michel and Chartres served the education of the public mind. But it cannot be said to have promoted by accident, still less by design, the actively responsive transformations needed to raise up what Montesquieu and Condorcet had considered the means and object of human happiness: "the general virtue which comprehends the love of all." Adams himself took and, as narrator, he provided several generations of readers the disengaged stance of *voyeur.*

Like other nineteenth-century "revivals"—including the classical and the oriental—the Gothic found its most permanent home in universities, which often proclaimed in architecture their own character as revivified creatures of medieval Europe, the lost and previously unsuspected self discovered by dominant orders in nineteenth-century America. In view of educational history since then, it might appear archly paradoxical to ask whether medieval studies are teachable. Are we too not teachers, the students of teachers, beneficiaries, heirs, and propagators of scholarly lineages?

Even allowing for the political and social ambitions that actually propelled Adams from the "social desert" of Cambridge, Massachusetts, to Washington, his resignation from Harvard, his impatience with circumstances of academic existence was authentic enough to pose the questions of whether history (including medieval history) could be taught at all and, if so, whether it could be taught in universities. Adams gained a considerable following among students. But, he concluded, he could teach them nothing. All but the fewest of the few passively received instruction. Method would not reduce the complexity of his antiquarian subject to order, nor make it actual for them. He esteemed his students. Yet, he was surprised by the gleeful mercantile expectations that they thought would repay their studies: "The degree of Harvard College is worth money to me in Chicago." His seven years' teaching seemed lost.[13]

It might be possible to dismiss Adams's words as an eccentric's warped and, in any event, out-of-date judgment, if there were no more recent testimonies to the same effect;[14] if, indeed, there were not very fresh counterparts in our own memories to Adams's encounter with passive ingestion, deafness to analytical and abstract reasoning, and, finally, weighing courses (and grades, their formal signs) against anticipated gains in the marketplace. The question is

not whether medieval studies constitute important pieces in the jig-
saw puzzle of knowledge without which the general pattern would
be incomplete and, to some degree, unintelligible. It is not about
facts or relations between areas of knowledge, or even technical
skills. It is whether a distinctive faculty of historical understanding
can be conveyed.

Montesquieu set forth one answer when, invoking the incom-
municable quality of genius, he applied to himself Correggio's
words, "Ed io anche son pittore." The creative intuition of artists,
historians, or painters, could not be taught; but, through representations in books or pictures others could apprehend the truth that
it had disclosed. The essential role of imagination in historical understanding might still be illustrated by analogy with painters; but,
now with reference to the lies, instead of the truthfulness, of art.
Reflections on historians' decipherment, explanation, and representation of materials have accented the fictive character of imagination and its malleability by various unseen hands, such as gender,
the intended audience, and the demands of literary (or rhetorical)
convention, not to mention the overt biases of class interest and
personal aspiration.

What is left, except to acknowledge that "history does not exist," any more than does truth?[15] All interpretation violates materials that exist without shape or form. In their parodic violations, art
restorers and forgers are not dissimilar to historians. (Of course,
this epistemological argument is quite different from the quasi-
metaphysical one that history has ended because historical processes have reached their limit, as in the apocalyptic Last Times or
in some political or social "steady-state."[16]) Consequently, there can
be no question of conveying historical understanding, except as a
branch of literary criticism, including subspecialties of criticism devoted to phenomena and theories of reception.

In fact, the entire history of medieval studies in North America
is an essay in discovery (or invention) and transmission. This is not
the occasion to develop, or apply, a theory of transmission. However, audits taken earlier in the career of American medievalism
provide some indications about the impulses and mechanics of
reception.

The actual reception was the change in public taste represented by the cults of Dante, Walter Scott, and Gothic architecture.

The stage with which we are directly concerned came later, when the maintenance of those cults was confided to professionally trained and certified specialists set apart in delegated institutions.

Ideals of forensic rigor in the evaluation of evidence and, consequently, authenticity of knowledge, demanded impartial, critical investigations. But the projects of knowledge for its own sake and of reconstituting the past as it really had been, opened a division that gradually widened between patterns of reception and levels of knowledge in public and academic medievalisms. Further, by looking outward to other continents, in the climate of political chauvinism before and after World War I, medievalists particularly and universities generally followed visions other than those of the political commonwealth. To be sure, there were ways in which, despite increasing esoterism, academic transmitters mirrored public convention. Here too, because social conventions have changed, we note differences between our inventory and earlier ones. It is time to draw up a balance sheet.

At this conference, we are engaged in a highly ritualized undertaking, one with a past. Much can be told even from small changes in ritual details. What will come of our discussions is yet to be seen. But, as an outline of ceremonies, the announcement of the conference presents interesting continuities and contrasts with comparable observances a generation and more ago. I take three (cited above, n. 4) as points of reference: conferences, or series of lectures, at the University of Wisconsin (1957), and at Rice (1962) and Carleton (1965) universities. To avert misunderstandings, let me explain that I have not taken moderators of sessions and commentators at this conference into my calculations because they have no known counterparts, and thus no points of reference, in earlier ones. I also acknowledge discrepancies between the ideal conferences that any past, present, or future sponsors could envision and what practical conditions allow.

What general framework do all four ceremonial occasions display? Most clearly, they have taken place in the middle section of the United States, three of them in the Middle West and (a different three) at private universities. Recognizing a Harvard parallax, I note that all conferences have been marked by a regional concentration of colleagues from universities in mid-Atlantic and midwestern states. The co-celebrants have all been from the professorate. Allowing for specialists here in the late Antique and in the Italian Renaissance, they have been professional medievalists, synods, as it were, of the anointed. As in classical drama, two-thirds of the enactment are lost—the song and dance. In all cases, the rituals have been completed by publishing only their lectionaries. The discrepancy between what was actually read and the reconsidered forms was recognized, never more clearly than when "exceptional difficulties" with two papers contributed to the lapse of almost a decade between reading and publication.[17]

There is an important spectral band in which differences infiltrate similarities and render them only virtual. Some of these have to do with places where transmission occurred. At all conferences, including our own, a sizable proportion of speakers received their professional educations in North America and were teaching in North America (before 1992: 11 out of 22; at Notre Dame, 1992, 16 out of 21). A conspicuous number consisted of scholars educated overseas, but teaching in North America (before 1992, 9 out of 22; at Notre Dame 5 out of 21).[18] At earlier conferences, two speakers educated overseas were teaching overseas; none here belongs to that category. Finally, at no conference, so far as I can determine, has there been a scholar educated in North America and teaching overseas.

A related point where similarity is only virtual consists in the exact institutions from which professional degrees were earned. In this regard, I leave aside degrees awarded overseas. Participants at earlier conferences held doctorates from Harvard (7), Princeton (1), and the universities of Toronto (2), Washington (1) and Wisconsin (1). Though two institutions from that list reappear, a wider distribution is represented at Notre Dame (1992): three each from Cornell, Harvard, Toronto, and Yale; two from Princeton; and one each from Stanford and the University of Texas at Austin. Here, one needs to recall that the proportion of those educated and teaching in North America to those educated overseas and teaching in North America was 1:1 at earlier conferences, but roughly 3:1 at Notre Dame.

The same verdict of quasi-similarity can be set on subjects of specialization represented. Numerous duplications underscore continuities in the histories of painting, the "framing" cultures (Byzantium, Islam, and Judaism), historiography, vernacular literatures, and philosophy. In 1992, musicology and certain so-called auxiliary disciplines (paleography and sfragistics) have been added to the list for the first time. One notes, however, two departures from earlier patternings that indicate changes in a collective definition of medieval studies. The first is the assignment of the late Antique and the Renaissance to the periphery as "neighboring disciplines," though previous medievalists cheerfully claimed both as their own. The second departure consists of numerous omissions from the checklists of earlier conferences, such as the histories of commerce, government (as such), science and technology, heresy, and monasticism.

One of these omissions—that of the liberal arts—I take together with the marginalization of late Antique and Renaissance cultures as particularly suggestive of a change in what we have in common and how we envision its future.

Finally, I come to spectral bands of difference. A number of changes relevant to the sociology of medieval studies are readily apparent. Generations pass. As nearly as I can determine, speakers at earlier conferences received their doctorates (or equivalent certifications) between 1921 and 1957, with, let us say, 1932 as a mean. At this conference, the range is approximately 1961–1982, with 1970 as the mean year. One participant here does not hold a doctorate, but hypothetically could have received one about 1960. (Since the 1961 doctorate is mine, I hasten to defer to Professor Bisson [formally excluded from the tally as the chair of a session], who received his doctorate in 1958, and, if possible, to Professor Sheehan, whose doctorate in 1962 was preceeded by an unusually long and varied professional career.) The magnitude of differences represented by these chronological brackets—in international and national politics, instruments of research, accessibility of data, educational opportunities, and formal organization of universities—cannot be concisely stated.

Still, two matters must be noted. The first pertains to the earlier conferences. They are characterized by the number of emigrée scholars attending with doctorates from Germany. The enrichment of American academic life and the impetus given various branches of medieval subjects by these scholars was ironic in several ways. For, as refugees, they imparted traditions which generations of North American scholars had sought by doctoral studies in Germany, but which had been abandoned by many of their American-educated colleagues, including some at these conferences, who, in the aftermath of World War I, reached out instead to France and Belgium. (To underscore the magnitude of this change, I provide one example: instruction at Concordia Seminary in St. Louis was entirely in the German language before the end of World War I.[19]) There is something to ponder in the conditions of so cosmopolitan a field in an isolationist society. At Notre Dame, the post-World War I pattern is repeated. For no lecturers hold German (or central European) doctorates. Among doctorates from outside North America, two are from England, one from Belgium, one equivalent certification from France. To these should be added the undoctored professional education of another colleague received in England.

The second matter to be noted briefly is the narrowing of professional opportunities in North America, which began to be acute in 1970. At that time, some qualified scholars were unable to find academic employment and either modified or abandoned their intended careers. Deliberately or by force of circumstance, enrollments in graduate programs were curtailed, reducing both the size of graduate cohorts and the variety of interests represented among them. Thus, we are as we are partly thanks to a combination of birth control and infanticide.

Other readily available sociological differences are apparent. Seven speakers here are women; fourteen are men. Among speakers at the earlier conferences, only one was a woman. In collaboration, a second woman organized a conference which engaged no woman speaker.[20] I am unable to speak numerically of other sociological categories meriting notice. One senses, for example, that a sizable proportion of colleagues at Notre Dame are the first in their families to attend college, much less pursue careers in higher education, and that this would not have been true at earlier conferences. It would not be amiss to recall a matter which changed during and after World War II: the general closure of private colleges and universities to all but wealthy and assimilated Jews, as undergraduates as well as members of the faculty.[21] The participants at this conference give a measure of the departure from this state of affairs, and an anticipation of a departure, which may be slowly beginning, from another closure against persons of color. It is unclear whether the tendency of present policies toward financial assistance of graduate students will continue to sustain such changes.

Social changes bear on the subject of this conference insofar as they illuminate how the nature and objectives of medieval studies are defined. The opening of professional doors has brought an indistinctness in these regards. In fact, one spectral band of greatest difference appears by comparing the statement of purpose and the procedure of this conference with those of earlier ones. Our predecessors did not lack clarity of purpose. Their object was to reveal the true beginning of Renaissance, and thus of modern European culture, which had come to dominate the world. They also wished to draw the attention of scholars and general readers to the proven capacities of medievalists to disclose the powers still quickening in the legacy of the Middle Ages.

While they came together to proclaim clear and generally accepted assumptions, we are called "to represent a diversity of views and to foster debate," each speaker proposing an individual "rationale" for medieval studies and, as well, addressing no fewer than seven general and exceedingly complex "questions." The modes of procedure also illuminate a major change in processes of definition. Participants at earlier conferences were lecturers. Each had sole charge for a different specialty; the lectures were regarded as "studies." They were intended to state, develop, and summarize a theme, within the space of an hour, and to stand, like works of art, complete in themselves.

By contrast, our procedure is collective and deliberative, rather than individual and declamatory. "Pluriform" as the subject may be, each speaker has twenty minutes in which to deliver a "talk," or protocol. The communicative unit is, not a sovereign address, but a composite of three protocols expanded by comments and discussion, almost certainly in ways unforeseen and unintended by the authors of the protocols. Instruction is sought from the collectivity, rather than from individuals, and by prospectively random and digressive ways. In a *pointillist* analogy, it is as though Seurat had been succeeded by a committee of Jackson Pollocks. However, since in the aftermath of Andy Warhol, our era disesteems the masterpiece, except for its market price, some other analogy to simultaneous narratives or performances might be more appropriate.

To my mind, this diffuseness of purpose and valuation of collective over individual judgment has less to do with the opening of academic opportunities since World War II (constricted in recent decades by general economic difficulties) than with general changes in thinking about society as a whole. The dispute over the statue of Alfred encapsulates some of these changes, which, I believe, are also related to the willing marginalization of late Antiquity and Renaissance, and the omission of the liberal arts at this conference.

As I said, the auditors at earlier conferences repeatedly alluded to medieval studies as ventures in self-knowledge, the appropriation of a lost European past. Even when they acknowledged the radical heterogeneity of society, they took for granted that all would be assimilated to the dominant culture, that all would find at least by adoption common origins and forebears in Europe, and a common destiny inscribed in Europe's career.[22]

The transmission of what was then called medieval studies moved in a cycle because, in the minds of potential receivers, there was inscribed, so to speak, a pre-text that found itself completed and exalted by medieval studies, a pre-existing need and desire. It remains to be seen whether others—some previously excluded from the paths leading to the professorate, some new to the continent—will be drawn in numbers to medieval studies and, if so, whether the desire for self-knowledge through the mirror of the European past will remain compelling to them or to those to whom they transmit medieval studies.

Equally, transmission in the first half of this century presupposed a Europe in which visual arts (including architecture), national literatures, and political and economic institutions revealed medieval "origins," "roots," or "sources." But now, literary critics and historiographers have displayed the fictive or mythic, character of historical writing, bent to serve those by and from whom the literary memory was made and leaving out others for the sake of the story. The arraignment of hegemonic culture, to which this conclusion belongs, has discounted the grandeur and beneficence of the European past, looking, not so much at the lilies, as at the acidic muck in which they grew.

Panofsky concluded in 1952 that the Renaissance had effected a permanent reconstitution of European culture, one that was "changeable only with our civilization as such." There is reason to think that such a change is now well advanced, making ever more distant "the Antique," which he judged had "been constantly with us" since the fourteenth century, and which had been temporarily reclaimed in what he called the "renascences" of the Middle Ages.[23] The Europe to which American medievalism looked in 1952 and earlier was that of the liberal arts, the Latin Mass, and the sovereign state. This Europe, which was also that of the shilling, in which our teachers found their roots and the hypothetical future of their world is passing away.

Consequently, recognizing one's own future in the European past lacks the reassurance that it gave endangered, though dominant, social orders during the late nineteenth and early twentieth centuries. In the present climate, an apocalypticist might well wonder what awaits those other protean institutions of medieval origin, universities.

As a study in desires, the career of medieval studies in North America offers numerous parallels to that of American studies in Britain and Europe. From the beginning, in the Enlightenment, America claimed attention because it stood for liberty, the same reason for which Montesquieu and Condorcet commended the Middle Ages. (The association with revolutionary ideologies was so close that Pope Leo XIII condemned the heresy of "Americanism" [1899].) American studies became a tool of self-knowledge and advancement for advocates of political liberalism. Here, too, there was a parallel to the Gothic revival. For wide public interest in aspects of United States history and literature came long before instruction in schools and universities. The beginning of academic instruction and the formation of research libraries in American studies in Europe began, as did those for medieval studies in the North America, after the War Between the States.

They continued to develop, increasingly mirroring different circumstances in each country. In some countries, they developed in isolation from dominant political tendencies and public interests. In others, as in Nazi Germany and the Soviet Union, they were tailored to government ideologies. Thus, the rule prevailed that what American studies were was in the beholder's eye or the desirer's heart, grist for the mills of critics convinced of history's fictive nature.

A reflowering of American studies in British and European universities began after World War II, though many universities and research libraries were still poor in holdings (especially archival ones), and though "the myth about America which we cultivate in Europe has a psychological reality which is much more important to us [Europeans] than the so-called truth about America."[24] The number of Americanists educated in Europe teaching in American universities is in scale with that of medievalists educated in North America and teaching in European universities. It is hard to imagine what reception would greet a proposal to take the image of any North American—according to current norms, Laura Secord, Sojourner Truth, or Sitting Bull might be candidates—into the iconology of a European university.

Finally, the coordination of American studies in British and European universities has become increasingly problematic as the function of the United States in the European myth of liberalism and its promise for the future have changed. As for medieval studies in North America, there have been for American studies in Europe two moments at which public and academic interests varied. In the mid-nineteenth century, universities were, on the whole, intellectual backwaters, far outstripped by public interest. Early in the twentieth century, they represented cosmopolitanism in a nationalist environment. The present day may be a third moment of divergence.

At any rate, by asking whether medieval studies can be taught and briefly noting the circumstances of their reception, we are able to conclude the obvious: that the transmission of medieval studies is configured with its context, the university, which, in turn, is configured with its social context. All are driven by multiple desires. Is the university a museum? We have exhibits of barbaric splendor. An intellectual caravansary or theme-park? We offer everything from bijoux to burlesque, not omitting banquets. A laboratory? We are accomplished experimenters in many fields. A golden door to new life? Our whole concern is the constitution of social worlds out of wreckage, ones that in art, music, and every branch of spirituality displayed, not only austere powers of invention, but an equally primordial force called by Newman "the gentleness and effeminacy of feeling which is the attendant on civilization."[25]

Plainly, an important segment of our appraisal is the character of universities in their social contexts. I cannot do more than observe that the auditors of our fields thirty years ago were already members of a learned culture that was being overtaken by new, and not always congenial, transformations. The development of a "mass university," administered by an elaborate bureaucracy largely cut off from the faculty was beginning. Subsequently, the increasing dependence of universities on financial subvention by others has accelerated general conformity of university policies and goals to administrative and legislative norms declared by national and state governments, with important results for teaching and research. Finally, while universities continue to be dominant centers for the pursuit and transmission of learning, experiences have left them places of "shaken morale," above all in areas known as "humanities" and "social sciences."

Ethical standards familiar to earlier generations continue to be enunciated and even acted upon, but this conservatism frequently clashes with the radically altered circumstances under which they are invoked.[26] The current sifting of the professorate in universities formerly in the German Democratic Republic offers many of these changes in a distorted, but magnified and therefore readily seen, problematic. Perhaps we have touched some reasons for the perceived disunity among the faculty at Alfred University, for the diffuseness of the call that has brought us here, and for our non-intersecting, if conceivably parallel, responses.

What rationale can be proposed in this uncertain moment for a subject so apt to mirror whoever is observing it at the time? The examples of the *philosophes* and of our more recent predecessors after World War II illustrate how *retardataire* any proposal must be, anticipating the future in the context of experience, by definition past. If each may call something else "medieval studies," each can present a distinctive rationale.

My medieval studies have to do with mediation—not with author-text-reader or artist-picture-viewer mediation, but with mediations among these coordinates. By "mediation," I do not have in mind "go-betweens" negotiating borders, such as another speaker cited. To be sure, negotiation—as brokerage, translation, or transit—connotes a variety of kinds of mediation between others. However, I have in mind different varieties, which include conversion and sacrifice. Negotiation implies a certain logic, in which the terms keep their otherness (no confusion of categories, no fallacy of the undistributed middle). Mediation by conversion and sacrifice produce phantasmagoric, logic-defying transformations in which the

"I" becomes the "you" while remaining itself. Conceptions may seem as eccentric to late twentieth-century people as it seemed miraculous to earlier ones. They are integral to the anti-classical mannerist strain of the classical tradition, now largely lost.

At any rate, from this perspective, one rationale does come to mind. The age with which we are preoccupied, unlike other historical periods, framed the doctrine of conscience. Though with many ironies, it taught ennoblement of human nature through compassion, as, in fact, a natural and supernatural act of conscience rightly ordered. Despite ancient precedents in Hebraic, Greek, and Roman traditions, the ideas of conscience and compassion as collective, social values in the European legacy cannot be credited to Antiquity. These achievements, the structures of thought that made them possible, and the institutions to which they were (sometimes all too imperfectly) confided are surely of value to our own age, in search as it is of mutual understanding: that is, of sympathy, whether malevolent or amorous.[27] They are not unrelated to the enfranchisements that Montesquieu and Condorcet regarded as milestones in the progress of human happiness.

To avoid misapprehension, I should emphasize that I am not advocating that historians apply empathy in assessing their evidence or in expressing their conclusions. What I do propose is an attempt to recover the character, range, and effects of empathy in creative processes of other societies. This is, I confess, an old objective, set forth even in Schleiermacher's goal of understanding the creative process better than did the maker of an artifact—whether artist or writer; but Schleiermacher postulated, as I do not, an empathetic power of divinatory intuition on the scholar's part. The "medievalist in search of the archetype from which he sprang" is all too likely to demonstrate the imagination's confinement to a vicious circle.[28] In a sentence omitted by Taylor, Guigo of La Grande Chartreuse commented on how syllables followed one after another in the song of life, and on the ill-judgments that came about if we expected later ones to conform with the ones that were ourselves: "The syllables that come after seem discordant to you because they jar upon the one which you badly loved."[29] To say this it to pose the enigma of discordant harmony (*concordia discors*).

What could be called the archaeology of empathies has not been much practiced, partly because the tyranny of the *Zeitgeist* or

Volksgeist has rushed in to explain all, stifling what is personal in a work, partly because the task requires observation of the artifact (which includes, but is not exhausted by, critical and exegetical "reading"), and partly too because it requires allowance for esthetic factors which, since they entail conflicting emotions, do not always conform with the academic demands of logic and syntactic order, however completely they satisfy those of art.

The habit of paradoxical or enigmatic thought and representation in the age with which we are preoccupied has prepared us for this task. So too has the fragmentary state of our evidence. We are enigmatologists by training, equipped through such disciplines as iconography, exegesis, and etymology to retrieve the unsaid in the said, to complete the depicted gesture. Because the formal codes at issue were so regularly directed at spiritual—which is to say, moral—sentiment, we are enigmatologists of emotion and desire as well as intellect. Since play is close to the heart of poetics, we must also recognize the foreignness of imaginations that, not only sensed, but also laughed differently from ours.

To assert the obvious: the sense of history is one characteristic peculiar to the human species. The glory of medieval history has always been in method, and this too has been what scholars in other fields have chiefly borrowed: first, the forensic investigation of texts; later, the quantitative analysis of data; and now, the restorations of hitherto historyless classes (including women) to history. Perhaps, the distinctive characteristics and deficiencies of evidence available to us gives promise of another method in the study of common human needs useful beyond our limited objectives, a method exploring the conflicted affective interplay (or synesthesia) among the arts, and thus how, in a way defining recognizably human existence, desires under suffering have been transformed into art.

The multiple decompositions of tradition in the present day pose a further Platonic question for us: When the lyre is broken, does harmony survive and not perish (*Phaedo* 86)? Plato applied this question to the body and soul. At least regarding societies whose lives are over, I am persuaded that harmony does survive the breaking of the lyre, that it survives between the lines of fragments known to us, and that to discover, arrest, and teach past harmonies is our care and delight, recognizing to be sure the possible incommensurability of transmission and reception.

All that I have said has been a frolic around King Alfred's statue. Amid the harrying distractions of his reign, Alfred realized "what punishments befell us in this world when we ourselves did not cherish learning or transmit it to other men."[30] I imagine that he would have found discourse about education stripped from the body of the liberal arts as limp and desiccated as the golden fleece. Transmission and reception of learning had failed, even among those charged with the instruction of others. Alfred's achievement was to restore both, however tenuously, and he himself taught children the liberal arts when the cares of day were past. The beginning was in poetry. For, illiterate until his twelfth year, he listened through all his waking hours to the Saxon poems—lays, chants, banqueting songs—of gleomen and scops, and learned them by heart, no doubt accompanied by the lyre or *hearpe*. He continued throughout his life to add English poems to his memory. In them, and in his own poetry and translations of Psalms and Boethius's meters, he apprehended through the dissonances a common harmony that arrested, exalted, and impelled his desires, and that, he sensed, must be declared, though it might not be received. There is some resonance with Montesquieu's idea that "in seeking to instruct human beings, one can put in practice that general virtue which comprehends the love of all." Alfred's lyre is cut; without transcription, his music is lost. His harmony, a *concordia discors,* ensnares us still.

> Thus Ælfred us
> Eald-spell reahte;
> Cyning West-sexna
> Cræft meldode.
> Leoth-wyrhta list.
> Him wæs lust micel,
> Thæt he thiossum leodum
> Leoth spellode,
> Monnum myrgen,
> Mislice cwidas. . . .
> Ic scal giet sprecan,
> Fon on fitte,
> Folc-cuthne ræd,
> Hælethum secgean,
> Hliste se the wille.[31]

Thus Alfred sang
to us a tale of old,
West-Saxon king,
displayed his art,
poet-skill.
His longing was great
to be the one
to deliver to his people
the interchanges of words,
joy to men like morning light...
I shall yet speak,
seize in verse,
counsel handed down from old time,
speak of heroic ones,
like it who may.

APPENDIX

Section I.

Doctorates Held by Lecturers at the University of Wisconsin (1957), Rice University (1962), Carleton University (1965)

Harvard	*Toronto*
1923, Holmes	1947, Maurer
1930, Strayer	1960, Mudroch
1931, Post	
1934, Salmon	*Washington*
1934, White	1951, Jackson
1940, Anastos	

Princeton	*Wisconsin*
1957, Cantor	1932, Krueger

Educated Overseas, Teaching in North America

1913 (?), Spitzer, Leipzig
1921, Kantorowicz, Heidelberg
1923, Thomson, Charles University, Prague

1924, Katzenellenbogen, Giessen (Dr. Jur.; see also 1933)
1926, Wilkinson, Manchester
1928, Klibansky, Heidelberg
1931, Thrupp, London
1931, Grunebaum, Vienna
1933, Katzenellenbogen, Hamburg (Ph.D.; see also 1924)

Educated Overseas, Teaching Overseas

1941, Crombie, Cambridge
1950, Folz, Paris (Doctorat ès Lettres)

Section II.

Doctorates Held by Participants at the Conference at the University of Notre Dame, 1992

Cornell	*Yale*
1961, Morrison	1965, Colish
1963, Rouse	1974, Geary
1978, Cohen	1976, Matter

Harvard	*Princeton*
1967, Bulliet	
1967, Starn	1967, Treitler
1969, Frank	1973, Jordan, W.

Toronto	*Stanford*
1962, Sheehan (M.S.D.)	1970, Bloch
1981, Bennett	
1982, Biddick	*Texas-Austin*
	1977, Jordan, M.

Educated Overseas, Teaching in North America

1974, MacCormack, Oxford
1977, Bedos-Rezak, École des Chartes
1979, McCormick, Louvain
1985, Camille, Cambridge
Without doctorate
Pearsall (educated at Birmingham)

NOTES

1. *New York Times,* 15 December 1991, a report of Alfred University at Alfred, New York.

2. John Henry Newman, *The Scope and Nature of University Education* (New York: Dutton, 1958), esp. 10–29.

3. The course listings were published in the *New York Times,* 6 January, 1992.

4. Some of these, in chronological order, are: Wallace K. Ferguson, *The Renaissance in Historical Thought: Five Centuries of Interpretation* (Boston: Houghton Mifflin, 1948); *Twelfth-Century Europe and the Foundations of Modern Society,* ed. Marshall Clagett, Gaines Post, and Robert Reynolds (Madison, Wisc.: University of Wisconsin Press, 1961) (papers delivered in 1957); Sidney R. Packard, *The Process of Historical Revision: New Viewpoints in Medieval European History* (Northampton, Mass.: Smith College, 1962), Katherine Asher Engle Lecture, 1960; *Perspectives in Medieval History,* ed. Katherine Fischer Drew and Floyd Seyward Lear (Chicago: University of Chicago Press, 1963); *Essays on the Reconstruction of Medieval History,* ed. Vaclav Mudroch and G. S. Couse (Montreal: McGill-Queen's University Press, 1974) (papers delivered in 1965); Karl F. Morrison, "Fragmentation and Unity in 'American Medievalism'," in *The Past Before Us: Contemporary Historical Writing in the United States,* ed. Michael Kammen (Ithaca, N.Y.: Cornell University Press, 1980), 49–77 (with bibliography); Norman F. Cantor, *Inventing the Middle Ages* (New York: William Morrow, 1991). From a more general view, see Geoffrey Barraclough, "What is to Be Done about Medieval History?" *New York Review of Books,* 4 June 1970.

5. Ferguson, *The Renaissance in Historical Thought,* 329–385.

6. Drew and Lear, *Perspectives in Medieval History,* esp. E. Dwight Salmon, "Medieval Foundations of Modern History," ix, 83.

7. Carl L. Becker, *The Heavenly City of the Eighteenth-Century Philosophers* (New Haven: Yale University Press, 1932).

8. Frederick Pollock and Frederic William Maitland, *The History of English Law Before the Time of Edward I,* vol. 2 (reprint, Cambridge: Cambridge University Press, 1968), 672–674.

9. Giles Constable, "The Study of Monastic History Today," in *Essays on the Reconstruction of Medieval History,* 24.

10. S. Harrison Thomson, "The Growth of a Discipline: Medieval Studies in America," in *Perspectives in Medieval History,* 17.

11. Translated in Henry Osborn Taylor, *A Historian's Creed* (Cambridge: Harvard University Press, 1939), 72. *Le Recueil des pensées du b.*

Guigue, ed. André Wilmart, Études de philosophie médiévale 22, (Paris: Vrin, 1936) nos. 56, 149, pp. 78, 93.

Pensée 56: "Facile est iter ad Deum, quoniam exonerando itur. Esset autem grave, si onerando iretur. In tantum ergo te exonera ut, dimissis omnibus, te ipsum abneges." *Pensée 149:* "Vix ex syllabis magni carminis adhesisti; ideo turbaris, cum canendo procedit cantor sapientissimus. Subtrahitur enim syllaba tibi quam solam amabas, et succedunt aliae suo ordine. Non enim canit tibi soli, nec tuae voluntati, sed suae. Quae autem succedunt syllabae, ob hoc tibi contrariae sunt, quia impellunt eam quam male amabas." See below, n. 29. Cf. Augustine, *Confessions,* 11.28.38. *Corpus Christianorum, series latina* 27, p. 214.

12. Ernst Robert Curtius, "The Medieval Bases of Western Thought," in *European Literature and the Latin Middle Ages,* trans. Willard R. Trask, Bollingen Series 26 (New York: Pantheon, 1953), 587.

13. Henry Adams, *The Education of Henry Adams* (New York: Modern Library, 1931), 302–307.

14. E.g., G. R. Elton, *The Practice of History* (New York: Crowell, 1967), esp. 144–146.

15. Paul Veyne, *Did the Greeks Believe in Their Myths?* trans. Paula Wissing (Chicago: University of Chicago Press, 1983), 115.

16. Francis Fukugama, *The End of History and the Last Man* (New York: Free Press, 1992).

17. Mudroch and Couse, *Essays on the Reconstruction of Medieval History,* xi.

18. Some anomalies result from using the source of the doctoral degree as a criterion. I have counted S. Harrison Thomson among those educated overseas and working in North America because he received a doctor of philosophy degree from the Charles University in Prague, not to mention a B. Litt. from Oxford. Despite his extensive studies at the École des Chartes, I have credited Michael Sheehan to the University of Toronto, from which he received the M. S. D.

19. I owe this information to Professor Louise Buenger Robbert, letter of 25 May 1993. Without suggesting how wide knowledge of German among undergraduates was throughout North America, one may still note, in association with its use as the language of instruction at Concordia, the considerable number of works in the German language recommended in a college textbook for further reading which Ephraim Emerton published when he was teaching at Harvard: *Medieval Europe (814–1300)* (Boston: Ginn & Co., 1896).

20. Sylvia Thrupp (Ph.D., University of London, 1931) lectured at the conference at the University of Wisconsin; Katherine Fischer Drew (Ph.D., Cornell, 1950) was a co-convener of the conference at Rice University.

21. William H. McNeill, *Hutchins' University: A Memoir of the University of Chicago, 1929–1950* (Chicago: University of Chicago Press, 1991), 53, 149–150.

22. Thomson, "The Growth of a Discipline: Medieval Studies in America," 1–2.

23. Erwin Panofsky, *Renaissance and Renascences in Western Art* (New York: Harper & Row, 1969), 108–113 (lectures delivered in 1952).

24. Sigmund Skard, *The American Myth and the European Mind: American Studies in Europe, 1776–1960* (Philadelphia: University of Pennsylvania Press, 1961), esp. 7, 16, 54, 62.

25. Newman, *The Scope and Nature of University Education,* 182.

26. Edward Shils, *The Academic Ethic* (Chicago: University of Chicago Press, 1983), esp. 20, 27, 38–40, 67–82, 94–96.

27. For these distinctions, see my study, *"I Am You:" The Hermeneutics of Empathy in Western Literature, Art, and Theology* (Princeton: Princeton University Press, 1988).

28. Thomson, "The Growth of a Discipline: Medieval Studies in America," 3.

29. Guigo of La Grande Chartreuse, *Pensées,* no. 149, Wilmart ed., p. 93. See above, n. 11.

30. Alfred's prose preface to the *Pastoral Care* by Pope Gregory I, trans. Simon Keynes and Michael Lapidge in *Alfred the Great: Asser's Life of King Alfred and Other Contemporary Sources* (Harmondsworth: Penguin, 1983), 125.

31. John Allen Giles, *Memorials of King Alfred* (London: John Russell Smith, 1863), 164.

Medieval Manuscripts
in the Modern Curriculum

RICHARD ROUSE

JULIAN BROWN DEVOTED HIS inaugural lecture as Professor of Paleography at London University to the contribution made to the study of paleography by Ludwig Traube, the first professor of medieval Latin at Munich.[1] Brown reminded us that it was Traube who first gave paleography, or the study of manuscripts, a proper purpose and place in the larger framework of historical and literary studies. "What distinguished him from other good editors of his own day, and from all too many since, was a lively historical sense which caused him to see the successive stages in the transmission of a text in human terms, not just as the groundwork for an edition, but as evidence for the cultural history of the centres through which that text had been transmitted."[2] To Traube, manuscripts properly dated and localized were the evidence through which to trace the passage of ideas across the face of the land, or from one generation to another through time. To this, Brown added that for himself paleography was a subject through which one learned how to observe, formulate, and express in precise terms what one saw; and that the possibility to see was open to anyone who wished to look, rather than just to repeat.[3]

In 1962, when Brown delivered this lecture, the British Isles supported seven positions in paleography at the reader and professor levels in five universities, not to mention other positions in diplomatic. Since that time there have been marked changes, instructive for American paleographers to ponder. The readership in paleography and diplomatic at Cambridge was frozen at the request of the history faculty—upon the retirement in 1975 of T. A. M.

Bishop, who, although a significant scholar, for the most part did not extend his teaching beyond the tenth century. In Oxford after Neil Ker's retirement in 1968, the reader in paleography was selected by the historians, who chose William Urry, better known as a diplomatist. After Urry's death in 1981, the post was frozen; for the historians found already in place an able lecturer in vernacular and Latin paleography appointed by the English Faculty and felt their interests adequately cared for by him. In 1988, in the face of cutbacks and retirements, the powerful University Grants Committee (UGC) commissioned a study to recommend where instruction in paleography in Britain should be funded.[4] The report recommended maintaining senior positions in paleography at the three large research universities with substantial collections of manuscripts in their libraries, namely, at London, Oxford, and Cambridge, and continuing instruction at lower levels of support elsewhere. To conserve funds, however, it recommended that both the Oxford and Cambridge appointments in paleography be positions shared with the university library, so that the university's paleographer, in addition to offering instruction in the subject, would carry out library duties. At Durham, although instruction in paleography continues to be available, the readership was frozen upon the retirement in 1990 of J. D. Thomas, who was the investigator of the most important western European paleographic find in living memory, the third-century documents written on wood found at Vindolanda. Belfast's lectureship was recently transferred by the UGC to Cambridge, but Cambridge did not accept the position, which was ultimately allocated to London University. The readership in paleography was recently reestablished in Cambridge but through the Department of Manuscripts at the University Library, following the recommendations of the 1988 UGC report. The London School of Archives closed its position in paleography on the retirement of Professor Andrew Watson in 1990. London University students seeking instruction in paleography are now served by the lectureship transferred from Belfast, and by the professor at King's. That professorship itself had been earmarked for closure before Julian Brown took early retirement. The post was retained only through the concerted efforts of Brown, Watson, and the members of the history and literature faculties in London and elsewhere. Now, thirty years after Brown's inaugural address, the King's College professorship is the only remaining position designated for the teaching of paleography in Great Britain.[5]

This is what was salvaged, through great effort on the part of an ever-diminishing number of manuscript scholars, of a tradition in manuscript studies reaching back to the early days of this century and before, with the likes of M. R. James, E. Maunde Thompson, and W. M. Lindsay. The easy thing to do is to blame the demise of paleography on Mrs. Thatcher and cut-backs in academic funding, but that is only part of the problem. It should not be used to camouflage the disturbing fact that paleography was voted out by one major university, that it was considered essentially nothing but a technique by another, and, worse yet, that it has been associated, by a national committee, with archival and library practice. It has been recommended that, when the lecturer at Oxford retires in 1997, his post be transferred to the Bodleian. Made with the good intent of saving paleography from extinction, this recommendation, in its broader application, would be the death-knell of paleography as a serious discipline, because it severs the link established by Traube between script form and human history. Paleography's purpose, in the view of the UGC report, is primarily to teach students how to extend abbreviations and correctly transcribe texts in order to be able to read them.

British paleographers have not succeeded in disabusing their colleagues of this notion, and only one or two among them were willing to risk drawing implications or essaying a broader generalization or two. The distance between correct transcription on the one hand, and the synthetic study of the development of writing, of the written page, of the book itself within the society that produced it, on the other, was not successfully bridged. There are too many academics, paleographers among them, who hold that the purpose of paleography is "to teach people how to read written texts" (without even a mention that it might teach people to date and to localize the manuscripts containing these texts). Certainly that goal must not be compromised; but if teaching students how to read medieval scripts is its only purpose, the subject will surely die, or at best survive only as a technical training to be found in European schools of archival management and library science. It is as if we considered the sole purpose of courses in medieval Latin or Middle English was to teach students to read medieval Latin or Middle English, never mind the culture they represent.

The paleographer must make an effort to be useful, and to do so it is necessary to enlarge the definition of paleography to encompass what is so well expressed by the German word "Handschriftenkunde," the study of manuscripts. I will not spend time discussing whether paleography should include codicology or whether codicology should be an independent discipline, since—especially in an American context—this is too silly to bother with. I am content with an approach to manuscripts that has no restrictions: if some approach renders service, use it. I use the term "paleography" here, partly from habit and mainly for convenience; but I disown the narrow connotations it implies even in Traube's use of the term. By paleography I mean "manuscript studies" without fixed boundaries.[6]

The lesson for American paleographers to learn from the British experience is that one can never teach only what one wants to teach, nor can one casually assume that paleography is necessary simply because it is there, or because Traube said it was necessary. To American academics in other fields, the ability to transcribe documents in medieval Latin or Middle English appears to be an archaic exercise like that of reading cuneiform tablets, one which in time will be rendered unnecessary because the important documents will all be edited—an exercise which, in any case, has little to do with the history and culture of the United States, North or South America, Africa, or Asia. Contrary to the paleographer's fondest daydreams, the importance of paleography is not one of those things that are patently self-evident to a world of busy academics with endlessly varied demands on their time and attention. Paleography's use and value to historical and literary studies must repeatedly be demonstrated in articles and books, and paleographers must constantly strive to be useful and valuable, or positions in paleography will be reallocated—Darwin said much the same thing in explaining why some species survive and others do not. Let us agree, then, that—while for paleographers personally, nearsightedness is just an occupational hazard—for paleography as a discipline, myopia is a mortal sin; and let us turn our attention to the place of manuscript studies in teaching and research.

Traube's formulation of the purpose of paleography was understood by some of his students and has from time to time been reformulated. It was, for example, reiterated by R. W. Hunt in his statement that "the books of the Middle Ages are the most enduring visible legacy of its flowering. Despite the losses caused by revolution and wars and periodic neglect, they have survived in their thousands, authentic witnesses, not doctored by the restorer's hand." But neither Traube's lesson nor Hunt's cogent observation has had the influence it deserves.

Traube's lesson, if it has largely been ignored on the research level, has been entirely forgotten on the teaching level, graduate and undergraduate alike. How manuscripts are employed in training students in historical studies, and to what degree students are taught to consider manuscript source materials and are instructed practically how to do so, will of course depend in part on the level of education with which we are dealing, undergraduate or graduate. But among both groups, the degree to which the manuscript basis of the study of the Middle Ages is incorporated into the presentation and teaching of the subject is minimal. A look at any standard textbook of medieval history or medieval literature will show that the role of manuscripts is limited to decorative pictures of the Strasbourg oaths, the Cotton Beowulf, Domesday book, the Digby Roland, a manuscript of Dante's Divine Comedy, the Ellesmere Chaucer, or a picture of Christine de Pizan writing. Nowhere does the textbook address the question of why any of these manuscripts were written, what audience each of them served, how one of them is different from another, or how each would in one way or another reflect the period or time which produced it and, thus, how it might serve as a window through which to examine the society which produced and used it. Nowhere does the textbook indicate that any critical reading of these texts must take into account the complex effect, on their content and composition, of their having been transmitted via manuscripts.

The role that the study of manuscripts should play in undergraduate or graduate instruction and in research depends in large part on what we feel to be the purpose of medieval studies in the undergraduate or graduate curriculum. The problem is not so difficult in the graduate curriculum where we might say for simplicity's sake that its purpose is to train productive researchers and writers and leave it at that, without raising the specter of which methodology or subject is "acceptable" or in current vogue. But on the undergraduate level, we cannot determine what the place of manuscript studies should be in the curriculum without knowing what our purpose is. We cannot assess how well manuscript studies helps us to achieve our goals until those goals are defined.

I will suggest what I consider to be four goals for an undergraduate curriculum and suggest how the study of manuscripts might be of value toward their attainment.

(1) Historical study, par excellence, is based on the careful reading of texts; the majority of these texts are written and can be both documents and narrative texts in verse or prose. Broadly interpreted, "texts" for the historian can also include images: pictures, wall paintings, stained glass, or carvings in stone, ivory, metal, or wood, or written musical notation as well. There are numerous questions that the historian may ask of a text in order to grasp what it meant, or could mean over time, to those who read it—for example, to whom is the text addressed, what literary devices are being used to convince, how would the use of such an expression of biblical echo have been perceived. But before the critical reader can interpret the words, he must know what the words actually are, and only then can he proceed to inquire what they meant. I acknowledge that in using the word "meant" I am saying that I belong to that group of people who believe that words have meanings that can be comprehended, and that it is a worthy enterprise to make an effort to understand them even if the effort is not always successful.

If students leave the university with an ability to read critically, the university will have taught them a great deal and gone far to achieving its purpose or producing a more discerning citizen. Historians, of course, have no monopoly, but share the emphasis on instruction in critical reading with literary critics and political scientists, among others; but the fact that we share it does not mean we can shirk it—it remains an inescapable responsibility of the historian's trade. Critical reading is no more important for medieval than for earlier or later texts, but it requires skills and provides challenges that perhaps are not there to the same degree for the modern historian—though I would not press this point. History is a medium, then, through which one learns how to think, and an early stage in learning to think is to read critically.

(2) The study of history should aid a student's perception and comprehension of the written text as text: to know what is meant by "the text," to know how this text came to be what it is. When a stu-

dent reads a text, all or in part—the Benedictine Rule, the Song of Roland, William of Malmesbury's History, Abelard and Heloise's letters, St. Thomas' *Summa,* Marco Polo's Travels, an English statute book, or the Lollard Bible—it should alter the student's perception of the text to know something of how that text has arrived at its present state. How was Marco Polo's Travels transmitted, how did the work's author mean it to be received, and, equally important, how was it actually received by its readers, and how did their attitude to the text change over time? Might not these later readers have changed the text or the image to adapt it to their own needs, so that it might be better understood? These questions could profitably be included in discussions of many literary works, since undergraduates tend to think that what one reads today is what Marco Polo actually wrote, and that all the manuscripts of the Travels look like Bodley 264, or that manuscripts of the Canterbury Tales all resemble the Ellesmere Chaucer—whereas the majority of the surviving manuscripts of both texts are quite plain and relatively small, and must have served a rather different audience from that served by those two grand manuscripts.

(3) Historians, if they are to shape the undergraduate's perception of the medieval past to any appreciable degree, must make that past graspable and tangible to students. A major challenge to North American medievalists, one which they have met with only mixed success, is to teach students how to examine and describe a world foreign to their own experience, how to accept that it actually had existed. American students, particularly undergraduates, are hampered by factors outside their own control:

1. the matter of language, even when they read and write English well—since almost everything essential is in a language other than modern English;

2. the matter of geographical distance—it is Europe's Middle Ages and Europe's map, not their own; and

3. the matter of religious practice—the Bible and the liturgy are foreign to the contemporary culture of most American students, a fact that every classroom instructor knows and no curriculum (adequately) acknowledges.

It is very difficult to teach such students how to investigate, understand, and describe aspects of the past. American students tend to read medieval history and medieval literature as if it had always existed in print, with notes; and they tend to describe medieval events largely in modern terms. This problem of distance can be countered in part by teaching through the reading and analysis of texts, literary and documentary, and the reading and analysis of images and music, with attention paid to their manuscript bases.

(4) Finally, I think we would agree that a goal of American undergraduate education is to encourage students to think on their own rather than to repeat previously memorized material, to sharpen the student's judgment, and to enhance the student's ability for precise self-expression. To ask students, as T. J. Brown suggested, to describe what they see in front of them[7] or to ask a student to define why one page is different from another is a useful exercise, as it is to ask a student to put into words why one script or page layout is effective with regard to achieving certain goals when another is not. True, this sort of exercise may be done with any artifact, not just with the written page, and it is one of the essential purposes of any course in the fine arts or literature; but why should historians not do it with manuscripts, and accomplish in part the other goals at the same time?

Let us be clear, I do not advocate a course in paleography for undergraduates. Instead, I have argued that knowing about its origin and transmission is an integral part of reading a text, of appreciating a literary work or an iconographic image; and that, more frequently and more deftly than at present, manuscript evidence should be the source through which a point is made or a question examined in the course surveying medieval history, literature, music, or art.

Let us turn from undergraduate teaching to the other end of the spectrum, research. What is the role of paleography or manuscript studies in research? The narrow view, that paleography is necessary in order to read texts, is generally accepted. Given that, do we envision a few paleographers surviving as vestigial organs, being kept alive on the academic equivalent of life-support systems into the next century? Historical research advances through discovery and interpretation. Without the discovery of new information one is left to interpret the same body of data according to different models or theories. Without the precise and cautious dating, localizing, and reading of the evidence that we do have, can useful interpretation follow? There is some truth in the statement that "new facts collected in old ways, under the guidance of old theories, rarely lead to any substantial revision of thought"; but there is still the inescapable fact that our field does advance in part by sheer discovery, whether it be the discovery of the Vindolanda fragments and the light they shed on conditions of life near Hadrian's wall in Britain, or the discovery of the origin of the eagle in Suger's treasure, or that of a hitherto unknown autobiographical work of Durandus of Huesca, or of a fragment of a poet's roll containing an unknown stanza of Reinmar von Zweter's lyrics, or the record of a payment of 125 pounds to Richard of Verdun, Master Honoré's son-in-law, for the making of a Bible, ten years after his supposed death-date. Each of these has altered in a small but significant fashion the way historians will interpret the subjects these discoveries affect. The paleographer, as a specialist in the "the circumstances in which texts were composed, copied and read," is well placed to add to the available documentation, both in the reinterpretation of existing data and in the discovery of new information.

If the manuscript foundation of medieval studies is to be brought into undergraduate instruction, and if there are to be further Lowes, Bischoffs, and Kers, then training in paleography must be offered at the graduate level, including fellowship support for thesis research in Europe. And equally important, medievalists in North American universities, at least those universities which profess to offer serious training in medieval studies, must be willing to devote positions to the subject. It will not be difficult to fill the seminar room with students, nor is there any lack of research to be done.

If manuscripts—along with other matters crucial to an understanding of the Middle Ages but at present largely ignored, such as liturgy—if these are subjects through which teachers are to present a more realistic picture of the Middle Ages to their undergraduates, those who teach will of course have to have had the proper components in their own professional training. Graduate training therefore will need to include both the necessary languages and the necessary skills to work effectively with whatever medieval materials and problems may confront them in the course of their work as productive scholars.

Having examined the place of manuscript studies in teaching and research, let me take up briefly in conclusion some of the specific questions posed by John Van Engen in his charge to the members of this symposium, insofar as they apply to manuscript studies.

I see no reason why the study of multiple cultures should diminish the importance of understanding the means by which members of a society communicate among themselves or between generations. Nor do I see it diminishing the necessity of having accurate editions of the texts through which we study a society. The reasons I have given for teaching through manuscripts in undergraduate and graduate curricula would apply equally well to studying the history of France, China, Peru, or Ethiopia.

I have always supported a "multiple key" approach to understanding a text or a historical situation and would not argue that one type of history is "better" or more valid then another. The field needs both interpretation and documentation. Ornato and Bozzola could not have produced their interpretive statistical study of dated manuscripts[8] had not others, with different interests and abilities, produced the catalog of dated manuscripts in the first place. Neither one of these works is "better" or more useful than the other. While in my opening remarks I reproached the paleographer who would not extend himself beyond the tenth century, I would also reproach those who cannot see beyond their own particular interpretive methodology. We can work effectively with Le Goff's formulation of examining a society through the careful analysis of the texts it has left behind, applying whatever tool is of help in elucidating their meaning.[9]

Medievalists have actively pursued interdisciplinary research and study in the application of anthropological and linguistic methodology, and paleographers are no exception to this. Paleographers are currently interested in the relationship between eye, brain, and hand, in why some cultures write from right to left and others from left to right,[10] in how children are taught how to write, and, most recently, in how people read. Codicologists from Russia, western Europe, and North America recently participated in a seminar at the Institute for Advanced Studies in Jerusalem devoted to the comparative study of Byzantine, Islamic, Armenian, Hebrew, and Western codicology and manuscript book production.[11] Scientific methods of digital image-enhancement and the examination of flat surfaces have been applied to reading erased inscriptions,[12] and to measuring the proportion of the surface of a page covered by the ink and the depth of the impression left by the quill in writing on parchment. It has been encouraging, from the opposite standpoint, to see those who study the history of literacy, reading, and graphology seek out the assistance of paleographers. Paleography has not normally been seen in this company, and paleographers might well be encouraged to exhibit some concern with enhancing their own image. If we are perceived as vestigial organs, it is in part our own fault.

Are the auxiliary disciplines, the tools necessary for basic research, still justifiable in the onslaught of interpretive studies? I do not see why they are any less important than they were twenty-five or fifty years ago, or than they remain to classical studies today. Paleography has not exhausted its subject, nor will it, as long as manuscripts exist to be examined. Whether manuscript studies will be considered useful depends upon paleographers making themselves useful to other disciplines and producing intelligent and intelligible work of their own. If they do not, they will be replaced by people working in other disciplines. I would like to see paleography as manuscript studies, as I have described it here, and I should think, for paleography's health, that the subject should be taught by people with a medieval history or literature training rather than a formation in classics. Part of the difficulty in which all the basic or auxiliary disciplines find themselves—papyrology, epigraphy, paleography, diplomatic, chronology, sigillography—is the legacy of their origin and existence in classical studies, interested in the written text alone. Since it is necessary to medieval studies that someone be able to read Latin and to decipher deeds and rent rolls, the field will have to sanction training in paleography if it wishes to continue effective teaching and research. It is up to the paleographers, however, to demonstrate that manuscript study has something substantive to offer, that it is not a peripheral luxury.

With regard to language preparation, medievalists must identify undergraduates who wish to continue in medieval studies and encourage them to consider where they are heading and to prepare themselves for the work that lies ahead. Intensive training in language as well as in basic disciplines has long been part of education in North America and should continue to be, in that we cannot each have a medieval Latinist or paleographer on our faculty. Those who have such specialists should shoulder this task; and I hope that the great private libraries and the various centers and institutes will continue their very useful contributions to providing training in special areas. Provision must undoubtedly be made, however, to make language training available to entering graduate students who are able but unprepared. Permitting students to change direction at the graduate level is a great weakness of the American university system; it is also one of its strengths.

I do not see it as harmful to medieval studies that they have emerged traditionally from the study of the church and of its writers or, more recently in North America, from the study of the Anglo-American legal tradition. That tools for the study of Merovingian charters were first formulated by a Benedictine monk, Jean Mabillon in 1681, has not affected their usefulness to Protestants, Jews, Muslims, or atheists. Rather than worry that we may have lost something by the fact that the discipline grew out of theology and church history, we might do better to be concerned with the tremendous change that has occurred in the nature of medieval studies with the disappearance—as a result of the decline in vocations—of the type of monastic and clerical scholarship which to a large extent defined and dominated medieval studies between c. 1870 and 1970. Where shall we find people profoundly familiar with the liturgy, the scriptures, or the works of the church fathers, who can identify echoes of the psalms or of Gregory's *Moralia on Job* in Middle English literature, or wherever else they might appear? Who will prepare sound editions of the works of St. Thomas when the Leonine Commission can no longer replace its aging members? The church has welcomed laymen to continue its tasks, but where in North America is liturgy taught for art historians, or for students in history and literature? This is all the more reason to see that students are made aware of the basics of medieval society from the start, that the role of liturgy and the cult of the saints, as well as the mean of communication, oral and written, be given their place in the undergraduate course in medieval history. Rather than short-changing undergraduates with a "taste of" or an "appreciation of" the Middle Ages, we might do well to let them see clearly that this was a culture different from our own, in Lynn White's words an "emerging" or "Third World" culture, with systems of communication and of belief and of basic assumptions different from ours. The medieval course will be the better for it, and so will the students.

NOTES

I shall concern myself with the role of paleography in the American curriculum of the future rather than the past, since I have discussed the latter
in "Latin Paleography and Manuscript Studies in North America," in *Un
secolo di paleografia e diplomatica (1887–1986)* (Rome, 1988), 307–327.
I am grateful to Mary A. Rouse for having read this essay in earlier stages
and discussed it with me.

     1. T. J. Brown, "Latin Paleography since Traube," *Cambridge Biblio-
graphical Society* 3 (1963): 361–381.

     2. Ibid., 366.

     3. Ibid., 381.

     4. Entitled *Palaeography: Report of the Working Party.*

     5. Paleography is taught elsewhere in Britain, but it is funded by soft
money, or annual rather than designated funds.

     6. This is how the term "paleography" has been understood in
Great Britain since at least the 1970s, a formulation again articulated in
Julian Brown's inaugural lecture, p. 364.

     7. Brown, "Latin Palaeography since Traube," 381.

     8. C. Bozzolo, E. Ornato, *Pour une histoire de livre manuscrit au
Moyen Age* (Paris, 1980).

     9. J. Le Goff, *Pour un autre moyen âge* (Paris, 1977).

     10. C. Sirat, J. Irigoin, E. Poulle, eds., *L'écriture: Le cerveau, l'oeil, et
la main,* Bibliologia 10 (Turnhout, 1990).

     11. Hebrew University, Jerusalem, 1 February–1 August 1991.

     12. J. Benton, "Digital Image-Processing Applied to the Photography
of Manuscripts . . . ," *Scriptorium* 33 (1979): 40–55.

Diplomatic Sources and Medieval Documentary Practices: An Essay in Interpretive Methodology.

Brigitte Bedos-Rezak

> Historians have their method, just like anyone else, and they're jealous
> of it, but the *Iliad* shames any history of Greece, and Dante stands su-
> preme above the world's collected medievalists. Of course, the me-
> dievalists don't know it, but everyone else does. As a way to arrive at
> the truth, exactitude and methodology are, in the end, far inferior to
> vision and apotheosis.
>
> Mark Helprin[1]

According to the Carolingian poet Raban Maur, writ-
ing served best the interests of the truth and was the perfect norm
of salvation.[2] At the beginning of the thirteenth century, Gerald of
Wales commented that "writing is an exacting business. First you
decide what to leave out, and then you have to polish up what
you put in."[3] Writing, from both perspectives, encompassed a wide
variety of forms: manuscripts, documents, seals, engraved metals
and stones. Such written sources are cited interchangeably by medievalists who use them as primary materials, as a solid basis from
which, and in continuity with which, to project their own historical
writings.

I propose to discuss a specific class of the documentary
sources available for Northern France between 1000–1230, so-
called documents of practice, pragmatic records, otherwise known
as charters.[4] Such documents have long been seen as records of
legal and economic activity, showing the world as it was, not as
it should have been. In reading charters, medievalists expect to
lift the ideological veil and to lay hold of the raw material of a ret-
rospective sociography.[5] In the age of postmodern criticism, how-

ever, an attempt has been made to erase presumptive distinctions
between ideologically distorted literary texts and transparent documents. This in fact has led to a redefinition of the same differ-
entiation but now oriented along a semiological cleavage. In
intellectual texts, processes of meaning production are the subject
matter which may thus be seen in direct operation. On the other
hand documents are the effects of meaning produced. Charters as
products, rather than as processes, readily lend themselves to a
content-oriented approach,[6] and having been left virtually untouched by the waves of textual criticism, are freshly available for
diplomatic analysis.

The centrality of documentary sources in the epistemology of
medieval history is best exemplified by what was, and still to a very
great extent is, a discipline proper to the field of medieval studies.
Diplomatics has long centered on a detailed examination of written
documents for the purpose of extracting what they say. This assumed epistemological centrality of the document, however, does
not correspond to the role, significance, and meaning of documentation in the time and place it was generated. I am not suggesting
that medieval historians reject written sources merely because they
were not central to the medieval mechanics of social action and
communication. I do suggest that recovery of medieval charters'
meaning and evidential capacity requires analysis of their operations within the society that produced them, operations that involved being marginal agents, forgeries, lexically imprecise texts,
linguistic (Latin) and semiotic (letters) mysteries, ineffective legal
tools, untrusted evidence, challenged receptacles of memory, un-
consulted archives, ambivalent symbols, ritual objects, or sacred
monuments. Many historians and diplomatists have listed these
many "dysfunctional" characteristics. Perhaps the time has now
come to consider not only the documents, but documentary practices, and not a failing system but one that worked; we need to explore how and to what effect. Northern French medieval charters
are available to us as material presences, as objects that were made
because desirable, that have since lived in oblivion, that have been
manipulated by silence. They were not produced as sources, and
diplomatics may not therefore dissociate the empirical examination
of documents from a three-tiered awareness: (1) of the principles of
historians' relation to the documents, (2) of the medieval idea of

the document, and (3) of the fact that in medieval times, everything was off the record so to speak save that which was read to an audience within earshot.[7]

The very concept of written source is fundamental in more than one way to the medieval historian, precisely because the balance between the sources and the gesture required to establish them is so tilted toward the founding nature of that gesture. The past that is being examined is the document, that is a material which is a product, an ongoing construct, and certainly not a given. Through the comprehensive taxonomy of diplomatics, the medieval status and role of charters, which has yet to be assessed, has been changed: from being social phenomena and cultural artifacts, charters have been rendered into data, no innocent term. Transformed into a "given," the very modalities of charters' creation and being no longer inhere in the medieval sphere of their use, but in their position within a reified sequence of types. The charter thus has come to derive meaning as a referential signpost within the larger class of documents. The multiplicity and redundancy of documentary signals have been condensed by diplomatists and historians who use various schemes of classification. But these classifications, having become the primary signals, are accepted and repeated at the cost of original detections. Medieval charters have partially been detached from their identities and are therefore of tremendously diminished evidential capacity. Because of the epistemic strategy of their very students they have been severed from many of their original functions and messages. Further consequences of such strategy are a narrowing of the already small pool of themes covered by scribal material, an obscuration of the implications of situated uses of literate modes, and a requirement that medievalists rely heavily on contexts as enabling analytical frameworks for charters that were long supposed to document precisely their own contexts and circumstances of production. In here proposing an agenda by which to learn directly from the product itself, to discover what allowed it to be conceived, to read the chain of its generative acts, I of course build on a rich legacy of diplomatic critique. But I wish also to suggest some newer avenues for future consideration.

Since Mabillon (1632–1707) first placed documentary criticism on a firm footing in the late seventeenth century, the discipline of diplomatics has been based upon specific set of assumptions. (1) Documents are to be considered from the viewpoint of their authors, so that categories include royal diplomas, aristocratic, or monastic, or episcopal charters, all of which may also be divided into the subcategories of public and private deeds. (2) Documents which contain the disposition and will of an agent are to be seen primarily as having been drawn up to serve probative juridical functions. (3) Documents were drawn up according to specific forms, and to particular sets of rules in order to achieve validity. (4) Documents are all part of archival deposits in an order that is historically significant because it was imposed by the institution that originally generated or received them. (5) Forged documents must be differentiated from genuine. Although current diplomatics embraces, in principle, every form of documentary evidence, it nevertheless focuses mainly upon juridical matters by confining most of its investigation to documents with legal implications and by emphasizing that these medieval charters have a primarily judicial function.[8]

In my own practice of diplomatics I began with the formulaic approach just outlined. But in studying Northern French documentary practices of the eleventh and twelfth centuries, I found that this formalization had imposed the shape of its own method upon the objects of its study; it obscured evidence of how these objects operated. Far from being confined to the juridical, the documentary practices that I identified suggest combined systems which are best analyzed without the preconception of an imaginary, unitary, reality.

Northern French charters are manuscript. By repeating this obvious characteristic, we are reminded that modes of documentary production were not mechanical; they always involved the mediation of a conscious intelligence, of a process of human creation at the material level. If historians organize their data in relation to conscious expressions and in the continuity of signs left by scribal activities,[9] then medievalists must be careful to distinguish within their documents the dual level of consciousness which informs the written characters and their semantics. Medieval self-consciousness about written modes of representation may be experienced through a work that is not only the residue of an event but is also an event in its own way, one that directly prompted other scribes to repeat or to improve its formulation.

Northern French charters between 1000–1230 yield up their full significance only when attention is paid to the circumstances of their production and conservation, to their diplomatic discourse, to the modalities and significance of their use, to their operations within society, and to the symbiotic relationship they entertain with yet other systems of signs: the heraldic emblems and images engraved on the seals attached to these charters.

Charters in the name of lay lords became more numerous during this period even as documentary practices extended from monastic to lay milieux. However, up until the beginning of the twelfth century, the process and control of written records had remained the monopoly of religious establishments which drafted and preserved those records of land endowments made to them and those acts which settled disputes over land ownership in their favor. The donor in whose name a charter records the decision to transfer land remains a problematic author from the viewpoint of the creation of the document: though he may have ordered the document to be made, as is sometimes specified in the charter, he is certainly not the one who composed and wrote it. Therefore, in addressing existing catalogues of the acts of the counts of Anjou, or of Flanders, or of Ponthieu, or of the lord of Montmorency, a critical early step should be establishment of the scribal provenance of such deeds. This is also true for royal diplomas which, too, between the tenth and the twelfth centuries, were drawn up primarily outside the royal chancery by their ecclesiastical recipients. Actually, it would be useful to conceive of charters and diplomas, and thus to organize their potential editions, from the viewpoint of their originating scriptoria. This would define spheres of scribal activity and serve to map their interactions with the zones and assertions of lay authorities. Such an approach suggests several lines of inquiry.

First, this approach shifts the emphasis from the charter as an act of individual or familial will to the charter as part of an archive. Here the historian and diplomatist must be cautious, for there may be no necessary contiguity between the archive of an abbey and documents drafted in its scriptoria. The archive might well, for example, include documents produced elsewhere, especially from other religious institutions endowed with their own writing bureaus. As a result, cartularies, which from the twelfth century onward registered copies of monastic title-deeds held in a particular archive, cannot be used systematically to document the output of its abbey's scriptorium. Nevertheless, the inclusion of a charter as part of a particular archive imparts to it a specific function, at the very least, preservation; but to what end? As discussed below, in cases of contested transactions, monks rarely referred to charters in trying to prove their rights, and these were often too vague about the property transferred. Even the witnesses listed in the charters were not those called for testimony; testimony and its authenticity still resided with people, not with charters.

Asking in the broadest terms what was meaningful in the very act of archiving, attention may be drawn to documentary practices in Northern French towns which reveal a formal requirement for city archives. Urban governments produced documents for their citizens who wished to put their contracts into writing. The format of these urban records, known as chirographs, consisted of several copies of a text recording that a covenant had been made in the presence of specifically named town officials. The identical texts were then cut apart along a marked incision so that parties to the conveyances could each receive an identical version of the text. Authenticity was to be proven by matching the cut edges of the copies with a reference copy deposited within the city archive, which served as a matrix from which the other versions of the transaction derived their authenticity. Chirographs were used to some extent by ecclesiastical institutions and by the nobility,[10] but not in the systematic way that came to characterize the documentary practice of Northern French towns. This has led to the veritable equation of chirographs with urban records.[11] When a portion of the chirograph bearing the names of all parties to the transactions was placed in the urban archive, these individuals were inscribed within the ongoing narrative of the city's history. This event made them part of the very substance of the collective identity from which they as individuals derived the means and meanings of their social behavior. Such archives, which were stored in the town hall, compelled a definition of this most urban of spaces, and ultimately of the town itself, as the very source for documentary authenticity, as the *locus credibilis*.[12] Archives thus played a critical symbolic role in marking the city as an authoritative center of credibility, and in imprinting its society with an authentic identity.[13]

Reconsideration of charters and diplomas from the perspective of their locus of production and conservation brings a different light to the medieval conceptualization of the public-private dichotomy. The applications to and implications of this dichotomy for the nature of aristocratic charters and of royal diplomas would thus bear reexamination if both types of documents indeed have a common monastic origin. During the tenth to the twelfth centuries, the distinction between private and public documents dear to diplomatists received a severe challenge when the quintessential public document, the French royal diploma evidenced the following symptoms of "privatization."[14] The early Capetians participated, as did their Robertian predecessors such as King Raoul,[15] in modes of documentary validation drawn from private procedures, including the exchange of symbolic objects and the addition of the *signa* of their entourage.[16] Perfectly authentic early Capetian diplomas survive which appear never to have been sealed.[17] Such unsealed diplomas, however, seem invariably to have been drafted outside of the chancery, for those drafted within appear always to have been sealed;[18] the seal remained an established formula of kingship for members of the royal chancery. Attempting to interpret these changes, diplomatists have postulated a corruption of the diploma by the diplomatic discourse of the private charter. This alteration has, in turn, been interpreted as a sign of the weakening of royal authority and indeed it corresponds temporally to the feeble rule of the early Capetians. Princely power as evoked with magnates' charters, which like royal diplomas of the period include lists of witnesses, has been assessed as essentially royal in nature, especially since the content of these charters, such as grants of immunity, indicate that princes were exercising regalian rights. One must of course ask why, if the presence of a witness-list does not expunge the quality of regality from princely charters, it should be presumed to do so from royal charters. Furthermore, those scribes who were also the composers and recipients of royal documents have been shown to have been scrupulous in emulating chancery standards while preparing these documents. Lastly, the texts of magnates' charters also confirm that such documents were drafted in imitation of the royal model.[19] The hypothesis of the "privatization" of the royal diploma must then be readdressed, not only from the point of view of the relationship between texts and power, but from that of the relationship between texts and writing. What appears to have happened is that both aristocratic and royal documents were written by the same scribes following a diplomatic formula of their own devising in which the importance attached to testimony. This is also reflected in a related change in the name by which the written charter was now known: *testimonium* or *memoriale*.[20]

Clerical scribes thus controlled the form, terminology, and language of the diplomatic discourse. They wrote in Latin, which they alone knew (the earliest preserved vernacular document is a 1205 city record from Douai). Charters originating from a single scriptorium tend to display standardized features but, and here diplomatics may have been guilty of over-categorization, standardization was specific to the locality, and the overall texture of scribal culture remained fluctuating, uneven, and multiform. As a result of this, and not merely because charters are rather few, quantification is of little value and ill suited to the conditions of scribal culture. Shared features within charters of identical scribal origin include lexical specificities, textual forms, traditions and topoi for the preambles. These articulate the cultural and ideological models ambient in a given scriptorium. They should consequently be analyzed with reference to the volumes produced by or kept in the library of the specific scriptorium in order to investigate the borrow-terms from classical texts and medieval treatises and their application in charters to the description of what was perceived as social reality. It would also be worthwhile to look at a scriptorium's textual production *in toto* so as to evaluate the extent to which Latin words were polysemic, and from which terminological traffic the ultimate patterns of semantic unity flowed. Such philological filiation, once established,[21] would allow one to address the question of how such diplomatic discourse engages reality which was its object. What was it within living experience that inspired such modes of representation but was yet not identical to it? Is the combination of themes (in preambles), titles (*nobilis, consul, miles*), acts (donation, exchange, agreement), a lexicon of what took place, or a structure within which might be organized a manifestation congenial to the relationships, imaginary or otherwise, which the scribes bore to their own social and cultural situations? With the general increase of written documents in the eleventh and twelfth centuries, there appeared all sorts of new elements, such as specific social categorizations and political definitions. Were these entirely new elements, or merely elements *newly* put into writing? Now that, by means of written artifacts, a medium for the preservation of complex context is made available, have we evidence for a new context, or for a new medium? We know that property was transferred previously without the benefit of charters; charters allowed new means for solemnizing, validating and executing the transfer, but the transfer itself was not new. Some social categories, among witnesses especially, appear so suddenly in eleventh-century charters that they are likely to have been consolidated over the years. Pushing the argument to an extreme, could we, in talking about a feudal revolution, for instance, be confusing the clarification of social concepts performed through writing with a possibly a-synchronous growth of specific social structure? If this were the case, might not the "feudal revolution" above all be a revolution in diplomatics?

The relationship between the social terminology used in these documents and constitutional reality, and the related question of the evidential capacity of charters, are perhaps best addressed by considering the charter as an agent for the structuring of society. In eleventh-century Northern France, diplomatic discourse extended far beyond the bare recording of transactions. It declared the donors' motivations, inscribing them within the rationale of Christian ethics and salvific eschatology. It garbed donors with titles of dignity, thus articulating a social system by which the donors' status was given definition, meaning, and precedence. It also shaped kin groups in reporting the modalities of the *laudatio parentum,* and networks of dependence and solidarity when listing witnesses. Documentary discourse and practice sacralized the whole process: thus a formula came systematically to accompany the autograph cross of the donor, stating that the cross strengthened the act, would prevent it from being attacked, or would bring excommunication or divine retribution upon whomever failed to respect the content of the charter.[22] Further sacralization was achieved by the custom of placing it on the altar.[23] The supernatural protection explicit in the deed's association with cross and altar implied that the written act functioned as representative of a superior, irrevocable order, and that the document itself might mediate divine punishment; threats of malediction and of excommunication were now regularly incorporated within final clauses.[24] These textual constructs in charter format might be, and were, read aloud in translation thus involving the audience in an oral experience which shaped and communicated awareness of their socio-cultural environment.[25] The charters themselves came to play a central part in the performance of rituals and social forms maintained in the oral tradition then prevalent in aristocratic lay culture. Many charters state that they have been touched by everybody's hand in order to prevent any quarrel, or refer to the *eloquia and gesta,* words and gestures of a donor, or have objects physically attached to them—knives or rods by conveyance of which acts of alienation had traditionally been performed.[26] By being spoken and manipulated, charters served to represent a particular order; they asserted control of time of space. They can be conceived as literally producing and organizing social meaning. Perhaps they should even be evaluated as products and instruments of power, on behalf of clerics who had the power and knowledge (a monopoly of literacy) to state the order of the universe, and on behalf of lay magnates who came to see the written word as symbolic of their power because it was a means for the representation and reinforcement of a social order in which they were accorded images of superior status.

The charters issued from and kept by a single monastery allow the identification of an aristocratic group unified by its gifts in its interactions with this monastery; perhaps it is possible here to perceive a medieval version of a clientele. By inscribing lay gifts, the titles of the donors, their family connections, the list of their witnesses, the scribes are also inscribing the social order, mapping zones of authority, organizing its hierarchy. In noting that eleventh- and twelfth-century donations to Ile-de-France abbeys register a sociological shift by which small landholders become totally excluded in favor of wealthy noble donors, I wonder whether it is possible to conceive that monks screened their donors, or at least the recording of gifts, so as to create through an archive that pattern of landholding and that structure of authority corresponding to their specific vision of social order; and they enacted this order through documentary practice and symbolic manipulation of charters.

Could this hypothetical performative function have been so central that adoption of its perspective may now be used to shed light on what appear to be charters' dysfunctional aspects? Although the land and property rights granted to monasteries and their saints are responsible for the documentary explosion in eleventh-century Northern France, a recent analysis of eleventh-century Norman charters shows how few charters describe the land transaction being recorded accurately; nor is it clear what witnesses were to do, or did, in defense of a challenged alienation.[27] In Anjou it appears that, even when a charter was contested in the lifetime of the listed witnesses, the witnesses called upon for testimony might actually be different from those listed.[28] There are virtually no records of written charters being cited as proofs against the challengers of their content. A substantial disjunction exists between text and life experience when the discursive claim is made by donors within charters that they wanted their gifts to be permanent for there is much evidence of other people's or even of the donor's own, challenges[29]to those very gifts whose permanency was presented as surrounded by various modes of assurance, among them the charter itself. The textually expressed purpose of the charter, initially, was to provide such assurance, but neither its recording of actions, nor of the names of those witnesses who would have to testify to these actions in case of a contestation, seem to have resulted in the completion of such actions. Though often denominated "obstacles to oblivion," charters nevertheless appear to have failed in their function of preserving memory and were not invoked when land transfers were actually challenged. This may indicate that, during the period under consideration, expert memory was continuously assembled in numerous settings where the working intelligence of daily life was repeatedly reshaped and constituted as the base of the knowledge of the past. Similarly, the permanence associated with a gift of land may not simply have involved possession of the land and its use. It also involved and required regular challenge, because in order to be preserved, ownership had to be seen as being preserved. Permanence also inhered in the very social relationships that were created, maintained, and continued to operate throughout the ongoing negotiations surrounding titles to land and revenues. For the negotiations and settlements of disputes involved both donors and beneficiaries, and their groups of witnesses as well, that is, a whole society addressing the complexity of its inner hierarchy and dynamics. The permanence of gifts was thus conceived as part of an ongoing process, not as a static situation, and was the necessary framework for the definition of social groupings.

In the eleventh and early-twelfth centuries, charters were part rather than proof of those processes by which land was transfered. To see this period of the Middle Ages as having a history without texts would indeed be excessive. Yet charters may be best considered as written objects rather than as texts since they were not produced by their lay donors, were written in a foreign language and could not be easily deciphered, since in short, as written texts, they existed outside the living experience of the great majority of medieval people. By considering their nature as objects, the medievalist elicits their role in rituals, in the visual, tactile, and auditory sensitivity of medieval people. This enables an understanding of documentary writing as a scripture, as an inscription of order, as a medium operating through a strong sense of the holy, and itself as a mediation between the earthly and the divine. If a function of communication is to be part of an understanding of these charters, medievalists must seek to uncover the various modalities of the non-literate legibility of such documents. Charters had levels of signification, since they were publicized, engraved on the doors of cathedrals or of city walls,[30] and since ultimately concrete writing of things ceased to be marginal and symbolic, but became for the lay aristocracy an integral and defining project of documentation. Charters progressively came to acquire those legal meanings and functions of proof and title deeds they were later analyzed as having, though never to the point, I think, where they should be considered mere repositories of evidentiary texts.

Any proper consideration of Northern French charters between 1000 and 1230 must take into consideration the fact of their rapid multiplication, the processes by which clerical scribes convinced non-literate laymen to transact affairs by means of writing, and by which the secular nobility came to adopt a literate mode, the ultimate success of which was clearly dependent upon their own willingness to participate. Ample evidence of vigorous monastic scribal activities testify, among other things, to the important role of monks in acculturating the laity to documentary practices. This role is increasingly obvious to us today, and it appears that the format of the lay aristocratic charter evolved in the specific historical and ideological context of the churchmen's need and preference for writing, but the modes of acculturation have yet to be unravelled from the evidences of empirical practices. A systematic study of aristocratic command within final clauses of charters that transactions or agreements be put into writing, would be instructive for tracing the increasing participation of the laity into literate modes, and the moments and circumstances of its initiative in the matter. Whether, and if so when, at some point monastic scriptoria acted on behalf of the nobility as writing bureaus even for those gifts not made in these monks' favor might also shed light on how the laity came to resort to literate modes and to conceptualize the notion of a chancery for its own use. Ultimately princely charters came to be drafted in princely chanceries. Evidence of a chancellor is attested c. 1080 in Anjou,[31] appears after 1101 in Champagne,[32] between 1106–1135 in Normandy,[33] and around 1136 in Flanders.[34] Though clerics continued to form the staffs of these secular chanceries, potentates nevertheless now secured for themselves control of those documents written in their own names which previously had typically been drawn up by the scribes of the recipient ecclesiastical institutions. But while it is clear that this evolution involved the increase, not of lay literacy but of an irreversible lay use of and accommodation to written documents, this sequence has been noted rather than analyzed. Cited as a *de facto* premise for studies on literacy, it has been considered as an epiphenomenon of administrative evolution, as a consequence of a revival of Roman Law, or simply as a by-product and the instrument of economic growth.[35] The lay adoption of literate modes has not been posited as a cultural reorientation with its own sphere of modalities and significance. Yet, in Northern France, lay aristocratic participation in documentary practices actually preceded all these administrative, legal, and economic developments. Having discussed the uses, meanings, and effects of charters within the society that produced them, I wish to outline further a few lines of inquiry. It was over gifts of land that the noble and the scribal worlds met, and noble assimilation to documentary forms cannot be separated from a consideration of the value system inherent in specific uses of landed property.[36] According to the charters, land, and therefore wealth, circulated through gift. Gift is a peace-time mechanism for the redistribution of landed wealth. It was through land alienation, and no longer through land plundering, that the nobles might enhance their prestige by behaving generously and by controlling the structure of their environment. Inspired by the Peace of God, a notion began to enter noble culture that rights won by arms could no longer provide an absolute and legitimate justification for status and land-holding. It is quite possibly in connection with this reassessment of the place of warfare within the noble ethos that the relevance of documentary modes for rights over the land established its importance within the lay aristocratic mentality. As a result of the zeal of tenth- and eleventh-century reformers, the monastic attitude to religion progressively penetrated the aristocracy which, by the eleventh century, was accustomed to be concerned about the day of judgment,[37] and to consider its penitential needs as being directly related to its proclivity for warfare. The crux of the issue seems to have been the redemptive significance achieved by pious gifts.[38] The relationship created between lay donors and religious institutions involved God and his saints, and ultimately was based on the lay concern for salvation. The eleventh and twelfth centuries were the great period of *donationes pro anima,* donations for the soul, which involved a lay gift of land to an abbey in exchange for the donor's and selected beneficiaries' redemption of sins and salvation after their deaths.[39] This linkage of and reciprocity between religious and lay interests was crucial for the development of the mechanisms of property transfer, principally by means of the written record. It is indeed in the area of property law that orality came largely to be superseded. Yet, in the twelfth century, writing did not secure the stability of gifts. Gifts were social actions which were represented not as abstract categories, but as events embedded in, and expressive of, a given social network. The referents of such social acts were actual circumstances which were to be remembered in the form of particular lived experiences. Charters articulated and gave meaning to a specific social structure. They had not yet evolved into trans-temporal abstractions functioning as their own referents; they encapsulated the present, but could not control the future, that is, provide permanence and stability, because they had not achieved self-referential authority.

A tendency toward such abstraction may be inferred from the evolving modes of documentary enforcement. Curses or the sign of the cross had attempted to bring supernatural sanctions to bear. Power for the maintenance of permanent donations came to be also vested in, or to be the responsibility of, a certain category of individuals termed *viri authentici,* or *viri boni,* or *viri legales,* or *viri legitimi.*[40] Whenever these individuals are identified, they are men, never women, of some authority and distinction, and they are specifically presented as known. They may include the local count, castellan, or bishop, dignitaries who exercised judicial functions. But, most often, they are invoked in the charters as an anonymous group of men, whose suitable presence and "authentic" quality gave worth to the alienation and to its written record. This anonymous rendering makes it difficult now to evaluate whether such worth derived from these individuals' moral, political, or military character. Local knowledge must have informed the specific composition of such groups whose members clearly enjoyed a local reputation. Their participation in the act, and in its recording, was as particular individuals, based on their status within the community which had faith in them. Yet, it was precisely as an anonymous group that these witnesses displayed an official character. They constituted a category, and although authenticity may also have emanated from their authority as individuals, it is possible to perceive here the use of an a-temporal category which extended living memory and its credibility across time, and which implied the abstract concept of office.

With the appearance of seals on aristocratic charters in the late eleventh century, the quality of authenticity became inherent in the seals themselves and in the sealed charters, that is, in objects.[41] The authentic charter was an iconic document in which several systems of signs—the letter, the image, the heraldic emblem—entertained a symbiotic relationship. The traditional scholarly view of the medieval seal has focused almost exclusively on its function in the authentication of written documents. This classical conception, while accurate, is perhaps incomplete for a phenomenon which presents much broader implications. For in the Middle Ages, the seal was a *fact of civilization,* and its perception merely as a means of documentary validation would fail to take adequate account of the additional dimensions which provide insights into the medieval construct of social identity. A new goal for medievalists, therefore, would be to present seals as a medium for several cultural discourses: political, familial, individual, and gender, and to assess seals' specific participation in the very social processes they expose.

Study of the social and cultural implications of seals must involve an understanding of the objects themselves. The seal presents a dualistic aspect. For the matrix, engraved intaglio, impressed a raised image upon a secondary surface, most often of wax or lead. This technical definition would appear to obscure many cultural nuances pertaining to seals as implements of social importance. But such a definition does underscore the essence of seals as active agents, the value of which lies in their creative capacity, in their power of becoming (the impressions) as well as simply of being (the intaglio matrices).[42] This regenerative potential lies close to the essence of living things—not of inanimate objects—and herein may lie the root of medieval man's intense psycho-social identification with his seal. I have developed from my own research the sense that in the Middle Ages seals were active extensions of the identities of their owners. For the medieval seal was a personal object incorporating both a text—the legend—and an image that, together, defined and represented the sealer. The seal matrix, designed to be impressed into a receptive surface, was carved in the negative. In this form seals were "inner-directed," functioning as quasi-amuletic objects, and as personal accoutrements of status. When impressed, the seal projected a three-dimensional image and any inscription included within the seal device became legible. In this outward-directed form, the seal functioned as a sign, conveying identity, status, prestige, and power-covenant. Since the seal operated through the medium of its progeny, as a progenitor, and was intended for repetitive use under a wide variety of circumstances, it had to display the most essential elements of a sealer's identity. This rendered the choice of titles especially significant, and the resultant textual impressions provide a coherent continuum of social vocabulary which may be analyzed by comparison with changing usages within charters and literary sources. The issue of identity also rendered the choice of image important,[43] for on seals in particular, text and image participate in a single discourse, the dialectic of which involves the linkage of a personal identity, specified in a seal's legend, to a more general group orientation, inherent in its iconography. On their seals kings invariably appear enthroned with regalia, lay magnates are equestrians in arms, noblewomen are endowed with attributes of virginity and fertility, and bishops and abbots are garbed in ecclesiastical vestments. For these social categories, the underlying convention dictated that seal owners be represented as concepts and not as individuals. The seal's iconography thus fostered a symbology of power and articulated organizing principles of society, while the personal identification of its individual owner was totally dependent upon an inscription. This relationship between a seal's text and image involved neither complete complementarity, nor redundancy, nor a tension of opposites; rather it created a space in which the particular (written legend) and the universal (image) combined to generate an identity that was operative in itself, and that constituted a mode by which medieval society could distinguish its essential elements. An extensive data base exists for the analysis of this particular representational system and its societal context, which analysis provides insight into the mechanisms of encodements.[44] And indeed a key question is: How much of a given social group's actuality depended upon the modalities of its representation?

Other critical elements of the sigillographic process include the modalities of sealing practice and the circumstances of their diffusion. I began to examine broad patterns of sealing after systematically gathering and analyzing an exhaustive corpus of French seals prior to 1200. This investigation revealed that, until the eleventh century, the use of seals for documentary validation was confined to the royal chancery. By the middle of the eleventh century, documentary seal usage spread from kings to the aristocracy.[45] The analysis of this movement has helped to define the relationship between social structure and the new ideological superstructure which informed aristocratic seal practice, rhetoric, and iconography. There is much evidence indicating a new consciousness within the nobility of its own relationship to signs. Indeed, a striking characteristic of the nobility during the eleventh and twelfth century is the way it constituted itself as a group in part through the agency of its seals. For seals served as symbols of this nobility's principles and self-image when displaying the equestrian warrior, of its kin structure when showing heraldic devices, of its members' sense of personal identity when rooting every perception of the self only within

the group, whether that of the functional order—those who fight—
or of the family. Aristocratic seals seem to indicate that the medieval
sense of self was about resemblance, that the self was itself the *sign*
that signs of representation were in conformity with reality.

But what reality? The interpretation that the assumption by potentates of the royal prerogative of sealing is evidence of a weakening of royal authority is correct, but too limited. It is worth
exploring, therefore, the linkages between new aristocratic sealing
practices and several other contemporary developments such as
the territorialization of lordly power, the patrilinear articulation of
noble kindred, and the increased participation of the lay nobility in
documentary practices, to which I will here limit myself. Seals,
while offering their owners a means of literate participation and operating as literate forms in a scribal context, also evoked and incorporated many elements of current practice and symbolism. In their
physicality they were successors to those symbolic objects that had
previously testified to transactions. And, as already mentioned, they
also included an image, as though an icon were needed to authen-
ticate writing in a society still predominantly oral. According to
Gilbert Crespin, Abbot of Westminster (1085–1117), "just as letters
are the shapes and signs of spoken words, pictures exist as the representations and signs of writing."[46] The power that came to inhere
in seals therefore had several dimensions: as an inscribed object,
the seal authenticated an individual; by its iconographic device, social structure and written language; by means of its impression, a
particular document.

Seals guaranteed participation to and absolute provenance for
the written records of any donor since no matter how many impressions might be needed over time its graphic consistency was more
reliable than the simple signs and impersonal subscriptions which
had been used by his predecessors. The unique personalization of
a sigillographic commitment also involved a greater allocation of
individual responsibility. The network of witnesses to a transaction
and to its drafting came to be replaced by the personal seal which
now was routinely announced in the charters as the witness to the
transaction.[47] In this way the written word was to some extent
emancipated from the limitations of direct human testimony just as
the legal rights and responsibilities of groups increasingly were
shifted toward individuals. So in the early steps of its dissemination,

documentary writing also bears upon the position of the individual within society, since the spread of written contracts led to a devaluation of traditional wider networks of kin or vassalic solidarities and interactions.

Seals, in embodying the characters of their owners, their fame, their authority, their authenticity (all three qualities are interchangeable in the period under consideration), communicated these strengths to the charter. Thus seals ultimately became, in Northern France, mandatory signs of documentary validation. By the thirteenth century, an authentic charter (that is a self-referential authoritative deed, which might also be a forgery)[48] had come into being through transfer to the sealed charter of the reliability that had previously inhered in individuals and in the circumstances of their status within a given community. As such, an authentic charter was secure, and unchallengeable, emancipated from the limitations of human and local memory. Sure signs of its reified status are the development of specific characteristics that defined its material essence. For instance, the notion of the authentic charter came to mean that it was an original document, and not a copy, that it displayed specific textual forms, and that it was in good condition.

In the next step of its dissemination, writing achieved, by a twofold reification, self-referential status. One involved material definitions of the charter. The other, an established order grounded in the written diplomatic discourse as it articulated stable and standardized social representations. These material and textual processes of reification operated reciprocally so as to create within the charter the seemingly self-evident cohesion upon which were predicated the workings of self-referentiality. In becoming a necessity for the operation of trust and credibility, the authentic charter replaced a structure of society in which the reliability of the written word and that of its contextual social organization more actively reinforced one another. In being axiomatically credible, the authentic charter became normative. The circumstances for its efficacy no longer required an integrated community remembering the forms of actions of particular groups. Rather the charter narrated specific circumstances in the formulaic terms of general truth. Once authenticity ceased to emanate directly from humans and became attached to law-bound objects, the segregation of domains of authorities came to be modified: the issue no longer was social groups vis-à-vis community, but parties vis-à-vis specific categories, ultimately that of the state. Increasing sensitivity to the problematics of evidence and of authority led medieval society on an experimental path that took it from recourse to the sacred to dependency on the human and the local to a concept of authenticity that had material form and abstract content. The construction of authenticity as a rule-referential quality generated and controlled by authority created an arena for the further development of such an authority the operative principles of which were also a category of law, state authority.

Because of our linear conception of history, medieval Europe has been primarily studied as an antecedent to, as the crucible of, the modern West, with a consequently strong emphasis on those issue that bear on the current problematics of contemporary Western life. It is true that whatever past may be their subject, historians write primarily the history of their own times. However the Middle Ages need not be seen in direct continuity or discontinuity with Western history. The ongoing, and felicitous, rapprochement with anthropologists has shown that even where differentiated modalities of human experience are not part of the past, interpretive methods devised for their study may be relevant for past societies. The anthropology of living societies has inspired many medievalists to turn a renewed attention to law, demography, kinship, urbanization, rituals, taboos, elite, marginals, emblems, and totems (heraldry). Medievalists can in turn contribute specific insights into the principles that govern their own relations to sources. Medieval historians have been accused of looking, not at the past, but at documents. Anthropologists have come to recognize that "doing ethnography is like trying to read (in the sense of 'construct a reading of') a manuscript—foreign, faded, full of ellipses, incoherences, suspicious emendations, and tendentious commentaries."[49] That which they call their data are their own constructions of other people's constructions. Understanding what is said by the occurrence and preservation of documents and artifacts and through their agency, the identification of structures of signification therein, the assessment of these structures', and of the modalities of their documentation's, social ground and import are all of primary concern for medievalists. They aim at the identification of the very terms of interpretation to which persons of the medieval past subjected their experience. Because of the nature of the medieval written word, as manipulated within a clerical monopoly, medievalists have more than other historians been accustomed to look for the obliquity of their written sources. As a result medievalists rarely have looked at any source without adopting a critical approach to it. Although, and perhaps because, the written word played so major a role for so small a part of medieval society, it is in the field of medieval studies that such techniques of documentary critique as codicology, paleography, sigillography, philology, and languages have been finely honed. That such critique, in traditional diplomatics, has produced a typology of charters and of their internal and external characters, mostly with a view toward the establishment and perfection of a grid that precisely ascertains documentary authenticity, is not enough. In traditional medieval studies, documents of practice, once their authenticity is established, have tended to emerge as transparent texts which can assert objective truth independent of the subjective act that intended the document and of the operations of language within it. Such concepts led scholars to believe that they might read directly about tangible aspects of past experience. As a documentary and representative text, the medieval charter has been seen less as the cultural artifact of than as the self-interpreting model created by a civilization for its economic, legal, and administrative purposes. Attention and explanation have therefore primarily focused on the actions the sources document. This attitude is of course shared by most historians of all places and periods who select their object of study, gather all documents relating to that object, study their documents from the viewpoint of this object with far less attention to the circumstances grounding documentary production, and try to resolve contradictions by applying the principles of authenticity and forgery, and by distinguishing legendary from historical documents.

This technique does not invalidate documentary critique itself, nor should it prevent medievalists from reflecting further on their sources, an action which constitutes one of their great contributions to the heuristics of history. For attention to sources is not simply a technique and a method. It is at the very center of historical interpretation, since any source is primarily a source about itself, a form that outlines the contour of an absence, a sign that projects in the present since no other plane of duration gathers the historian and her source into the same instant, a text concerned with appearances noted in the present but occurring in the past, and an event carried by a material arranged in a pattern that still makes sense today.[50] Acceptance and analysis of the source's self-reflective nature enables medievalists to grasp the specific process of meaning production implied by the discursive and existential mode of that source and permits the retrieval both of the ideological and evidential status of the text, and of the ideological and social standards from the past. Our recognition of past events is conditioned by the ideologies and assumptions of the scribes from the past, but it is still debatable whether what we retrieve is the medieval axis of reference and intelligibility. In fact the medieval conceptual and textualized categories (God, land, salvation, proof, authenticity) that we use as representations of that society, as explanation that make it intelligible to us, were in effect the very questions they had to explain through axiomatic truths. For the medievalist, all documents should be seen as at once true and false (a construct). They should inspire a dialectic between those operations of language that represent events and the modalities of documentary fabrication and conservation. Special concern is required for what the document chooses as worthy of (e.g., pious gifts of land) or excluded from discourse and for the crucial yet unyielding mimetic engagement between documentary form and that of society.

In my department I currently serve as Graduate Director for about 280 graduate students, 75 percent of whom are involved in U.S. history. In my interactions with them and with their advisors, I often discuss the relationship between their interpretive positions and their theoretical approach to sources. I often get nowhere. The source is there, somehow to be shaped by the conceptual approach to which it will be subjected, and is treated only from the viewpoint of its thematic content, not from that of its functional, symbolic, and cultural dimensions. It is not surprising that to this day diplomatics, even in its most positivist formulation, has not become part of the locus of concern or armamentarium of modern historians. Yet the problematization of sources may become increasingly central to the epistemological and heuristical apparatus of a discipline increasingly aware that archival work is fragmentary, and that history's synthesizing formations are shaped by a research that remains specific, partial, selective, and an uncomfortable equilibrium between the aura of the documents and the discourse that names them and dictates their reception. The erudition associated with medieval studies need not alone lead to a substantiation of fact, but might also prompt attention to the material sense of writing, to the residual presence in it that informs our relation to, and our construction of, the past.

In my graduate seminar on "Script and Society (Medieval Europe 500–1500), I train students in paleography and diplomatics. The main issue of the seminar is the shape, place, and meaning of the written word in medieval society, and their implication for the reading and analysis of sources. Increasingly this seminar has attracted a large number of students from the fields of modern and contemporary European history, who often select medieval history as a minor field to study the methodologies for the interpretation of sources which they associate with that field.

With my colleagues in non-western history, especially with one in African history, exchanges are smooth, particularly with regard to the use of polarized partitions that serve as models of investigation: political-sacral, aesthetic-functional, word-image, abstract-symbolic, emblematic-symbolic, oral-written, memory-imagination, town-countryside, law-custom, nomadic-sedentary. As a medievalist, I am accustomed to a field that offers heterogeneous surfaces of functioning, and variations in these systems and their associations. For instance a charter is an iconic written document in which the polarized word-image does not operate. Emblems as they refer to individuals, and symbols to concepts, are conflated, perhaps interchangeable entities in the medieval mind, as are, up to a point, the aesthetic and the functional.[51] The prominent place occupied by the sacred in the substantiation of medieval political power has been well identified. Such associations and dissociations underline the nature of medieval studies as a pluridisciplinary enterprise for they do not at all correspond to the current epistemological partitions of the discipline. My Africanist colleague has made me aware of how, in her experience, cultural systems may organize abstraction as different from symbolism, but at the same time equate memory with imagination, and kinship with urbanization. We plan to team-teach a course on African and medieval Western urbanization.

Universities have shied away from practice and technicalities to the point where almost anything that places history in rapport with them has been classified as "auxiliary science."[52] As a new faculty member I myself was introduced as a dabbler "in all kind of antiquarian things." Yet history, medieval and other, is a practice mediated by technique, be that of deciphering and reading foreign languages, editing, encoding and decoding. None of these activities preclude the interpretive activity that is conventionally associated with the noble making of *H*istory. To the contrary. I hope I have demonstrated, and will continue to argue, that Northern French charters reveal their fullest significance when analytical and interpretive attention is given to, and inspired by, their technicalities. A source must have objective materiality in order to be here. It denotes a past insofar as it refers to an absence, so historians of all hues must make as much of this presence as possible when the rest of their object of study is well beyond physical recovery.

NOTES

1. Mark Helprin, *A Soldier of the Great War: A Novel* (New York, 1991), 30.

2. *P.L.*, CXII (*Carmen ad Bosonum*), quoted by Robert Favreau, "Fonction des inscriptions au Moyen Age," *Cahiers de civilisation médiévale* 32 (1989): 204–232, at p. 224.

3. Gerald of Wales, *The Journal Through Wales and the Description of Wales* (New York, 1978), quoted by Marc Drogin, *Biblioclasm: The Mythical Origins, Magic Powers, and Perishability of the Written Word* (Savage, Md., 1989), vii.

4. The following sources have been used in this essay: Albert Bruckner and Robert Marichal, *Chartae Latinae Antiquiores.* Vol. XIII: France, ed. Helmut Atsma and Jean Vezin (Zurich, 1981); Clovis Brunel, *Recueil des actes des comtes de Ponthieu* (Paris, 1880); Marie Fauroux, *Recueil des actes des ducs de Normandie de 911 à 1066* (Caen, 1961); P. Gasnault, "Les actes privés de l'abbaye de St Martin de Tours du 8e au 12e siècle," *Bibliothèque de l'Ecole des chartes* 112 (1954): 24–66; Olivier Guillot, *Le comte d'Anjou et son entourage au XIe siècle*, 2 vols. (Paris, 1972), vol. 2: *Catalogue d'actes;* Walter Prevenier, *De Oorkonden der graven van Vvlanderen, 1191–1206*, 3 vols. (Brussels, 1964–1977); F. Vercauteren, *Actes des comtes de Flandre. 1071–1128* (Brussels, 1938).

I have already addressed the context for and implications of increasing lay documentary practices in "The Confrontation of Orality and Textuality: Jewish and Christian Literacy in Eleventh- and Twelfth-Century Northern France," *Rashi, 1040–1990.* Congrés europeén des Études juives, ed. Gabrielle Sed-Rajna (Paris, 1993), 541–558, and "Civic Liturgies and Urban Records in Northern France (Twelfth-Fourteenth Centuries)," *City and Spectacle in Medieval Europe,* ed. Kathryn Reyerson and Barbara Hanawalt (University of Minnesota Press, forthcoming).

5. Georges Duby, *The Three Orders: Feudal Society Imagined* (Chicago, 1980), 147.

6. This contradictory argument is Hayden White's, "The Context in the Text: Method and Ideology in Intellectual History," *The Content of the Form: Narrative Discourse and Historical Representation* (Baltimore, 1987), 187, 210–211.

7. In the striking wording of Elizabeth Eisenstein, *The Printing Press as an Agent of Change,* 2 vols. (Cambridge, 1979), 10.

8. The best discussions of diplomatics are found in Robert-Henri Bautier, *Chartes et chancelleries. Etudes de diplomatique et de sigillographie médiévales* (Paris, 1990), especially 3–33, 167–182; in Leonard Boyle, "Diplomatics," *Medieval Studies: An Introduction,* ed. James Powell (Syracuse, 1976), 69–101; and in Georges Tessier, "Diplomatique," *L'histoire et ses méthodes,* ed. Charles Samaran (Paris, 1961), 633–676.

9. In the word of Michel de Certeau, *The Writing of History* (New York, 1988), 210, who has inspired much of my own consideration of the craftsmanship of my discipline, as has George Kubler, *The Shape of Time: Remarks on the History of Things* (New Haven, 1962), and to some lesser extent *Tendances, perspectives, et méthodes de l'histoire médiévale. Actes du Centième congrés national des Sociétés savantes,* vol. 1 (Paris, 1977).

10. Michel Parisse, "Remarques sur les chirographes et les chartes-parties antérieures à 1120 et conservées en France," *Archiv für Diplomatik* 32 (1986): 546–567.

11. Fifty thousand urban chirographs from the thirteenth century onward are still extant in the city archives of Douai, as well as several thousands each in the city archives of Valenciennes and Abbeville, R.-H. Bautier, "L'authentification des actes privés dans la France médiévale," *Notariado publico y documento privado: de los origines al siglo XIV. Actas del VII Congreso Internacional de Diplomatica* (Valencia, 1986), 701–772, at p. 744.

Article 4 of the 1352 charter of the town of Saint-Josse reads: "et porra on par devant eulx [the *échevins*] passer et faire toutes obligations, acors, recognoissanches faites entre parties; et de ychelles feront chartres ou chirograffes, dont il tenront une des parties, et en bailleront à cascune partie autant se elles le requierent." Augustin Thierry, *Recueil des documents inédits de l'histoire du Tiers Etat. Tome quatrième: pièces relatives à l'histoire municipale d'Abbeville . . .* (Paris, 1870), 638.

The urban chirograph remained in use through the second half of the fourteenth century. The later-developed system of registering deeds of title from which were issued as many originals as needed also involved the maintenance of these registers in urban archives. See mention of registers in the 1343 statute for the administration of Rue, article 3: "Item, que les escriptures des chartes de le dite ville et des autres coses seront faites à l'anchien usage, et y ara caier propres pour les chartes, et seront passées en plain eskevinage, et les chirographes recordées, et les chartes seelées; et y ara propre caier as causes, as mises et as recheptes, chascun a l'ordenanche, et un pour les plais, prochiés et arrés." (Thierry, *Recueil des documents inédits* 4: 672.)

12. A. de Boüard, *Manuel de diplomatique française et pontificale. Tome II: L'acte privé* (Paris, 1948), 238–241; Bautier, "L'authentification des actes privés," 739; Georges Espinas, *La vie urbaine de Douai au Moyen Age,* 4 vols. (Paris, 1913) 1: 536; Henri Sellier, *L'authentification des actes par l'échevinage* (Lille, 1934), 144, quoting an article from the customal of Cambrai: "Lettres en ferme [i.e., in city archives] sont mères en elles, faisantes plainte foy de ce qu'elles contiennent."

13. This argument has been further developed in Bedos-Rezak, "Civic Liturgies and Urban Records in Northern France."

14. B. Bedos-Rezak, "Ritual in the Royal Chancery: Text, Image and the Representation of Kingship in Medieval French Diplomas (700–1200)," in *European Monarchy: Its Evolution and Practice from Roman Antiquity to Modern Times,* ed. Heinz Duchhardt, Richard A. Jackson, and David Sturdy (Stuttgart: Franz Steiner, 1992), 28–40.

15. Raoul's documents with appeals for potentates' *signa,* and with knife, were not written in the royal chancery, see Jean Dufour, *Recueil des actes de Robert Ier et de Raoul rois de France, 922–936* (Paris, 1978), p. xliv, n. 12 p. 47–52 (*nostrosque primates subsignare jubemus,* 927), p. xli, n. 8 pp. 34–38 (*Rodulfus, gratia Dei rex. . . . nostrum accepimus cultellum et, misso super altare Sancti Symphoriani, reddimus eamdem terram,* 925).

16. With Hugh Capet, witness-lists begin to appear regularly in royal charters as well, as if the king's personal action was no longer sufficient to render the royal deed authoritative. See a witness-list in a diploma (925) from the Robertian king Raoul in Dufour, *Actes de Robert et de Raoul,* n. 8 p. 34. On the general appearance of witness-list in early Capetian documents, see Jean Dunbabin, *France in the Making, 843–1180* (Oxford, 1985), 129–130; Léopold Génicot, *Les actes publics* (Brepols-Turnhout,

1972), 41; Jean-François Lemarignier, *Le gouvernement royal aux premiers temps capétiens, 987–1108* (Paris, 1965), 73–75, 136–139.

17. Charles Pfister, *Etudes sur le règne de Robert le Pieux* (Paris, 1885), xxv–xxxii.

18. Olivier Guyotjeannin, "Les actes d'Henri Ier et la chancellerie royale dans les années 1020–1060," *Comptes-rendus de l'Académie des inscriptions et belles-lettres* (1988); 81–97, at p. 91.

19. Guyotjeannin, "Les actes d'Henri Ier," 94; Paul Bonenfant, *Cours de diplomatique. Deuxième partie: Diplomatique spéciale* (Liège, 1948), 51.

20. O. Guyotjeannin, "Les actes établis par la chancellerie royale sous Philippe Ier," *Bibliothèque de l'Ecole des chartes* 147 (1989): 29-48, at pp. 31 (*testimonium*) and 45 (*memoriale*).

21. See an instance of this in Bernard S. Bachrach, "Neo-Roman vs. Feudal: The Heuristic Value of a Construct for the Reign of Fulk Nerra, count of the Angevins (987–1040)," *Cithara* 30 (1990): 3–30, at p. 9.

22. Guillot, *Le comte d'Anjou*, 2: 9, note 21 in which is quoted a 1056 donation of Count Geoffrey to the abbey of Marmoutiers *cartam istam . . . sacratissime crucis in eadem effigiato vexillo quo adversus omnem possit esse tuta calumniam munivimus;* Fauroux, *Recueil des actes des ducs de Normandie,* no. 43 p. 148, 1015–1026 donation of Duke Richard II to the abbey of St Ouen: *. . . per signum crucis cum excommunicatione hanc cartam firmavit. . . .*

23. Fauroux, *Actes des ducs de Normandie,* for instance no. 149 p. 334, 1040–1050 confirmation by Duke William of a donation in favor of the abbey of St Léger, *. . . pro sua suorumque salute, donationem supra altare posuit, de his omnibus que Hunfridus dederat. . . .* See also a discussion of placing charters on altars in Boüard, *Manuel de diplomatique,* 2:112–114.

24. Yvonne Bongert, *Recherches sur les cours laïques du Xe au XIIIe siècles* (Paris, 1949), 43, indicates several instances of such threats in tenth- and eleventh-century charters. There is scholarly consensus on the fact that the use of documentary clauses involving spiritual maledictions against betrayers of a charter's content grew numerous during the tenth and early eleventh century and declined in the later part of that century; see a review of the evidence in Lester K. Little, "La morphologie des malédictions monastiques," *Annales. E.S.C.* 34 (1979): 43–60, at 47; on French southern documents, see Michel Zimmermann, "Protocoles et préambules dans les documents catalans du Xe au XIIe siècle: évolution diplomatique et signification spirituelle," *Mélanges de la Casa de Velasquez* 10 (1974): 41–76, 11(1975), 51–79, at 10: 51–54.

25. On the charters being read aloud and on the vocal participation of its audience, see Little, "Maledictions monastiques," 48; Stephen White,

Custom, Kinship, and Gifts to Saints (Chapel Hill, 1988), 37, 208; Emily Tabuteau, *Transfers of Property in Eleventh-Century Norman Law* (Chapel Hill, 1988), 207, 212–215, 220. On lay donors gaining social identity through their patronage of religious houses, see the comments of John Howe, "The Nobility's Reform of the Medieval Church," *American Historical Review* 93 (1988): 317–339, at p. 334.

26. Quoted in Bedos-Rezak, "The Confrontation of Orality and Textuality," 549; Boüard, *L'acte privé*, 112–120.

27. Tabuteau, *Transfers of Property*, 11–12, 148–149, 212.

28. Guillot, *Le comte d'Anjou et son entourage* 2: 18–20.

29. See cases in Tabuteau, *Transfers of Property*, 113, and in White, *Custom, Kinship, and Gifts to Saints, passim.*

30. See examples in Arras, Blois, and in Germany in Favreau, "Fonction des inscriptions au Moyen Age," 210–214. Greater links should exist between epigraphy and diplomatics.

31. Guillot, *Le comte d'Anjou* 1: 420, 422.

32. Michel Bur, *La formation du comté de Champagne* (Nancy, 1977), 425.

33. W. Prevenier, "La chancellerie des comtes de Flandre dans le cadre européen à la fin du XIIe siècle," *Bibliothèque de l'Ecole des chartes* 125 (1976): 34–93, at p. 46.

34. Prevenier, "La chancellerie des comtes de Flandre," 34 sq; Th. de Hemptine, W. Prevenier, M. Vandermaesen, "La chancellerie des comtes de Flandre (12e–14e siècle)," *Landesherrliche Kanzlein im Spätmittelalter* (München, 1984), 433–454. Both these studies qualify some of the earlier remarks by Henri Pirenne, "La chancellerie et les notaires des comtes de Flandre avant le 13e siècle," *Mélanges Julien Havet* (Paris, 1895), 733–748.

35. The following studies, based on an implicit acceptance of a revival of documentary modes in tandem with general legal, economic, or administrative developments, provide excellent insights into the operation of literate modes within the medieval mentality from the eleventh century onward: Brian Stock, *The Implications of Literacy* (Princeton, 1983) 32–34, who is sensitive to the fact that the process by which the medieval literate culture shaped itself is poorly understood; Franz H. Baüml, "Varieties and Consequences of Medieval Literacy and Illiteracy," *Speculum* 55 (1980): 237–265; Michael T. Clanchy, *From Memory to Written Record. England, 1066–1307* (Cambridge, 1979). For a study on literacy that concludes that "literacy was there to be simply acquired, and it was acquired simply because it was there," see Simon Franklin, "Literacy and Documentation in Early Medieval Russia," *Speculum* 60 no. 1 (1985): 1–38, quotation p. 38.

36. For an analysis of the uses made of property as part of a history of ideas, see Barbara Rosenwein, *To Be the Neighbor of Saint Peter: The Social Meaning of Cluny's Property, 909–1049* (Ithaca and London, 1989).

37. On the centrality of salvation within aristocratic spirituality, see Constance Bouchard, *Sword, Miter and Cloister: Nobility and the Church in Burgundy, 980–1198* (Ithaca and London, 1987), 225–229, 241–246; Howe, "The Nobility's Reform of the Medieval Church," 333–334; G. Tellenbach, *Church, State and Christian Society* (Oxford, 1959), 84.

38. White, "*Pactum . . . legem vincit . . . :* The Settlement of Disputes by Compromise in Eleventh-Century Western France," *American Journal of Legal History* 22 (1978): 281–308, at pp. 302–306, who enlarged his argument in *Custom, Kinship and Gifts to Saints,* chapter 5, with specific developments on the extra-economic significance of land and land transactions in medieval society.

39. Gasnault, "Les actes privés de St Martin de Tours," 43; Brunel, *Recueil des actes des comtes de Ponthieu,* p. xl; Vercauteren, *Actes des comtes de Flandre,* pp. viii, xx, xlv; Fauroux, *Recueil des actes des ducs de Normandie,* 29, 35; Guillot, *Le comte d'Anjou,* II, *passim.*

The formulae *pro anima* and lay eschatological concerns were already present in early medieval charters, also expressing the notion that gifts of earthly property involved heavenly salvation: *Marculfi Formulae,* ed. Karl Zeumer, *Monumenta Germaniae Historica, Legum V. Formulae* (Hanover, 1886), 74, 75, 76, 78, 98, 100, H. Fichtenau, *Arenga. Spätantike und Mittelalter im Spiegel von Urkundenformeln* (Cologne, 1957), 143–144. What is new in eleventh-century charters is the systematic association between gifts of land to saints, their redemptive effects, and concerns for their memory and stability.

See an analytical survey of the purposes and functions of gifts to saints in White, *Custom, Kinship and Gifts to Saints,* 74–76, 154–156; Bouchard, *Sword, Miter and Scepter,* 225–246; Rosenwein, *To Be the Neighbor,* 41, 136–139.

40. Charters containing mention of *viri authentici* have been identified in the card catalogue of the Nouveau Du Cange. The specific function of the *homo legitimus* in England has been analyzed by C. Odegaard, "Legalis Homo," *Speculum* 15 (1940): 186–193. Discussions about *viri authentici* have remained inconclusive with regard to their status and function. No in-depth study of the topic is available; see the few comments in Guillot, *Le comte d'Anjou* 2: 16–18; Auguste Dumas, "Etude sur le classement de la forme des actes," *Le Moyen Age* (1933): 81–97, 145–182, 257–264, at 153–157; Boüard, *L'acte privé,* 142, 230, 266; Tabuteau, *Transfers of Property,* 151–153, 156; Bernard Guenée, "Authentique et approuvé. Re-

cherches sur les principes de la critique historique au moyen âge," *La lexicographic du latin médièval* (Paris, 1981), 215–229, at 216–217; Bongert, *Recherches sur les cours laiques,* 257.

41. On the diffusion of seal usage within French society, see Bedos-Rezak, "The Social Implications of the Art of Chivalry: The Sigillographic Evidence (France, 1050–1250)," *The Medieval Court in Europe,* ed. Edward Haymes, *Houston German Studies* 6 (1986): 142–175.

42. On seals as active agents, see Margaret Cool Rost, *The Art of Seals: Aesthetic and Social Dynamics of the Impressed Image from Antiquity to Present* (Ann Arbor, Mich.: Kelsey Museum of Archaeology, University of Michigan, 1984), 8–9, 17, 18.

43. Pictorial renderings on seals are referred to by the sealer as *imago mea;* I would like to explore this concept, and practice, of *imago* with reference to the contemporary theological category of likeness.

44. Bedos-Rezak, "Les sceaux juifs français," *Art et archéologie des Juifs en France médiévale,* ed. B. Blumenkranz (Toulouse: Privat, 1980), 207–228; *eadem,* "Signes et insignes du pouvoir au Moyen Age: le témoignage des sceaux," *Comité des Travaux historiques et scientifiques. Section de philologie et d'histoire jusqu'en 1610. Actes du Cent Cinquième Congrès national des Sociétés Savantes* [Caen, 1980] (Paris: CTHS, 1984), 47–62; *eadem,* "Women, Seals and Power in Medieval France, 1150–1350," in *Women and Power in Medieval and Early Modern Europe,* ed. M. Erler and M. Kowaleski (Athens and London: University of Georgia Press, 1988), 61–82; *eadem,* "Medieval Women in French Sigillographic Sources," in *Women and the Sources of Medieval History,* ed. Joel T. Rosenthal (Athens and London: University of Georgia Press, 1990), 1–36; *eadem,* "The Town on French Medieval Seals; Representation and Signification," in *Town Life and Culture in the Middle Ages and Renaissance: Essays in Memory of J. K. Hyde,* ed. Brian Pullan and Susan Reynolds, *Bulletin of the John Rylands Library of Manchester,* 72 (1990): 35–48; and my forthcoming volume of collected essays: *Form and Order in Medieval France. Studies in Social and Quantitative Sigillography* (London: Variorum, 1993).

45. This movement and related phenomena are the focus of my book in progress *Seals and Social Structure: New Evidence for the Transformation of the French Nobility in the Eleventh and Twelfth Centuries,* for which I have assembled a corpus of some 500 seals prior to 1200, *terminus ad quem* of the proposed work. Preliminary conclusions can be found in Bedos-Rezak, "The Social Implications of the Art of Chivalry: The Sigillographic Evidence (France, 1050–1250)," 142–175, and *eadem,* "Medieval Seals and the Structure of Chivalric Society," *The Study of Chivalry: Resources and Approaches,* ed. Howell Chickering and Thomas Seiler (Kalamazoo, 1988), 313–372.

46. Quoted in Michael Camille, "The Book of Signs: Writing and Visual Differences in Gothic Manuscript Illumination," *Word and Image* 1 (1985): 133–148, at p. 135.

47. The list of witnesses had disappeared by the early thirteenth century and from then on the seal *is* the only witness to the charter: ... *in cujus rei testimonium* (or: ... *in cujus rei memoriam* ...) *presens sriptum sigillo nostro fecimus roborari*. ... On the appearance of these formulas see Brunel, *Recueil des actes des comtes de Ponthieu,* p. cx, and A. Giry, *Manuel de diplomatique* (Paris, 1894), 575.

48. On the distinction between diplomatic authenticity which deals with forged documents, and legal authenticity which deals with documents having intrinsic legal force, see Tessier, "La diplomatique," 671.

49. Clifford Geertz, "Thick Description: Toward an Interpretive Theory of Culture," *The Interpretation of Cultures* (New York, 1973), 10.

50. This formulation is strongly inspired by Kubler, *The Shape of Time,* 17, 19–20.

51. Bedos-Rezak, "Form as Social Process," forthcoming in *Artistic Integration in Early Gothic Churches,* ed. Virginia Raguin et al. (University of Toronto Press).

52. This remark is from Certeau, *The Writing of History,* 69.

Inventing a European Music Culture—Then and Now

Leo Treitler

I SHALL TRY TO EMBED what I have to say about the general issues that have been put before us in a concrete description of the long-term project that I would like to accomplish in my medieval studies, if I can. In doing so I have two related objectives (how they are related will shortly emerge): (1) to show that those general issues are not to be evaded in a genuinely historical study; (2) to address head-on the lack of awareness within medieval studies outside my field about the historical materials that abound in the domain of music and about what the interpretation of those materials can contribute to the understanding of medieval culture—from the most detailed and specific to the most general.

Here is a partial list of opportunities that have been missed so far: medieval poems that were sung, edited without taking account of what the melody can tell, like a native informer, about the phrase articulation and versification and therefore, ultimately, about meaning; studies written about medieval punctuation without a good understanding of the intimate involvement of musical notation in the history of that practice; a literary historian publishes a comprehensive book about words and music in the Middle Ages that is uninformed by any real consideration of music's resources for reflecting the form and meaning of language at its several levels; studies about the functioning of memory in the Middle Ages written from a literary background with no account taken of what was surely the most spectacular of all memory feats, the chanting of the divine office through the day, throughout the year, year in, year out. We could be, if we wanted to be, witness to the large-scale recording of that chanting tradition in a newly invented writing system (at whose birth we could almost be in attendance), and we could learn what the oral culture wanted to encode in writing, and how, and what reading was in relation to remembering. Homer-scholars and their medieval progeny could be green with envy. . . .

So while many at this conference have addressed themselves to the need for public relations with deans and provosts on behalf of medieval studies, I am here to do a bit of public relations with adepts of medieval studies on behalf of music; for the picture of medieval studies that I have seen in three days of this conference, unlike the Middle Ages, has no music in it.

Why is that? It is of course another case of disciplinary isolation: medieval studies has been charted as an interdisciplinary domain, but with firm geographical and disciplinary boundaries that have, in any case, excluded the musical and visual arts (just as these have been symbolically marginalized by their location as afterthoughts on the program for this conference).

Medievalists, like scholars in all humanistic fields, are intimidated by music's specialized technical-analytical apparatus. The preciseness of some of our methodologies can be a curse as well as a blessing and we musicologists can be seduced by it to formulate questions just because we can answer them. But I would not want to pretend that the opportunities that I have just enumerated have been taken up by musicologists. We have all in some measure been practicing what, since Gilbert Ryle, has been called "thin description" whereas it is only through efforts at "thick description" that we can hear the resonance in one another's work.[1] That means attention to two things we have in common: our interest in medieval cultures, and our participation in contemporary culture as interpreters of medieval culture.

I study the oldest European music that we can know: the chanting traditions of the Latin liturgy of the medieval Western church—centrally what is called "Gregorian Chant." I shall try to outline the range of phenomena and issues that a study of this subject must ultimately touch if it is to produce understanding in the broad cultural context that I believe historical understanding requires. And as I go I shall try to keep my eye on the problems of trying to view my distant object from the needs and assumptions, the habits and thinking patterns of the present, which have a tendency to make all historical objects conform to them. I think we learn best about medieval culture when we also learn from the same effort about our participation in contemporary culture.

An exemplification of this just slipped past you: I said "chanting traditions," then "Gregorian chant." The difference is considerable. "Gregorian" stands for a patently false but revealing legend of ninth-century invention (the context will become clear) that identifies the sixth/seventh-century Pope Gregory the Great as the composer, or compiler, of the music of the Roman church. In that context "chant" is heard as a noun, objectifying the object of the inquiry—*chants* rather than chanting *practices* or *traditions*. That polarization of meaning is encouraged by a conception of the closed musical work that has been in control in talk about music since the nineteenth century, when the study of this subject went into full swing. It is at odds with the early medieval reality, and it obscures the shift toward such a conception later on when it comes. But "chant" is only the English word for *cantus* and, like its Latin original, can mean either "song" *or* "singing." It is the singing traditions of the church that I study, and they have given us the oldest music we can know because it is the oldest music that has come down in musical notation.

The written transmission begins for us in the 10th century, with about fifteen surviving books, to which about ninety representing all regions of Western Europe and the British Isles are added in the eleventh century. The notational system was invented sometime between the late eighth century and the mid-ninth (848 is the probable terminal date for what is probably the oldest surviving specimen), somewhere in the Frankish domain. The notation of chant melodies had become a regular practice in some places by the late ninth century. The books of the tenth and eleventh centuries transmit with striking uniformity musical texts for a repertory that had already reached that degree of stability in its unwritten tradition by the time the notation was invented.

These facts reflect the Carolingian court's will to uniformity in chanting the liturgy, about which Charlemagne seems to have been as insistent as he was about uniformity in the number and species of herbs to be grown in imperial gardens.[2] It was his project to spread the singing of what was regarded as the *Cantus Romanus* throughout his domain, replacing local practices that had evolved out of no-longer-identifiable originals, as local Romance dialects had evolved out of Roman Latin. Anecdotal and musical evidence testifies both to the earlier diversity of local practice and to the resistance against the imposition of foreign practices. Now Romans did not write down their music before the eleventh century, and when they did it was not the music that was diffused through the Carolingian monasteries and cathedrals. The "Cantus romanus" was probably as much a Carolingian, i.e., Frankish, creation as was "Classical Latin."[3]

I am interested in this process of diffusion, adaptation, invention, appropriation, and displacement, and the process of propagandizing, mythologizing, and rationalizing that accompanied it initially and that accompanies each era's reception of the chant tradition according to its own needs and self-image. It is a process directed initially from a center preoccupied with the deliberate integration of a cultural system from which we can see a continuity to our own. The congeries of circumstances that drove it is plausibly interpreted as the beginning of a European musical culture, just as one speaks of the beginning of Europe at this time. There is musical evidence in abundance that testifies to it, and it is one of my purposes here to advertise that fact. It is the musical reflection of the drive for political hegemony and, in association with that, cultural uniformity. I do not hesitate to characterize this as a "world in motion," about which we are challenged to write "essential narratives . . . devoted to showing how the present world was shaped by its emergence from a very different past and hence concentrated on critical transitions from the past toward the present." These are the hortatory words of Bernard Bailyn, spoken in his Presidential Address to the American Historical Association meeting in 1981.[4]

The ambition to describe such a world in motion carries risks. It places a very heavy burden of responsibility on an early cultural practice to claim that it is the beginning of our own: a responsibility to be itself potent and fertile, and a responsibility to adumbrate qualities that we like to think of as characteristic of our own culture. Such expectations are immanent in the role that histories play as celebrations of myth, as rituals of the assertion of cultural self, and the risk is that an engagement with the past in search of beginnings becomes a solipsistic engagement with the present.[5]

In the case of the history of Western music, medieval chant must play the role that Greek tragedy and sculpture play for Western literature and art, marking the beginning of the tradition and displaying what are held to be the essential characteristics of Western music. In the beginning of the modern reception history of medieval chant (in the late eighteenth century), that fact alone led scholars to assume an ancient Greek patrimony for the chant and to invest the chant with the classical aesthetic values of simplicity, grandeur, balance, reason, sobriety, and the absence of levity, licentiousness, and effeminate qualities. (One of the most prominent of modern chant scholars has characterized Gregorian chant as "music for a world power" and found in it "clear, sculpted configurations, systematically chiselled, disciplined and ordered, a product of thorough rational thinking."[6]) The first challenge to the assumption of descent from Greek antiquity came in the early 1830s in the first book of the genre "History of Western Music," not on empirical grounds, but on the national- or ethnic-ideological ground that "our contemporary European-Western" music (by then and since then most fully represented by the music of Beethoven) could not possibly be modeled upon and continuous with the music of the Greeks. The meaning of history, as this story demonstrates, is partly supplied through its reception by the community to which it is addressed, according to the way that it answers to the needs and beliefs of that community.

The idea of Greek patrimony did not survive, but the expectations about the aesthetic values that would be displayed by the chant by virtue of its founding role did survive. And when chant styles were found in the sources that violated those standards, they were accommodated through a duality of "Western" vs. "Oriental" (near-Eastern) with overtones of "masculine" vs. "feminine," both well-exercised and linked ways of asserting the identity of a Western cultural self through contrast with the other. (This produced the oddity that the Roman chant that was finally written down in the eleventh century came to be characterized, as recently as the 1960s and 1970s, as Mediterranean or Oriental because of a certain ornate character.)

What is to be learned, I think, is not only that those interpretations need correction on the basis of a closer look at the evidence—although that, certainly; and not discouragement altogether of flirtation with such large-scale questions of interpretation; but that interpretation is episodic and entails risks—in this case the risk that once we conceive our subject to be something like "the beginning of Western musical culture" the story writes itself, guided by imperatives that accrue, like barnacles, to each one of those words and steer their meanings, like it or not. To be in charge as authors requires conscious awareness about those imperatives and how they work, not giving up such grand ideas because they have been treated in unappealing, self-serving ways. It requires tolerance for the uneasy feeling of teetering on the edge between myth and reportage.

Unity in the Carolingian Empire was to be achieved in large measure through the spread of language literacy, and it is in the context of this centrally directed phenomenon that we can understand the invention of systems of music writing specifically, and their use in the diffusion and practice of liturgical chant. This is so in two respects: transference of the prestige that writing had been given through its role in administration and in the establishment of a uniform spoken language, and more specifically, derivation of significant aspects of the technology and functioning of music writing from the technology and functioning of aspects of language writing. I itemize the second of these.[7]

(1) The adaptation of the highly differentiated Carolingian system of punctuation, in place since the late eighth century, for a system of musical neumes, both in the form of the signs and in their role in articulating the sense units of language for comprehension in reading. The first principle in setting a liturgical text (or any other kind, for that matter) to music was to fit melodic phrases to such sense units. The role of melody was thus parallel to that of punctuation; both worked as ways of articulating, hence interpreting, language.

(2) At least one very early system of musical notation was based on the concept of accent as the rising and falling of the voice in speaking, a concept that was transmitted in grammar treatises of late antiquity that were widely copied and recirculated in Carolingian times even though, paradoxically, the spoken language was by then not inflected and the written language was not marked with accents.

(3) Some early notational systems simply used letters of the alphabet as characters. This was advocated as early as the late ninth century by the music master Hucbald of Amand, and it reflects two major shifts in thinking and practice: toward an analytical under-

standing of melody—note by note—as against the aggregative conception of melody embodied in the neumes that represent the
note-groups that constituted the units of melody in the performance tradition; and toward a more precise denotation of pitch intervals, which would assure a reliably accurate reproduction of the
melodic line with each performance (this purpose was ultimately
better served by staff notation, which proved, as we know, to have
the greater survival value). These changes are easily described, especially as they are in the direction of our way of thinking about
music. It is too easy to miss their deep radicality as technical inven-
tions, but even more as mental reorientations.

Tracing the connections between the technologies of music-
and language-writing has been mainly an achievement of musical
paleography. But alongside the paleographic task there are questions that engage us in a more active visualization of the prehistory
and the history of musical notation in the context of a user-
community that is affected by other historical factors, i.e., *semiotic*
questions.

(1) How did the performance tradition function before the
time of its representation in books with the use of musical notation?
The conceptions through which this question has been addressed
in much of the modern literature exemplify as well as anything I
can think of the need for a "self-reflective impulse" and "reassessment" that John Van Engen has asked us about. Where the fact of an
unwritten tradition has not been altogether repressed by insinua-
tions of a centuries-older writing practice than can be demonstrated, largely, I think, out of ideological repugnance toward the
thought that the music of the Church should have been apprehended and transmitted only through an oral tradition, like nothing
more dignified than folk traditions. Where that idea has not been
altogether repressed, two modern vernacular conceptions have
come into play, arranged in a polarity of opposites: improvisation
and memorization.

"Improvisation" is generally used in the sense of unplanned,
capricious, free, fantasy-like performance, and as such it belongs to
the conceptual instrumentarium of a nineteenth-century musical
aesthetic with the work concept at its center—the improvisation or
caprice or impromptu or fantasy contrasts with the closed, organic,
unified work. Late eighteenth- and nineteenth-century music dictio-

naries uniformly explain improvisation as a practice of Italian character and origin, and the implication is not far beneath the surface that it is a Mediterranean practice to be contrasted with the rational, unified, and planned character of the music of northern countries. But it has no counterpart in either medieval practice or description.

"Memorization" has stood for a conception about the passive storage and retention of material in a fixed state and its equally passive reproduction or retrieval, depending on a mental faculty that mimics the clay tablet, the book, or the computer hard disk. It is a conception that accommodates itself, like "improvisation," to the "work" concept, and it is too narrow an idea to describe the medieval situation.

A more fitting image of the medieval performance tradition can be gained, on one side, from the much richer medieval conception of memory as an active, creative faculty that has recently been explicated in Mary Carruthers's *The Book of Memory*,[8] which is consonant with the prevailing conception of memory in the modern cognitive sciences (recently summarized in Israel Rosenfield's book *The Invention of Memory*[9]) and, on the other, from the conception of "oral composition," the paradigm developed by Milman Parry and Albert Lord to account for the extempore performance of epic poems of great scope and stable traditions (most recently summarized by John Miles Foley[10]). I adapted the main principles of that paradigm in the first effort to propose a detailed model for extempore chant singing before the age of writing.[11] Carruthers associates memorial performance in the Middle Ages with the art of oratorical discourse. Harold Powers, a student of Indian classical performance traditions, has generalized that "a musical improvisation is an extempore oratorical discourse on a traditional theme which is elaborated and ordered using traditional rhetorical forms and techniques," noting that the Indic term *ālāpa,* denoting the principal genre for presenting a *rāga* extemporaneously, simply means "discourse."[12] If we regard the early written transmission of medieval European chant as an essentially accurate representation of the unwritten performance tradition—as I believe we should do with confidence—then it provides an abundance of evidence instantiating this general idea.[13]

(2) The second in my list of questions about the history of the writing practice concerns the actual initial acts of writing down. We

are accustomed to speaking rather easily of the "transcription" or "redaction" of the unwritten tradition into written form, as though in a modern dictation class or editorial office, and once again that ease must be associated with the influence of the work concept on our thinking. But it must have required overcoming the most severe sort of cognitive disjunction to settle the flow of melody that had repeatedly come into existence only through the ongoing performance act into the fixed, synchronic notational matrix, especially when that matrix was quite specific with respect to pitch intervals. That process provoked for the notators questions and conflicts about the interval contents of melodies that had not troubled singers in the unwritten tradition, and in making choices about these, they left abundant detailed evidence about the cognitive process itself, evidence that, as far as I know, has no counterpart in any other domain of medieval intellectual or artistic activity.

(3) On what semiological principles did the notations function? What was the nature of the relationship between signs and what they signified: representation? reference? denotation? imitation? There has been a tendency to treat these as synonyms, but they are not. Did the signs function as prescriptions or descriptions, as instructions for what was to be done or as protocols of what had already been done (the way some early maps were protocols of trips taken, and some early recipes were protocols of feasts)? This is a major question about the degree to which signification referred to an experiential field or to some abstract cognitive space. What was the conception of the reference of notation? In some situations the notated score seems to have been regarded as representation of a melody as a whole object; in others the notation was regarded as referring to a movement of the voice. In still others the reference was to the constituent notes of melodies, an idea that had first to be invented and legitimated. What knowledge on the part of the reader did the signs engage? The modern reader of music is likely to believe that he or she is simply decoding notational signs as instructions to perform certain digital or vocal acts or as representation of a work for study. But there is copious evidence to show that musical notations were read as reminders, either of whole melodies that singers already knew how to sing, or of melodic intervals in which they had been drilled, or something in between (for example, well-known melismas that could be sung in different melo-

dies). Musical sources provide rich evidence for Mary Carruthers's assertion that reading in the Middle Ages was a memory procedure, and some intimately detailed demonstrations of how it functioned. No single answer to any of these questions will do for all medieval situations. But any history of early medieval notation must be couched in terms of the particular and changing answers to all of them.

The same first wave of notated books that make the old chant melodies present for us also brings liturgical and religious songs that are new to the time, not descendants of an older oral tradition—tropes, sequences, versus, many with poetic texts. It is the oldest music we know that was written down at the time of composition, more or less. The comparative study of the transmission of these repertories with that of the chant affords us an opportunity to compare music from an oral tradition with music from a written one under very closely related cultural circumstances, and thus to test the efficacy of the oral-written dichotomy as a descriptive critical tool. What this shows is that writing did not offer a fundamentally different way of organizing material than memory or oral composition, and certainly not a superior (more rational, unified, etc.) way, although the *act* of writing down constituted a major cognitive disjunction. This complements the conclusion already stated, that reading was not a fundamentally different performance act from remembering or extempore composition. I am encouraged by the resonance between these conclusions and the caveats uttered by scholars in such diverse fields as social anthropology (Ruth Finnegan) and literary history (Mary Carruthers).

At the center of what is new in these new songs is poetry. While the composer-singer of chant was accountable to the scriptural language in the sense of rendering it with clarity according to principles of phonetics and grammar (in modern language I would say "syntax"), composers of song were confronted with the constraints of poetic processes that were themselves new—accentual patterns, syllable-counting, rhyme, for example—and we see them kneading melody with poetry on the plane of rhetoric as well. In brief, music and poetry constitute at this time a single expressive medium. I say this against a strong tradition for holding that music and poetry co-habit in medieval song with but a formal relationship. This idea has been given its most elaborate formulation recently by John Stevens.[14] He writes "In plain language, the musician did not set the words of the poem to music, he set its pattern. . . . The notes and words are not so much related to one another as related both to a single numerical idea. . . ." This is as though one would claim that the notes and words of Mozart's operas are not related to one another, without paying any attention to such matters as vocal tessitura, direction of vocal line, phrase rhythm, harmonic action and contrast, and musical intertextuality.

The most direct indication that what we have in view is the integration of a music-cultural system continuous with our own is in the tradition of writing about music with reference to the contemporary practice that began in the ninth century—at most fifty years after the invention of the first notational systems. It is the fact of reference to the contemporary practice—describing, explaining, rationalizing, systematizing, classifying—that most sharply distinguishes the ninth-century writers from earlier transmitters of classical doctrine about music—Boethius, Cassiodorus, Isidore of Seville, for whom reference to any practice would have been irrelevant—and that is the basis of continuity in writing about music to the present. Medieval writing about music begins in the ninth century.

One of those modern conceptual guy-wires that I referred to at the beginning has confined such writings to the category of "music theory;" that is how you will most often find them identified in the literature. The authors are identified as "theorists" and their texts as "treatises." A clue to the distorting effect of that is in some of the labels actually carried by the texts: "handbook," "instructions," "compendium," "discipline," "art" (the latter to be understood in the sense of a body of precepts, rules, conventions that apply in a practice, or "usage" [*usus*]). That is they are more practically oriented than contemplative or speculative. But their ambition is to elevate the practice and practitioners so that they may be informed by truly theoretical doctrine.

In the seventh chapter of the *Musica disciplina,* a mid-ninth-century pedagogical book that is either the oldest or next-oldest of these texts (it vies for this honor with the *Musica enchiriadis* [*Handbook of Music*]), Aurelian of Rêome wrote "There is as much difference between a musician and a singer as there is between a grammarian and a mere reader. . . . Every art and discipline has naturally a more honorable character than a handicraft, which is performed by hand and toil. For it is a much greater thing to know what someone does than to do what someone knows. . . . *A musician is one who has with well-weighed intellect attained the knowledge of singing not by the servitude of labor but by the rule of contemplation.* . . . The singer seems to stand before the musician like a prisoner before the judge."[15] The sentence that I have emphasized speaks of the author's ambition to formulate an art with respect to what had been until then an unreflected traditional oral practice, taught more by rote than by rule, and to elevate the singer to the status of musician. The very idea of a role for someone with such an overview is prime evidence of an awareness that it is an integrating music-cultural system that is at play here. ("Musician," by the way, is what we ought to call the authors of such texts.) Aurelian's distinction speaks for the ambition—and the radical achievement—of the literature as a whole. This has been formulated very well in a recent book about the relation between music and grammar in the Middle Ages: "Medieval music pedagogy, to a not inconsiderable degree through reliance on the extramusical conceptual system of grammar, attained to the formulation as 'music' (*musica*) of an orally transmitted 'song' (*cantus*) previously dependent on speech structures, and beyond that, to the notion of 'music' as composition also obeying formal laws."[16]

Among the main preoccupations of the earliest medieval writings on music, there are two that circle back to some of the central matters that I have already described: mode and tone system.

Mode. The chants of all the liturgical repertories transmitted with notation in the oldest music books fall into classes that can be described in terms of two intersecting dimensions: liturgical genre and what I shall call "tune type" for the moment, borrowing a phrase from folkloristics. By "liturgical genre" I mean those categories specialized for different liturgical functions (Introit, Alleluia, Antiphon, Hymn, etc.). The liturgical genre has a musical character through the determination of who is singing (the cantor, who is an experienced and skillful solo singer, the trained *schola cantorum,* the priest or deacon, whose skills may rise to the level of a psalm tone but hardly beyond, the congregation); and the liturgical act that the chant accompanies (e.g., the Introit for the celebrant's entrance into the church). By "tune type" I mean a distinct cluster—

among several such clusters—of interconnected melodic properties that can include pitch-ambitus, central tone of reference or resolution, stereotyped melodic patterns or formulas used especially at points of articulation in the melody that correspond to points of articulation in the text, characteristics of tessitura (e.g., melodies that tend to begin at the top of the ambitus and descend to the bottom, or melodies that begin by dipping into the bottom of the ambitus), etc.

Looking at the repertories that have come down from the Middle Ages, we can recognize multiple instances of the same tune type within any liturgical genre, and the melodic differences among them can be understood as results of the fact that they intoned texts of different lengths and accentual patterns, with syntactical structures calling for different emphases. But on the whole we would not find the same tune types in different liturgical genres.

Sometime in the second half of the eighth century, Western practitioners of ecclesiastical chant copied the system of eight church modes from the practice of the Eastern church and undertook the classification of the received traditional chants according to the modes. That is, they divided the chants of each of the liturgical genres into eight modal categories. This two-dimensional classification system would be reflected in such—nowadays—commonplace designations as "second mode gradual," "fifth-mode antiphon." The melodic categories that I have called "tune type," they called "mode," or sometimes "tone." Whatever the origins and history of the eight-mode system may be, and whatever the reason for eight modes rather than some other number, there is no reason to think that there would have been eight tune types represented in each liturgical genre, ready to be labeled mode 1, mode 2, etc. By the same token, there is no reason to expect that just because one now refers to "mode 1" introits, graduals, and alleluias they should share melodic properties ("mode-1-ness") that they did not share as tune types. And indeed on the whole they do not, except for properties as general as the location of the final tone within the ambitus.[17] Putting this more formally, we cannot abstract from the collection of chants of all liturgical genres assigned to the first mode a consistent tonal configuration that controls them all. It required a good deal of squeezing and reshaping and arbitrary labeling to produce those classes; even as they are, the distribution of chants among them is irregular (the extreme case is that of the tracts, of which there are chants in only the second and eighth modes, which is to say that there were just two tune types represented in the liturgical genre of tracts).

No doubt this massive classification project was undertaken in the effort to gain control over the huge traditional repertory—another manifestation of the ambition to proceed by rule and system rather than by rote. But there was a very specific practical purpose. A major constituent of the ritual of the mass and office was the singing of the psalter. Psalm verses were chanted to standard recitative patterns called "psalm tones." Many of the chants of the liturgy are actually refrains for such psalm singing. The classification of the refrain chants according to the modes was a way of systematizing the matching of refrains with psalm tones with respect to their melodic polarities.

My report that we cannot abstract from the collection of chants assigned in medieval books to the first mode any sort of tonal aggregate that controls them all may come as a surprise to anyone familiar with the way that the ecclesiastical modes function as paradigms in late medieval and Renaissance polyphony, roughly corresponding to the way the keys function in music from *c.* 1600 to *c.* 1900. The modal configurations that are represented by eight different octave scales are the products of a long history,[18] which begins with efforts to describe and differentiate the modes, not as abstract principles but as *collections* of chants.

The oldest surviving descriptions are in Aurelian's book, and they read like an invention of Borges: "Sweet voices that are thin and intense, clear voices which sustain fairly long like the trumpet, thin voices like those of infants, fat like the voices of men, a hard voice that is emitted violently, like hammers on an anvil." Difficult as it may be for us to imagine how such characterizations could have helped anyone, we should not overlook the historical significance of the effort itself. It is an axiom of classification theory that while some classification systems have as their principal function the sorting and indexing of their objects, others serve a theoretical purpose: by partitioning whole collections or populations of things into natural classes they make a theoretical or explanatory assertion about the entire collection, something about how it works. By partitioning the repertory of chants according to eight modal classes the musicians were in effect interpreting that repertory as a complete, i.e., a perfect, system. And in that they were reaffirming the apprehension that they also manifested by putting the repertory in a book, which they identified as a "book of musical art." This, too, is a very remarkable cognitive invention, the first time in European music history, evidently, in which a repertory is identified as a closed, systematically ordered corpus.

In order to understand the situation that I have briefly summarized here, it has been necessary to adopt an interpretive mode that is closely related to those of musical ethnology and folkloristics. This recognition constitutes a radical shift in a field that has from the beginning been informed by the philological stance and goals learned from Classics and tied to written texts. One of the most important experiences in the history of musical medieval studies has been the failure of our text-critical methods to produce archetypes, best texts, source-stemmata, etc. The field as a whole has not yet assimilated that. I think it would not be exaggerating to interpret this experience in Thomas Kuhn's sense of a paradigm shift that has brought us to a fork, with one branch continuing with a work- and text-grounded orientation aiming for "truth" and the other developing an orientation toward the study of culture and aiming for "certainty," to borrow an old distinction from Vico. There are ramifications far beyond medieval studies, for example, to the study of nineteenth-century composers like Chopin and Liszt, for whom the concept of a single authoritative text representing a fixed work makes no sense.[19] But it is the confrontation with the problems of textual editing that has brought us to this point. So I want to reassure John Van Engen that from the point of view of my experience, while textual editing is "out" at the MLA, doggedly pursued it leads to some of the very subversions that are "in."

Tone system. With a little reflection about our modern notational system we can recognize that, while we may be accustomed to thinking of those round note-heads as direct signs for pitches, they are really signs for positions in a tone system that we take for granted (if we think of it at all it is as a diatonic or chromatic scale, or a keyboard on which we play these). That has been so for all Western notations that encode the intervallic contents of music. The need to explain a tone system was instantly created by the intention to create such a notation, and the ninth-century *Musica enchiriadis* has that as its main purpose. It was the task of conceiving melodies in terms of such a tone-system, and pinning them down to a notation that referred to it, that forced people to think about intervals (and, among other things, stirred up the confusions of which I spoke before). As Lawrence Gushee has put it, "... notation and harmonic science go together ... notation was the conceptual tool which could bridge the gap between harmonic science and traditional church music, not merely a practical tool."[20] Bringing them all together was another of the remarkable cognitive achievements of medieval musicians.

The dynamic, revolutionary character of what I have been describing is brought home by a fact that rather brings me full circle: these earliest medieval books about music are themselves among the earliest documents containing musical notation. We cannot rule out the possibility that support of precepts through musical examples and illustrations of identifications and differentiations in pedagogical texts were the first uses of notation in the Middle Ages. Other cultures have used musical notation for such purposes without writing down their repertories (ancient Chinese, medieval Arabic, Ancient Greek). The *Musica enchiriadis* depends heavily on notation—not just for illustration but for carrying the argument, and its author is an enthusiast about its potential, as well as an advocate for its use. In writing that "practice will make it possible to notate and sing sounds as easily as we write and read letters" he explicitly confirms the context of language writing in which music writing was embedded, and he articulates for the first time a music-language analogy that has been influential in the theory and interpretation of music down to the present. On a more general level, he gives evidence of consciousness about the integration of different cultural manifestations and about innovation in the technology of musical practice, both leading values of the new music culture.

NOTES

1. See Clifford Geertz, "Thick Description: Toward an Interpretive Theory of Culture," in *The Interpretation of Cultures* (New York: Basic Books, 1973), 3–32.

2. Sarah Garland, *The Complete Book of Herbs and Spices* (New York: Viking Press), 120.

3. Details can be found in two essays of mine: "Reading and Singing: On the Genesis of Occidental Music Writing," in *Early Music History* 4 (1984): 135–208, and "The 'Unwritten' and 'Written Transmission' of Medieval Chant and the Start-Up of Musical Notation," in *Journal of Musicology* 10 (1992): 131–191. There is a built-in paradox in this study that is always ready to mislead us. We may insist that it is *singing practices* we want to study, but the evidence for them that comes down looks like the scores of *songs*. The temptation is to study and compare them in their fixed, written aspect, both note by note and synoptically, approaching them like modern scores and with unwarranted assumptions about their status and functions for the user communities of their time.

4. Published as "The Challenge to Modern Historiography," *American Historical Review* 87 (1982): 1–24.

5. See my essay "The Politics of Reception: Tailoring the Present as Fulfilment of a Desired Past," in *Journal of the Royal Musical Association* 116 (1991): 280–298.

6. Bruno Stäblein, *Die Gesänge des altrömischen Graduale Vat. lat. 5319* (Kassel, 1970), 38, and "Die Entstehung des gregorianischen Chorals," in *Die Musikforschung* 27 (1974): 17.

7. Details can be found in Treitler, "Reading and Singing," and "The 'Unwritten' and 'Written Transmission' of Medieval Chant."

8. Mary Carruthers, *The Book of Memory* (Cambridge, Cambridge University Press, 1991).

9. Israel Rosenfield, *The Invention of Memory,* With a New Forward by Oliver Sacks, M.D. (New York: Basic Books, 1989).

10. John Miles Foley, *The Theory of Oral Composition: History and Methodology* (Bloomington: Indiana University Press, 1988).

11. "Homer and Gregory: The Transmission of Epic Poetry and Plainchant," *Musical Quarterly* 60 (1974): 333–372.

12. Harold Powers, "Language Models and Musical Analysis," in *Ethnomusicology* 24 (1980): 1–60.

13. Models of chant transmission have turned out to be useful for the understanding of musical traditions as diverse as those of jazz and Troubadour songs. See Gregory E. Smith, *Homer, Gregory, and Bill Evans? The Theory of Formulaic Composition in the Context of Jazz Piano Improvisation.* Doctoral dissertation, Harvard University 1983 (University Microfilms International, Ann Arbor DEU83–22445 [1984]); and Robert R. Labaree, *"Finding" Troubadour Song: Melodic Variability and Melodic Idiom in Three Monophonic Traditions.* Doctoral dissertation, Wesleyan University 1989 (University Microfilms International, Ann Arbor 3919962 [1990]).

14. John Stevens, *Words and Music in the Middle Ages* (Cambridge: Cambridge University Press, 1986).

15. *Aureliani Reomensis Musica Disciplina,* ed. Lawrence Gushee (Rome: American Institute of Musicology, 1975) p. 77.

16. Mathias Bielitz, *Musik and Grammatik* (München and Salzburg, 1977), 10.

17. But even to speak of a "final" with reference to a performing tradition without a notation and without any discussion of a tone system is anachronistic.

18. It is well told in Harold Power's article "Mode" in volume 12 of *The New Grove Dictionary of Music and Musicians* (London, 1980), 376–418.

19. Regarding Chopin, see Jeffrey Kallberg, "Are Variants a Problem? 'Composer's Intentions' in Editing Chopin," *Chopin Studies* 3 (1990): 257–267.

20. Lawrence Gushee, "Questions of Genre in Medieval Treatises on Music," in *Gattungen in der Musik in Einzeldarstellungen I, Gedenkschrift L. Schrade* (Bern-München 1973), 385.

Art History in the Past and Future
of Medieval Studies

MICHAEL CAMILLE

As USUAL, pictures have been deemed supplements, extras, "rounding-off" something more substantial or illustrating the already written text. Being last I feel somewhat like an after-dinner speaker having to delight and entertain an audience now well-fed on the Word. Why do I follow the papers delivered on medieval literature, philosophy, history, and documents in a conference that has moved from these deeply discursive realms to culminate in that which is on the borders of language—the figural? I suspect that it has something to do with the things I deal with which have a somewhat liminal status within the academy. I am at yet another disadvantage standing as I do between two blank screens. I want to bring something physically before you as I speak. I want to show you images. This is the first time I have ever addressed an academic audience without the props of slides. Because I work through and with these strange simulacral representations in the form of miniaturized, transparent icons, I sometimes feel that I cannot speak without them. They are images of the images which are my sources and documents. The slide presentation, whose ancestor is the phantasmagoric Victorian magic lantern show, allows you, the audience to sleep or dream in the dark, and me the speaker to stand safely aside from my material and let *it* become the object of your gaze. But the slide lecture is also a paradigm for a more disturbingly negative view of images as divorced from the verbal, as superficial *simulacra,* like the reflections in Plato's cave or the dangerously false *phantasmata* feared by the early Church Fathers. The noncognitive status of images was most influentially formulated for the Middle

Ages by St. Augustine when he wrote: "a picture is looked at one way, and letters in another. When you see a picture, the matter is ended: you have seen and you praise. When you see letters this is not yet the end, because you also have to read." Ernst Robert Curtius made the same point earlier this century when he said "knowing pictures is easy compared with knowing books."[1] This pronouncement might seem absurd today but I continue to attend many conferences on a whole variety of medieval topics where I am often the only "visual" aid. Whether it be on Aristotle, agrarian life, or the status of women, I am often asked to provide the pictures to "see and praise" some always already established set of issues. Well-meaning friends and academic colleagues write and ask me for ideas for their book jackets, as though I were some advertising executive for the thirteenth century. On the other hand I *could* argue that my place here today is final in the sense of climactic, a culmination which gives visual art the "last word" or if you will, image. It might be said that like music (which shares the final stage of this conference with art), pictures go "beyond" words to some higher realm of "pure form." Yet this dangerous idealism, rooted as it is in the Romanticism of the last century has been as much a cause of the isolation of the visual from history as Augustine's separation of it from language.

The question of why the so-called "Fine Arts"—a category invented in the late nineteenth century—are the final disciplines to be discussed on this program might be answered by their relatively late entry into the academy as subjects of historical inquiry.[2] During the Middle Ages, of course, there were no such things as the "fine arts" and certainly not as part of the university curriculum (although neither was literature and history). And yet if we are to follow the scholastic philosophers and perspectivists of the thirteenth century who at the universities of Oxford and Paris rediscovered the Aristotelian primacy of the sight—scholars like Roger Bacon and Aquinas—all cognition is rooted in *phantasmata* perceived through the senses.[3] The visual was a crucial aspect of medieval theories of cognition, theological speculation, and social and political order especially after the impact of Aristotelianism. In every sphere of life from the mania for heraldry to the theology of the eucharist, images were on the ascendent. If we live in an image-saturated world as many argue we do today, the beginnings of that bombardment are medieval. Most people then inhabited a richly coded and patterned "image-world" as against our "information world" and yet as with our computer screens and terminals, they saw the Logos in images just as much as in words. Some of the most innovative recent research in the history of medieval art has focused on exactly this power inherent in images, looking at how icons, relics, and devotional images worked not to "reflect" some previously constructed historical context but helped shape history itself. Art no longer has a "background" which is "history" but for our period has been shown to be the very matrix of ideology and action in society. As Hans Belting has argued, we can dispense with the notion of "art" altogether before the sixteenth century and focus rather on the history of these important and active "images."[4]

In terms of the place of visual studies within the university of the third millennium it is indeed ironic that many scholars in the humanities continue to see the visual as abject and lacking when our own post-modern, video-computerized culture with new tools like magnetic resonance imaging, artificial intelligence-linked graphic manipulation systems, and computer-aided tomography scanners is dependent more than ever before on the visual. The university of the future will be a place where people do more looking than reading, more imaging than writing. Knowledge will be stored in radically new spatial ways and retrieved differently with image-making "mice" rather than linear tools of inscription. It will be created not upon the page but upon the screen. Virtual reality machines will transport us and our students directly into the nave of Chartres Cathedral to study its construction and imagery in the space of a hypertextual visual world rather than in the sequential forms of language. If the cathedral were a "book," a "summa in stone" for the nineteenth century, it will be an interface in the next. In this scenario, no doubt frightening to our text-bound colleagues, the place of the figural in history and the capacity of images to communicate about the past, will be crucial to the survival of the humanities in post-book culture.[5]

If, as Lee Patterson has argued, medieval studies today occupies a marginal place in the university as a whole, from my opening argument it might seem that I occupy the margins of the margins.[6] But not really. I have another hat. As an art historian I am placed within a comparatively powerful and influential strata of the humanities. Where I teach at the University of Chicago, art history is the largest graduate program after English (history is in social sciences). Most universities in the United States have art history programs, where many lack proper modern language teaching facilities and philosophy departments. This is partly because of the status of "art" as a commodity fetish in our current consumer culture and the elite associations of museums with prestige, power, and money. But it is also because of the great tradition of the academic discipline in universities in the United States which in many ways is stronger than anywhere in Europe. The study of medieval art can be shown to have played a major role in the founding of art history departments early this century. Precisely because this country did not have monuments of the Middle Ages, their recreation in texts and in institutions was all the more important. Scholars like Charles Rufus Morey and Kingsley Porter, together with the historian Charles Homer Haskins, created a focus on the "twelfth century" which still endures today. Medieval art in the United States was long synonymous with "romanesque art" as can be seen from the early issues of *Gesta,* the organ of the International Center for Medieval Art.[7] Oddly split from the study of Byzantine art, which has its pentagon at the elite and powerful, Constantinople-like "second Rome" of Dumbarton-Oaks in Washington, the institution of medieval art history has a large and thriving constituency to judge by the number of art-historical sessions at the annual meetings of the Medieval Academy of America and the increasingly popular International Congress of Medieval Studies at Kalamazoo with its less exalted but marvellous mix of the monastic and the democratic. If art history had been a powerful historical paradigm early this century for scholars as diverse as Porter and Panofsky, the impact of the social sciences in the 1950s and 1960s saw the social science model of history take over as the leading discipline. But today with the advent of "cultural studies," postmodernism's embrace of the phantasmic image and theoretical disruption in the universities, the paradigms of knowledge are changing once again and the visual gaining ground. My use of the word "visual" rather than "art" here is significant.

In my more powerful mode as an art historian I play something of a double-agent in rejecting many of the paradigms of traditional connoisseurship-based art history and joining my colleagues, most of whom are in twentieth-century art history, in the rush towards theory. It would be unfair to think of medieval art historians as being backward-looking however. Historians of medieval art have been among the most vociferous critics of traditional museum and "profit-based" art history partly because we have always been excluded from the games of genius-display that motivated the connoisseurs. We have always had to be more contextual, language-based, and historical compared to scholars of Renaissance and Baroque art, bound by the tyranny of the image of Vasarian models of artist-idolatry and by the market to the individual dollar-sign of genius.

Like many scholars of my generation I am interested in crossing boundaries. But I am stepping out of my field in two separate directions. In one to enter the smaller interdisciplinary world of a period label—medieval studies—and in the other to enter a larger interdisciplinary arena, the politically embattled discursive spaces of contemporary postmodern theory. I must admit that of the two directions I have most problems about positioning myself in medieval studies where the visual is still relegated to second-order status. This is in marked contrast to the arena of theory. In the vanguard areas of today's humanities in critical theory, anthropology, film studies, feminist and gay and lesbian studies—the visual is at the very center.[8] In these areas of inquiry it is through the image that we construct the imaginary and in psychoanalytic terms, the subject. New kinds of historical methods are being developed which are simultaneously historically specific and theoretically focused, many of them utilizing the visual as the very medium of knowledge.

Of course the visual arts were not always supplementary in modern historical discourse. Earlier this century the work of influential scholars like Ernst Kantorowicz and Erwin Panofsky put images at the very center of medieval studies, if not the humanities as a whole.[9] They could only do so because of the modernist paradigms within which their particular form of German idealist *Geistesgesichte* worked. If one believes in a realm called "the history of ideas," images are kings; drained of their materiality, they can float above events and map out the past as manifestations of historical consciousness. Part of the confusion felt by many in the discipline today is a result of the fragmentation and erosion of traditional humanist ideas about history and the subject. Large numbers of art historians have not only rejected connoisseurship but they also no longer accept iconography—the smooth explanation of image through text.[10] Icon and logos have been split apart after three decades of postmodern "isms" and the so-called "new art history" has reshaped and invigorated our discipline mostly through its incorporation of theoretical models from linguistics, anthropology, literary theory, and post-Lacanian psychoanalysis.[11] While some in art history look back with nostalgia at the superb syntheses of thinkers like Panofsky, most of us can no longer believe in doing such things ourselves, nor do we even want to.

The problem is that these recent reformulations in art-historical thinking have not yet had an impact upon many medievalists in other disciplines who utilize visual materials. While historians and literary scholars have turned to visual images as never before, it is all-too-often to the worn-out word and image of iconographic models. The two controlling paradigms in medieval studies that have served to perpetuate this state of affairs are *art as text* and *art as mirror.* Both approaches are dangerous, a-historical, and essentialist, continuing to promulgate the subaltern status of the visual as supplement.

ART AS TEXT

Frederick Jameson has described how "textuality may rapidly be described as a methodological hypothesis whereby the objects of study in the human sciences are considered to constitute so many texts that we decipher and interpret, as distinguished from the older views of those objects as realities or existants or substances that we in one way or another attempt to know."[12] This approach has been most influential among scholars of literature, being rooted in a Romantic nineteenth-century myth, fostered by Victor Hugo and later developed by Emile Mâle that medieval pictures and buildings can be read like "a book, index, a symbolic code."[13] Iconography, literally collapsing iconic image and graphic writing, developed into the most popular mode of decoding images as unproblematic text-alternates. Now problematized in art-historical thinking, iconography is still all the rage in medieval studies. There are medievalists who today still seek to "read" pictorial signs, collapsing crucial differences between verbal and visual communication and flattening or simplifying the complex web of pictorial marks and styles that make up the history of the visual arts. The days of Robertsonian moral "readings" of medieval texts using iconography as the argument for a narrow Augustinian exegesis are now thankfully over but the trend continued under the trendier guise of semiotic theory. Jesse Gellrich's *The Idea of the Book in the Middle Ages,* to take just one example, uses manuscript images like St. John eating the book from a thirteenth-century Apocalypse to bolster his Derridian thesis about the totalizing textuality of medieval culture, as if visual signs were just another form of quotation. Moreover his superficial visual argument, such as it is, depends solely upon secondary sources that are totally textual and moreover half a century old, like Von Simson and Panofsky.[14] The visual is merely another semiotic source to be tapped without an awareness of its materiality or its site.

Ironically it is the language-driven, theoretical movements in medieval studies, which have in themselves been liberating and exciting for us all, that have often furthered this logocentric appropriation of the visual. This is the case with the "new philology" where a whole issue of *Speculum* devoted to rethinking manuscript culture contains nothing about the visual page itself. In his Introduction Stephen J. Nichols pays some lip-service to art history by talking about "the manuscript matrix" and the image as the text's "unconscious" (but once again therefore submerged and inarticulable). I personally welcomed these wide-ranging and fascinating essays as a medievalist but felt short-changed as an art historian, for images, as usual, were only addressed in the already worn-out terms of text and image (note that text always comes first). The denigration of vision in French twentieth-century thought, as studied by Martin Jay, perhaps accounts for the ways in which these French-inspired medievalists, brilliantly opening up their texts to new strategies of reading have foreclosed their ultimate visibility. Representing the excess and force of libidinal desire to disrupt the text, the visual is in this tradition of scholarship, rendered readable only as unconscious trace, excess, or simulacra.[15] The danger is that with the increasing undermining of philological reference and secure subject-positions, the image will be left as the easy articulable center, the only object left from which meanings can still be read-off. I am not arguing that there are special skills that only an art historian can have; that we are the only people qualified to speak for images. On the contrary some of the best recent work on medieval visual strategies and signs has been undertaken from outside the field itself. Rather I am arguing that literary scholars who go to great lengths to problematize the textual all too often take visual images for granted. Pictures are still "easy" in Augustinian terms, which means that ultimately they are still superficial simulacra.

ART AS MIRROR

If the problem with the literary appropriations of art in medieval studies is that these scholars often treat art as text, for historians using the visual, it is more often that they treat art even more naively, as the "real." Willibald Sauerlander in a review of a major exhibition of medieval art, *The Age of Chivalry* held at London's Royal Academy, which tried to represent peasant life through manuscript illuminations, made the point that "At best art functions only indirectly as a mirror of the past because art has its own language. Any effort to put medieval works of art back into historical or social context faces delicate problems of translation."[16]

Historians tend to think of images not as material visual objects, with cash value, sitting in bank vaults or behind museum vitrines but as disembodied reflections in what Michel de Certeau calls "the picture-gallery of history."[17] Think about how images are used naively, as if they were photographs of some current "reality" to illustrate history books. This is true not only of popular history texts like Georges Duby's flashily illustrated series on *The History of Private Life,* but some of the most sophisticated historical minds of the current generation. Caroline Bynum's book *Holy Feast, Holy Fast,* an otherwise brilliant and influential analysis, places images in a central "picture-section" separate from the text. These captioned images (often from periods and contexts quite different from the focus of her text) are never discussed in the body of the book, being literally a supplement to it. Pictures are totally separate from her discourse, acting like a surface floating above the real bodies of the women she is taking about. As Kathleen Biddick cogently argues, they are part of a failure to explore difference, between text and image, male and female, at the core of Bynum's project.[18] It is important to point out that art history, unlike medieval studies, is a field dominated by women. Gender is a powerful metaphor for other cultural codes, not the least being text and image. The male text still rules and controls the image and woman is culturally constructed as image and mirror just as art history is also positioned in this subservient role, as "feminine."[19] Yet today, thankfully, the fact that more than three-quarters of our graduate students and hopefully more and more faculty are women is not only because it was once considered socially acceptable as a so-called "women's field" but also because of the enormous impact of feminist art history in the past two decades. Likewise one can say that much of the best recent scholarship on the Middle Ages has been within or felt the impact of the intersection of history and gender studies, opening up fascinating areas of research that go beyond the function of images in female spirituality to deal with gender and space and the whole issue of sexuality. There are only a handful of women out of the fifty tenured faculty in the history department at the University of Chicago. In the art history department, by contrast over half of its faculty are women. Here art history "mirrors" a welcome trend that has to continue if the humanities are to flourish and medieval studies along within them.

MEDIEVAL IMAGES IN CONTEMPORARY CULTURE

Hans Belting, a leading German medieval art historian, has argued in a book called *The End of Art History,* that if the discipline is to survive we must also seek to understand, whatever our specialization, contemporary works of art, advertising images, and other visual technologies produced by our culture.[20] I too believe that this contemporaneity is crucial if we are to attract students to think about the role images play in history and in my view provides a crucial role for what I have been calling "visual studies" rather than "art history" in the future. In Europe professors of art history specialize much less than those in the Anglo-American tradition, which I think has a positive effect upon the discipline. The greatest failure of this overspecialization in medieval art history can in my opinion be attributed to the subfield of medieval architectural history which has not only isolated itself as an area of "expertise," but refused to engage with the dynamics of the lived environment and the social meaning of buildings and spaces in medieval culture. By contrast to new methods developed by scholars in medieval painting, sculpture, and manuscript studies, medieval architectural historians in the past twenty years have concerned themselves almost totally with problems rooted in the nineteenth century; the cathedral as beautiful formal machine (as did Viollet le Duc) and as clearly readable book (as did Emile Mâle). Medieval architectural history has clung not only to positivist visual theories of style, "development" and the genius of the great "architect" as author, but also it has retained modernist paradigms that isolate the object in plans and cross-sections that have nothing to do with medieval subject positions, rooted as they are in production and not reception. With a few exceptions there seems to be no new generation of younger architectural historians in the United States comparable with other fields, notably within architectural history itself. Ironically students of nineteenth-century medieval revivals are, by contrast, thriving and influential in the academy. Fearful of interdisciplinarity medieval architectural historians still run for the measuring-rod, with a few exceptions such as the recent work of German Marxist-inspired social historians of Gothic.[21] The danger of this situation is that we have micro-histories of media like stained-glass, manuscripts, and metalwork but lack the spatial context for their function in the church itself. Our overspecialization fragments the synchronicity of all media in the liturgy of the cathedral. The same can be said of the secular sphere in the castle and manor-house, where tapestries and goblets worked similarly within a visual realm we still hardly understand. One of the trends in the next generation, one hopes, will be studies that cross boundaries between media within art history and not just disciplinary ones. We need studies of sexuality and space, boundaries and social codes in medieval institutional architecture like hospitals and town halls, more research on urbanism and city planning as well as a total rethinking of the cathedral as a site of contestation and not just an empty symbol of architectural genius or social unity.

Interdisciplinarity has become an all-too-easy buzz-word which requires institutional and not just individual commitment for it to work effectively. If students of the visual and the textual are to interconnect and training in medieval studies not to prioritize one mode over another, it is not at some "interzone," some "in between," where we should position ourselves, but at a site where we can take up a variety of subject-positions and disciplinary axes. Researchers of the past often believed that interdisciplinary work in medieval art involved reading texts, usually theological. But no matter how much one reads Hugh of St. Victor or Pseudo-Dionysius their texts cannot explain the structure of the Abbey Church of St. Denis or of Chartres cathedral.[22] As Belting argues in his most recent book *Bild und Kult* theologians are the last people the historian should turn to in order to understand the way divine images functioned in history.

Being interdisciplinary as an art historian today means being able to engage in truly theoretical work, reading not just in another disciplinary language or, as I have argued, across boundaries and sub-specialities within the discipline itself, but sometimes in a totally new, in another medium. Film studies has had far more influence upon my vision of the Middle Ages than theology because it has shown me how to think about visual narrative, the flow of signs and the framing of icons of power. Many of my students learn more about relics through taking courses in anthropology than in history. This is true interdisciplinarity—not falling back on the copied codes of another traditional method but embracing multiple media and learning to use new tools and modes of analysis.

The future of medieval studies will depend to a large extent on whether our vision of the medieval past can be reshaped by our present concerns. A hundred years ago the *fin-de siecle* turmoil of industrialization and ebbing Romanticism produced a diverse medievalism embracing Huysman's symbolist cathedral, Emile Mâle's ordered "summa in stone," Viollet le Duc's rationalist machine, and Henry Adams' Virgin-worship. All these writers found the Middle Ages through an awareness of images—the cathedrals—but saw them through the lens of their own political positions. In our present *fin-de-siecle,* less idealistic and no less tumultuous in terms of cultural transformation, another Gothic revival is not necessary but analysis of the way our culture is and has been shaped by images seems to me more crucial than ever before. This analysis is happening in the universities and colleges in the United States, where I believe there is a great deal of interest in things medieval, but is sadly missing from those institutions in which medieval objects are actually kept—the museums. The future of medieval studies depends just as much on these places and on the ways in which manuscripts, reliquaries, and statues housed in American collections are displayed and made available to a culture which, unlike Europe, did not itself experience the Middle Ages. Sadly this long-distant "other" is presented in ways that make the art of the past dead and uninteresting to most young people. Non-Western art, by contrast, is far more powerfully presented in the Metropolitan Museum than the objects in the medieval galleries, which present statues and altarpieces unproblematically as "our heritage" in ways which have not changed since the beginning of the century. Yet for most Americans these things are just as alien as Oceanic masks and need to be contextualized far more. Only by bringing together medieval things and the theories that describe them in new ways and in radically new public displays that describe their function and not only their beauty as "art" will interest in the period be fostered for future generations of museum-goers as well as art historians.[23]

In conclusion I am going to try and practice what I preach. I want an image to have the last word. It is a miniature from a manuscript in Brussels Bibl. Royale MS 9548, entitled the *Li Ars d'Amour de Vertu et de Boneurte* which is an unusual thirteenth-century translation of parts of Aristotle's Ethics into a vernacular courtesy book, made for a Picard courtier at the very end of the thirteenth century. The miniature depicts a typical "chivalric" image of a young nobleman out hawking on his horse. It is the kind of picture reproduced in history books like Duby's *History of Private Life* with the caption "the nobility" underneath it. All too easily it comes to stand for a historical or a textual category. If we read the red rubric above it however, we see that it does not depict a class of society but a period of time—"le moyen eage." "Cis capiteles devise la maniere de caius ki sunt ou moien eage qui on apele estat."[24] But this cannot be a medieval vision of the Middle Ages as the term "moyen age" used to describe a historical epoch "between" ancient and modern times only came into use during the sixteenth century.[25] This is an image of "moyen age" not as a period but as a stage of the life cycle. Yet I still think it true to say that the image *does* tell us something about what we call the "moyen age" as a period in historical time as well as in an individual life. It is still an

Brussels, Bibliotheque Royale Ms 9548, *Li Ars d'Amour, de Vertu et de Boneurté*, fol. 21v.

image of "the Middle Ages." But to get at that we have to understand its dependence on certain traditional pictorial types from calendar illustrations, which often depict a youth out hawking for the month of May, to various images in the tradition of depicting the various ages of life.[26] It is also important to know the conventions of costume and how bodily ideals and expectations inform representations of behavior in this period. Moreover we have to understand not only how it was received but also how it was produced, the patterns, codes, and practices used by the illuminator in putting it together in this particular site, the economic significance of its lavish gold background, the various divisions of labor between scribe, rubricator, and illuminator.[27] If we are to understand this image we have to learn to "read" it—not in the Augustinian linguistic sense, but as a process of performance in both production and reception.

But this little scene, only a few inches square, also has a context that opens into our own world. If in conclusion I might be allowed to be playful with this image, to do what I think medievals did with pictures and invest them with current significance, even to "misread" them, I might want to interpret it not just as the Middle Ages but as emblematic of medieval studies. As the text tells us "moyen eage" is the culmination and highpoint of life. It is not just something between youth and old age but a period of real accomplishment and import on its own terms. As medievalists we have to champion this view of a vibrant, animated, and above-all colorful "Middle Ages," urging our students to see that it is just as relevant to them as the "ancient" childhood myth of origins or the much-flaunted modern age after the non-existent Renaissance (which in this trajectory would be decrepit old age anyway). Medieval studies is perhaps suffering from that modern malaise of the "moyenne"—the mid-life crisis. We have the established authority of the well-endowed male rider (all too male perhaps); having left behind youthful "Romantic" indiscretions, we are preparing to grow old gracefully but on our heels are the younger, fashionable, more energetic disciplines. I could carry my fantastic exegesis further. If the riding figure is the scholar, whose nobility is threatened by the foot-soldiers of theory, the falcon can represent his or her "objective" tools and methods which catch and retrieve pieces of living history, prey which the bird's eagle eye *sees* before it swoops. Are the sniffing dogs our long-suffering students who often catch the scent before we do? This example, perhaps playing into the very trope of the entertaining image I argue so strongly against at the outset, nonetheless shows us how a picture can be viewed, "read," and "misread" on multiple levels. Texts, by contrast, are much more constrained, linear, univocal, and directed. With an awareness of its historical conventions we can all of us say something about this miniature, for being an image it can become a point of view and a departure for discussion, not only of a historical period but also of current methodological concerns, bringing together theory and practice, image and text. My association of theory with the image and practice with the text is not perverse, since the word *theoria* means in Greek, "looking at, viewing, beholding, observing, or being a spectator."[28] So much for those academics who inhabit every discipline, not only medieval ones, and who are threatened by and are constantly castigating theory—for they are showing themselves to be terrified of something else, something much more dangerous, primal, and psychoanalytically significant and which today does indeed threaten their logocentricism—the image.

NOTES

1. Augustine, *In Iohannes Evangelium Tractatus CXXIV,* Corpus Christianorum Series Latina XXXVI (Turnholt, 1954), tractatus XXIV, 224. "Aliter enim uidetur pictura, aliter uidentur litterae. Picturam cum uideris, hoc est totum uidisse, laudasse; litteras cum uideris, non hoc est totum; quoniam commoneris et legere." The passage has often been quoted by medievalists; notably Meyer Schapiro used it to end his famous essay "On the Aesthetic Attitude in Romanesque Art" to argue for a modernist "art for art's sake" approach to twelfth-century images (M. Schapiro, *Romanesque Art* [New York, 1977], 25). E. R. Curtius makes his very Augustinian remark in a diatribe against the powerful tradition of art history in early twentieth-century Germany in *European Literature and the Latin Middle Ages* (Princeton, 1953), 26.

2. See *Early Departments of Art History in the United States,* ed. Craig Hugh-Smyth, Peter Lukehart, and Henry A. Millon (forthcoming). For a critical analysis of the field see Donald Preziosi, "The Question of Art History," *Critical Inquiry* 18 (1992): 364–385. For the place of medieval art history in this historical perspective the best resource is W. Eugene Kleinbauer, *Modern Perspectives in Western Art History* (New York, 1971), 1–105. Princeton University with its Index of Christian Art as well as the German emigres like Panofsky became the major center for medieval art history earlier this century. With the advent of interdisciplinarity and medieval studies the geopolitics of the discipline has much altered (moving West) and is not explained by the nostalgic musings of Norman Cantor, *Inventing the Middle Ages: The Lives, Works and Ideas of the Great Medievalists of the Twentieth Century* (New York, 1991), 429. One gets a sense how rapidly things have changed in the United States since Karl F. Morrison, "Fragmentation and Unity in American Medievalism," in *The Past Before Us,* ed. Michael Kammen (Ithaca, N.Y., 1980), 69, where Millard Meiss, *French Painting in the Time of Jean de Berry* published in 1974 is described as "collating" manuscript miniatures as if they were "written texts"! For a survey of recent work in the field, see Herbert J. Kessler, "On the State of Medieval Art," *Art Bulletin* 70, (1988): 166–187.

3. David C. Lindberg, "The Sense of Vision and the Origins of Modern Science," in *Studies in the History of Medieval Optics* (London, 1983).

David Summers, *The Judgement of Sense: Renaissance Naturalism and the Rise of Aesthetics* (Cambridge, 1987) is in fact more about the medieval foundations of visual empiricism and an excellent introduction to the priority of vision. For a stimulating series of essays on the modern period see *Vision and Visuality*, ed. Hal Forster (Bay Press, 1988). Two recent books by medievalists that have the ambitious aim of highlighting the visual in historical research seem to my mind to fail because of their untheorized and essentialist notion of images as ineffable, almost mystical modes, de-politicized and therefore ultimately useless except as hermeneutic ladders of ascent: Margaret Miles, *Image as Insight: Visual Understanding in Western Christianity and Secular Culture* (Boston, 1985) and Karl F. Morrison, *History as a Visual Art in the Twelfth-Century Renaissance* (Princeton, 1990). Morrison reproduces on the cover of his book and discusses a fake Mosan sculpture (which he does not problematize as a fake) suggesting that he is not really interested in the materiality of images as objects, only as ideas, arguing that visualization comes *before* understanding (49–53). Miles, on the other hand, has a more thorough knowledge of recent image theory and semiotics but gets it confused with a similar immaterial theology of images (15–41).

4. The most comprehensive and strongly argued of a recent series of books is Hans Belting, *Bild und Kult: Eine Geschichte des Bildes vor dem Zeitalter der Kunst* (Munich, 1990). See also David Freedburg, *The Power of Images: Studies in the History of Response* (Chicago, 1989); Michael Camille, *The Gothic Idol: Ideology and Image-Making in Medieval Art* (Cambridge, 1989); Jean Wirth, *L'Image Medievale: Naissance et developments* (*VIe–XVe siecle*) (Paris, 1989). I discuss this revival of interest in medieval image-theory in a review of Belting's book, *Art Bulletin* 74 (September 1992): 514–517.

5. This has been argued by historians of science, notably Donna Haraway, "Situated Knowledges," in *Simians, Cyborgs, and Women: The Reinvention of Nature* (London, 1991), 189–193 but see also the recent art historical argument for the future priority of vision in Barbara Maria Stafford, *Body Criticism: Imaging the Unseen in Enlightenment Art and Medicine* (Cambridge, Mass., 1991), 465–475. An excellent general introduction to the impact of the computer in the humanities with many references to medieval culture is Jay David Bolter, *Writing Space: The Computer, Hypertext, and the History of Writing* (New Jersey, 1991), who notes on page 74 that "only in the medieval codex were words and pictures as unified as they are on the computer screen."

6. Lee Patterson, "On the Margin: Postmodernism, Ironic History, and Medieval Studies," *Speculum* 65 (1990). For the importance of margins, see my *Image on the Edge: The Margins of Medieval Art* (Cambridge, Mass.: 1992).

7. The recent survey of medievalists by the International Center for Medieval Art discovered more Romanesque specialists than any others. See Ilene H. Forsyth "The Monumental Arts of the Romanesque Period: Recent Research," in *The Cloisters Studies in Honor of the Fiftieth Anniversary,* ed. Elizabeth C. Parker and Mary B. Shepard, (New York, 1992), 3–4. I have not attempted in this essay to discuss the strengths of various subfields within medieval art history, for example, the still relative dearth of scholars studying the important but neglected areas of Early Christian and Early Medieval art and architecture.

8. The work of anthropologist James Clifford has raised questions about what we consider museum "art" objects, see *Predicaments of Culture* (New York, 1989). We could ask the same questions of relics and cult statues from the Western Middle Ages in our museums as he asks of so-called "Primitive" products. For film studies, journals like *Screen* in the 1970s and 1980s and now *Camera Obscura* have been crucial in the creation of "cultural studies." For gay and lesbian studies see the many visual essays in *Inside/Out Lesbian and Gay Theories,* ed. Diana Fuss (New York, 1991).

9. For these scholars see Kleinbauer, *Modern Perspectives in Western Art History.* The epistemological context for Panofsky's work in Hegelian thought has been studied by Michael Ann Holly, *Erwin Panofsky and the Foundation of Art History* (Ithaca, N.Y., 1984). Kantorowicz's contributions to art history as well as political history are collected in *Selected Studies* (New York, 1965).

10. For a problematization of iconography, see W. J. T. Mitchell, *Iconology: Image, Text, Ideology* (Chicago, 1986) and many of the essays of the proceedings of the conference held at Panofsky's shrine—Princeton in 1989, *Iconography at the Crossroads,* ed. Brendan Cassidy (Princeton, 1993). The rise of new journals in the field of the humanities that treat images seriously, such as *Word and Image* and *Representations,* suggests that there are new ways of linking icon and logos.

11. Donald Preziosi, *Rethinking Art History: Mediations on a Coy Science* (New Haven, 1989) and *The New Art History,* ed. A. L. Rees and Frances Borzello (Atlantic Heights, N.J., 1988). The latter has no essays dealing with medieval subjects, typical of the modernist bias in recent theory.

12. Frederick Jameson "The Ideology of the Text," *The Ideology of Theory: Essays 1971–1986* (Minneapolis, 1988), 18.

13. Victor Hugo, *Notre Dame de Paris,* first published in 1831 popularized the idea of the cathedral as a "book of stone." The history and impact of this metaphor in medieval art history will be further explored in Michael Camille, "Reading and Writing Amiens Cathedral" in *Audiences*

of Medieval Art, Michael Camille, Robert Nelson, and Linda Seidel (Chicago, forthcoming).

14. Jesse M. Gellrich, *The Idea of the Book in the Middle Ages: Language, Theory, Mythology and Fiction* (Ithaca, 1985). This scholar's use of images is basically no different from the influential work of D. W. Robertson, Jr., *A Preface to Chaucer* (Princeton, 1962), always seeking legitimation of a prior argument through a picture. Though more complex and introduced by a much more subtle chapter on the importance of vision in medieval culture, V. A. Kolve, *Chaucer and Imagery of Narrative: The First Five Canterbury Tales* (London, 1984) has similar problems of generalizing literary concepts from extraneous visual materials, often far apart in time and place. A more successful study of the interaction of poetry and visual narratives and one in my view, embedded far more richly in the manuscript locus, in Sylvia Huot, *From Song to Book: The Poetics of Writing in Old French Lyric and Lyric Narrative Poetry* (Ithaca, 1987).

15. See "The New Philology," ed. Stephen J. Nichols, *Speculum* 65 (1990). For a discussion of "manuscript matrix" and its "multiple forms of representation," see pp. 5–6. "A miniature we admire as a work of art in its own right also represents a scene in the poetic narrative, now transposed from the verbal to the visual medium." Nichols's view of the image as unconscious is influenced by recent French philosophers, particularly Lyotard, whose *Discours, figur* (Paris, 1971) is a key text. Martin Jay has a series of articles on the anti-visual tradition in French thought, see especially "The Rise of Hermeneutics and the Crisis of Ocularcentrism," in *The Rhetoric of Interpretation and the Interpretation of Rhetoric,* ed. Paul Hernadi (Durham, N.C., 1989). For a set of essays exploring the relation between verbal and visual in medieval culture see the special issue of *Yale French Studies, Contexts: Style and Value in Medieval Art and Literature* (1991). A forthcoming set of essays, *Medievalism and the Modernist Temper: On the Discipline of Medieval Studies,* ed. R. Howard Bloch and Stephen G. Nichols (Stanford University Press), includes a piece in which I make a more thorough critique of the philological attitude towards images in manuscript editing.

16. Willibald Sauerlander, review of *The Age of Chivalry* exhibition, in *Burlington Magazine* 130 (1989): 149.

17. Michel de Certeau, *The Writing of History* (New York), 100. For a critique of the way historians use images, see M. Camille "Labouring for the Lord: The Ploughman and the Social Order in the *Luttrell Psalter,*" *Art History* 10, no. 4 (1987): 423–427.

18. Caroline Walker Bynum, *Holy Feast, Holy Fast: The Religious Significance of Food for Medieval Women* (Berkeley, 1987). For a brilliant and more thorough critique of Bynum's use of images see Kathleen Bid-

dick, "Genders, Bodies, Borders: Technologies of the Visible" in *Speculum* 68 (1993), 389–418.

19. For woman as image, see Joan M. Ferrante, *Woman as Image in Medieval Literature from the Twelfth Century to Dante* (New York, 1985) and R. Howard Bloch, *Medieval Misogyny and the Invention of Western Romantic Love* (Chicago, 1991). For an overview of the rapid developments in feminist approaches in art history, see Thalia Gouma-Peterson and Patrician Matthews, "The Feminist Critique of Art History," *Art Bulletin* 69 (1987): 326–358, and for medieval studies, the essays in *Speculum* 68 (1993).

20. Hans Belting, *The End of Art History* (Chicago, 1987): "Discourse today seems to cluster around two poles: the definition and structure of images throughout history, and the problem of the visual and mental reception of such images by the historical and the contemporary beholder. Such topics have been accompanied by a new curiosity about past creations, a curiosity we might even characterize as 'postmodern' " (53).

21. Stephen Murray describes the two approaches that have dominated the study of medieval buildings as "feeling" and "rationality" in "Plan and Space at Amiens Cathedral: With a New Plan Drawn by James Addiss," *Journal of the Society of Architectural Historians* 49 (1990): 44–45. For a strong argument that "scholars of medieval art today do not recognize the dependency of their practice upon nineteenth and twentieth-century modernism," see Maija R. Bismanis, "The Necessity of Discovery," *Gesta* 28 (1989): 115–121. An exception to my negative view are Dieter Kimpel and Robert Suckale, *Die Götische Architektur in Frankreich 1130–1270* (Munich, 1989).

22. Conrad Rudolph, *Artistic Change at St. Denis: Abbot Suger's Program and the Early Twelfth-century Controversy over the Arts* (Princeton, 1990) is an example of the theological "reading" of a building. Rather than the inscribed theology of books, the enacted social performances of textual liturgies is surely a more fruitful area for further research. A fundamental and new study is Jane Welch Williams, *Bread, Wine and Money: The Windows of the Trades at Chartres Cathedral* (Chicago, 1993).

23. The role played by museums, the only places where our students can see medieval objects, is crucial to any account of the future of medieval studies in the United States. As the remarks above suggest, in my opinion these are lagging behind their European counterparts in presenting the past to young people as "high art" and not as history or social experience. The lack of historical emphasis in great medieval collections like the Metropolitan Museum in New York with its unimaginative and old-fashioned presentation of the past as glass case after glass case and its unwillingness to rethink categories of art in its pseudo-medieval Romantic idyll at the Cloisters Museum will have more negative impact on the art

history of the future than anything happening in universities. In Europe (and I am thinking most of France and Germany) the universities are (often) the deadening places of tradition and conservation and it is the museums that are the exciting centers of research with marvellous public-funded exhibitions, juxtaposing their permanent collections with contemporary artists and doing research dealing with historical and social issues and not just "famous artists." The opposite is true in the United States where museums are, for political reasons, far too involved with private fund-raising and popularizing shows of "great art" to think about history or about teaching the American public about other places and periods. Thus we have had no major "historical" exhibitions of medieval art in recent years on a par with the great displays of twenty years ago, like *The Year 1200* exhibition in 1975 which helped shape the ideas of a whole generation of scholars, only "blockbusters" and nationalist surveys. This tragic failure of museums in the United States to present the pre-modern past in a stimulating way is, in my view, partly responsible for the retreat from history in society as a whole as well as the turn away from the object toward theory in the discipline of art history and the increasing separation/isolation of museums from universities as sites of cultural negotiation. Students avoid museums and prefer libraries to learn about the past. Fifty years ago it was exactly this distance from Europe as "other" that gave young American scholars like Meyer Schapiro, the framework for radically new approaches to Romanesque sculpture (see my forthcoming essay "How New York Stole the Idea of Medieval Art" in the *Oxford Art Journal,* special issue on Schapiro) while today we are in danger of mummifying medieval objects in museums that have become all too securely "ours."

24. Brussels Bibliotheque Royale MS 9548 see C. Gaspar and F. Lyna, *Les Principaux manuscrits a peintures de la Bibliotheque Royale de Belgique,* Paris 137–147, no. 90, p. 209.

25. Nathan Edelmann, "The Early Uses of Medium Aevum, Moyen Age, Middle Ages," in *The Eye of the Beholder: Essays in French Literature* (Baltimore, 1974), 58–80.

26. This example is not included in the excellent survey of the theme by Elizabeth Sears, *The Ages of Man: Medieval Interpretations of the Life Cycle* (Princeton, 1986).

27. An exemplary new study of the techniques and mechanics of manuscript image-making that integrates a theoretically sophisticated notion of production with a dynamic sense of historical meaning is Jonathan J. G. Alexander, *Medieval Illuminators and Their Methods of Work* (New Haven, 1993).

28. According to Hans Blumenberg, *The Genesis of the Copernican World,* (Cambridge, Mass., 1989), 692 notes b and e, *theoria*'s "indissoluble combination of aesthetic, moral and scientific aspects" has been "nar-

rowed down to the mere preview of the collection of visual 'data' which are instrumentalized for the nonvisual functioning of modern 'theory'." For the idea as it was instrumental in the Middle Ages, see Olaf Pedersen, "Theorica: A Study in Language and Civilization," *Classica et Medievalia* 22 (1961): 151–166. No matter how much vivified by "presentist" concerns and politicized by necessary deconstructive turns, theoretical approaches to medieval images must, in my view, take more into account the theoretical strategies and negotiations at work in *medieval* theories of language and representation.

Medieval Studies and Medieval Art History

Jeffrey Hamburger

IF MICHAEL IS LAST, where does that leave me? I hope not as the apocalyptic Christ-figure who at the end of time must provide both redemption and judgment! It may not be our collective task to establish "new heaven, new earth," but I cannot resist wondering whether in the final reckoning, "the first shall be last and the last, first." Why, in this triumphal procession of disciplines, which it seems my duty to bring to a close, do the so-called "fine arts" bring up the rear?[1] I do not want to make more of this than it is worth: otherwise I risk sounding like a negotiator obsessed with the shape of the table. But, if I can be tendentious for a moment, consider whether our priorities would have been shared by a medieval audience. Or, to put it more pointedly, by which medieval audience?

Since the arts deal, *inter alia,* with concrete imagery, let me use an exemplum to illustrate my point. In 1469, when the Abbess Gertrude von dem Brake undertook the reform of the Benedictine nunnery at Ebstorf, her first act was to confiscate all existing choir books—be they lectionaries, graduals, or antiphonaries—declare them corrupt, and, to the consternation of her charges, have them cut to shreds.[2] In the following weeks, the community spent the night hours writing out a rough script for the following day's services, performed by a skeleton staff of twelve specially trained nuns. Until they learned the new liturgy, all others were barred from participation. And over the next three years, the community painstakingly produced a new set of choir books, in the words of the chronicle, "cum litteris aureis et pictatis."[3]

No exemplum would be complete without a gloss. For the reformed nuns at Ebstorf, if not for us, the liturgy came first. The liturgy required the production of manuscripts, which, in turn, were

383

illuminated. Note the sequence: from chant to so-called "sources and materials" to images—I will not work my way backwards through the whole of the program. But as a hypothetical I think it worth contemplating in what ways our discussions of the last few days might have differed had we begun with the so-called "sources." Manuscripts provide a common denominator linking many, if not all, of the sessions, not just music and the visual arts. With Richard Rouse, I would argue that they are more than mere accessories or "tools of the trade." Old-fashioned as it might sound, we should remind ourselves of the value of studying the sources, especially at a time when our preoccupation with historiography threatens to encourage not merely a necessary skepticism, but in some quarters an indifference bordering on solecism. If the past is only what we make of it, why bother studying it at all?

As an art historian, I have been trained to be exquisitely sensitive to matters of form—perhaps excessively so. But can we separate form from substance, or ideas from the means of their transmission? Consider, for example, the changing shape of the medieval gloss or else the origins of musical notation as noted by Leo Treitler. And, for all the enthusiastic discussion of CD-ROM systems and computerized databases, might they not represent the fallacy of the facsimile writ large? In our age of mechanical reproduction— witness H. Bloch's discussion of Migne's industrialization of the Church Fathers—we tend to forget that in the Middle Ages every work of art—even a so-called copy—was not just an "image," but a unique object.[4] In the end, there is no substitute.

Having stressed the importance of manuscripts, it is worth remembering that the nuns at Ebstorf put their outmoded liturgical library through the shredder. So much for the "fine arts." But here, too, we have a reminder of different priorities. We would have enshrined the discarded codices in a museum or library. Just as, according to Leo Treitler, concepts such as "memorization" and "improvisation" are of limited utility in approaching medieval music, so too the notion of the "fine arts" is predicated on a conception of the artist, an opposition between "high" versus "low" culture, a hierarchy of genres, and divisions among media that have little if any bearing on medieval patronage and practice. Take, for example, that touchstone, the writings of Abbot Suger, the supposed "founding father" of Gothic. Our textbooks herald his abbey church as the birthplace of Gothic architecture and sculpture. Yet in his writings Suger hardly mentions the former, the latter not at all. Instead, he is transfixed by relics, reliquaries, and glass—"minor arts" in the modern scheme of things. As for "aesthetics," in the Middle Ages, the objects and images we call art were used in anything but a disinterested manner. To paraphrase David Freedberg and Leo Steinberg, we need to remind ourselves of the "power of images in the Middle Ages and in modern oblivion."[5]

My theme of "first things first" also has implications not only for what we study, but also for how we study it. To stay for a moment with manuscripts: like philologists, art historians have often been fixated on sources and stemmata. In hunting down elusive exemplars, we have overlooked the trees, let alone the proverbial wood, in our search for the roots. Today, however (and to judge from Treitler's remarks, in musicology as well as art history) a novel pluralism has displaced privileged prototypes. Each version—one hesitates even to speak of copies—is considered a valuable witness in its own right. In this vein, art historians might profit from musicologists by thinking of copying and viewing as kinds of performance, without, however, getting trapped in the hunt for such bugbears as "definitive" renditions or "authenticity."[6]

All this, of course, is part of a turn from intention to reception, from artists (and authors) to audiences, and it is in that direction that I, too, would now like to turn. Art history, musicology, all the humanities are in the midst of a sea-change in their approach to the object—indeed, many of us spend too much time worrying if we have missed the boat.[7] From Coleridge to the New Criticism, we were taught to begin with the work of art, to treat it as an organic unity, as Treitler said, a "closed, fixed" entity, subject to disinterested perception or, at least, formal analysis. Such modernist assumptions are often entirely at odds with medieval objects, many of which—just think of reliquaries or cathedrals—are better characterized as cumulative works, forever being completed by accretion.[8] In contrast, today we tend to view the object not as closed but open—a "site," to use the new jargon—at which all manner of discourses intersect, but especially those of the postmodern Trinity: race, class, and gender—not always, I might add, the most pertinent categories within a medieval framework. It would, I think, be rash to write theology, the liturgy, and religious experiences entirely out of the picture.[9] Rather than an endpoint, a distillate of styles and sources, we envisage the work as a catalyst to an open-ended series of responses and interpretations.

No area of research better illustrates this shift in perspective than that of Byzantium and the West. The art of the Byzantine East has often been characterized as if it were no more than a prestigious model for passive emulation or else a grab bag of iconographic motifs and stylistic devices, to paraphrase my colleague, Marcia Colish, a "conduit" or a "bundle of sources." Art history has been slower in shaking off these fallacies than intellectual history. Yet today we read the Western reception of Byzantine art in terms of active appropriation, even productive misprision.[10]

Key terms quickly become irritating buzz-words, but three rubrics summarize this shift of emphasis: "audience," "function,"and "context."[11] If integrating monuments in their context is a desideratum, then, as Michael Camille noted, architectural history is an area ripe for reform, especially as architecture provided the governing context for sacral and liturgical performance as well an overarching metaphor for the sacred. Symptomatic of the situation is the self-imposed isolation created by Panofsky's abridged translation of Suger's writings (occasionally referred to as if its original title were "Abbot Suger on the Art Treasures of St. Denis"!). But even within our own discipline, architecture is isolated. Today, art and architectural historians have separate journals, separate conferences, and separate academic appointments.

Let me quickly add a *mea culpa*. Those of use who do not specialize in architecture specialize in other media: manuscript illumination, metalwork, sculpture, and stained glass. Who of us, for example, could have written the treatise, *Of Diverse Arts*? As John Van Engen has shown, its author, the self-styled Theophilus, was a Jack-of-all-trades with theological as well as artistic pretensions.[12] The mixing of media and the emulation of other art forms were essential ingredients of medieval art. Blinkered by our own areas of expertise, we need to look to interdisciplinarity within art history, as well as outside it. As Aby Warburg once said, we need to disregard the academic "border police."[13]

The impoverishment of architectural history is particularly regrettable when one considers that, for better or worse, the battle over "The Gothic" used to be the proving-ground of much of medieval art history.[14] Once the mainstream, architectural history is now often marginalized. That said, I would add that the historiography of medieval architecture teaches lessons that we would be foolish to ignore. As the rest of us move away from a narrow focus on the object, architectural history has all but completed the reverse trajectory, leaving behind grand syntheses and speculations.[15] Otto von Simson's classic, *The Gothic Cathedral,* is now often subjected to scorn; consider, also, the critical fate of Gunther Bandmann's *Mittelalterliche Architektur als Bedeutungsträger.*[16] If architectural historians have "run to their measuring rods" (and, one should add, their computers) it is in part because earlier generations so studiously avoided them. They were arm-chair archaeologists. At the very least we should acknowledge that architectural historians beat the rest of us to the mark in exorcising the ghosts of "Geistesgeschichte." And, while recent work is often monographic in focus, to paint it as altogether arid is at best a caricature. In a recent review of the literature on Early Christian and Byzantine architecture, Cyril Mango identified four strains: "typological," "symbolic-ideological," "functional," and "social-economic."[17] As a subcategory of the "functional," one might add the "topographic-liturgical."[18] Had his subject been Gothic, no doubt he would have added the "structural." Symbolic interpretation, however, rooted in scriptural analogies, remains a valid approach.[19] Assessments of architectural finance, changes in building technology, and the affiliations of patrons provide an indispensable foundation for any study of the meanings and social functions of medieval buildings and their programs.[20] And while archaeological surveys may hardly be glamorous, or, in career terms, produce immediate pay dirt, we should acknowledge that they can transform our approach to major monuments. Take Cluny, for example. After decades of efforts to decode the presumed program of the choir capitals, painstaking surveys of production methods and sculpture surviving from other monuments, some of them previously dismissed as "minor," has undermined the validity of entire enterprise.[21]

Art in context sounds like a failsafe formula, but context itself is proving a problematic notion.[22] What do we meant by it? Usually a very specific setting, particular to a place or a patron. Yet contexts for objects do not come ready made like display cases. We should no more allow historians to establish contexts for us than they, in turn, should assume that images provide a unmediated "window" onto the medieval world. In this view of things, the very concept of context as all that which frames or informs an image is itself under challenge. Instead of placing images in their contexts, like jewels in their settings, art historians now speak of objects constructing their context in complex interactions with changing audiences. Images structure experience rather than embodying it, and, rather than "reflecting" nature or society, they project power, serving, for example, as instruments of propaganda, indoctrination, or instruction. In this way they perform as agents, active protagonists on the historical stage.

In a sense what we have here is art history inside out: instead of images in contexts, we have contexts in images, in short, the "new historicism." Less a return to history than a rereading of history in terms of representation, the "new historicism" enlarges the art historian's disciplinary domain. No wonder art history has been receptive to this trend. But is the notion that there is "nothing beyond the image" any better than the catchphrase that there is "nothing beyond the text?"[23] I am concerned that, as images are merged into discourse, the tyranny of codes and conventions is in danger of imposing a new kind of isolation and self-referentiality on the object. Moreover, is the new notion, "art as instrument," any less fallacious than "art as reflection?" In our eagerness to hitch images to the bandwagon of discourse, do we not often underestimate their individuality and, at the same time, overestimate their efficacy? Even in an age of miraculous images, medieval viewers occasionally had their doubts.[24] Images played many roles—from didactic to devotional—but church and state had other, more effective means of enforcing their will.

On the subject of efficacy, let me offer you yet another exemplum, in this case not one of my own devising, but drawn from a sermon delivered by the cardinal, Eudes de Châteauroux, during a visit to Assisi in the mid-thirteenth century.[25] Given his audience of Franciscan friars, his theme, appropriately enough, is poverty; his illustration, the parable of the Good Samaritan. The cardinal recounts that, on arriving in Assisi, "I was reminded that when I was a child and was looking at a certain window in which was depicted this parable or story, I did not understand what it was. Standing next to me was a certain young lay person, whom I did not know. And he said to me: 'this picture greatly upsets the clergy and religious in comparison with the laity because they have no mercy on the poor and indigent; the laity, however, have mercy on them and aid them in their need.' And he recounted to me the story of the Gospels."[26]

As an art historian reading this text my first instinct is to try to identify the site of the story: in his mind's eye the cardinal might reflect on the famous window of the Prodigal Son in the cathedral at Bourges, not far from Châteauroux.[27] Be that as it may, neither Eudes nor his youthful guide have much use for the literal sense of the parable. The lay viewer identifies the indifference of the Levites in Luke 10 with the cruelty of the Christian clergy, giving the lie to the Gregorian dictum that monumental narrative imagery served as the "Bible of the illiterate."[28] And in the reading offered by Eudes to his audience at Assisi, the image merely serves as a pretext for lengthy allegorical moralizations: the parable is fulfilled in the time of the blessed Francis; the man who goes down from Jerusalem to Jericho and who fell among robbers represents men who have fallen from a state of grace and sunk into sin.[29]

We can draw other lessons from this tale. Why should we be more literal in reading medieval imagery than were medieval viewers themselves? The cardinal privileges one set of meanings, but his story reminds us that a work—in this case, a monumental window—admits of various interpretations, none of which need be normative. Had he been speaking to an audience of Dominicans or else to a lay congregation he might have offered radically different readings. Making an exemplum of Eudes's sermon also teaches us that in interpreting works of art, misinterpretations can be as informative as intentions. The sermon itself offers multiple misreadings that open themselves to readings of their own, some deliberate, others unenvisaged by its author. For example, Eudes's reference to childhood is both deliberate and loaded, recalling traditional monastic teaching, which characterized imagery, whether real or imagined, as an infantile prop, necessary for novices, but cast aside by the mature monk or cleric in pursuit of imageless devotion.[30] Like Paul in 1 Corinthians 13:11, Eudes has given up childish ways of seeing. Yet his allegorical insights, elaborated in ever more intricate distinctions, effectively blind him to the narrative structure and surface of the window. Regardless of the self-conscious care invested in its fabrication, no one seems to have grasped its straightforward scriptural message, let alone other levels of content or association.[31] Whatever scenarios we envisage for the complex interplay between patron and artisans, meanings escaped the control of their makers.[32]

This type of reading could be dismissed as no more than speculation in a dark glass. It also represents a type of interpretation that would have been unthinkable without the productive example of other disciplines. Yet even as we break down the boundaries of the so-called "old" art history, I think it worth asking what, if anything, is intrinsic to our discipline as art historians that we, in turn, can lend to others? Nothing, perhaps. Born in the eighteenth century—some would say the sixteenth—art history may have a fixed lifespan. In fact, Hans Belting has already pronounced it dead.[33] If, as applied to the Middle Ages, the discipline's disease is an anachronistic model of progress and development, focused exclusively on problems of style and representation, then I concur in diagnosing it as fatal. Applied to architecture, similar models, combined with the persistent Gallocentrism that plagues our field, have produced such constructs as the German "Sondergotik," by definition an aberration.[34] In this kind of analysis, as all too often in art history, periods, styles, and influences have acted as if they were disembodied agencies. The grand stylistic unities that remain the stock-in-trade of survey books never worked well for medieval art (Romanesque and Gothic were denigrating terms to begin with).[35] Models of organic, biological development continue to compel us to see the later Middle Ages in terms of decline and decay, yet, to judge what I hear from all quarters, *pace* Huizinga, the "waxing Middle Ages" might have been a better concept.[36] Certainly, scholarship on the period is waxing.[37]

Art history as style history, especially when reduced to formalism, may be moribund—deservedly so if in trusting the eye alone its practitioners became blinkered to all that can inform and mediate visual experience. In other respects, however, I am not quite ready to give up the art-historical ghost. We are still left with the problem of change, which need not be defined in teleological terms. As we all know, historical change does not admit of easy explanation. But as we adopt contextual models of interpretation that emphasize horizontal, synchronic perspectives, we risk losing sight of the vertical or diachronic perspective.

Michael Camille spoke of the importance of the visual and the dangers of automatically privileging the Word. Yet it might be argued that, in taking a methodological lead from literary studies, we are sometimes in danger of doing just that. In the words of the proverb, "if all the arts were the same, we would need only one." The so-called "old" art history is sometimes defined as defending a distinct visual sensibility against encroachments from the "new" linguistically oriented art history. From the medievalist's perspective, however, the "new" art history places far more emphasis on the visual experience of medieval audiences, whereas older, now less fashionable forms of iconographic analysis tend to assimilate medieval images to the texts adduced to interpret them.[38]

It might seem self-evident that the history of art would privilege the visual. Too often, however, we have read medieval art as a text.[39] More recently, historians of late medieval and early modern Europe have championed the importance of ocular experience in pre-Reformation spirituality, but in ways that themselves are problematic.[40] With a propensity inherited from Protestant apologetics, they tend to see in the visual a manifestation of the popular, and therefore, the vulgar. In the history of art, as in the history of spirituality, the vulgarization of the visual has produced dramatic distortions: on the one hand, we have underestimated the importance of visual experience in mainstream monasticism;[41] on the other hand, at least until recently, we have marginalized such areas as female spirituality, in which the visual and the visionary played central roles.[42] "Popular" has proved such a problematic term that, unless carefully qualified, it might best be discarded.[43]

Even if, as Camille suggests, "visual studies" are the wave of the future, we need to keep firmly in mind that the "visual" also has its past. In a time in which we are inundated with images, visual experience has a different valence than it did in medieval cultures.[44] The eye-witness accounts of medieval visionaries testify to a synesthetic interpenetration of visual and verbal experience in which, as in a historiated initial, we cannot speak of text and image, but only of text as image (or vice versa).[45] At a time when our analyses are in danger of submerging images in text and context, how are we to redeem the visual without, however, lapsing into formalism? As early as 1974 David Rosand remarked that, "historicism, unfortunately, tends to avoid confronting some fundamental issues of hermeneutics. Our methods of style description, iconographic interpretation, and contextual commentary, depend upon external comparison—with other works of art, cultural conventions, and social situations. Hardly do we ever attempt to deal with the communicative functioning, the visual mechanics, so to speak, inherent in the work of art itself."[46] In terms of what I have already said about context, Rosand's dialectic between elements intrinsic and extrinsic to the work of art is problematic, but the point he raises is valid nonetheless: objects are more than the sum of their parts, and style more than pretty packaging. We need to recall that "forms can support a variety of meanings"—the phrase is Paul Crossely's—and that, as Michael Baxandall has reminded us, "forms may manifest circumstances, but circumstances do not coerce forms."[47]

Since I have spoken of multiple meanings, I would like to offer an alternative allegory of the image that Michael presented, no less facetious. Here is his rider once again, but in a different context: in this case, Hugh of Fouilloy's moralized *Aviary* (Stift Heiligenkreuz, Ms. 18 [226], f. 129v).[48] Now it is the cleric at his desk who personifies the *vita contemplativa* of academe. In contrast, the knight, his horse, the falcon, and the hound stand for the active life. In this version, the knight—not the foot soldiers (who are nowhere to be seen)—represents the new aristocracy of theory, riding high, confronting the sedate scholar. The horse, the beast of burden, stands, say, for the curators and cataloguers who support the theoreticians' enterprise; the falcon for the connoisseur, his keen eyes now a means to end, rather than an end in itself; and the dogs—not, as Michael suggested, for graduate students or research assistants— but for the archaeologists, their noses close to ground. In the end, however, the knight and the cleric, the active and the contemplative, the "theorist" and the "positivist," the "New" and the "Old" Art History, coexist in perfect harmony within the same frame of reference. Depending on one's point of view, this reading offers either an ideal or an idealized vision.

"The last shall be first and the first, last": back to the beginning. As I said at the outset, the structure of our program can serve as an emblem of how little, in fact, may have changed in medieval studies. Yet no matter how many of us have touched on the parlous state of medieval studies, with regard to art history, medievalists are confronted with tremendous opportunities.[49] As the discipline sets

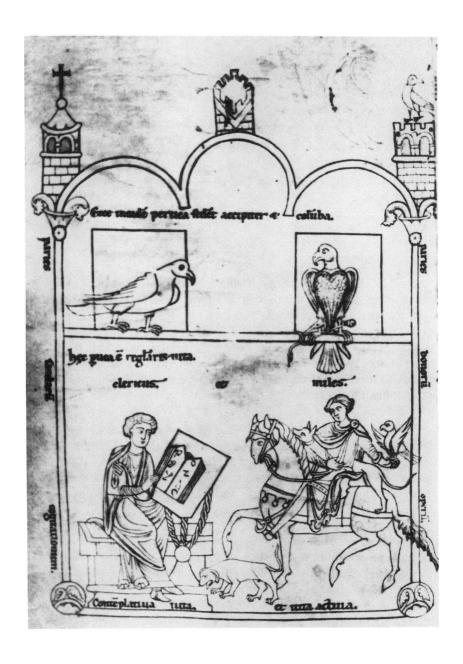

Hugh of Fouilloy, *Aviary*, Stift Heiligenkreuz, Ms 18 (226), fol. 129v.

aside paradigms that trace their ancestry to the Renaissance, medieval art need no longer serve simply as a foil for earlier and later developments.[50] Is it too much to hope that the study of medieval art, which in the past as well as the present has been highly interdisciplinary in nature, now might provide methodological exempla for the field as a whole? If so, medieval studies can return to the center that its name—no matter how anachronistic—implies is its rightful place.

NOTES

My thanks to John Van Engen for having invited me to participate in the symposium, as well as to the participants for sharing their thoughts both during and after the conference. With their usual generosity and insight, Marcia Colish, Gil Miranda, and Grover Zinn commented on earlier drafts of this paper. As I had no chance to review the revised remarks of the participants, I have made few changes to my comments, in which, as the last discussant, I tried to address issues raised by the program as a whole, not just the concluding session.

1. In this respect, little has changed since the publication of M. D. Burno, "Duplicating Medieval Art: Accuracy and Design," in *Medieval Studies in North America Past, Present, and Future,* ed. F. G. Gentry and C. Kleinhenz (Kalamazoo, Mich., 1982), 243–250, which offers no more than a postscript to the other papers and a guide to archival sources for photographic reproductions.
2. Some scraps survive due to their having been used as binding materials. See B. Uhde-Stahl, "Drei Miniaturen aus den ehemalige Klöstern Lüne und Ebstorf," *Niederdeutsche Beiträge zur Kunstgeschichte* 15 (1976): 63–70; eadem, "Figürliche Buchmalereien in den spätmittelalterlichen Handschriften der Lüneburger Frauenklöster," *Niederdeutsche Beiträge zur Kunstgeschichte,* 17 (1978) 25–60, and A. L. Leber, *Kloster Lüne,* Königstein im Taunus, n.d. (1991), 23, 26 and 32.
3. C. Borchling, "Litterarisches und geistiges Leben in Kloster Ebstorf am Ausgange des Mittelalters," *Zeitschrift des Historischen Vereins für Niedersachsen* (1905): 361–420, esp. 389–392. I discuss this episode at greater length in "Art, Enclosure and the *Cura monialium:* Prolegomena in the Guise of a Postscript," *Gesta* 31 (1992): 108–134.
4. See H. Swarzenski, "The Role of Copies in the Formation of the Styles of the Eleventh Century," in *Romanesque and Gothic Art: Studies in*

Western Art, Acts of the Twentieth International Congress of the History of Art (Princeton, 1963), I, 7–18, and J. J. G. Alexander, "Facsimilies, Copies, and Variations: The Relationship to the Model in Medieval and Renaissance Illuminated Manuscripts," in *Retaining the Original: Multiple Originals, Copies, and Reproductions,* Studies in the History of Art 20 (Hanover, N.H., 1989), 61–74.

 5. D. Freedberg, *The Power of Images: Studies in the History and Theory of Response* (Chicago, 1989), and L. Steinberg, *The Sexuality of Christ in Renaissance Art and in Modern Oblivion* (New York, 1983).

 6. Cf. the remarks of H. R. Jauss, "Alterität und Modernität der mittelalterlichen Literatur," in *Alterität und Modernität der mittelalterlichen Literatur: Gesammelte Aufsätze 1956–1976* (Munich, 1977), 9–47, esp. 17. J. Lowden, "Concerning the Cotton Genesis and Other Illustrated Manuscripts of Genesis," *Gesta* 30 (1992): 40–53, paradoxically proves able to challenge the philological method championed by Weitzmann by taking into consideration philological evidence too often overlooked by art historians.

 7. For two recent overviews, see J. Kerman, *Contemplating Music: Challenges to Musicology* (Cambridge, 1985) and P. Burke, "The Social History of Art or the History of Images," *Budapest Review of Books* 2, no. 1 (1992): 9–12.

 8. Not a new idea; compare V. Hugo's remarks in *Notre Dame de Paris,* trans. J. Sturrock (Harmondsworth, 1978) , 129: "Great buildings, like great mountains, are the work of centuries." More recently, see X. Barral y Altet, "Définition et fonction d'un trésor monastique autour de l'an mil: Sainte-Foy de Conques," in *Haut moyen-âge: Culture, éducation et société. Études offertes à Pierre Riché,* ed. M. Sot (La Garenne-Colombes, 1990), 401–408.

 9. D. A. Wells, "Die Allegorie als Interpretationsmittel mittelalterliche Texte," in *Bildhafte Rede in Mittelalter und früher Neuzeit: Probleme ihrer Legitimation und ihrer Funktion,* ed. W. Harms, K. Speckenbach, and H. Vögel (Tübingen, 1992), 1–24, surveys the *status quaestionis* regarding the application of patristic and medieval exegesis to medieval literature. The lack of any recent comparable essay on medieval art history and exegesis reflects the degree of disinterest in the approach, at least in this country, due in large part to the discrediting of the iconographic method.

 10. H. Belting, *The Image and Its Public in the Middle Ages: Form and Function of Early Paintings of the Passion,* trans. M. Bartusis and R. Meyer (New Rochelle, N.Y., 1990), and idem, *Bild und Kult; Eine Geschichte des Bildes vor dem Zeitalter der Kunst* (Munich, 1990).

 11. Terms that loom large in an anthology of essays written by some of Germany's leading art historians, *Funkkolleg Kunst: Eine Geschichte der*

Kunst im Wandel ihrer Funktionen, ed. W. Busch, 2 vols. (Munich, 1987). Would that an anthology of similar breadth and quality were available for American undergraduates in place of the anodyne surveys that, no matter how frequently revised, are rooted in a discredited geneological approach to the history of art—an approach that from Vasari on has never served medieval art well.

12. J. Van Engen, "Theophilus Presbyter and Rupert of Deutz: The Manual Arts and Benedictine Theology in the Early Twelfth Century," *Viator* 11 (1980): 147–163.

13. Cited by P. Crossley, "Medieval Architecture and Meaning: The Limits of Iconography," *Burlington Magazine* 130 (1988): 116–121, without, however, giving the source: Aby Warburg, "Arbeitende Bauern auf Burgundischen Teppichen," *Zeitschrift für bildende Kunst,* n.f. 18 (1907), reprinted in *Gesammelte Schriften,* vol. 1 (Leipzig, 1932), 221–229 and 383, esp. 227: "das einflußreiche Grenzwächtertum in unserer heutigen Kunstgeschichtsschreibung." On the subject of interdisciplinarity, looking to the discipline's past might also illuminate its future; see, e.g., D. Wuttke, *Aby M. Warburgs Methode als Anregung und Aufgabe: Mit einem Briefwechsel zum Kunstverständnis* Gratia: Bamberger Schriften zur Renaissanceforschung 2 (Wiesbaden, 1990 [1977]), esp. 71.

14. See P. Frankl, *The Gothic: Literary Sources and Interpretation Through Eight Centuries* (Princeton, 1960).

15. In addition to Crossley, "Medieval Architecture and Meaning," see a trio of articles by E. C. Fernie: "Contrasts in Methodology and Interpretation of Medieval Ecclesiastical Architecture," *Archaeological Journal* 145 (1988): 344–364, "Archaeology and Iconography: Recent Developments in the Study of English Medieval Architecture," *Architectural History* 32 (1989): 18–29, and "The History of Medieval Architecture from Carolingian to Romanesque: Criteria and Definitions from 1925 to the Present Day," *Muqarnas* 8 (1991): 36–39. M. Trachtenberg, "Some Observations on Recent Architectural History," *Art Bulletin* 70 (1989): 208–241, esp. 228–230, sets the study of Gothic architecture within the context of architectural history as a whole.

16. Otto von Simson, *The Gothic Cathedral* (Princeton, 1962) and Gunther Bandmann, *Mittelalterliche Architektur als Bedeutungsträger,* 7th ed. (Berlin, 1981).

17. C. Mango, "Approaches to Byzantine Architecture," *Muqarnas* 8 (1991): 40–44.

18. For an overview of the vast and growing literature in this field, see S. de Blauuw, "Architecture and Liturgy in Late Antiquity and the Middle Ages: Traditions and Trends in Western Scholarship," *Archiv für Liturgie-wissenschaft* 33 (1991): 1–34. W. Sauerländer, "Façade ou façades

romanes?" *Cahiers de civilization médiévales* 135–136 (1991): 393–340, also explores the possibilities of this approach.

19. See, for example, R. Suckale, "Aspetti della simbologia architettonica del dodicesimo secolo in Francia: il santuario," *Arte cristiana* 78 (1990): 111–127.

20. Here D. Kimpel and R. Suckale, *Die gotische Architektur in Frankreich 1130–1270* (Munich,1985), breaks new ground. An English translation that would make this work accessible to students would be a great boon.

21. See, e.g., N. Stratford, "Romanesque Sculptors in Burgundy: Reflections on its Geography, on Patronage, on the Style of the Sculpture, and on the Working Methods of Sculptors," in *Artistes, Artisans et Production Artistique au Moyen Age*, vol. III Fabrication et Consommation de l'Oeuvre, ed. X. Barral i Altet (Paris, 1990), 235–263. W. Jacobsen, *Der Klosterplan von St. Gallen und die Karolingische Architectur: Entwicklung und Wandel von Form und Bedeutung im fränkischen Kirchenbau zwischen 751 und 840* (Berlin, 1992) offers another recent example of how an unabashedly positivist and archaeological approach can reinvigorate an old debate.

22. See most recently M. Bal and N. Bryson, "Semiotics and Art History," *Art Bulletin* 73 (1991): 174–208, esp. 176–180. The critique of context can, however, be taken to extremes; see, e.g., D. Preziozi, *Rethinking Art History: Meditations on a Coy Science* (New Haven, 1989), and K. Moxey, "The Social History of Art in the Age of Deconstruction," *History of the Human Sciences* 5 (1992): 37–46.

23. Cf. the remarks of G. Spiegel, "History, Historicism, and the Social Logic of the Text in the Middle Ages," *Speculum* 65 (1990): 58–86.

24. See. e.g., A. Vauchez, "Les stigmates de saint François et leurs détracteurs dans les derniers siècles du moyen âge," *Mélanges d'archéologie et d'histoire* 80 (1968): 595–625.

25. Cited by J. Hubert, "La place faite aux laïcs dans les églises monastiques et dans les cathédrales aux XIe et XIIe siècles," *I Laici nella "Societas Christiana" del secoli XI e XII: Atti della terza Settimana internazionale di studio Mendola, 21–27 agosto 1965,* Miscellanea del Centro di Studi Medioevali 5; Pubblicazioni dell'Università Cattolica del Sacro Cuore, III/5 (Milan, 1968), 470–487, esp. 474–475, after J. B. Pitra, *Analecta Novissima: Spicilegii Solesmensis altera continuatio* (Tusculana, 1888), II, 270.

26. Pitra, *Analecta Novissima,* 270: "Luc. X. 'Homo quidam descendebat de Hierusalem in Jericho, et incidit in latrones. . . . Cum venirem modo ad locum istum, recordatus sum, quod cum essem puer, et inspicerem quamdam vitream, in qua depicta erat ista parabola sive historia, et

nescirem quid hoc esset, stetit juxta me quidam juvenis laicus, quem non cognoscebam. Et dixit mihi: Ista pictura valde confundit clericos et religiosos in comparatione laicorum, quia ipsi non compatiuntur pauperibus et indigentibus, laici autem eis compatiuntur et juvant eos in necessitatibus suis. Et exposuit mihi historiam evangelii."

27. Already suggested by Pitra, *Analecta Novissima,* 270, note 2.

28. In addition to L. Gougaud, "Muta Praedicatio," *Revue Bénédictine* 42 (1930): 168–171, recent studies include M. Camille, "Seeing and Reading: Some Visual Implications of Medieval Litteray and Illiteracy," *Art History* 8 (1985): 26–49; C. Chazelle, "Pictures, Books, and the Illiterate: Pope Gregory's Letters to Serenus of Marseilles," *Word & Image* 6 (1990): 138–153; H. L. Kessler, "Pictorial Narrative and Church Mission in Sixth-Century Gaul," in *Pictorial Narrative in Antiquity and the Middle Ages* ed. H. L. Kessler and M. S. Simpson, Studies in the History of Art 16 (Washington, D. C., 1985), 75–91, and M. Curschmann, "*Pictura laicorum litteratura?* Überlegungen zum Verhältnis von Bild und volkssprachlicher Schriftlichkeit im Hoch- und Spätmittelalter bis zum Codex Manesse," *Pragmatische Schriftlichkeit im Mittelalter: Erscheinungsformen und Entwicklungsstufen,* ed. H. Keller, K. Grubmüller, and N. Staubach, Münstersche Mittelalter-Schriften 65 (Munich, 1990), 211–229.

29. Pitra, 270: "Mihi videtur quod temporibus beati Francisci fuit impleta ista historia. Per istum hominem, qui descendit de Hierusalem in Jericho, designantur homines qui a statu gratiae cadunt et incidunt in peccata."

30. See J. Hamburger, "A *Liber precum* in Sélestat and the Development of the Illustrated Prayer Book in Germany," *Art Bulletin* 73 (1991): 209–236.

31. For the complex narrative structures of medieval windows, see W. Kemp, *Sermo Corporeus: Die Erzählung der mittelalterlichen Glasfenster* (Munich, 1987), and M. H. Caviness, "Biblical Stories in Windows: Were They Bibles for the Poor?"in *The Bible in the Middle Ages: Its Influence on Literature and Art,* ed. B. Levy, Medieval and Renaissance Texts and Studies 89 (Binghampton, N.Y., 1992), 103–147.

32. For what we can glean of relations between patrons and artists, see P. Skubiszewski, "L'intellectuel et l'artiste face à l'oeuvre à l'époque romane," in *Le travail au moyen âge: Une approche interdisciplinaire,* Actes du colloque international de Louvain-la-Neuve, 21–23 mai 1987, ed. J. Hamesse and C. Muraille-Samaran, Université Catholique de Louvain, Publications de l'Institut d'Études Médiévales: Textes, Études, Congrès, 10 (1990), 262–321.

33. H. Belting, *The End of Art History* (Chicago, 1987).

34. K. Gerstenberg, *Deutsche Sondergotik: Eine Untersuchung über das Wesen der deutschen Baukunst im späten Mittelalter,* 2nd ed. (Darmstadt, 1969).

35. As noted by H. Kessler, "On the State of Medieval Art History," *Art Bulletin* 70 (1988): 166–187.

36. For a challenge to Huizinga on his own turf, see F. P. van Oostrom, *Court and Culture: Dutch Literature, 1350–1450,* trans. A. J. Pomerans (Berkeley, 1992).

37. Witness the emergence of the *Bibliographie annuelle du moyen âge tardif: auteurs et textes latins, ca. 1250–1500* (Turnhout, 1992—).

38. D. Kuspit, "Traditional Art History's Complaint Against the Linguistic Analysis of Visual Art," *Journal of Aesthetics and Art Criticism* 45 (1987): 345–349, discusses some of the issues raised by this type of critique. For a medievalist's viewpoint, in retrospect remarkably prescient, see A. Grabar, "Peut-on parler de l'acte d'écrire lorsqu'il s'agit d'images?" *Cahiers internationale du symbolisme* 15–16 (1967–1968): 15–27.

39. Cf. the formulation of O. Pächt in his classic study, *The Rise of Pictorial Narrative in Twelfth-Century England* (Oxford, 1962), 58: "For what stimulated the artist's imagination in the first place was not visual experience. The primary creative impulse seems to have come from the talking world." D. de Chapeaurouge, *"Das Auge ist ein Herr, Das Ohr ein Knecht":* Der Weg von der mittelalterlichen zur Abstrakten Malerei (Wiesbaden, 1983), also emphasizes the primacy of hearing over seeing in medieval experience.

40. In addition to A. L. Mayer, "Die heilbringende Schau in Sitte und Kult," in *Heilige Überlieferung* (Beiträge zur Geschichte des alten Mönchtums und des Benediktinerordens), ed. I. Herwegen (Münster, 1938) 235–262, an early and often overlooked study, see the work of B. Scribner, "Popular Piety and Modes of Visual Perception in Late-Medieval and Reformation Germany," *Journal of Religious History* 15 (1989): 448–469; "Das Visuelle in der Volksfrömmigkeit," in *Bilder und Bilderstrum im Spätmittelalter und in der frühen Neuzeit,* ed. Bob Scribner, Wolfenbüttler Forschungen 46 (Wiesbaden, 1990), 9–20; and "Zur Wahrnehmung des Heiligen in Deutschland am Ende des Mittelalters," in *Das Mittelalter: Unsere Fremde Vergangenheit,* ed. J. Kuolt and others (Stuttgart, 1990), 241–267. Also of importance is E. Benz, *Die Vision: Erfahrungsform und Bilderwelt* (Stuttgart, 1969).

41. For two contrary views, see G. Constable, "A Living Past: The Historical Environment of the Middle Ages," *Harvard Library Bulletin* n.s. 1 (1990), 49–70, and K. F. Morrison, *History as a Visual Art in the Twelfth-century Renaissance* (Princeton, 1990).

42. See J. Hamburger, "The Visual and the Visionary: The Changing Role of the Image in Late Medieval Monastic Devotions," *Viator* 20 (1989): 161–182, and idem, *The Rothschild Canticles: Art and Mysticism in Flanders and the Rhineland circa 1300* (New Haven, 1990).

43. As suggested by L. Boyle, "Popular Piety in the Middle Ages: What is Popular?" *Florilegium* 4 (1982): 184–193, kindly brought to my attention by Diane Phillips.

44. Cf. Jauss, "Alterität und Modernität," esp. 16: "Auch wenn uns moderne Massenmedien der mittelalterlichen Erfahrung einer nicht durch das Buch vermittelten Dichtung wieder näher gerückt haben sollten, als es die einsame und stumme Visualisierung einer individuellen Lektüre tat, kann sich der moderne Hörer doch schwerlich in ein Bewußtsein zurückversetzen, das keine andere Wahl hatte, als hörend aufzunehmen."

45. See Hamburger, *The Rothschild Canticles,* and, for an overview of the literature, P. Dinzelbacher, *Revelationes,* Typologie des sources du Moyen Age occidental 57 (Turnhout, 1991).

46. D. Rosand "Art History and Criticism: The Past as Present," *New Literary History* 5 (1974): 435–445, esp. 437.

47. M. Baxandall, *The Limewood Sculpture of Renaissance Germany* (New Haven, 1980), 164.

48. See W. B. Clark, *The Medieval Book of Birds: Hugh of Fouilloy's Aviarium,* Medieval and Renaissance Texts and Studies 80 (Binghampton, N.Y., 1992).

49. It is striking to what extent the optimism and confidence expressed in *Medieval Studies in North America Past, Present, and Future,* has given way to widespread pessimism. Who now would say with Wheeler, 201, that Medieval Studies are the "Sunbelt of academe?"

50. As it continues to do in N. Bryson, *Word and Image: French Painting of the Ancien Régime* (Cambridge, 1981), 1–4. In contrast, see L. Patterson, "On the Margin: Postmodernism, Ironic History, and Medieval Studies," *Speculum,* 65 (1990): 87–108, and J. M. Bennett, "Medieval Women, Modern Women: Across the Great Divide," in *Culture and History 1350–1600: Essays on English Communities, Identities and Writing,* ed. D. Aers, (Detroit, 1992), 147–175.

An Afterword on Medieval Studies, Or the Future of Abelard and Heloise

John Van Engen

"GOD GRANTED IT TO ME to serve the greatest people of France." So reads the will of Jean de Meun, famed continuator of the *Romance of the Rose*. About 1302, presenting one of his works to King Philip the Fair, Jean explained that he had served the great of the land by providing vernacular translations of Vegetius, the *Marvels of Ireland,* Ailred's *Spiritual Friendship,* Boethius' *Consolation,* and *The Life and Letters of Pierre Abelard and Heloise his Wife.*[1] What Jean de Meun looked back upon as his life's work medievalists might well take up as matter fit for an afterword on Medieval Studies. A medievalist would want to ask, among other things, why the nobility of France in the later thirteenth century patronized this combination of imaginative fiction, military strategy, fantastic travelogue, spiritual counsel, philosophy, and letters. An essayist on Medieval Studies in turn would ask where these six works get studied in the modern academy and how, and whether they ever fit into the same course of study. Such an essay, perhaps the more interesting one, will not be attempted here—or rather, will be left to the imagination of readers. This essay will take as its point of departure just one of the translated works. For while the other four had already circulated widely in Latin, the letters of Abelard and Heloise remained, so far as scholars can determine, unknown before Jean de Meun translated them around 1290.

He worked from a Latin manuscript, now lost, judged comparable in quality and content to two others copied in Jean's lifetime, the earliest extant witnesses to the letters. One (A) came into the hands of Petrarch around 1337, who made a number of textual an-notations; another (T) belonged to the chapter at Notre Dame in Paris and was sold in 1347 to the chancellor of the university.[2] Two more can be dated to the generation after 1300. After five generations of neglect stretching to 150 years, in other words, this correspondence suddenly came into vogue among Latin intellectuals, and that vogue persisted, attested by five more Latin manuscripts and evidences of another fourteen, one ordered up by Coluccio Salutati, the humanist chancellor of Florence. Jean de Mcun's vernacular version, by contrast, survived in a single poor copy made approximately a century after his original translation.

So what is a medievalist to make of these late manuscripts, this newfound interest? Jean's work may represent unique vernacular testimony to wider enthusiasm for a recently recovered work, including a new and more general receptiveness to the rhetoric of these letters; or Jean may have initiated that recovery by retrieving a Latin manuscript from the Paraclete;[3] or he might himself have authored the Latin correspondence. Scholars have reached no agreement.[4] In the larger perspective of medieval studies, however, one thing seems certain: in Paris, about 1290, fascination with the lives, loves, and letters of Abelard and Heloise, attested earlier only in glancing references to their affair, first began, and was never again wholly to abate. In some larger sense, modern medievalists are the heirs to this work of reinscribing, translating, and interpreting.

But disruption and discontinuity are as much a part of the story as continuity and inheritance. This holds true for the Paraclete itself, the presumed source or repository of any authentic correspondence. Only two generations after Jean de Meun, war with the English brought destruction, possibly leveling the cloister in 1356 (the reference is vague) and emptying the house for a decade. More than a century later, on 2 May 1497, the abbess of the Paraclete had the bodies of Abelard and Heloise translated from their original burial site in Abelard's oratory (a place called le Petit-Moustier, located alongside the river Arduisson on convent property near the cloister) and entombed on either side of the high altar in the convent church.[5]

Discontinuity holds as well for access to copies of these letters. The first edition appeared a full 150 years after Gutenberg. In 1616 François d'Amboise, a lawyer and royal counselor, initiated the first edition of Abelard and Heloise's *Opera Omnia,* inspired to do so by reading a manuscript copy of their letters. Heloise received almost equal billing on the title page (a difference only in type size: *et Heloisae coniugis eius primae paracletensis abbatissae*). But d'Amboise apparently found, or was given, no copy of the correspondence at the Paraclete, though he was given and he included in his edition copies of Abelard's liturgical and philosophical works. The edition promptly landed on the Index, even though he had taken care to print the medieval censures of Abelard's thought at the beginning.[6] One generation before this edition and d'Amboise's request for everything the Paraclete had on Abelard and Heloise, the convent itself had been occupied by a Protestant abbess during the wars of religion. She, it was rumored, had seized and sent to England all of Abelard's works.

For its last two centuries the convent was ruled by abbesses from the La Rochfoucauld family; the first of them patronized d'Amboise. It was not their social acclaim, however, but a poem written in English by Alexander Pope, a century after the first edition (1717), that attracted new attention to the letters, and made sentimental depictions of Heloise all the rage:

> Soon as thy letters trembling I unclose,
> That well-known name awakens all my woes.
> Oh name for ever sad! for ever dear!
> Still breathed in sighs, still usher'd with a tear.
> I tremble too, where'er my own I find,
> Some dire misfortune follows close behind.
> Line after line my gushing eyes o'erflow,
> Led through a sad variety of woe;
>
> . . . .
>
> When at the close of each sad, sorrowing day,
> Fancy restores what vengeance snatch'd away,
> Then conscience sleeps, and leaving Nature free,
> All my loose soul unbounded springs to thee.
>
> . . . .
>
> Provoking demons all restraint remove,
> And stir within me ev'ry source of love.
> I hear thee, view thee, gaze o'er all thy charms,
> And round thy phantom glue my clasping arms.
>
> . . . .

Sudden you mount, you beckon from the skies;
Clouds interpose, waves roar, and winds arise.
I shriek, start up, the same sad prospect find,
And wake to all the griefs I left behind.

· · · · · · · · · · · · · · · · · · ·

Come, Abelard! for what hast thou to dread?
The torch of Venus burns not for the dead.
Nature stands check'd; religion disapproves:
Ev'n thou art cold—yet Eloisa loves.[7]

For the following century, romantic images of Abelard and Heloise,
as represented in sculpture and painting, in poems and plays, rendered them an unavoidable presence in aristocratic and bourgeois
culture. After the Revolution, the dismantling of cloister and church
resulted in the removal of their bodies to a Parisian cemetery (Père-
Lachaise).[8] The cult of Abelard and Heloise, as the martyrs of romantic love, peaked in the mid-nineteenth century. Almost all of it
rested, in that age of letters, upon their letters, reproduced in nearly
a hundred editions, translations, and versions over about seventy-
five years. In the midst of the cult's popularity, in the year 1857,
there appeared, in a new journal devoted to literary correspondence, the first scholarly article questioning the authenticity of
those same letters.[9] And in the succeeding one hundred years
scholarly and other reconstructions have enlivened each succeeding generation, becoming the occasion in this last generation for
new editions (one still in progress), for learned disputes over authenticity, and for nude scenes of love-making and violation on
stage and screen.

The letters of Abelard and Heloise, and the corresponding images, cults, and reconstructions over the past centuries, may stand
as emblematic for a pattern that could be traced out for many other
medieval figures. In the case of Abelard's equally famous adversary,
Bernard of Clairvaux, Giles Constable has pointed up a remarkably
intense recopying of his works (and those of many other twelfth-
century spiritual writers) two centuries later by the so-called Modern Devout and the Observants,[10] a pattern of reappropriation
which could be followed into the reading of Bernard by John Calvin
or by seventeenth-century Trappists or by nineteenth-century restorers of the religious life or indeed by nineteenth-century secular
humanists, down to the reading and re-editing undertaken by Jean

Leclercq in our own day which played so significant a role in the flowering of monastic studies. Patterns of recovery and transmission have plainly manifested themselves differently in the cases of Bernard and Abelard, betraying differing avenues and purposes at work in the preserving and appropriating. Real differences in the medieval materials being preserved or appropriated are also disclosed.

Medievalists have generally left it to "medievalism" to study the patterns of transmission, those framing images of the Middle Ages, while Medieval Studies has gone after that on which such reconstructions rest. But medievalists must be reminded from time to time of their intellectual debt to medievalism: what they are attempting to recall or represent or reconstruct is not so easily or naively separated from that framework, which is to say, from their overarching purposes ("why") or their chosen means ("how"). Popular, even vulgar, forms of medievalism may often occasion serious scholarly study, either to clarify or to disabuse, and the scholarly interpretations of one generation may well persist, in attenuated or fancified forms, as the popular images of the next. It is not so easy to separate out and describe in some ideal way, uncluttered by past or present purposes, the presumptive original content ("what") of medieval studies.

Medieval Studies[11] is said to be interdisciplinary, a relatively new word in the educator's vocabulary, as Roberta Frank has taught us.[12] A discipline is an acquired body of learning which, as its name suggests, shapes the mind. The disciplines, as educators use the word in university jargon today, represent intellectual conventions for the dividing up of human knowledge and expression. With the professionalization of higher education over the past century those conventions have acquired institutional form and interests as departments. The disciplining inherent in these disciplines comes quickly to light when two differently disciplined scholars discuss the same matter. What one, say a person disciplined in history, finds insightful or persuasive or helpful may well leave the other, say a person disciplined in philosophy, largely unmoved or unconvinced. What one sees, say a person disciplined in art history, is invisible to or has no persuasive effect upon someone otherwise disciplined. And when one enters the sphere of another, say literary critics working out a philosophy-like conceptual apparatus, those disciplined in the sphere encroached upon, say philosophers, can prove quick to dismiss the others as amateurs or not clear-headed. To break out of or transcend these disciplinary mind-sets, in other words, requires a difficult and risky undertaking, both intellectually and institutionally.

A long view of the history of education may well disclose near constant motion between disciplining, the shaping of the mind and the affections toward certain ends, and the discipline, understood as the *scientia* or body of knowledge which is to be conveyed— with the emphasis tending toward one or the other in differing eras and circumstances. Except for a few remarkable figures like Dilthey or Weber or Durkheim at the turn of the century, humanists, until recently and for the most part, have waxed eloquent about the ends of their disciplining and largely presupposed as self-evident the object of their discipline: to shape literate or sensitive people, to form good or thoughtful citizens, historians treat the past, philosophers treat thought, musicologists treat music, English teachers treat grammar or composition or literature written in the English language, and so on. Each of these recognized "disciplines" appears to carve out or claim for itself, even "name," some particular facet of human experience or expression or cognition in which its professors claim expertise.

But to what does a medievalist lay claim? What object does he or she name and to what end? Medieval Studies was not conceived in its origins as a discipline or a department. It arose as a challenge to existing or newly forming intellectual conventions, an alternative way to hold together bodies of knowledge becoming separated or to pursue matters being neglected. Though individual champions of Medieval Studies certainly had particular subject-matters in mind, the proffered rationale intentionally did not specify any one aspect of human experience and expression across time and space, as did other disciplines. The first bulletin for Notre Dame's Medieval Institute declared its intent in 1947 as "to acquire exact information about, and accurate knowledge of, Mediaeval life, thought and history by utilizing every method and device known to modern scholarship." Stated generically, then, Medieval Studies is—potentially—the study of any and all peoples, societies, languages, cultures, and material artifacts found on one continent (Europe) during the course of one-thousand years (500–1500). As an ideal conception or as annually embodied at the Kalamazoo Congress, Medieval Studies takes in all aspects of human thought and experience and expression, literally everything, as the student of past Kalamazoo programs knows, from theology to scatology.

The act of segmenting off those thousand years, moreover, was not inspired by the perception of some internal dynamic or manifest feature. It was born rather of nostalgia and contempt, nostalgia on the part of European humanists and reformers for an earlier and better time, Antique or Early Christian, and an accompanying contempt for what separated them from that lost age. The temporal divider, that is, came first, segmenting off as "middle" all the years that divided humanists and reformers from a presumed better time; what unified those Middle Ages was not some essential internal characteristic—though several were soon ascribed to it—but rather the perception that they had intervened or disrupted. An exact reversal of this interplay of nostalgia and contempt came later, especially following the French Revolution, and it inspired another generation to repudiate reason, industrialization, democracy, or secularization in order to seek again all that had been lost, or an image of what had been lost. For these people the temporal divider was explicitly assumed to have encompassed an age possessing thematic unity—a time of faith, social order, courtesy, closeness to nature, simpler human relations—which they desired to reclaim, in spirit or in deed.

The spatial divider was largely finessed, for while the first reformers looked back mainly to Rome, Athens, and Jerusalem (also at times to, say, the Africa of Augustine), they presupposed as the locus of their endeavors the lands in which they lived. The spatial boundaries represented a still living cultural reality, a product in fact of those Middle Ages. For that cultural unit they had many particular and few general names. They increasingly substituted the classicizing "Europe" for the widespread but—to the good Latinist—embarrassing "*christianitas.*" Christendom, a complex term common in medieval sources and common still in the nineteenth century, referred essentially to the peoples, cultures, and lands of Latin Christianity, effectively overlooking or repudiating the Jews within and the Muslims or non-Christians beyond its borders. The "Europa" of ancient and medieval cartography took as its boundaries the Mediterranean and the rivers of Russia. But cartographers and humanists endowed that geographical space initially with the cultural force of *"christianitas,"* and latterly with overtones of scientific technology or state building or political expansion. The "West," a much vaguer term found occasionally in ancient sources, inevitably took its meaning from an explicit or implied contrast with the "East." Other terms, "gothic" in particular, occasionally transformed a cultural smear into a spatial reality, as in "the gothic North."

In recent years, the dividers have increasingly been dissolved. Late Antiquity (250–650) has acquired an epochal life of its own, neither medieval nor antique but with features reminiscent of what came before and what came after. Renaissance and Reformation have been drawn back into the Middle Ages, or the late Middle Ages forward into the early modern. Students of the long view have interposed new dividers (1000/1200–1800) and a new name (Old Europe), arguing that social and economic relations in particular retained medieval features into the nineteenth century. Students of culture, both high and low, have preferred to emphasize continuous appropriations and reappropriations, with persisting patterns or predispositions rather than the sharp breaks suggested by terms like "renaissance," "reformation," or "enlightenment." All this is justified by greater attention to medieval peoples' own sense of living on the cusp between the "ancient" and the "modern" (meaning, their own day), protected by the authority of "tradition" and carried forward by the force of "innovation" or "reform."

There is then no neutral or self-evident term for this thousand-year segment of European history and culture, for the object of the medievalist's discipline, since each term comes laden with meaning implicit in the dividers or imposed by cultural appropriations, including our own. Abelard, too, repudiated essentializing universals, though he held that the matter (*res*) was prior to a concept of it (*intellectus*) expressed by the voice in words (*vox*). For the modern scholar, difficulties persist in using any word whose past cultural overtones may be perceived, for instance, to exclude Islam or the Jewish peoples from medieval studies or indeed the eastern Christian peoples and cultures. Yet arguing terms apart from investigating peoples and cultures, a grave temptation at times, will not resolve the difficulty. And, again following Abelard, both the words and the concepts presuppose social patterns and cultural unities necessary to render individual items from the medieval past intelligible, patterns which, though widely varying, remain distinguishable from those of antiquity and modern Europe. The "Middle Ages," used in the plural and without singular thematic attributions, may prove, however artificial in origin, the most capacious term for the object of our study. But is that not simply to return to our starting-point?

The point in creating an all-encompassing definition is not to posit a meaningless general term but an object of study full of materials potentially productive of meaning. One volume entitled *Medieval Studies* has divided its subject-matter into 137 bibliographical subfields, each in itself capacious ("canon law" or "social history").[13] The true nominalist would be required to list each of the possible items for inclusion; here a rhetorical gesture must suffice. Medieval Studies must equip scholars to teach and write about Beowulf, Dante, and Chaucer but also about writings not recognized as literary set texts; about Christendom but also about a Middle Ages not limited to Latin Christians; about kings and lords and peasants but also about a range of events and social relations with no direct connections to the modern state or parliaments; about Anselm and Aquinas and Ockham but also about thinkers not accounted anticipatory of modern thoughts; about Sutton Hoo or the Mystical Lamb but also about innumerable objects not idolized in modern museum or museum-like settings. The object of Medieval Studies is then as large and as pluralistic as the writings and artifacts of the Middle Ages themselves—and so conceived it allows, even encourages, medievalists to disrupt or to combine patterns that may elsewhere have hardened into disciplines or departments.

This may sound too platitudinous or self-evident, until working medievalists apply it to cases they know. Since about 1290 Europeans and their cultural heirs have known about, and have given various meanings to, the Abelard and Heloise of the letters, above all, the first letter, titled in manuscripts a "consolatory [letter] to a friend," together with Heloise's "deprecatory" reply (both rhetorical categories), and the double exchange that followed. Medieval Studies must continue to make ample room in its teaching and study for those first six letters. But there is as well the complicated letter of spiritual guidance, a virtual rule for nuns, which has gained more careful attention in the debates of the last generation (and was in fact translated into medieval French, though not included in Monfrin's widely used "standard edition" in 1959). There is Heloise the abbess, said at her death to be "outstanding in letters and religion" (*prima abbatissa documentis et religione clarissima*)[14] and "equal to her Peter in sensibility, moral action, and intellectual skill and without equal in her knowledge of Scripture" (*Illa suo Petro par sensu, moribus, arte,/Scripturas omnes noverat absque pare*),[15] whose work establishing the institutions, prayer-life, and properties of the Paraclete can be partially reconstructed from letters, rules and cartularies. That prayer-life elicited from Abelard 129 strikingly original hymns for the Paraclete, several of them translated into French by the later thirteenth century.[16] There is Abelard the musician, of whom at least one melody has survived intact. There is Abelard the homilist; to Heloise, notably, Abelard explained in his prefatory letter that he was not an orator and that she would find the rhetorical style plain.[17] There is, as Abelard's letter presupposes, Heloise the master of Latin letters, who could cite ancient florilegia to express modern emotion. There remains throughout Abelard the arrogant master whose presumed self-depiction has governed most historical reconstructions of the early university.[18] At the same time there is Abelard the Benedictine monk, who castigated the self-righteousness of the canons regular and the White Monks, likened contemporary monks to ancient philosophers, and died at Cluny.[19] There is Abelard the scriptural exegete, provoked to some of his most intriguing interpretations not by students in Laon and Paris (famous scenes in the correspondence) but by "problems posed by Heloise." Heloise, the student of exegesis, seems to have compiled the forty-two "problems" and "solutions" in their extant form, complete with a rhetorically sophisticated prefatory letter declaring that she and the sisters were following his exhortations in attempting to understand Scripture. It was for them, too, that he interpreted the opening of Genesis, providing in effect reflections on cosmography.[20] There is Abelard the Christian who self-consciously raised in a "soliloquy" and in a "conversation" the question of his faith stance alongside that of a Jew and a "philosopher" (Arabic/Aristotelian natural philosophy).[21] There is Abelard the ethicist who wrote the first medieval Latin book on ethics as such, choosing for his title the Socratic "know yourself" (*Scito teipsum*), treating not the intricacies of love but—among other things—the nature of

penance, an issue raised with respect to Heloise in his poem to
their son Astrolabe. There is Abelard the thinker whose investigations into the nature of words and things were, it now seems, the
product of his own original reflection, not of access to more Aristotelian sources. There is Abelard the theologian, whose attempts to
rethink the central mystery of the Christian faith, to construe the
Trinity in terms of concepts drawn from fresh philosophical reading
(the Holy Spirit likened to Plato's world soul, and so on), drew
down the ire and condemnation of those who had never heard or
conceived such thoughts and felt compelled to protect the received
language.[22] And there is the human couple who wrote nearly all
their extant works as castrated master and monk, as willing student
but less than willing nun. The forms of address in their other letters
intriguingly mirrored the contrasting *personae* of the correspondence, she addressing him as "beloved to many but most beloved
to me" (*dilecte multis sed dilectissime nobis*) and he her as "dear in
the world but most dear in Christ" (*soror Heloissa, in saeculo
quondam cara, nunc in Christo carissima*).[23] All these differing
images of Abelard and Heloise, all the sources and disciplines required to reconstruct them—that is the Middle Ages envisioned by
Medieval Studies.

No single discipline in the modern university would accommodate all that is required to approach Abelard and Heloise as
letter-writers, much less as poets, philosophers, liturgists, and eth-
icists; and therein remains the foundational justification for pursuing Medieval Studies, whether as a degree-granting program, a
curricular arrangement, a gathering of like-minded people, or a
personal scholarly ideal. But such differing images depend only in
part upon the range of sources, or our means of access to them, the
factors recent medievalists have tended to emphasize (and to which
this essay will return). They depend as well upon our purposes,
some conscious, some arising unconsciously from cultural or social
givens. It is essential, but not enough, to say that we intend to understand Abelard and Heloise in the fullness of their own world.
For, colloquially put, what we find has much to do with what, and
especially why, we are seeking. Dronke noted tellingly that opinions about the authenticity of the letters rested importantly upon
whether scholars imagined such a love affair, such a troubled, even
unrepentant, Heloise, as possible in the Middle Ages—or rather

dismissed it all as some rhetorician's naughty exercise, some celibate cleric's erotic fantasy.[24]

All scholarship, we have been told repeatedly in the last years, is driven as much by the "why" as the "what" questions, the disciplining intent as much as the disciplinary content. Here too, Abelard and Heloise offer rich illustration.[25] A century ago scholars sought and found in Heloise the champion of "free love," in Abelard the champion of "free thinking," a half-century ago in them both "Christian humanism" or in their ordered letters mutual movement from physical love to spiritual care.[26] In our own generation Le Goff has seen in Abelard "the first professor," Dronke in Heloise a "woman writer"; Brooke in their letters an early theology of love and marriage; Nichols in Heloise the first woman to articulate an anthropology that credited sensual perception by way of the body;[27] and so on.

It may well be that in those areas of the academic enterprise which we Americans call "studies" the "why" questions play an even larger role in giving shape to the "what." Where the subject matter is by definition capacious and amorphous, with no long tradition of set texts or set questions or set paths of pedagogy, the purposes that animate study will inevitably serve even more to structure the materials and matters studied. In our day, accordingly, questions animated by feminist concerns, by efforts to deal justly with Judaism and Islam, by sympathies with the "people," by curiosity about non-Christian religious practices, by fascination with hermeneutic issues or linguistic interactions have done as much as new sources or new disciplinary approaches to enlarge our sense of the "what" of the Middle Ages.

The declared goal of Medieval Studies was at its origins to pursue a disinterested or "scientific" approach to Europe's medieval past. Such declarations were (and are) sincerely made and to a degree truly practiced. Some students of neo-scholastic philosophy and theology hold, for instance, that the undoing of their modern forms came in part from the careful historical laying bare of their scholastic beginnings, even as the philologists and new critics who prepared editions opened the way for wholly opposing approaches to those same texts. Yet in the work of most scholars there have also pulsed deeper purposes, usefully distinguished as personal, public, and academic.

Personal purposes are as various as we are. We cannot escape ourselves as interpreters, though we may strive for a certain reflective or ironic distance. Our sources do not discover or interpret themselves. Some scholars therefore have taken up a more confessional mode, saying upfront what they are seeking and why. Sixty years ago Carl Becker coined the slogan "every man his own historian," and we might similarly encourage everyone to become their own medievalist, in effect to construct their own Middle Ages. But for all the reality of these personal purposes, and their effect upon our reconstructions, our teaching, writing, and intellectual exchange also presuppose common material, common language, common questions, even common conclusions. For the personal questions often merge, to greater or lesser degrees, into public questions; audiences require and expect that they will. For a generation or two medievalists, together with their students and readers, were interested, perhaps disproportionately, in the self as spirit, particularly as thinking or questing spirit, now increasingly in the self as body, especially engendered body; for many years in the self as bound up in political and social collectivities, now increasingly in the self as material agent; for many years in the self as giving expression in words or images to larger perceived realities, now more to the self as verbal signifier or image-maker creating realities; for many years to the self as absorbed into a comprehensive culture, now more to the self as participating in competing or overlapping cultures.

This way of putting it takes the orientations of the self, individual or collective, as the point of departure, as shaping the framing interpretive structures we bring to bear upon our medieval materials. Another approach presupposes a public medieval culture with which individual medievalists become engaged. In the realm of politics, positions were argued by way of medieval precedents, adjudged good or bad, well into the nineteenth century, past the French Revolution's repudiation of "feudalism" and the English Reform Bill's revision of county privileges, with the search for, say, representative government or constitutional precedents or women's legal status in the Middle Ages continuing into our day. In the realm of religion, down into the 1960s members of the Catholic church, and most outside it, saw in her Latin liturgy, Gregorian chant, devotional art, religious orders in their varied habits, canon law, Thomistic theology, Aristotelian philosophy, and devotional practice a living extension of the medieval past. In the realm of culture, many early twentieth-century educators saw in the monuments of the European past the foundations of a high culture they were concerned to pass on, whether in the field of national literatures, or philosophical reflection, or artistic monuments, or universities, or medieval Latin literature, the avowed purpose for the founding of the Medieval Academy of America. To engage in medieval studies was one way of understanding, participating in, even influencing, that public culture.

In North America, however, Protestant, enlightened, and revolutionary founders sowed serious doubt early on about the "culture" to be found in medieval Europe. A century ago Henry Adams (and others) rethought those doubts and embraced new visions of medieval culture; waves of European immigrants—ironically, from the vantage point of Adams's class—strengthened the sense of connection, and in 1949 Curtius believed he saw in American medievalists a conscious effort to reappropriate that culture. Then in 1958 Lynn White in turn rethought Henry Adams and rewrote medieval culture to approximate American dynamism.[28] But, for all these impulses to distance or to reappropriate, it remains true that Americans call medieval culture theirs only at several removes: removed in time, as it also is for modern Europeans; removed in space, present to us only in books or museums; still farther removed, if our familial or cultural roots are not European. Even Americans with familial or cultural roots in Europe sprang themselves mostly from among peasants, the unfree or dispossessed, those holding little personal stake in the old European order. The sting of that removal was real: asked why he had left, my grandfather, landless in the Dutch village of Kampernieuwstad, his only ambition and desire to work the land, replied brusquely that he had no land; so he left, never to see his native land again. But what such European immigrants carried to America was no less real: language and food, social behaviors and expectations, cultural commitments, religious beliefs. The heirs to those immigrants have never been able to decide whether they should spitefully keep their distance, avoiding that old corruption, or return to Europe with pent-up intensity, reclaiming or making space for all that was once denied them. The study of the European Middle Ages remains for Americans a con-

tinuing dialectic between connection and disjunction, the tug of social and cultural features still influential among us and the shimmer
of something totally and yet perceptibly other.

The sense of distance has its advantages. Call it the outsider's
or the peasant's perspective. We can raise any question, pursue any
subject-matter, without regard for party or religious affiliation, for
regional or national loyalties, for school networks or university patronage. For some Americans, it is true, the European Middle Ages
have functioned mostly as the Happy Isles, the totally (but appreciably) other. Others have exercised benign neglect or sharp critique or focused upon that which fell outside the Old Order, the
peasants, the marginalized, the Jews, the dissidents, the heretics—
evident, for instance, in the work of Henry Charles Lea. But the issue for our generation—given changing demographic patterns, a
deeper embedding of distinctly American social and cultural patterns, and access to a variety of cultures around the world—is
whether medieval Europe has still the compelling quality of connectedness, of something worth studying and quarreling about,
whether indeed it has any noteworthy function in public culture, or
is merely one possible "origin," one possible figure of the distantly
"other," among many from which Americans could choose. Despairing medievalists can easily summon up numerous arguments on
the negative side. Yet it is worth noting all the work that rests upon
a conviction of something worth recalling or representing differently: feminist scholars tracing back into the Middle Ages the dilemmas faced by women in their social roles and self-understanding,
students of Jewish history tracing back into Christendom the social
and cultural position of that people, scholars of sexuality tracing
back into the Middle Ages moral expectations and surprising possibilities; students of philosophy tracing logical and metaphysical
foundations back into a rewritten history of medieval philosophy;
and much more.

Whatever medievalists may understand to be their personal
and public purposes and however those may influence their sense
of what the Middle Ages encompass, their work is carried out in the
world of the academy. Their representations of the Middle Ages
must intersect and shape those of students. As late twentieth-
century Americans, students too are alternately fascinated and put
off by the European Middle Ages. The reasons are easily stated: peo-

ple reared in mass democracies have little taste or understanding for monarchical or lordly institutions; a materialistic age finds the preoccupations of a religious age hardly intelligible; an "updated" church finds its medieval past mostly embarrassing; popular culture finds the artifices of noble courts or the elitist culture of Latin clerics incomprehensible. Or students may be drawn precisely to that which was configured so differently, and by other equally plausible attractions, including a concern to understand the sources of their own culture and the nature of the world's "Europeanization." In either case the teacher is left with a challenge, to render more intelligible what seems at first a wholly other world populated by wholly other people, or to render more complex what has been too comfortably and superficially appropriated. But this is only to state for Medieval Studies the tasks peculiar to good pedagogy.

The more appropriate questions may be those we put to ourselves as professionals: have we exaggerated our own scruples about what we are doing as medievalists and why, and in effect foisted them upon our audiences? Patent dangers loom at either extreme. If the formative stage in the making of European culture and society is studied only as the distant past, and for its own sake, the learning has no power of disciplining, little or no formative meaning for the present-day student or reader. But if the European past is rendered only through the framing lens of present-day questions, making it largely an additional tool or weapon in contemporary cultural or social disputes, the learning loses much or most of its disciplinary content, becoming thereby, ironically, equally dispensable or irrelevant. To justify our enterprise in the world of higher education, our approach to the Middle Ages must proceed in tension, must make its way through a kind of magnetized force-field, with the past "in its own right" as one imaginary pole and the present in its own right as the other.

As professionals, medievalists must address not only questions of content and purpose but also questions of technique (the "how"), of the expertise appropriate to their intellectual labors. This essay will conclude by saying something about five marks found, it seems to me, in professional medievalists, though not all necessarily in the same scholar.

There is, first, expertise in the materials remaining to us from medieval cultures and societies. Virtually all those materials were hand-made, from the codices containing written works (manu-scripts) to the visual images, from the buildings to the furrowed fields. Medievalists, oriented early on toward philology, have virtu-ally transformed their subject by focusing ever greater attention on the material transmitters of medieval cultural and social life: the manuscripts themselves in codicology, their scripts in paleography, documents in diplomatics, material remains in archeology, seals in sphragology, coins in numismatics, images in catalogues and icon-ographic indices, and so on through an ever longer list. Out of this arose, in the minds of some, notions of the medievalist as a high-powered technician, a person whose claim to *scientia* rests upon an acquired expertise in handling materials as arcane to most people as quantum physics.

Medievalists forego acquiring such skills at their peril, at the risk indeed of laying any foundation for their interpretive endeav-ors. This is not to sacrifice the intellect to technique, or meaning to method. For most medievalists it remains clear that the materials, however fascinating in themselves, are not the end, neither for our students nor for our readers, that the foundation is not the building. Just as importantly, careful attention to medieval materials renders the act of interpretation more complex, not less, makes it palpably plain that ordered photographs or printed editions may radically foreshorten contextual realities and possibilities. This holds true for major and oft-edited literary monuments like *Beowulf* or the *Canterbury Tales,* as it does for the notes taken by schoolmen, the lists kept by stewards and merchants, the images fabricated for churches, the tapestries woven for castle walls. Scholarly produc-tions too far abstracted from the material realities have regularly created "works" or "units" or "languages" or "cultural intentions" or "social groups" that never existed as such. On the other hand, to yield entirely to the particular, to make as many editions as there are manuscripts, or to make no edition at all—the temptation of our age—is no less an act of interpretation, albeit a despairing one.[29] Rendering medieval cultures and societies more complex— if you prefer, "problematizing" its literary works or social configu-rations—has arisen, in short, as much from more careful attention to the materials as from latter-day questions.

Expertise in medieval materials must comprise more than a pious sentiment, a rhetorical flourish, a quick glance at a manuscript, image, or charter "in the original" before publishing. It must be born of practice: tracing out the scripts of more than one manuscript, reading visually the textures and lines of more than one local image, reconstructing more than one manuscript from loose quires or leaves to bound codex, choosing among several variants to construct a text. Only at that point does the medievalist come face to face with the nature of the medieval materials in which he or she claims expertise. This requires that medievalists have opportunities to learn, extending to the equivalent of apprenticeships in classrooms or less formal settings. It means too that the profession must continue to make space for those whose life's work consists in developing, teaching, or applying such skills. Most medievalists can attain, with effort and practice, at least artisan levels of skill; those who achieve, or are gifted with, truly genial expertise remain few. Moreover, few medievalists will attain multiple such competences—a reality brought home painfully when a child or friend asks about some object in a museum or book, and we know only as much as the curators or editors have explained to us.

At the risk of overstating the point, and making this essay too long, the general claim may be tested again on Abelard and Heloise. For all the attention paid to their letters and love life, serious research into the manuscript transmission has been undertaken only in the last generation. It was twenty years ago, in 1972, that John Benson first asked pointedly why, if they were authentic, Abelard and Heloise's letters had remained hidden for 160 years (from 1130–1290)? Where had the original pieces gone (none survive)? And who made of them an ordered correspondence?[30] Is not Heloise, in the Paraclete, the most likely keeper and the most likely editorial hand—quite the opposite of arguments a generation ago from printed text that Abelard had composed hers, or even Benton's notion of the correspondence as a celibate's fantasy? But what purposes, private or public, should be read in this rhetorical exchange? What signs of editing—of her editing—remain? Should it be compared to her editing of the forty-two questions and answers on scriptural interpretation,[31] of which we have still no critical edition?

The questions are no less basic about Abelard's production. His philosophical and theological works have survived mostly in one to four manuscripts. Why? Do they represent the fragments of a restless teacher who never properly wrote out his teaching? Scraps copied on the run by students in different times and places? The inevitable aftermath of heresy charges? Or the lack of a religious order interested enough to preserve and transmit his works? The works of Bernard of Clairvaux and Hugh of St. Victor have come down to us in the hundreds of manuscripts. Should we conclude that Abelard's influence and personage have been wholly exaggerated by modern interpreters reading only printed editions and his own arrogant accounts?[32] Is it significant that Abelard's "apology" (the public defense of his faith) has come down in the most copies (14), with his poem to his son Astrolabe, his challenging repository of *Sic et Non* authorities, and one version of his theology all tied for second (12 each)? Does this transmission tell us about Abelard, his times and his influence, or about the avenues of transmission, also an aspect of medieval culture? Careful attention to the materials, in short, offers no way out, and certainly no end in itself. It necessarily forms the basis, however, for whatever representations medievalists may choose in the future to make of Abelard and Heloise.

The second mark of medievalists is attentiveness to language. Inherited from earlier philologically oriented scholars, it has been sustained by necessity. Whatever medievalists choose to study, they must deal with materials written in languages that are not modern, whether medieval Latin, Greek, Hebrew, Arabic, or the medieval vernaculars. This is not peculiar to the literary scholar; the economic historian dealing with financial records, the art historian pursuing patronage, the musicologist reading lyrics, the philosopher interpreting thought in its original formulation—all must deal with medieval languages simply to do their work. And since medieval societies and cultures were at once international and local, modern studies appear in all the European languages.

This, too, has required a degree of specialization that may make the medievalist look more like a technician than a scholar. All the learned multi-volume dictionaries and glossaries contain indispensable scholarship, which may appear to be more enabling than interpretive and enticing. American institutions in particular may struggle to justify expensive enterprises which have no apparent bearing upon the national language. The Medieval Academy of America, ironically, was founded precisely to protect learning in the language fundamental to western medieval culture, medieval Latin, which now has no obvious heir or protector. Each medievalist must additionally find ways to achieve competence in the particular sub-fields, whatever the languages, in which he or she works. Thus the social historian must know the vocabulary for farm implements or positions at court, the musicologist the words for musical in-struments and styles, the historian of medicine the language of bodies and herbs, the legal historian the nuances of law and the courts, and the literary historian more capaciously all the lan-guage's possibilities.

Increasing mastery, once again, is not a matter of technique alone but of gaining an interpretive capacity essential for access to medieval cultures and societies. Echoes and reminiscences from the Scriptures, rhetoric patterned on schoolbook or classical mod-els, divisions drawn from legal or economic records, and much more must become recognizable to the medievalist, for these were the presumed framework, at times the unconscious givens, of me-dieval cultural expression. But for the medievalist working back-wards through the language toward those social and cultural givens, rather than outward from them, the language presents an additional problem. It is the fundamental question about whether and how so-cial and cultural realities can be reconstructed by way of linguistic expression. To a degree all scholarly work presupposes it.[33] Al-ready in medieval times, when the Word was the presumed access to or expression of Ultimate Reality, differing philosophical views developed—Abelard was himself a contributor—on the relations between words and things. The pendulum has swung steadily, also in our own day, between notions of the text as disclosing only the text or relations with other texts and the text as disclosing realities beyond. While there may be general disciplinary inclinations— broadly speaking, historians to infer social and cultural realities, lit-erary scholars to infer internal or intertextual references—all scholars incline one way or the other not just according to mood or conviction but, it must be conceded, according to what proves use-ful to a given argument. Both extremes remain in high fashion, to read realities directly out of the words, even as being shaped by the words, and to read the words mostly as words, as intertextual play. Even if medievalists temper extreme claims in practice, the evi-dence they cite to elicit a more contextualized reading itself rests on readings of medieval language.

Language in the Middle Ages also had an interactive social function. Medieval societies were necessarily multi-lingual and multi-cultural. The language of religion, often of the state and of institutions, of higher learning, of medicine, and more was at one remove at least from the language of the home, the street, and the field, a lesser remove in the case of the romance-speaking countries, a near total remove in the case of germanic, slavic, or celtic countries. But the vernacular language of the courts or the cities, and eventually of the written literatures, was itself at some remove from the countless regional and local dialects of village and home. Medievalists must therefore sort out not only the written and the oral languages, with the varying social and cultural roles assigned to each, but must also attempt to reconstruct various layers of understanding or comprehension in the interaction of all these languages—with their own conclusions drawn from the reading of extant written texts and without forgetting that medieval Latin was itself a spoken language. Here too, some simple social division or univocal linguistic theory will not do the job. Careful and thoughtful reading in more than one medieval language will help. Analogies from multi-lingual, multi-cultural America may prove helpful, if discerningly applied.

From Abelard and Heloise we have only Latin works, though Abelard was originally from Brittany and Heloise from Paris. Was their love-making conducted in the Latin which the master taught his student, or in the Old French of the Parisian streets? Initially their exchanges were more brazen in writing than in speaking (*pleraque audacius scribere quam colloqui = et moult de choses plus hardiment escripre que de bouche dire*). But when Abelard teasingly recalled the seduction (assuming he wrote this), should we think it in his labored Latin or Jean de Meun's French? With the books lying open, he tells us, more words were exchanged about love than about the reading, more kisses than learned sayings; hands reached more for breasts than for books, and eyes mirrored love more than they were directed to the reading.[34] But how should we reconstruct intentions out of these words? Abelard introduced it all as a conquest born of the pride that leads to a fall; Heloise described it as a love that emptied itself and transcended all forms to gain the beloved. But when she declared the name "friend," even "concubine" or "courtesan," dearer to her than "wife," was she thinking those words in the schoolmen's Latin or the Parisians' Old French?[35] Whichever the case, Abelard thought that Heloise, amidst the love-making, learned her Latin rhetoric well: he introduces her as not the least in beauty but the best in letters (*Que cum per faciem non esset infima, per habundantiam litterarum erat suprema = Et comme ceste ne feust pas basse par beauté, par habundance de lettres estoit la souveraine*).[36] He assumed that she had also learned her technical theology well. To reassure her in the midst of troubling charges about her husband's heterodoxy—or as he ambiguously put it, so that all worry and shadow might be driven from the white splendor of her breast (*a candore tui pectoris explodantur = soient desploiees de la beauté de ton couraige*)—Abelard set out for her his confession of faith, a technical statement requiring real theological understanding to read, let alone to grasp.[37] The future of Abelard and Heloise, in short, as theologians or as lovers, rests upon our ability to grasp their language in all its nuances.

The third mark of medievalists is interdisciplinarity. If the first two marks suggested something of the technically learned, the mastery of materials and languages, the third must reclaim all the intellectual liberty originally associated with the notion of not being bound, intellectually or institutionally, by the conventions or orthodoxies of a single discipline. This is much easier to say than to do, either in the classroom or in research or in the disciplining of one's own mind and sensitivities. The temptation is to reach for face-saving shortcuts, a little poetry thrown into a work of history, a little history into a study of literature, and inevitably these days an exemplary image or two.

The most general temptation of late is to combine disciplinary work with one or another framing conceptual apparatus called generically "theory." The principle is clear and not unwelcome to an interdisciplinary medievalist: to address the larger questions of knowing, interpreting, and perceiving which help scholars escape the traps of disciplinary conventions. In practice, however, "theory" has become virtually another discipline with its own canons of authors, its own sets of assumptions and intellectual conventions (generally present-minded in the extreme), and its own discourses. At best it becomes thus another discipline with which multidisciplinary medievalists might choose to intersect; at worst another set of strictures to escape or rise above. To speak the language of Beowulf and of Foucault, of the Anglo-Saxon chronicle and Derrida, is indeed to speak two languages,[38] and thus perhaps one form of interdisciplinarity. By acting as a kind of leaven in the academic dough, by raising fundamental questions about how texts mean, what can be inferred from them, and the like, theoretical discourse may form some kind of useful preamble, putting questions into play—not just about language, but about social configurations, and the like—that might otherwise get overlooked. The exercise has missed something, however, if the confrontation is not tense, even explosive, for the presuppositions about the nature and ends of human life in medieval texts and in contemporary theories are frequently, perhaps mostly, in tension or even directly at odds.

Interdisciplinarity cannot be reduced to a single definition, or it would mark the beginning of a new discipline. It cannot mean without discipline, the opportune seizing upon one or another image or representation that happens to suit or to please. It must mean mastering, or at least moving comfortably, in more than one discipline. The habits of mind, the tenor of questions, the method of thought, associated with a given discipline must be acquired, and yet worn lightly enough to make room for those of another, if not several others. An interdisciplinary scholar refuses to be trapped by the modes of a single discipline but draws appreciably, not superficially, upon several. Curricular programs may help, but finally this must be a personal achievement. It requires double duty in the mastery of materials and paths of pedagogy. More than that, it requires living with honest intellectual tension. The literary scholar, the historian, and the art historian will not think or see the same objects in the same way. To reproduce that tension in a classroom is most instructive for students (and for the instructors). To reproduce that tension in a single mind, to interpret and to write intelligibly in the midst of that tension, is another matter and a far greater challenge.

One crucial element in medieval interdisciplinarity is the effort to contextualize, or as Lee Patterson has argued "to historicize."[39] The latter term has come to assume many meanings, particularly in the work of literary scholars. In this context, however, while allowing for all the complexities of historical understanding and reconstruction, it means that whatever habits of mind are brought to bear upon the materials and languages of the Euro-

pean Middle Ages, the results must be disciplined by an attempt to
measure them against the possibilities of the medieval context. It
means as well that the personal, the contingent, the subjective,
whether in thought or action, must receive its due, as must the political and social circumstances within which the personal is played
out. This introduces an additional tension in the interpretive act:
not all the possibilities generated by multidisciplinary work, but all
the possibilities measured against, disciplined by, the context. Nothing will so quickly discredit interdisciplinary work as the impression that it offers up glib comparisons or flattened generalities that
no disciplined scholar would accept. It will require scholars who
can live with and reproduce those tensions, the tensions inherent
in differing habits of mind, and the tensions between all the possibilities and the contextual possibilities, to represent justly Heloise
the writer, the lover, the nun, the exegete, and the mother; or
Abelard the master, the monk, the hymn-writer, the philosopher, the
castrated lover, and the preacher. It deserves note in this regard that
one of the recent series of books on Abelard and Heloise was devoted almost entirely to questions of context.[40]

The fourth mark of a medievalist is, ironically and more
briefly, disciplinarity. A generation ago medievalists took great intellectual pleasure in linking up with colleagues outside their own
discipline (as is evident still at Kalamazoo). But where medievalists
are present in sufficient numbers and with a vital program they may
well begin to think of other medievalists as their natural colleagues.
And within departmentalized disciplines modernists may be only
too happy to relegate medieval colleagues or medieval subject-
matters to Medieval Studies. Some medievalists may also hide behind their interdisciplinarity as an excuse to avoid questions, texts,
or methods within a discipline which they find repugnant or irrelevant. It was against all these tendencies, and in behalf of medievalists willing to address contemporary issues, that Lee Patterson
spoke out in his critique of a—sometimes willfully—marginalized
Medieval Studies.[41]

Reclaiming or insisting upon disciplinarity is not just a pragmatic move, a way to find a job or a departmental home or a contemporary voice. It is an intellectual necessity, both with respect to
our medieval materials and to our academic responsibilities. One
cannot take on the question of Heloise's rhetorical expertise or

Abelard's concept of moderate realism unless one has been formed in the deeper and longer traditions of Latin literature or western philosophy. Moreover, if medievalists expect to be heard, they must also listen: they must be open, horizontally and diachronically, to the questions and observations of their disciplinary colleagues. Of late, however, this argument has become somewhat one-sided, exhorting medievalists to take over and apply the questions, the method, or the jargon which other colleagues find compelling. Medievalists certainly should not be afraid to confront such questions; it was in many cases the Middle Ages that first laid the philosophical or literary foundations that made possible the asking of such questions in modern western culture. But by the same token, medievalists should not fear to take on their colleagues, ancient or modern, on the basis of questions, cultural concerns, and social configurations peculiar to medieval Europe. The intellectual exchange must go both ways, within and beyond the disciplines, if Abelard and Heloise are in the future to be taken seriously both in their own right and in contemporary culture.

The fifth mark of a medievalist, lastly and also briefly, is that he or she is, by instinct, a comparativist. The same impulse of mind that makes someone unsatisfied with the conventions or strictures of a single discipline will also incline them to seek points of comparison, a means to triangulate on the subject-matter they are attempting to understand and communicate. This instinct has at times been channeled off too quickly into set paths, the legal historian turning to comparative constitutions (when "constitution" may require a wholly different sense in a medieval context), the literary or religious historian manipulating indo-germanic myths. But the instinct remains an important one, which, soundly practiced, medievalists must encourage in one another.

The difficulty in making comparisons, as in developing interdisciplinarity, is to get beyond the superficial fix, the all too easy likening of one motif or rhetorical pattern or folkloric story to another. A self-conscious comparativist must seek to grasp genuine differences in mental or cultural patterns, while allowing for, say, transferences between the vernacular of the court and the Latin of the cleric. The same applies to philosophers: it is one thing to note the role of Jewish and Arabic thinkers in shaping the conceptual apparatus Latin Christians brought to Aristotle; it is another to highlight the differences that persisted, and to seek out their sources in larger cultural or religious predispositions. Self-conscious comparativists must choose points of comparison apt for medieval studies. Anthropological studies of non-literate societies on the edge of modernity, viewed through the lens of modern examiners, have inspired medievalists to reexamine the cultural and ritual histories of medieval Europe's non-literate peoples, often quite fruitfully. But it may be that comparisons to a society such as that in Hindu India may be more apt; there too was a relatively common sacred text, protected and interpreted by a sacred caste, producing a relatively common veneer of culture, beneath which there developed a congery of differing peoples, languages, and societies. The tensions in such a society between the sacred and the profane, the literate and the non-literate, the socially privileged and the unprivileged, may offer far more fitting points of comparison for the situation in medieval Christendom. To make such comparisons meaningfully will require more than seizing upon some neat structure provided by Geertz or Turner; it would require steeping one's self in another language and culture. But that should be the impulse of a medievalist, sensitive to the distinct cultural worlds that competed or blended in the making of Europe. The movement of modern Americans and Europeans onto a global stage represents no threat as such to the study of Europe in its formative stage. Danger lies more in the direction of that homogenization of all cultures promoted by the popular media and encountered by Americans mostly in the comfort of their couches or their theater seats. Where the full reality of cultural and social difference becomes manifest, with their consequences for peoples' lives, questions about the origins of various western societies in the European Middle Ages will, if properly dealt with, only become more interesting.

Medievalists, to conclude, must find their way through—to return to an earlier image—a kind of forcefield: constrained by medieval materials, by medieval words, and no less by modern-day questions and assumptions, drawn by interpretive questions from multiple perspectives, no less by comparative questions that put early Europe into comparative settings. At the center of this imaginary forcefield there must be scholars and teachers who are imaginative, thoughtful, and critical. For in the end no amount of expertise or methodology, interdisciplinary or otherwise, directed at sources or at interpretation, will yield compelling insights. That comes only from the quality of mind and imagination, however dependent upon fundamental skills. The ends to which those qualities of mind are directed must likewise arise from subjective powers of judgment and discernment. For many those ends remain the pleasure of scholarly work, the *scientia,* of acquiring multidisciplinary learning, about the medieval European past. For many it is the self-conscious pursuit of a particular political, cultural, or religious agenda. For some academics, more openly stated these days, it is the pursuit of power and influence (Abelard's own self-confessed aims). And for some it is *sapientia,* wisdom or insight into the human condition, born of thoughtful multidisciplinary reflection on the achievements, dilemmas, and perceptions of human beings in medieval Europe. Those methods and ends have to do not only with ourselves and our students and our readers; they have to do as well with the future of Abelard and Heloise.

NOTES

In memory of Lynn White, Jr., and Michael Sheehan

1. Cited here from Eric Hicks, ed., *La Vie et les Epistres Pierres Abaelart et Heloys sa fame*, Nouvelle bibliothèque du moyen âge 16 (Paris-Geneva, 1991), xxvii (with further references).

2. For the manuscripts, see Jacques Monfrin, *Abélard, Historia calamitatum* (Paris, 1959), 9–31; David Luscombe, Julia Barrow, and Charles Burnett, "A Checklist of the Manuscripts Containing the Writings of Peter Abelard and Heloise and Other Works Closely Associated with Abelard and His School," *Revue d'Histoire des Textes* 14–15 (1984–1985): 244–245; and Hicks, *La Vie et les Epistres,* xliv–liv. On fourteenth-century humanist readers of the correspondence, see Peter Dronke, *Abelard and Heloise in Medieval Testimonies*, W. P. Ker Lecture 26 (Glasgow, 1976), 55–60. Because this is not an essay on Abelard and Heloise as such, I will cite literature only for illustrative purposes.

3. Jacques Monfrin, "Le problème de l'authenticité de la correspondance d'Abélard et d'Heloise," in *Pierre Abélard—Pierre le Vénérable* (Paris, 1975), 415f., has argued that the entire transmission rests on a single, now lost, exemplar, which he presumes came from the Paraclete.

4. For the arguments, which have taken many twists and turns, see John Benton, "Fraud, Fiction, and Borrowing in the Corresponence of

Abelard and Héloïse," in *Pierre Abélard,* 469–506, followed by his retraction in "A Reconsideration of the Authenticity of the Correspondence of Abelard and Heloise," and the further commentary of D. E. Luscombe, "The *Letters* of Heloise and Abelard since 'Cluny 1972'," and Peter von Moos, "*Post festum:* Was kommt nach der Authentizitätsdebatte über die Briefe Abaelards und Heloises?" in *Petrus Abaelardus (1079–1142): Person, Werk und Wirkung,* ed. Rudolf Thomas, Trierer Theologische Studien 38 (Trier 1980), 41–52, 19–40, 75–100. The strongest defender of "fraud" is now Hubert Silvestre, "L'Idylle d'Abélard et Héloïse: la part du roman," *Bulletin de la Classe des Lettres et des Sciences Politiques de l'Académie Royale de Belgique* 5e série 71 (1985): 157–200.

5. A photograph of the original document recording the translation reproduced in Charlotte Charrier, *Héloïse dans l'histoire et dans la légende* (Paris, 1933), facing p. 306.

6. Ibid., 403–406, with a reproduction of the title page.

7. Alexander Pope, "Eloisa to Abelard," 11. 29–36, 225–28, 231–34, 245–48, 257–60.

8. The story of their various sepulchral monuments is a long and interesting one, well told by Charrier, *Héloïse,* 309–365.

9. L. Lalanne, "Quelques doutes sur l'authenticité de la correspondance amoureuse d'Héloïse et d'Abailard," *La Correspondance litteraire* 1 (1856–1857): 27–33.

10. Giles Constable, "The Popularity of Twelfth-Century Spiritual Writers in the Late Middle Ages," in *Renaissance Studies in Honor of Hans Baron,* ed. Anthony Molho-John Tedeschi, (Florence-DeKalb, Ill., 1971), 5–28; and "Twelfth-Century Spirituality and the Late Middle Ages," *Medieval and Renaissance Studies* 5 (1971): 27–60.

11. In this essay I try to maintain a distinction between "medieval studies" (lower case), meaning any and all possible study of the European Middle Ages, and "Medieval Studies" (upper case), meaning some curricular or degree-granting arrangement. The latter is obviously some specific or institutionalized form of the former. But in my experience nearly every institutional arrangement of Medieval Studies varies, depending upon the local constellation of departments, colleges, programs, and budgets, even the force of local personalities and patrons.

12. Roberta Frank, " 'Interdisciplinary': The First Half-Century," in *Words for Robert Burchfield's Sixty-Fifth Birthday,* ed. E. G. Stanley and T. F. Hoad (Cambridge, 1988), 91–101.

13. Everett Crosby, Julian Bishko, and Robert Kellogg, *Medieval Studies: A Bibliographical Guide* (New York, 1983).

14. From a necrology, still in manuscript (Troyes 2450), cited in Charrier, *Héloïse,* 301.

15. This epitaph edited and discussed in Dronke, *Abelard and Heloise,* 21–22, 49.

16. Chrysogonus Waddell, *Hymn Collections from the Paraclete,* Cistercian Liturgy Series, nn. 8–9 (Trappist, Ky., 1987–1989)

17. PL 178.379–80

18. Essential, for instance, to Jacques Le Goff, "How Did the Medieval University Conceive of Itself?" in his *Time, Work and Culture in the Middle Ages* (Chicago, 1980), 122–134; but likewise to most other depictions.

19. Letter 12, ed. E. R. Smits, *Peter Abelard, Letters IX–XIV* (Groningen, 1983), 257–269, with commentary 153–172; and the sermon against the Cistercians published by L. J. Engels, *"Attendite a falsis prophetis:* Un texte de Pierre Abélard contre les Cisterciens retrouveé?" in *Corona Gratiarum: Mélanges E. Dekkers* (Bruges, 1975) 2.195–228; and more generally, David Luscombe, "Pierre Abélard et le monachisme," in *Pierre Abélard,* 271–278.

20. PL 178.677–78, 731–32. Eileen Kearney is preparing an edition of this text.

21. *Collationes* or *Dialogus inter philosophum, Iudeum et Christianum,* ed. Rudolf Thomas (Stuttgart, 1970). In the opening of the dialogue he could also label Christians, from the philosopher's stance, as "insane."

22. Orientation to the latter two aspects now by David Luscombe, in *A History of Twelfth-Century Western Philosophy,* ed. Peter Dronke (Cambridge, 1988), 279–307.

23. PL 178.677, 375, 731, 1771. Good orientation by Mary M. McLaughlin, "Abelard as Autobiographer: The Motives and Meaning of his 'Story of Calamities'," *Speculum* 42 (1967): 463–488, and "Peter Abelard and the Dignity of Women: Twelfth-Century 'Feminism' in Theory and Practice," in *Pierre Abélard,* 287–334

24. Dronke, *Abelard and Heloise,* whose entire lecture, with its various partial editions, aimed to establish what contemporaries and near contemporaries held to be believable about Abelard and Heloise.

25. Besides Charrier, *Héloïse,* see Peter von Moos, *Mittelalterforschung und Ideologiekritik: Die Gelehrtenstreit um Heloise* (Munich, 1974), which perceptively reviews the interpretive attitudes scholars have brought to their philological discussions of authenticity. His 135 pages all treat the controversy before Benton, "Fiction, Fraud, and Borrowing," set it in motion anew!

26. E. Gilson, *Heloise and Abelard* (Ann Arbor, 1968), which grew out of a course at the Collège de France in 1936–37 on "The Medieval Origins of Humanism." The notion of the ordered correspondence as illustrating a spiritual progression was suggested by Richard Southern, *Me-*

dieval Humanism (New York, 1970), 86–104, in a paper first read in 1953, and was argued more fully by D. W. Robertson, *Abelard and Heloise* (New York, 1972).

27. Jacques Le Goff, *Les Intellectuels au moyen âge* (Paris, 1957), 40; Peter Dronke, *Woman Writers of the Middle Ages: A Critical Study of Texts from Perpetua to Marguerite Porete* (Cambridge, 1984); Christopher Brooke, *The Medieval Idea of Marriage* (Oxford, 1989), 93–118; Stephen Nichols, "An Intellectual Anthropology of Marriage in the Middle Ages," in *The New Medievalism*, ed. Marina S. Brownlee, Kevin Brownlee, and Stephen G. Nichols (Baltimore 1991), 85–88.

28. A lecture on "The Medieval Bases of Western Thought," included in Ernst Robert Curtius's *European Literature and the Latin Middle Ages* (New York, 1963), 585–596. Lynn White, Jr.'s "Dynamo and Virgin Reconsidered," first published in the *American Scholar* (1958), reprinted in White's essays, published as *Machina ex Deo* in 1968 and republished as *Virgin and Dynamo Reconsidered: Essays in the Dynamism of Western Culture* (Cambridge, Mass, 1971), 57–74.

29. See for instance, David F. Hult, "Reading it Right: The Ideology of Text Editing," in *The New Medievalism,* 113–130.

30. Benton, "Fraud, Fiction, and Borrowing," 471–473 (the first point in his challenging essay).

31. See Peter Dronke, "Heloise's *Problemata* and *Letters:* Some Questions of Form and Content," in *Petrus Abaelardus,* 53–73.

32. Nikolaus M Häring, "Abelard Yesterday and Today," in *Pierre Abélard,* 341–403, with the provocative summary (based on the number of extant manuscripts), ". . . Abelard's original popularity was of very short duration. . . . We know much more about Abelard today than scholars of many centuries before us knew or cared to know about him. They considered their parchment too precious to 'waste' it on Abelard, whereas we admire the manifold and many-sided revelations of his genius."

33. A point well made by Gabrielle Speigel, "History, Historicism, and the Social Logic of the Text in the Middle Ages," *Speculum* 65 (1990): 59–86.

34. "Apertis itque libris, plura de amore quam de lectione verba se ingerebant, plura erant oscula quam sentenie; sepius ad sinus quam ad libros reducebantur manus, crebrius oculos amor in se reflectebat quam lectio in scripturam dirigebat." = "Quant li livre donquez estoient ouvert, plus de parolles s'embatoient entre nous d'amour que de leçon; plus y venoient baissiers que sentences; plus souvent getions les mains es saings que aus livres; plus souvent reflechisoit amour les yeulx de l'un a l'autre que la leçon ne faisoit a l'escripture." (Hicks, *La Vie et les Epistres,* 11.)

35. "Et si uxoris nomen sanctius ac validius videtur, dulcius michi semper extitit *amice vocabulum,* aut—si non indigneris—concubine vel scorti...." = "Et se li noms d'estre appellee ta femme me semblast plus sains et mielx vaillans, *li noms d'amie* me fust tousjours plus dous, ou se tu n'en as desdaing, le nom de meschine ou de ta soingnante...." (Hicks, *La Vie et les Epistres,* 49. My italics.)

36. Ibid., 10.

37. Ibid., 149–150. It is disputed whether the French translation of this *confessio* and of two other pieces came from Jean de Meun.

38. See the interesting examples in Allen Frantzen's *Speaking Two Languages: Traditional Disciplines and Contemporary Theory in Medieval Studies* (Albany, 1991), particularly Frantzen's own "Prologue: Documents and Monuments: Difference and Interdisciplinarity in the Study of Medieval Culture" and Martin Irvine's "Medieval Textuality and the Archaeology of Textual Culture," 1–33, and 181–210.

39. "Critical Historicism and Medieval Studies," in Lee Patterson, ed., *Literary Practice and Social Change in Britain, 1380–1530* (Berkeley, 1990), 1–14.

40. *Abélard et son temps,* ed. Jean Jolivet (Paris, 1981).

41. Lee Patterson, "On the Margin: Postmodernism, Ironic History, and Medieval Studies," *Speculum* 65 (1990): 87–108, and *Negotiating the Past* (Madison, 1987), 37–38.